THE EUROPEAN UNION AND HUMAN RIGHTS

This open access book provides a comprehensive exploration of the EU's role, as a regional international organisation, in the protection of human rights within national legal orders.

Emphasising the distinctive features of this contribution, it brings clarity for both EU and non-EU lawyers, particularly scholars of public and human rights law. By taking a cross-cutting approach – examining the capacity, nature, and adjudication of EU Fundamental Rights Law – it expertly navigates the intricacies of this system. Moreover, it advocates for a political turn in EU Fundamental Rights Law – one that enables European society to meaningfully engage with the deeper issues underpinning this legal framework.

This is an invaluable tool for scholars and practitioners in the fields of European law, public law, human rights, and International law.

The European Union and Human Rights

Understanding a Singular Regional Player

Cecilia Rizcallah

•HART•
OXFORD • LONDON • NEW YORK • NEW DELHI • SYDNEY

HART PUBLISHING

Bloomsbury Publishing Plc

Kemp House, Chawley Park, Cumnor Hill, Oxford, OX2 9PH, UK

1385 Broadway, New York, NY 10018, USA

Bloomsbury Publishing Ireland Limited, 29 Earlsfort Terrace, Dublin 2, D02 AY28, Ireland

HART PUBLISHING, the Hart/Stag logo, BLOOMSBURY and the Diana logo are trademarks of Bloomsbury Publishing Plc

First published in Great Britain 2026

A catalogue record for this book is available from the British Library.

A catalogue record for this book is available from the Library of Congress.

ISBN: HB: 978-1-50998-910-2
ePDF: 978-1-50998-912-6
ePub: 978-1-50998-911-9

Typeset by Compuscript Ltd, Shannon

For product safety related questions contact productsafety@bloomsbury.com

To find out more about our authors and books visit www.hartpublishing.co.uk. Here you will find extracts, author information, details of forthcoming events and the option to sign up for our newsletters.

To Sébastien Van Drooghenbroeck

Virtuoso of human rights, maestro of humanity,
May your work continue to inspire –
Like a lighthouse in the night,
Guiding us towards your ideals of justice, equality, and dignity.

PREFACE

There is no doubt today that the European Union (EU) has grown to become a key player in the protection of fundamental rights in Europe. In recent years, EU institutions have adopted a remarkable number of legislative instruments directly relevant to fundamental rights protection, such the European Media Freedom Act[1] or the Artificial Intelligence Act.[2] The Area of Freedom, Security and Justice – relating to border checks, asylum, immigration, judicial cooperation in civil and criminal matters, and police cooperation, which are often salient fundamental rights policy areas – has come to rank first among the themes the Court of Justice of the EU deals with, ahead of economic policies such as state aid or consumer protection.[3]

The European Union has indeed been called upon to take up a growing role in matters of fundamental rights protection. A combination of political factors, such as rule-of-law backsliding across several EU Member States and beyond, and contextual changes, in particular the growing influence of digitization in our daily lives, have pushed EU institutions to take action. The EU has been an obvious ally in the quest for further protection of rights, as it is often a much better-suited level of governance than the national one for that purpose. This is either because threats are generated by national institutional dynamics themselves, or because such threats fully escape the boundaries of national law-making for reasons of scale as in the digital sphere. Furthermore, the EU is able to autonomously generate legal norms, either through legislating – think of the web of EU directives prohibiting discrimination – or international law-making – consider the EU's active role in the negotiations of the Council of Europe Framework Convention on Artificial Intelligence and Human Rights, Democracy and the Rule of Law.[4] The EU also relies on a dual system of vigilance to protect rights, with both private and public

[1] Regulation (EU) 2024/1083 of the European Parliament and of the Council of 11 April 2024 establishing a common framework for media services in the internal market and amending Directive 2010/13/EU (European Media Freedom Act) (OJ L, 2024/1083, 17.4.2024).

[2] Regulation (EU) 2024/1689 of the European Parliament and of the Council of 13 June 2024 laying down harmonised rules on artificial intelligence and amending Regulations (EC) No 300/2008, (EU) No 167/2013, (EU) No 168/2013, (EU) 2018/858, (EU) 2018/1139 and (EU) 2019/2144 and Directives 2014/90/EU, (EU) 2016/797 and (EU) 2020/1828 (Artificial Intelligence Act) (OJ L, 2024/1689, 12.7.2024).

[3] Court of Justice of the European Union, Annual Report 2024: The Year in Review, available at curia.europa.eu, p. 25.

[4] The EU's ratification is still pending, see Proposal for a Council Decision on the conclusion, on behalf of the European Union, of the Council of Europe Framework Convention on Artificial Intelligence and Human Rights, Democracy and the Rule of Law (COM(2025) 265 final).

enforcement resulting from the combined workings of the principles of primacy and direct effect on the one hand, and the EU's sophisticated judicial machinery, on the other.

The EU was, however, not initially designed to engage in such a large attempt at protecting fundamental rights in Europe. This observation comes with two types of problems that the RESHUFFLE project, devoted to reshuffling our understanding of fundamental rights law in Europe and to which Cecilia Rizcallah's monograph belongs, has sought to address.[5] First and foremost, the EU is often not yet perceived as a possible source of protection of rights. This is in many ways understandable. The trajectory of the EU has primarily been marked until fairly recently by its contribution to European economic integration. Furthermore, the EU is sometimes perceived as a threat to rights rather than a source of protection – a concern related to Cecilia Rizcallah's earlier work on mutual trust.[6] Yet, this limited interest in the EU as a source of rights protection is regrettable because the EU's sophisticated legal machinery could be put to better use to enhance rights protection. Cecilia Rizcallah's second monograph goes a long way toward addressing this first problem.

This book indeed acts as a bridge between students and stakeholders eager to enhance their knowledge of European human rights law and of the specifics of EU law. The book is particularly valuable in that it provides both an accessible overview of the key features of the EU legal order relevant to human rights experts, and an introduction to more recent and technical developments in the field. Non-experts in EU law will thus value being guided through the evolution of the EU from a 'norm-taker' to a 'norm-maker' in the field, and being reminded also of the limits of EU law and of the coexistence of fundamental rights protection with competing interests at the level of EU primary law. Those already familiar with EU law, as well as human rights lawyers willing to make the very best of the potential of EU law for their field, will further appreciate being taken through the meanders of multiple contemporary developments: ranging from the technicalities of direct effect and of levels of harmonisation to the relevance of governance through funding, all specifically applied to the context of fundamental rights protection.

The second problem created by the growing role of the EU in matters of fundamental rights protection is the possible mismatch between the existing machinery of the integrated EU legal order and its new tasks in matters of fundamental rights. First, one may ask how this transformation impacts the relationship between stakeholders and key institutions at the national level, on the one hand, and their counterparts at EU level, on the other hand.[7] Second, one could question the extent

[5] The RESHUFFLE project (2020–2026) has received funding from the European Research Council (ERC) under the European Union's Horizon 2020 research and innovation programme (grant agreement n° 851621).

[6] C Rizcallah, *The Principle of Mutual Trust in European Union Law: An Essential Principle Facing a Crisis of Values*, Larcier, 2022.

[7] This has been explored in other contributions to the RESHUFFLE project. On the role of national courts, see L van der Meulen, *National Courts as EU Fundamental Rights Courts: An analysis of Dutch,*

to which the design and workings of EU political and judicial institutions have been fully adjusted to enable them to take up their new tasks. This is discussed, for instance, in the section of the present monograph devoted to "Rethinking the EU's Capacity in the Field of Fundamental Rights Protection," where the author explores how to improve the use of Article 114 TFEU as a legal basis for legislative intervention in the field as well as how to improve the legislative process to enhance fundamental rights protection.

Thirdly, and this is an aspect of the RESHUFFLE project to which the present monograph makes an important contribution, one could wonder how the role of the EU compares and relates to that of the Council of Europe, which was initially designed to protect human rights on the continent. As Cecilia Rizcallah rightly shows, although the EU is not a human rights organization, it can contribute to the protection of human rights. It should do so within the framework of international human rights law, and that of the European Convention on Human Rights in particular. We can thus only rejoice that the Commission has recently asked for the Court of Justice of the EU to examine the compatibility of the latest version of the draft agreement organizing accession by the EU to the ECHR, in light of recent conciliatory case law by that same Court.[8]

If the growing role of the EU in matters of fundamental rights protection deserves to be highlighted more often, as this monograph does, one can only agree with the epilogue warning against complacency on the part of the EU. EU institutions should be further invited to enhance their own efficiency and legitimacy to enhance fundamental rights' protection, and to work toward greater complementarity with other key regional players such as the European Court of Human Rights.[9] I can only hope that Cecilia Rizcallah's book will contribute to indeed making EU fundamental law yet stronger.

Elise Muir,
KU Leuven,
13 January 2026

German and Belgian adjudication on fundamental rights exceptions to transfer decisions under the European Arrest Warrant and Dublin Regulation (Asser Press, forthcoming in 2026, open access). On how the growing body of EU fundamental rights law may affect federal systems more generally, see O. Scarcello, *Contestatory Federalism and Rights: Resisting Incorporation in the US, Canada, and the EU* (Oxford University Press, forthcoming in 2026, open access).

[8] The request was filed by the Commission to the Court of Justice of the EU on 21 November 2025.

[9] See further V Davio, *EU fundamental rights as a special source for the European Court of Human Rights* (Larcier Intersentia, forthcoming in 2026, open access) and E Muir, S Garben & I Govaere (eds), *Activating human and fundamental rights before the European courts* (Hart, forthcoming in 2026, open access).

FINANCIAL ACKNOWLEDGEMENT

The completion of this book was funded by the European Research Council (ERC) under the European Union's Horizon 2020 research and innovation programme (grant agreement No. 851621) in the framework of the RESHUFFLE project led by Professor Elise Muir at the Institute for European Law of the KU Leuven. Additional support was provided by the Belgian National Fund for Scientific Research (F.R.S.-FNRS) through a fellowship held at UCLouvain Saint-Louis Bruxelles and the Université libre de Bruxelles, during which the manuscript was finalised. Financial support for the editorial work was also provided by the Centre interdisciplinaire de recherches en droit constitutionnel (CIRC) and the Institut d'études européennes (IEE) of the UCLouvain Saint-Louis Bruxelles.

ACKNOWLEDGEMENTS

February 2013, Université Saint-Louis, Brussels. I took my seat for the very first session of 'Libertés publiques approfondies', an elective course taught by Professor Sébastien van Drooghenbroeck. The seminar focused largely on the protection of human rights within the European Union – a topic I had been keen to begin. My favourite professor, a small lecture hall, and the chance to delve deeper into the field of human rights law that had already fascinated me in his constitutional law classes: all the ingredients were there. What I did not yet know was that this course would stand at the intersection of my two greatest academic passions – human rights and European Union law – and that it would prove decisive for my future career and, indeed, for much more than that.

November 2025, UCLouvain Saint-Louis, Brussels. I now find myself writing the closing pages of this book on *The European Union and Human Rights*. Much has changed. A few weeks ago, Sébastien passed away. The sense of joy that usually accompanies the completion of a book is, this time, absent – a mere detail in comparison with the profound sadness his passing has caused among so many people, yet one that I feel compelled to acknowledge in these pages. If the completion of this book marks a significant milestone in my career, it is equally important to recognise the extent to which it is indebted to the teaching, guidance, and inspiration of Sébastien van Drooghenbroeck.

Through that 'Libertés publiques approfondies' course, he introduced me to EU Fundamental Rights Law – not only to its technical complexity, but, more importantly, to its political meaning for us, as European citizens. Sébastien conveyed the profound shift represented by the EU's engagement in this field – a commitment that has, regrettably, grown increasingly weak.

I was later fortunate to complete my doctoral thesis under his co-supervision, together with Professor, and now constitutional judge, Emmanuelle Bribosia, on the principle of mutual trust in EU law and the crisis of values it faces – a crisis that remains with us still. In the acknowledgements of the monograph that arose from that thesis,[1] I emphasised that they both stood as unwavering points of reference throughout the journey that doctoral research represents – a voyage shared between the Université Saint-Louis and the Université libre de Bruxelles.

After the PhD, I entered the postdoctoral years. First, a fellowship with the Fonds national de la recherche scientifique (F.R.S.–FNRS), obtained again under

[1] C Rizcallah (2022). *The Principle of Mutual Trust in European Union Law: An Essential Principle Facing a Crisis of Values*, Bruylant.

the support and mentorship of my tireless allies, Sébastien and Emmanuelle, this time on the protection of judicial independence in the European Union.

A new opportunity then opened up, a little further down the Boulevard du Jardin Botanique and Avenue Franklin Roosevelt: a postdoctoral position at the Institute for European Law at KU Leuven, as part of Professor Elise Muir's ERC project RESHUFFLE, dedicated to reshaping our understanding of EU Fundamental Rights Law. Encouraged by my mentors to take flight and find my own path within this new environment, I embarked upon the adventure – and was welcomed by Elise.

That experience proved to be one of immense intellectual and human enrichment. Yet it was by no means an easy journey.

I was often told that the real challenge lies with the second child. With the first, all your attention is devoted to a single being; with the second, one must care for the newborn while tending to the eldest – a double load, mental and physical alike. When the first child slept, you could sometimes rest; with two, that is nearly impossible. This, in truth, captures quite well my experience of writing this second monograph. Still engaged in research on mutual trust and in teaching in my two alma maters, I had to pour myself entirely into this new project at the KU Leuven. I can only hope that the result is worthy of your attention – and of those who guided me here. No project of this scale is ever a solitary endeavour. I therefore wish to express my sincere gratitude to the many friends and colleagues who supported me throughout this journey.

My heartfelt thanks go to my colleagues in the RESHUFFLE project – Elise, of course, as well as Orlando Scarcello, Victor Davio, and Lucia Vandermeulen – and to others at the Institute whose collaboration I deeply appreciated, among whom are Ilaria Gambardella, Robin Gadbled, and Teresa Cabrita. The RESHUFFLE project culminates in the publication of four monographs, including the present volume.

From that bubble of knowledge in the heart of Flanders, I also had the privilege of spending several weeks in Milan – Italy's capital of creativity – where part of this book took shape. My warmest thanks go to Professor Eleanor Spaventa for welcoming me at Bocconi University. Crossing the Alps from Milan to Paris, my sincere gratitude extends to Professor Laurence Burgorgue-Larsen, who, through the prism of her distinguished expertise in international human rights law, so kindly agreed to write the foreword to this book. Her contribution is both an honour and a profound source of inspiration. I am also deeply grateful to Marc Errera and Lorence Vaïsse, whose generosity allowed the final stretch of this writing journey to unfold in the quiet seclusion of Rhuat, in Brittany. Immersed in its turquoise waters and accompanied by the distant calls of does, thought seemed to slow, deepen, and find its own rhythm. This landscape did not merely host the work; it gently shaped it, offering a rare and enduring source of intellectual and creative nourishment.

I would also like to express my special thanks to those who generously read and commented on parts of this manuscript, thereby improving it substantially: Elise Muir, Antoine Buyse, George Letsas, Ilaria Gambardella, Orlando Scarcello, Norman Vander Putten, Sélim Hamzaoui, Camille Bertaux, Julian Clarenne, Eleni De Becker, Séréna Menzione, Rémy Rizzo, Pauline Thinus, and Yann Lorans. My warmest thanks to Clara Guéguen and Anjum Shabbir for their invaluable editorial work, and to Hart Publishing, in particular Sinead Moloney and Verity Stuart, for their confidence in this project and their exemplary professionalism and responsiveness throughout the publication process.

I am moreover indebted to the authorities and my colleagues at Université Saint-Louis Bruxelles, now UCLouvain Saint-Louis – Bruxelles, for granting me the time and space to nurture this 'second child', notwithstanding my appointment as professor at this university. My sincere thanks go to Isabelle Hachez, Vice-Rector of Saint-Louis, whose courage in continuing to uphold the value of research in an academic world under growing pressure truly deserves recognition and applause. I am also profoundly thankful to Pierre-Olivier De Broux and Antoine Bailleux, (former) deans of the Law Faculty and the Institute for European Studies, for making this project possible – and, indeed, for the audacity of their encouragement. Warm thoughts also go to my colleagues at the CIRC (Centre interdisciplinaire de recherches en droit constitutionnel), in particular Norman Vander Putten, Julian Clarenne, and Mathias El Berhoumi, as well as to my colleagues at the two Institutes for European Studies in Brussels, especially Antoine Bailleux and Ramona Coman, with whom it is such a pleasure to work and to push our reflections further. I also wish to thank Céline Frémault and Véronique Lamquin, who have already opened pathways for this work beyond the boundaries of academia.

Finally, I wish to express my deepest gratitude to Maxence, who patiently endured the sleepless nights – not yet those of a crying child, but those caused by the silence that stems from the anguish of the blank page. These projects, at times overwhelming, never obscure what truly matters. His love, unwavering and quietly present, is the anchor that carried me through it all.

Until the very final stages of this book – particularly the writing of chapter four – I had the privilege of exchanging ideas with Sébastien. Though much has changed since 2013, I can only restate how profoundly this book owes a debt to his mentorship and guidance. Sébastien, this book is dedicated to you. This work does not aspire to rival your virtuosity, but I hope it may, in its own way, honour its light.

Cecilia Rizcallah
Brussels, 19 November 2025

CONTENTS

Preface ..... *vii*
Financial Acknowledgement ..... *xi*
Acknowledgements ..... *xiii*
Table of Cases ..... *xxiii*
Avant-propos by Laurence Burgogue-Larsen ..... *xxxv*

Introduction 1
Section I – An Active Role in Fundamental Rights Protection 4
Section II – A Singular (Supranational) Regional Player 6
Section III – A Common Area of Fundamental Rights Protection 9
Section IV – Relationship to Existing Literature 12
Section V – Why Studying the Role of the EU in Protecting Fundamental Rights Matters Now 14
Section VI – Structure of the Book 15

1. A Simultaneously Strong and Limited Human Rights Protector 17
Introduction 17
Section I – Deference: The European Communities as 'Norm-takers' 18
Section II – Consolidation: Elevating Fundamental Rights 20
Section III – Indispensability: EU Fundamental Rights Protection, an Essential Condition for EU Integration 23
Section IV – Limitation: A Paradoxically Restricted Mandate 26
IV.1. The Absence of a General Mandate for Fundamental Rights Protection 26
IV.2. Limits to the Scope of the EU Charter and the General Principles of EU Law 28
IV.3. The Constraints Limiting the Exercise of EU Competences 30
Section V – In Search of a Human Rights Telos? 34
V.1. The EU's Human Rights Commitment: A Fake Narrative? 34
V.2. The EU's Competing Objectives and the Specific Characteristics of EU Law 38
V.3. Not a Traditional 'International Human Rights Organisation' 42

Section VI – Emancipation: A New 'Norm-maker' 45
VI.1. The EU's Harmonisation Power....................45
VI.1.a. EU 'Self-standing' Fundamental Rights Competences: Non-discrimination and the Protection of Personal Data....................47
VI.1.b. Fundamental Rights Harmonisation and the Development of the Internal Market 51
VI.1.c. Fundamental Rights Harmonisation as a Key to Unlocking the Area of Freedom, Security and Justice....................55
VI.1.d. The Slow Development of a Social Policy Shaping the Emergence of EU Fundamental Social Rights 66
VI.2. The Emancipatory Interpretation of the CJEU....................70
VI.3. A Constitutional Balance under Tension 76
VI.3.a. The Ambit of EU Fundamental Rights Law in the Absence of EU Harmonisation....................77
VI.3.a (i) The Scope of Application 77
VI.3.a (ii) The Level of Protection....................79
VI.3.b. The Ambit of EU Fundamental Rights Law where there is EU Harmonisation....................82
VI.3.b (i) The Scope of Application 82
VI.3.b (ii) The Level of Protection....................83
Conclusion....................89

2. The Power of EU Fundamental Rights Law....................91
Introduction....................91
Section I – The Special Characteristics of EU Fundamental Rights Law 92
I.1. The Special Characteristics of EU Law: A 'Unique' International Organisation....................93
I.1.a. The Principle of Primacy 95
I.1.b. Direct Effect....................97
I.1.c. The Principle of Effectiveness 98
I.1.d. The Uniqueness of EU Law and its Specific Characteristics....................100
I.2. The Supreme EU Fundamental Rights Law System....................105
I.3. The Individual-rights-based EU Fundamental Rights Law 108
I.3.a. The Vertical Direct Effect of EU Fundamental Rights Law 108

I.3.b. The Horizontal Effects of EU Fundamental Rights Law 112
I.3.b (i) Horizontal Effects Through Legislation 112
I.3.b (ii) Horizontal Effects Through the CJEU's Case Law 114
I.4. An Effective EU Fundamental Rights Law System 123
I.4.a. Effectiveness Through Legislation 123
I.4.b. Effectiveness Through the CJEU's Case Law 130
Section II – A Strong System of Judicial Remedies to Enforce EU Fundamental Rights Law 140
II.1. Individual Vigilance and National Judges as EU Fundamental Rights Guarantors 141
II.2. Institutional Enforcement to Protect EU Fundamental Rights Protection 145
Conclusion 156

3. A Sophisticated Oversight Over Fundamental Rights 159
Section I – Political Oversight 160
I.1. Using the Accession Procedure as a Political Means to Impose EU Fundamental Rights 160
I.2. Permanent Political Oversight of Respect for Fundamental Rights 164
I.2.a. The European Parliament's Oversight 165
I.2.b. The European Commission's Oversight 167
I.2.b (i) The Annual Report on the Application of the Charter 167
I.2.b (ii) The EU Justice Scoreboard 168
1.2.b (iii) The Annual Rule of Law Report 169
I.2.c. The Council of the EU's Oversight of Respect of Fundamental Rights by the Member States 170
I.3. Political Sanctions in Case of Serious and Persistent Breach of Fundamental Rights 171
Section II – Financial Tools Supporting EU Fundamental Rights Protection 173
II.1. The Protection of Fundamental Rights within the EU Budget 175
II.1.a. Shared-management Funds Impacting the Protection of Fundamental Rights 176
II.1.a (i) CPR Funds Supporting Fundamental Rights Protection ('Carrot') 178

II.1.a (ii) Sanctions to Ensure Respect of Fundamental Rights under the Common Provision Regulation ('Stick') 182
II.1.b. The Justice, Rights and Values Fund Supporting Fundamental Rights Initiatives 194
II.2. The Role of Fundamental Rights in the Recovery and Resilience Facility 197
II.2.a. Fundamental Rights Milestones Supported by the RRF ('Carrot') 198
II.2.b. Sanctions to Respect Fundamental Rights under the RRF ('Stick') 199
II.3. The Conditionality Regulation 203
II.4. EU Spending Powers and Fundamental Rights: A Cross-cutting Analysis 205
Section III – Independent Monitoring and Supervision of EU Fundamental Rights Protection 208
III.1. The Fundamental Rights Agency 208
III.2. Sector-specific Human Rights Monitoring Bodies 212
III.2.a. Equality Bodies 213
III.2.b. Data Protection Authorities and Officers 215
III.2.c. Frontex's Fundamental Rights Officer and Fundamental Rights Consultative Forum 218
Conclusion 220

4. EU Fundamental Rights: A Political Project for the European Society 223
Introduction 223
Section I – A Key Voice in the Human Rights Polyphony 224
I.1. A Resonance Chamber 225
I.2. A Ground for Growth 226
I.3. A Strategic and Relevant Arena 228
Section II – A Field of Tensions and Contradictions 229
II.1. A Fragmented Layer of Protection with Blurred Boundaries 230
II.2. A Site of Conflict 232
II.3. The Challenge of Unity and Diversity 235
II.4. The Fragile Effectiveness of (EU) Fundamental Rights Law 236

Section III – Fundamental Rights as a Political Project for the EU 237
III.1. Towards a Political Turn in EU Fundamental Rights Law 239
III.1.a. The Politicisation of EU Fundamental Rights Law 240
III.1.b. A Political Project for the European Demoï-cracy 243
III.1.c. The EU Charter and the European Convention on Human Rights as a Framework 246
III.2. Rethinking the EU's Capacity in the Field of Fundamental Rights Protection 250
Conclusion 254

Concluding Remarks: EU Fundamental Rights Law, a Cluster of Raw Diamonds 257

Epilogue: A Risky but Vital Wager 261

Selected Bibliography in EU Fundamental Rights Law *263*
Index *269*

TABLE OF CASES

National Courts

1. German Federal Constitutional Court – Bundesverfassungsgericht

BVerfGE 37, 271, 2 BvL 52/71 *Solange I-Beschluß*, 29 May 1974, ECLI:DE:BVerfG:2020-05-29:2BvL52/71. 19

BverfGE 73, 339, 2 BvR 197/83 *Solange II*, 22 October 1986, ECLI:DE:BVerfG:1986:rs19861022.2bvr019783. 20

2. French Court of Cassation

French Court of Cassation, 4 December 1996, *Cass. soc.*, n°93-44.907 226

French Court of Cassation, 10 September 2025, *Cass. soc.*, n°791 FP-B+R 226

International Courts

1. Inter-American Court of Human Rights

Inter-American Court of Human Rights, Case of *Almonacid Arellano et al v Chile.* Judgment of September 26, 2006 (Series C, No. 154) 102–03

Inter-American Court of Human Rights, Case of the *Dismissed Congressional Employees (Aguado-Alfaro et al.) v Peru.* Judgment of November 24, 2006 (Series C, No. 158). 103

Inter-American Court of Human Rights, Case of *Gelman v Uruguay.* Judgment of February 24, 2011 (Series C, No. 221) 103

2. Permanent Court of International Justice (historical)

Permanent Court of International Justice (1922–1940), *Jurisdiction of the Courts of Danzig (Pecuniary Claims of Danzig Railway Officials who have Passed into the Polish Service, against the Polish Railways Administration)*, Advisory Opinion of 3 March 1928 (PCIJ Series B, No 15, ICGJ 282) 95

3. European Court of Human Rights

Airey v Ireland, App no 6289/73, Series A No 32, ECLI:CE:ECHR:1979:1009JUD00062897, (1979) 2 EHRR 305 100
The ECtHR's Decision as to the Admissibility of *Banković and Others v Belgium and Others*, App no 52207/99, ECLI:CE:ECHR:2001:1212DEC005220799 (ECHR, 12 December 2001) 30
Broniowski v Poland, App no 31443/96, ECLI:CE:ECHR:2004:0622JUD003144396 (ECHR, 22 June 2004) 101
Democratic Republic of the Congo v Belgium, App no 16554/19, ECLI:CE:ECHR:2020:1006DEC001655419 (ECHR, 6 October 2020) 74–75
Dumitru Popescu v Romania (No 2), App no 71525/01, ECLI:CE:ECHR:2007:0426JUD007152501 (ECHR, 26 April 2007) 101
Giuseppe Mostacciuolo v Italy (No 2), App no 65102/01, ECLI:CE:ECHR:2006:0329JUD006510201 (ECHR, 29 March 2006) 101
Hovhannisyan and Shiroyan v Armenia, App no 5065/06 ECLI:CE:ECHR:2011:1115JUD000506506 (ECHR, 15 November 2011) 101
Ilias and Ahmed v Hungary, App no 47287/15 ECLI:CE:ECHR:2017:0314JUD004728715 (ECHR, 14 March 2017) 73
Ilias and Ahmed v Hungary, App no 47287/15 ECLI:CE:ECHR:2019:1121JUD004728715 (ECHR, Grand Chamber, 21 November 2019) 73
Islamic Republic of Iran Shipping Lines v Turkey, App no 40998/98, ECLI:CE:ECHR:2007:1213JUD004099898 (ECHR, 13 December 2007). 74
Kuric and others v Slovenia, App no 26828/06, ECLI:CE:ECHR:2012:0626JUD002682806 (ECHR, 26 June 2012) 100
Marckx v Belgium, App no 6833/74, Series A No 31, ECLI:CE:ECHR:1979:0613JUD000683374, (1980) 2 EHRR 330 138–39
Romeo Castaño v Spain & Belgium, App no 8351/17, ECLI:CE:ECHR:2019:0709JUD000835117 (ECHR, 9 July 2019) 232
Scozzari and Giunta v Italy, App nos 39221/98 and 41963/98, ECLI:CE:ECHR:2000:0713JUD003922198 (ECHR, 13 July 2000) 100
Slovenia v Croatia, App no 54155/16, ECLI:CE:ECHR:2020:1118DEC005415516 (ECHR, 18 November 2020) 75
Soering v UK, App no 14038/88, ECLI:CE:ECHR:1989:0707JUD001403888 (ECHR, 7 July 1989) 100

Swedish Engine Drivers' Union v Sweden, App no 5614/72, Series A No 20, ECLI:CE:ECHR:1976:0206JUD000561472, (1979–80) 1 EHRR 617 100
Verein Klimaseniorinnen Schweiz and Others v Switzerland, App no 53600/20, ECLI:CE:ECHR:2024:0409JUD005360020 (ECHR, 9 April 2024) 248
Zehnalova and Zehnal v the Czech Republic, App no 38621/97, ECLI:CE:ECHR:2002:0514DEC003862197 (ECHR, 14 May 2002) 122

Court of Justice of the European Union

1. Judgments of the Court of Justice

Joined Cases C-148/13 to C-150/13 *A and Others v Staatssecretaris van Veiligheid en Justitie* ECLI:EU:C:2014:2406 [2014]. 64
Case C-617/10 *Åklagaren v Hans Åkerberg Fransson* ECLI:EU:C:2013:105 [2013]. 29, 77
Case C-556/17 *Alekszij Torubarov v Bevándorlási és Menekültügyi Hivatal* ECLI:EU:C:2019:626 [2019]. 134
Case 106/77 *Amministrazione delle Finanze dello Stato v Simmenthal SpA* ECLI:EU:C:1978:49 [1978] ECR 629. .... 92, 96
Joined Cases C-6/90 and C-9/90 *Andrea Francovich and Danila Bonifaci and others v Italian Republic* ECLI:EU:C:1991:428 [1991]. 107
Case C-621/18 *Andy Wightman and others v Secretary of State for Exiting the European Union* ECLI:EU:C:2018:999 [2018]. 8
Joined Cases C-133/93, C-300/93 and C-326/93 *Antonio Crispoltoni v Fattoria Autonoma Tabacchi and Giuseppe Natale and Antonio Pontillo v Donatab Srl* ECLI:EU:C:1994:364 [1994] ECR I-04863. 33
Case C-64/16 *Associação Sindical dos Juízes Portugueses v Tribunal de Contas* ECLI:EU:C:2018:117 [2018]. 151
Case C-78/11 *Asociación Nacional de Grandes Empresas de Distribución (ANGED) v Federación de Asociaciones Sindicales (FASGA) and Others* ECLI:EU:C:2012:372 [2012]. 226
Case C-236/09 *Association Belge des Consommateurs Test-Achats ASBL and Others v Conseil des ministres* ECLI:EU:C:2011:100 [2011] ECR I-773. 122
Case C-176/12 *Association de médiation sociale v Union locale des syndicats CGT and Others* ECLI:EU:C:2014:2 [2014]. 115–16, 120

Case C-507/18 *Associazione Avvocatura per i diritti LGBTI* ECLI:EU:C:2020:289 [2020]. 85
Case C-554/14 *Atanas Ognyanov* ECLI:EU:C:2016:835 [2016]. 98
Case C-233/19 *B v Centre public d'action sociale de Liège (CPAS)* ECLI:EU:C:2020:757 [2020]. 110
Case C-83/20 *BPC Lux 2 Sarl and Others v Banco de Portugal, Banco Espírito Santo SA, and Novo Banco SA* ECLI:EU:C:2022:346 [2022] 80
Case C-361/12 *Carmela Carratù v Poste Italiane SpA* ECLI:EU:C:2013:830 [2013]. 117
Case C-336/19 *Centraal Israëlitisch Consistorie van België and Others v Vlaamse Regering* ECLI:EU:C:2020:1031 [2020]. 84
Case C-304/02 *Commission of the European Communities v French Republic* ECLI:EU:C:2005:444 [2005] ECR I-06263. 152
Case C-193/85 *Cooperativa Co-Frutta Srl contre Amministrazione delle finanze dello Stato* ECLI:EU:C:1987:210 [1987] ECR 2085. 115
Case C-193/17 *Cresco Investigation GmbH v Markus Achatzi* ECLI:EU:C:2019:43 [2019]. 115
Case C-377/18 *Criminal proceedings against AH and others (Presumption of Innocence)* ECLI:EU:C:2019:670 [2019]. 59
Case C-345/89 *Criminal proceedings against Alfred Stoeckel* ECLI:EU:C:1991:324 [1991] ECR 1991 I-04047. 86
Case C-573/17 *Criminal proceedings against Daniel Adam Popławski* ECLI:EU:C:2019:530 [2019]. 105
Case C-646/17, *Criminal proceedings against Gianluca Moro* ECLI:EU:C:2019:489 [2019]. 59, 130
Case C-564/19 *Criminal proceedings against IS (Illegality of the removal order)* ECLI:EU:C:2021:949 [2021]. 135
Case C-467/19 PPU *Criminal proceedings against QR* ECLI:EU:C:2019:776 [2019]. 59
Case C-206/13 *Cruciano Siragusa v Regione Sicilia – Soprintendenza Beni Culturali e Ambientali di Palermo* ECLI:EU:C:2014:126 [2014]. 29, 43
Case C-441/14 *Dansk Industri (DI), acting on behalf of Ajos A/S v Estate of Karsten Eigil Rasmussen* ECLI:EU:C:2016:278 [2016]. 119
Case C-122/17 *David Smith v Patrick Meade and Others* ECLI:EU:C:2018:631 [2018]. 107, 115
Case 30/59 *De Gezamenlijke Steenkolenmijnen in Limburg v High Authority of the European Coal and Steel Community* ECLI:EU:C:1961:2 [1961] ECR Special Edition 1. .... 92, 95

Joined Cases C-293/12 and C-594/12 *Digital Rights Ireland Ltd v Minister for Communications, Marine and Natural Resources and Others and Kärntner Landesregierung and Others* ECLI:EU:C:2014:238 [2014], para 47. 34
Case C-128/18 *Dumitru-Tudor Dorobantu* ECLI:EU:C:2019:857 [2019]. 20
Case C-792/22 *Energotehnica* ECLI:EU:C:2024:788 98
Case 29/69 *Erich Stauder v Ville d'Ulm – Sozialamt* ECLI:EU:C:1969:57 [1969] ECR 419 19
Case C-518/07 *European Commission v Federal Republic of Germany* ECLI:EU:C:2010:125 [2010]. 217
Case C-286/12 *European Commission v Hungary* ECLI:EU:C:2012:687 [2012]. 147
Case C-288/12 *European Commission v Hungary* ECLI:EU:C:2014:237 [2014]. 147, 217
Case C-769/22 *European Commission v Hungary (Union values)*, OJ 2023/C 54/19 (judgment pending) 150
Case C-66/18 *European Commission v Hungary (Higher Education)* ECLI:EU:C:2020:792 [2020]. 72, 149
Case C-78/18 *European Commission v Hungary (Transparency of associations)* ECLI:EU:C:2020:476 [2020] 148
Case C-204/21 *European Commission v Poland (Independence and Privacy of Judges)* ECLI:EU:C:2023:442 [2023]. 150
Case C-619/18 *European Commission v Poland (Independence of the Supreme Court)* ECLI:EU:C:2019:531 [2019] 150
Case C-791/19 *European Commission v Republic of Poland (Disciplinary regime for judges)* ECLI:EU:C:2021:596 [2021] 150
Case C-540/03 *European Parliament v Council of the European Union* ECLI:EU:C:2006:429 [2006] ECR I-5769 64–65
Case C-473/16 *F v Bevándorlási és Állampolgársági Hivatal* ECLI:EU:C:2018:36 [2018]. 64
Case C-376/98 *Federal Republic of Germany v European Parliament and Council of the European Union* ECLI:EU:C:2000:544 [2000] ECR I-8419 51–52
Case 6/64 *Flaminio Costa v ENEL* ECLI:EU:C:1964:66 [1964] ECR 585. .... 19, 92, 94
Joined Cases C-924/19 PPU and C-925/19 PPU *FMS and Others v Országos Idegenrendészeti Főigazgatóság Dél-alföldi Regionális Igazgatóság and Országos Idegenrendészeti Főigazgatóság* ECLI:EU:C:2020:367 [2020]. 73–74
Case 103/88 *Fratelli Costanzo SpA v Comune di Milano* ECLI:EU:C:1989:256 [1989] ECR 1839 96–97

Case 43/75 *Gabrielle Defrenne v Société anonyme belge de navigation aérienne Sabena* ECLI:EU:C:1976:56 [1976]....114
Case 149/77 *Gabrielle Defrenne v Société anonyme belge de navigation aérienne Sabena* ECLI:EU:C:1978:130 [1978] ECR 1365....47
Case C-537/16 *Garlsson Real Estate SA and Others v Commissione Nazionale per le Società e la Borsa (Consob)* ECLI:EU:C:2018:193 [2018]....106, 109, 116
Case C-131/12 *Google Spain SL and Google Inc v Agencia Española de Protección de Datos (AEPD) and Mario Costeja González* ECLI:EU:C:2014:317 [2014]....121
Case C-117/14 *Grima Janet Nisttahuz Poclava v Jose María Ariza Toledano* EU:C:2015:60 [2015]....232
Joined Cases 46/87 and 227/88 *Hoescht AG v Commission of the European Communities* ECLI:EU:C:1989:337 [1989]....225
Case C-156/21 *Hungary v the European Parliament and Council of the European Union* ECLI:EU:C:2022:97 [2022]....23, 203–04, 244
Case C-19/21 *I and S v Staatssecretaris van Justitie en Veiligheid (Refusal to take charge of an unaccompanied Egyptian minor)* ECLI:EU:C:2022:605 [2022]....133
Case C-289/21 *IG v Varhoven administrativen sad* ECLI:EU:C:2022:920 [2022]....132
Case C-268/06 *Impact v Minister for Agriculture and Food and Others* ECLI:EU:C:2008:223 [2008] ECR I-2483....131
Case C-438/05 *International Transport Workers' Federation and Finnish Seamen's Union v Viking Line ABP and OÜ Viking Line Eesti* ECLI:EU:C:2007:772 [2007] ECR I-10779....39
Case 11/70 *Internationale Handelsgesellschaft mbH v Einfuhr- und Vorratsstelle für Getreide und Futtermittel* ECLI:EU:C:1970:114 [1970] ECR 1125....20, 94
Case C-68/17 *IR v JQ* ECLI:EU:C:2018:696 [2018]....115
Case 105/14 *Ivo Taricco and others* ECLI:EU:C:2015:555 [2015]....42, 81
Joined Cases C-804/18 and C-341/19 *IX v WABE eV and MH Müller Handels GmbH v MJ* ECLI:EU:C:2021:594 [2021]....33, 87
Case C-601/15 PPU, *J. N. v Staatssecretaris van Veiligheid en Justitie* ECLI:EU:C:2016:84 [2016]....71
Case C-715/20, *KL v X sp (absence de motif de résiliation)* ECLI:EU:C:2024:139 [2024]....120, 136–37
Case 4/73 *J Nold, Kohlen- und Baustoffgrosshandlung v Commission of the European Communities* ECLI:EU:C:1974:51 [1974] ECR 491....2, 20
Case C-168/13 PPU *Jeremy F v Premier minister* ECLI:EU:C:2013:358 [2013]....144

Case C-491/10 PPU *Joseba Andoni Aguirre Zarraga v Simone Pelz* ECLI:EU:C:2010:828 [2010] ECR I-14247.......144
Case C-660/21 *KB and FS (Official record in criminal matters)* ECLI:EU:C:2023:498 [2023].......136
Joined Cases C-29/22 P and C-44/22 P, *KS and KD v Council and Others* ECLI:EU:C:2024:725 [2024].......250
Joined Cases C-8/15 P to C-10/15 P, *Ledra Advertising Ltd v European Commission* ECLI:EU:C:2016:701 [2016].......28
Case C-341/05 *Laval un Partneri Ltd v Svenska Byggnadsarbetareförbundet, Svenska Byggnadsarbetareförbundets avdelning 1, Byggettan and Svenska Elektrikerförbundet* ECLI:EU:C:2007:809 [2007] ECR I-11767.......39
Case C-562/12 *Liivimaa Lihaveis MTÜ v Eesti-Läti programmi 2007–2013 Seirekomitee* EU:C:2014:2229 [2014].......232
Case C-107/23 PPU *Lin* ECLI:EU:C:2023:606 [2023].......81
Case C-426/11 Mark *Alemo-Herron and Others v Parkwood Leisure Ltd* ECLI:EU:C:2013:521 [2013].......86
Case 42/17 *MAS and MB* ECLI:EU:C:2017:936 [2017]....... 42, 81
Case C-528/21 *MD (Prohibition of entry into Hungary)* ECLI:EU:C:2023:341 [2023].......111
Case 152/84 *M H Marshall v Southampton and South-West Hampshire Area Health Authority (Teaching)* ECLI:EU:C:1986:84 [1986] ECR 723.......117
Case 222/84 Marguerite *Johnston v Chief Constable of the Royal Ulster Constabulary* ECLI:EU:C:1986:206 [1986] ECR 1651.......131
Case C-282/10 Maribel *Dominguez v Centre informatique du Centre Ouest Atlantique and Préfet de la région Centre* ECLI:EU:C:2012:33 [2012].......107
Case C-170/11 *Maurice Robert Josse Marie Ghislain Lippens and Others v Hendrikus Cornelis Kortekaas and Others* ECLI:EU:C:2012:540 [2012].......56
Case C-362/14 *Maximillian Schrems v Data Protection Commissioner* ECLI:EU:C:2015:650 [2015].......217
Case C-684/16 *Max-Planck-Gesellschaft zur Förderung der Wissenschaften eV v Tetsuji Shimizu* ECLI:EU:C:2018:874 [2018].......68, 115–16
Case C-252/21 *Meta Platforms and Others (General terms of use of a social network)* ECLI:EU:C:2023:537 [2023].......217
Case C-614/11 *Niederösterreichische Landes-Landwirtschaftskammer v Anneliese Kuso* ECLI:EU:C:2013:544 [2013].......117
Case C-26/62, *NV Algemene Transport- en Expeditie Onderneming van Gend & Loos v Netherlands Inland Revenue Administration* ECLI:EU:C:1963:1 [1963] English Special Edition 1.......91, 93–94, 109, 114, 141

Joined Cases C-508/18 and C-82/19 PPU *OG and PI (Lübeck Public Prosecutor's Office)* ECLI:EU:C:2019:456 [2019]..........135
Case C-33/22 *Österreichische Datenschutzbehörde* ECLI:EU:C:2024:46 [2024]..........110
Case C-91/92 *Paola Faccini Dori v Recreb Srli* ECLI:EU:C:1994:292 [1994] ECR I-3325..........117
Case C-73/16 *Peter Puškár v Finančné riaditeľstvo Slovenskej republiky and Kriminálny úrad finančnej správy* ECLI:EU:C:2017:725 [2017]..........132
Case C-406/18 *PG v Bevándorlási és Menekültügyi Hivatal* ECLI:EU:C:2020:216 [2020]..........134
Case C-332/11 *ProRail BV v Xpedys NV and Others* ECLI:EU:C:2013:87 [2013]..........56
Case C-158/21 *Puig Gordi and Others* ECLI:EU:C:2023:57 [2023]..........144
Case C-432/22 *PT (Accord entre le procureur et l'auteur d'une infraction)* ECLI:EU:C:2024:987 [2024]..........78–79
Joined Cases C-465/00, C-138/01 and C-139/01 *Rechnungshof v Österreichischer Rundfunk and Others and Christa Neukomm and Joseph Lauermann v Österreichischer Rundfunk* ECLI:EU:C:2003:294 [2003] ECR I-4989..........57
Case C-896/19 *Repubblika v Il-Prim Ministru* ECLI:EU:C:2021:311 [2021]..........164
Case C-157/21 *Republic of Poland v the European Parliament and Council of the European Union* ECLI:EU:C:2022:98 [2022]..........203–04
Case C-872/19 P *République bolivarienne du Venezuela v Council of the European Union* ECLI:EU:C:2021:507 [2021]..........75
Case 33/76 *Rewe-Zentralfinanz eG et Rewe-Zentral AG v Landwirtschaftskammer für das Saarland* ECLI:EU:C:1976:188 [1976] ECR 1989..........99, 131
Case 36/75 *Roland Rutili v Ministre de l'intérieur* ECLI:EU:C:1975:137 [1975] ECR 1975-01219..........225
Case 14/83 *Sabine von Colson and Elisabeth Kamann v Land Nordrhein-Westfalen* ECLI:EU:C:1984:153 [1984] ECR 1984-01891..........97
Case C-157/15 *Samira Achbita and Centrum voor gelijkheid van kansen en voor racismebestrijding v G4S Secure Solutions NV* ECLI:EU:C:2017:203 [2017]..........86
Case C-555/07 *Seda Kücükdeveci v Swedex GmbH & Co KG* ECLI:EU:C:2010:21 [2010] ECR I-365..........118
Case C-585/16 *Serin Alheto v Zamestnik-predsedatel na Darzhavna agentsia za bezhantsite* ECLI:EU:C:2018:584 [2018]..........134
Case C-369/17 *Shajin Ahmed v Bevándorlási és Menekültügyi Hivatal* ECLI:EU:C:2018:713 [2018]..........63

Joined Cases C-704/20 and C-39/21 *Staatssecretaris van Justitie en Veiligheid (Examen d'office de la retention)* ECLI:EU:C:2022:858 [2022]. 64, 129, 134

Joined Cases C-569/16 and C-570/16 *Stadt Wuppertal v Maria Elisabeth Bauer and Volker Willmeroth v Martina Broßonn* ECLI:EU:C:2018:871 [2018]. 68, 106, 115–16, 119

Case C-399/11 *Stefano Melloni v Ministerio Fiscal* ECLI:EU:C:2013:107 [2013]. 41, 80

Case C-285/98 *Tanja Kreil v Bundesrepublik Deutschland* ECLI:EU:C:2000:2 [2000] ECR I-69. 105

Joined Cases C-609/17 and C-610/17 *Terveys- ja sosiaalialan neuvottelujärjestö (TSN) ry v Hyvinvointialan liitto ry and Auto- ja Kuljetusalan Työntekijäliitto AKT ry v Satamaoperaattorit ry* ECLI:EU:C:2019:981 [2019]. 68

Case C-213/89 *The Queen v Secretary of State for Transport, ex parte: Factortame Ltd and others* ECLI:EU:C:1990:257 [1990] ECR I-02433. 99

Case C-242/22 PPU *TL (Absence d'interprète et de traduction)* ECLI:EU:C:2022:611 [2022]. 111, 136

Case C-432/05 *Unibet (London) Ltd and Unibet (International) Ltd v Justitiekanslern* ECLI:EU:C:2007:163 [2007] ECR I-2271. 145

Case C-414/16 *Vera Egenberger v Evangelisches Werk für Diakonie und Entwicklung e.V.* ECLI:EU:C:2018:257 [2018]. 109, 115–16, 121, 132

Case C-198/13 *Víctor Manuel Julian Hernández and Others v Reino de España (Subdelegación del Gobierno de España en Alicante) and Others* ECLI:EU:C:2014:2055 [2014]. 43, 78

Case C-247/23 *VP v Országos Idegenrendészeti Főigazgatóság [Deldits]* ECLI:EU:C:2025:172 [2025]. 51

Case C-144/04 *Werner Mangold v Rüdiger Helm* ECLI:EU:C:2005:709 [2005] ECR I 9981. 117

Case C-356/12 *Wolfgang Glatzel v Freistaat Bayern* ECLI:EU:C:2014:350 [2014]. 115

Case C-621/21 *WS v Intervyuirasht organ na Darzhavna agentsia za bezhantsite pri Ministerskia savet* ECLI:EU:C:2024:47 [2024] 66

Case C–638/16 PPU *X and X v État belge* ECLI:EU:C:2017:173 [2017]. 144

Joined Cases C-615/20 and C-671/20 *YP and Others (Lifting of a judge's immunity from prosecution and his or her suspension)* ECLI:EU:C:2023:562 [2023]. 107

Case 41/74 *Yvonne van Duyn v Home Office* ECLI:EU:C:1974:133 [1974] ECR 1337. 111

2. Judgments of the General Court

Case T-10/13 *Bank of Industry and Mine v Council of the European Union* ECLI:EU:T:2015:235 [2015]......75

3. Orders of the Court

Order of the Court of the Grand Chamber of 20 November 2017 in Case C-441/17 R *European Commission v Republic of Poland* ECLI:EU:C:2017:877 [2017]......152–54
Order of the Vice-President of the Court of 19 October 2018 in Case C-619/18 R *European Commission v Republic of Poland* ECLI:EU:C:2018:852 [2019]......153
Order of the President of the Court of 15 November 2018 in Case C-619/18 R *European Commission v Republic of Poland* ECLI:EU:C:2018:910 [2019]......153
Order of the Court of 17 December 2018 in Case C-619/18 R *European Commission v Republic of Poland* ECLI:EU:C:2018:1021 [2019]......153
Order of the Vice-President of the Court of 14 July 2021 in Case C-204/21 R *European Commission v Poland (Indépendance et vie privée des juges)* ECLI:EU:C:2021:593 [2021]......154
Order of the Vice-President of the Court of 27 October 2021 in Case C-204/21 R *European Commission v Poland (Indépendance et vie privée des juges)* ECLI:EU:C:2021:878 [2021]......154

4. Opinions of the Court

Opinion 2/94 of the Court, *Accession by the Community to the European Convention for the Protection of Human Rights and Fundamental Freedoms* ECLI:EU:C:1996:140 [1996] ECR I-01759......27
Opinion 2/13 of the Court, *Accession of the European Union to the European Convention for the Protection of Human Rights and Fundamental Freedoms* ECLI:EU:C:2014:2454 [2014]......6, 8, 23, 38, 40–41, 249
Opinion 1/19 of the Court, *Istanbul Convention* ECLI:EU:C:2021:198......65

5. Opinions of Advocates General

Opinion of Advocate General Bot, Case C-216/14 *Criminal proceedings against Gavril Covaci* ECLI:EU:C:2015:305 [2015]......60
Opinion of Advocate General Ruiz-Jarabo Colomer, Joined Cases C-187/01 and C-385/01 *Criminal proceedings against Hüseyin Gözütok (C-187/01) and Klaus Brügge (C-385/01)* ECLI:EU:C:2003:87 [2003] ECR 2003 I-01345......9
Opinion of Advocate General Saugmandsgaard Øe, Case C-235/17 *European Commission v Hungary* ECLI:EU:C:2018:971 [2019]......148

Opinion of Advocate General Kokott, Case C-66/18 *European Commission v Hungary (Enseignement supérieur)* ECLI:EU:C:2020:172 [2020]. 149
Opinion of Advocate General Pikamäe, Joined Cases C-924/19 PPU and C-925/19 PPU, *FMS and Others v Országos Idegenrendészeti Főigazgatóság Dél-alföldi Regionális Igazgatóság and Országos Idegenrendészeti Főigazgatóság* ECLI:EU:C:2020:294 [2020]. 73
Opinion of Advocate General Poiares Maduro, Case C-465/07 *Meki Elgafaji and Noor Elgafaji v Staatssecretaris van Justitie* ECLI:EU:C:2009:94 [2009] ECR 2009 I-00921. 10
Opinion of Advocate General Bot, Joined Cases C-609/17 and C-610/17 *Terveys- ja sosiaalialan neuvottelujärjestö (TSN) ry v Hyvinvointialan liitto ry and Auto- ja Kuljetusalan Työntekijäliitto AKT ry v Satamaoperaattorit ry* ECLI:EU:C:2019:459 [2019]. 119

AVANT-PROPOS

Why a new book on fundamental rights within the European Union? Specialist literature on these issues is indeed abundant and has been for many years. The answer is given by Cecilia Rizcallah herself from the very introduction of her book. She seeks to situate her reflections within the many pre-existing doctrinal works in order to account for an exceptional evolution, without sidestepping its blind spots, and ultimately to propose a political shift.

First and foremost, the author aims to take stock of the long path travelled by the European Union, which has evolved from norm taker to norm maker, to the point where, in her view, the protection of fundamental rights has now become part of its very identity. In this respect, her book is didactic, as it places the evolution of the European Union in a long-term perspective and reminds the reader – or allows them to discover – the extraordinary metamorphosis of this international organisation, which was never originally created to protect fundamental rights. Initially and fundamentally anchored in economic matters, its DNA was exclusively that of the market. In this sense, she develops her argument within a doctrinal current that does not present the Union as a *sui generis* organisation (a debate that fuelled many lively discussions in the French-speaking doctrinal field in the early 1990s), but within the framework of orthodox public international law. The European Union is an international organisation, created by international treaties, whose action is strictly governed by the principle of conferral. However, and this is one of the original features of the book, once this premise is laid down, Cecilia Rizcallah continually shows – indeed demonstrates – to the reader that, despite the EU's transformation in this field, since its institutions harmonise entire areas affecting fundamental rights and the CJEU act as watchdog in this respect, the Union is not an international organisation for the protection of human rights *like the others*. This analytical perspective had never, in reality, been systematised in this way in a monograph. While one can find here and there in the literature articles that adopt this approach, what was missing was a substantial study that would explain, in concrete terms and for each issue addressed, why – although anchored in international law by virtue of its mode of creation – the Union cannot be compared to international organisations whose intrinsic vocation is the protection of fundamental rights. This gap has now been filled.

As an established specialist in EU law, Cecilia Rizcallah is fully aware of its shortcomings, in particular those stemming from its highly complex institutional structure, underpinned by an especially singular system of competences. She tackles these elements head-on and does not fall into a naïve or uncritical approach to the study of the Union's legal system. She also knows and presents without circumlocution the *disputationes* on whether the European Union instrumentalises fundamental rights in order ultimately to serve interests that are far removed from them. This is important. For a professor of my generation – trained by the pioneers of EU law in France, who ardently wished to make it a major and autonomous discipline – criticisms of the system were rare and often diluted in an overwhelmingly laudatory discourse. Today, more than ever, an objective and critical approach to the European project is necessary. Such an approach runs throughout the book, including in the essential account of the eruption of illiberalism at the very heart of the European continent and of the CJEU's ensuing defence of the values of the European Union. The critical perspective could admittedly have been taken even further – in particular by engaging more closely with recent historical work on the links between the creation of the European Economic Community and colonialism, or on current asylum policy – but this does not detract from the fact that, from a technical point of view, the aporias of EU law are addressed head-on, which enables the author to frame her final proposal.

Cecilia Rizcallah indeed calls for a political shift: she argues for a politicisation of debates on fundamental rights within the Union so that every citizen who is the addressee of EU law is aware of what it offers them – of their rights, but also of their duties. Creating a European society of shared values, based on a relational approach, is the ambition, indeed the dream, of the author. In the wake of the work of Loïc Azoulai and Édouard Dubout, she seeks to breathe new life into the European project by insisting that political debates about the content and scope of rights must not be avoided. I shall leave it to the reader to discover her concrete proposals, which give substance to her final analytical bouquet, so as not to spoil her approach. These proposals will undoubtedly serve as the basis for further research by authors who will in turn follow in her footsteps. This is the very essence and beauty of academic enquiry.

Cecilia Rizcallah's book invites us to appreciate – despite the flaws, shortcomings and biases of EU law – its concrete importance for the lives of European citizens. At a time of global bewilderment, when the post-war international order is disintegrating, she rightly reminds us that Europe remains, for the time being, a democratic space that must be praised, preserved and improved.

Laurence Burgorgue-Larsen,
Université Paris 1 Panthéon-Sorbonne,
22 January 2026

Introduction

The European Union (EU) has not traditionally been seen as a major player in the international human rights arena. In recent years, though, it has stepped up, and now plays an increasingly pivotal role in protecting fundamental rights. It has transformed into an international organisation that significantly influences human rights protection in Europe.

It is no longer questionable that the protection of these rights constitutes an important feature of European integration. As one of the EU's founding values,[1] which it shall promote,[2] the protection of fundamental rights has acquired undeniable importance within the EU legal order over time. Still, the idea that the EU could play a role in safeguarding individual rights may sometimes appear counter-intuitive, given its historical focus on other objectives at the time of its inception, and the ongoing criticism it faces as constituting a potential threat to individual rights. Nonetheless, it is becoming increasingly evident that the EU now has a crucial position in shaping the landscape of human rights in Europe.

This is indeed a remarkable development, given that initially the European Communities did not, as such, intend to directly contribute to the protection of individual rights. After the Second World War, this was a task assigned to another international organisation in the European sphere – the Council of Europe – which oversees the commitment of states, primarily responsible for protecting human rights within their territories.[3] The founding treaties of the European Coal and Steel Community – established in 1951[4] – and of the European Economic Community – established in 1957[5] – remained silent on the question of fundamental rights protection. There were a couple of exceptions to that general situation: the right to equal pay for women and men – although this was mainly devised to avoid distortion of competition between Member States[6] – and the prohibition of

[1] Consolidated Version of the Treaty on European Union [2008] OJ C115/13 (TEU), art 2.

[2] TEU, art 3(1).

[3] On the context of the establishment of the Council of Europe and the enactment of the European Convention on Human Rights, see, among others, FG Jacobs and RCA White, *The European Convention on Human Rights*, 2nd edn (Clarendon Press; Oxford University Press, 1996); and DJ Harris (ed), *Harris, O'Boyle & Warbrick: Law of the European Convention on Human Rights*, 2nd edn (Oxford University Press, 2009). Even if it is agreed that the EU plays an increasingly important role in the field of fundamental rights protection, it is not acknowledged that the EU would, therefore, be generally competent in this field.

[4] Treaty establishing the European Coal and Steel Community [1951] (Treaty of Paris).

[5] Treaty establishing the European Economic Community [1957] (Treaty of Rome).

[6] Treaty of Rome, art 119; D Beck, 'Equal Pay and the Implementation of Article 119 of the Treaty of Rome' (1978) 13 *Irish Jurist* 112.

discrimination on grounds of nationality,[7] which served as the cornerstone of the emerging common market.

Gradually, however, the need for protection of fundamental rights within the Community legal order became apparent. The story is well known:[8] it emerged from a challenge to the primacy of Community law by certain national constitutional courts due to the lack of protection of fundamental rights at Community level, which prompted the European Court of Justice (ECJ, as it was then described) to address this shortcoming.[9] By enshrining general principles of law, the Court of Justice of the European Union (CJEU)[10] has, over the years, built up an extensive catalogue of fundamental rights in Community law, drawing on the 'common constitutional traditions' and the international treaties ratified by the Member States, including, first and foremost, the European Convention on Human Rights (ECHR).[11]

Although fundamental rights thus emerged within the Community legal order relatively early on, the European Communities' role in this respect remained, at the outset, mainly passive. Indeed, it was a matter of the European Communities 'respecting' these rights, as a limit to the exercise of their competences.

Nevertheless, there were soon calls for EU leadership in this area.[12] The shift from the EU's more passive to more active role in the protection of fundamental rights has long been and still is contested.[13]

The EU became more active in this area following a political will to give greater visibility to this catalogue. The case law-based catalogue of fundamental rights was codified and consolidated in the Charter of Fundamental Rights of the European Union in 2000 (EU Charter). When the Treaty of Lisbon was agreed, this EU Charter was given the same legally binding value as the EU Treaties.[14] Little by little, the EU has also acquired specific competences in the field of fundamental rights protection, enabling it to positively adopt measures in this area. As stated by the Hague Programme in 2004, this framework meant that the EU was, from

[7] Treaty of Rome, art 7; and see, with regard specifically to workers, Treaty of Rome, art 48(2).

[8] See, among others, G de Búrca, 'The Evolution of EU Human Rights Law' in G de Búrca and P Craig (eds), *The Evolution of EU Law* (Oxford University Press, 2021) 480; and E Spaventa, 'Fundamental Rights in the European Union' in C Barnard and S Peers (eds), *European Union Law*, 3rd edn (Oxford University Press, 2020).

[9] S Kadelbach, 'The European Court of Justice and Human Rights Law' in S Kadelbach et al (eds), *Judging International Human Rights* (Springer, 2019) 171–72.

[10] In this book, this term mainly refers to the Court of Justice part of the CJEU, the name by which the overarching institution has been known since 2009.

[11] Case 4/73 *J. Nold, Kohlen- und Baustoffgrosshandlung v Commission of the European Communities* ECLI:EU:C:1974:51 [1974] ECR 1974 00491.

[12] See, among others, S Besson, 'The European Union and Human Rights: Towards A Post-National Human Rights Institution?' (2006) 6 *Human Rights Law Review* 323; P Alston and JHH Weiler, 'An "Ever Closer Union" in Need of a Human Rights Policy' (1998) *European Journal of International Law* 658; and A Cassese and others, *Leading By Example: A Human Rights Agenda for the European Union for the Year 2000* (Academy of European Law, 1998).

[13] A Williams, *The Ethos of Europe: Values, Law and Justice in the EU*, 1st edn (Cambridge University Press, 2010) 110 et seq.

[14] TEU, art 6.

then on, placed 'under a legal obligation to ensure that in all its areas of activity, fundamental rights are not only respected but also *actively promoted*'.[15] The EU started legislating in this field, moving from passive actor and 'standards-receiver' to a more active actor, as 'standards-setter'.[16] The links with the ECHR were also specified in the EU Treaties, which now make the EU's accession to the ECHR an obligation.[17] The EU has thus now acquired a clear role in the European fundamental rights landscape, and it takes action in this field on the basis of a 'plurality of sources'.[18]

Many texts have traced these developments. Recently, the 10th anniversary of the EU Charter acquiring binding value, and the 20th and 25th anniversaries of its proclamation, have led to a great deal of research on the subject.[19]

This book builds on and goes beyond the scope of the existing literature. More precisely, it seeks to examine the singular characteristics of the EU's contribution to the protection of human rights in Europe – in particular, its purported added value within national legal orders – as well as acknowledging its limits. By doing so, it aims to provide a comprehensive analysis of the EU legal framework protecting fundamental rights. The objective of this book is, thus, to serve the beneficiaries of fundamental rights by enabling them to better understand the scope of the protective layer of those rights provided by EU law. In view of this, it provides a comprehensive, cross-cutting, case-based, and practice-oriented understanding of the EU's unique system of fundamental rights protection.

The central argument of this book is that the EU's approach to protecting fundamental rights stands apart from traditional international human rights organisations. In certain instances, this distinction allows the EU to provide added value to the broader framework of protection. EU law, rich in complexity, indeed operates under a distinctive logic owing to singular characteristics that set it apart from traditional international organisations. However, this book does not claim that EU law offers, from a universal point of view, a 'superior' level of protection compared with other international instruments. Instead, it acknowledges that the EU's unique characteristics can provide notable *advantages* in safeguarding fundamental rights, while also recognising its inherent weaknesses. There is

[15] Emphasis added. The Hague Programme: Strengthening Freedom, Security and Justice in the European Union [2005] OJ C53/01; Annex I to the Conclusions of the Brussels European Council of 4–5 November 2004 [2004] 14292/04, para 2 (general orientations).

[16] O De Schutter, 'The Division of Tasks between the Council of Europe and the European Union in the Promotion of Human Rights in Europe: Conflict, Competition and Complementarity' (2007) Working Paper Series (REFGOV-FR-11) 1, 3.

[17] TEU, art 6.2.

[18] K Lenaerts and JA Gutiérrez-Fons, 'The Place of the Charter in the European Legal Space' in S Peers et al (eds), *The EU Charter of Fundamental Rights: A Commentary*, 2nd edn (Bloomsbury, 2021) 1711.

[19] See, among others, R Tinière and C Vial (eds), *Les dix ans de la Charte des droits fondamentaux de l'Union européenne: bilan et perspectives* (Bruylant, 2020); A Iliopoulou-Penot and L Xenou (eds), *La Charte des droits fondamentaux, source de renouveau constitutionnel européen?* (Bruylant, 2020); E Bribosia, C Rizcallah, and S Van Drooghenbroeck (eds), 'La Charte a 20 Ans. Regards Croisés Pour Un Anniversaire' (*Numéro Spécial des Cahiers de droit européen*, 2021).

thorough examination of these limitations, along with the legal challenges posed by the EU's evolving role in human rights protection. By analysing these aspects, it addresses significant legal questions arising from the EU's distinctive system, and its implications for the broader landscape of fundamental rights protection. Given the relatively recent active character it has in safeguarding fundamental rights, human rights practitioners often overlook the wealth of resources nestled within EU law, but also the limits circumventing this new layer of protection.

In view of this, this Introduction will first explain how the EU has acquired a significant and active role in the landscape of protecting fundamental rights in Europe (section I). It will then clarify why the EU's contribution in this area cannot be equated to that of traditional international organisations for protecting fundamental rights, due to its unique characteristics, and why it is therefore necessary to provide an in-depth study of these singularities (section II). The discussion will then turn to the emergence of a genuine 'Common Area for the Protection of Fundamental Rights' within the wider EU legal framework, along with the difficulties and challenges it entails (section III). Finally, it will expand on how this book contributes to the existing literature (section IV), why it is timely to conduct this research now (section V), and the structure of the book (section VI).

Section I – An Active Role in Fundamental Rights Protection

The EU has not been given a general mandate to protect human rights either at the EU level or within its Member States. The implementation of these rights remains the primary responsibility of the Member States, under the supervision of the non-EU entity that is the separate Council of Europe.[20] The only exceptions provided for in the EU Treaties that allow the EU to generally monitor Member States' compliance with fundamental rights are of an institutional nature and concern the accession procedure provided for in Article 49 of the TEU, and the procedure provided for in Article 7 of the TEU. The latter theoretically permits the EU to take action in response to serious and persistent breaches by Member States, or the risk thereof, of EU values enshrined in Article 2 TEU, including those related to human rights. However, experience has demonstrated that the effectiveness of this procedure remains highly debatable.[21]

Although the EU gradually began to engage with fundamental rights, their role within the EU legal order was initially perceived more as one marked by limitation or constraint rather than of pursuing a proactive policy objective or

[20] E Muir, *EU Equality Law: The First Fundamental Rights Policy of the EU*, 1st edn (Oxford University Press, 2018) 1.

[21] See Chapter 3, I.3 and D Kochenov, 'Article 7: A Commentary on a Much Talked-About "Dead" Provision' in A von Bogdandy and others (eds), *Defending Checks and Balances in EU Member States*, vol 298 (Springer, 2021).

driving positive action. Tawhida Ahmed and Israel De Jesus Butler summarised, in 2006, that:

> The EU is seen to be under a duty not to violate human rights when it takes steps to fulfil the obligations arising from the Treaty. It is considered to be under a duty not to violate human rights whenever it takes action, but without any general competence to take positive action on human rights.[22]

A significant transformation has occurred since then: despite lacking general competence in this area, the EU has emerged as a pivotal and fully-fledged player in the protection of fundamental rights in Europe. This evolution did not occur spontaneously, but was driven by strong political will within the EU and among its Member States, which progressively recognised the need for a coherent and visible human rights framework at the EU level. This political momentum culminated in the adoption and, later, the recognition of the binding force of the EU Charter of Fundamental Rights, marking a decisive step in elevating the EU's role from an economic to a political and normative actor.

Indeed, alongside the economic integration pursued through the establishment of the Internal Market, the EU has been entrusted with increasingly political missions, which have involved, among other things, integration to a certain extent in the field of fundamental rights protection. The CJEU played a particularly innovative role in this evolution: even before the Charter became legally binding, it carefully crafted a body of case law that transformed general principles of EU law into a de facto catalogue of fundamental rights. Through this jurisprudential creativity, the CJEU not only ensured the protection of individual rights within the EU legal order but also laid the groundwork for the Charter's later consolidation.

Today, the EU possesses its own catalogue of fundamental rights enshrined in the Charter, which has the same legal value as the EU Treaties and constitutes one of the most modern and comprehensive collections of fundamental rights worldwide.[23] Several positive obligations on the EU to protect fundamental rights are embedded in this instrument.[24] Moreover, the EU has been granted specific competences to safeguard particular rights, enabling the harmonisation of national standards.[25] Following this, several fundamental rights have now been fleshed out by a large amount of EU legislation.[26]

Despite its limited mandate in the field of fundamental rights, the EU has, thus, gradually positioned itself as a significant protector of these rights within Europe. This has resulted in the addition of a new layer of protection,

[22] T Ahmed and I De Jesus Butler, 'The European Union and Human Rights: An International Law Perspective' (2006) 17 *European Journal of International Law* 771, 794.

[23] M Beijer, *The Limits of Fundamental Rights Protection by the EU: The Scope for the Development of Positive Obligations* (Intersentia, 2017) 110.

[24] Charter of Fundamental Rights of the European Union [2000] OJ C364/01, arts 1, 8, 24, and 25.

[25] See, among others, J Wouters and M Ovádek, *The European Union and Human Rights: Analysis, Cases, and Materials* (Oxford University Press, 2021) 147 et seq.

[26] Muir, *EU Equality Law* (n 20) 29.

complementing the frameworks already in place at the national level and within the Council of Europe.

Section II – A Singular (Supranational) Regional Player

Understanding the EU's contribution to protecting fundamental rights involves taking into proper account the singularities of its architecture and functioning due to its supranational nature. Indeed, it is through these unique features that the EU's contribution provides a protection of fundamental rights different from, or complementary to, that offered by more traditional sources of protection, especially national constitutions and the ECHR. In this particular context, this book focuses on the distinctive features of the protection provided by EU law in the landscape of international protection of fundamental rights.

While the EU's layer of fundamental rights protection could have been examined through the lens of federal law,[27] I have chosen to approach this study from the perspective of international law, as it offers a viewpoint more fitting to the aims of this analysis. The objective is, indeed, to examine the unique contributions of the EU as a regional international organisation in terms of fundamental rights protection.

This ambition is primarily based on the fact that, despite having specific characteristics, the EU remains a fully-fledged international organisation. In this regard, as Bruno de Witte has emphasised, the EU 'came into being as [a creature] of international law, as [it was] established by means of international treaties concluded by States'.[28] These international treaties still form the foundation of the EU legal order, and the validity of EU secondary legislation has its roots in them. In its famous *Opinion 2/13* about EU accession to the ECHR, the CJEU, sitting in full court, underlined very explicitly in that regard that 'the EU is, under international law, precluded by its very nature from being considered a State'.[29] The EU is also still missing a means of coercion in comparison with traditional states, as it remains a 'community of law' and did not become a 'community of coercion, implying a distinction between the origin of the authority to legislate and the one to enforce'.[30]

[27] See, among others, P Pescatore, 'International Law and Community Law – a Comparative Analysis' (1970) 7 *Common Market Law Review* 167; GF Mancini, 'Europe: The Case for Statehood' (1998) *European Law Journal* 29; R Schütze, *From Dual to Cooperative Federalism: The Changing Structure of European Law*, 1st edn (Oxford University Press, 2009) and O Scarcello, *Contestatory Federalism and Rights: Resisting Incorporation in the US, Canada, and the EU* (Oxford University Press, forthcoming in 2026).

[28] B de Witte, 'EU Law: Is It International Law?' in C Barnard and S Peers (eds), *European Union Law*, 3rd edn (Oxford University Press, 2020) 210.

[29] Opinion 2/13 *Accession of the European Union to the European Convention for the Protection of Human Rights and Fundamental Freedoms – Compatibility of the draft agreement with the EU and FEU Treaties* [2014] (Opinion 2/13), para 156.

[30] A von Bogdandy, 'Founding Principles' in J Bast and A von Bogdandy (eds), *Principles of European Constitutional Law*, 2nd edn (Hart, 2011) 30.

Moreover, the EU's contribution in the field of fundamental rights very much reflects the limitations inherent to its non-state nature. In particular, it does not enjoy full competences in the field of fundamental rights protection and can only intervene in the areas of competence that have been conferred on it. This reflects the more general principle of specialty in international law.[31] It cannot, therefore, act in an unlimited and cross-cutting manner in this area. The EU's action is limited by the competences it has been granted, as well as by its institutional framework.

Having noted that, the EU has not become a traditional international human rights organisation either, despite the growing importance of fundamental rights protection within its realm.[32] In using the concept of 'traditional international human rights organisation', I am referring to intergovernmental organisations – thus, subjects of international law[33] – primarily dedicated to promoting and protecting human rights worldwide or in a particular region of the world, and whose principal tasks include the monitoring of human rights violations, providing assistance and support to victims of human rights abuses, and the promotion and the implementation of international human rights standards.

The United Nations (UN) constitutes one of the main international organisations in the field of human rights protection, even though it pursues other objectives too, such as peace, security, and development.[34] It was, indeed, under its ambit that the Universal Declaration on Human Rights was adopted in 1948, and later the International Covenant on Civil and Political Rights and International Covenant on Economic, Social and Cultural Rights, in 1966. Many other subsequent international treaties protecting human rights in particular fields have also been concluded under the auspices of the UN,[35] some of which have a proper institutional system to enforce them.[36]

Three main human rights organisations have also been established regionally.[37] In Africa, the African Commission on Human and Peoples' Rights was established for promoting and protecting human rights in Africa.[38] In the Americas, the Organisation of American States created the Inter-American Commission on

[31] M Shaw, *International Law* (Cambridge University Press, 2021) 998.

[32] Lenaerts and Gutiérrez-Fons, 'The Place of the Charter in the European Legal Space' (n 18) 1712. On this topic, see also A von Bogdandy, 'The European Union as a Human Rights Organization? Human Rights and the Core of the European Union' (2000) 37 *Common Market Law Review* 1307.

[33] M Cogen, *An Introduction to European Intergovernmental Organizations* (Routledge, 2016) 2.

[34] Pescatore, 'International Law and Community Law' (n 27) 7.

[35] See, among others, the Convention on the Elimination of all forms of Discrimination against Women, adopted by the General Assembly [1979]; the Convention on the Rights of the Child, adopted by the General Assembly [1989]; the Convention on the Rights of Persons with Disabilities [2006].

[36] See, eg the Committee on the Rights of Persons with Disabilities, established under art 34 of the Convention. It is composed of 18 independent experts who are elected by States Parties to the Convention.

[37] On these regional systems, see L Burgorgue-Larsen, *The 3 Regional Human Rights Courts in Context. Justice That Cannot Be Taken for Granted* (Oxford University Press, 2024).

[38] R Murray, *Human Rights in Africa: From the OAU to the African Union* (Cambridge University Press, 2004).

Human Rights, also in charge of the promotion and protection of human rights.[39] In Europe, the pre-eminent international organisation in this area is undoubtedly the Council of Europe, which 'became a standard-setting organisation in the fields of good governance, democracy and human rights'.[40]

Yet, despite its growing role in the field of fundamental rights protection, the EU cannot be equated with such organisations, partly because it pursues, as already underlined, many other objectives that can directly conflict with fundamental rights protection, and partly because its competences in this field remain limited.

Although the EU is an international organisation, it is widely acknowledged that it possesses distinctive features that make it a truly unique entity, setting it apart from traditional intergovernmental organisations.[41] As underlined by Andrew Moravscsik, 'the EU has successfully expanded its substantive mandate and institutional prerogatives to a level without parallel among international organisations'.[42] The CJEU considers, in this respect, that

> the founding Treaties, which constitute the basic constitutional charter of the European Union … established, unlike ordinary international treaties, a new legal order, possessing its own institutions, for the benefit of which the Member States thereof have limited their sovereign rights, in ever wider fields.[43]

As observed by Stephen Gardbaum, the EU responds to a paradigm of a 'constitutionalised regime of international law'.[44] In this context, the EU has governance tools distinct from those of traditional international organisations, which also support the protection of the fundamental rights it provides. The EU indeed stands as a genuinely supranational organisation, and remains, to this day, the only example of such a structure in the world.

The starting point of this book is, therefore, this in-between position: the EU is not a traditional international organisation for the protection of human rights and nor is it a state: it is a regional organisation with unique characteristics that plays an increasingly important role in the field of fundamental rights protection. The hypothesis put forward is that these specific features influence the role played by the EU in the field of individual rights protection within national legal orders.

[39] DJ Harris and S Livingstone (eds), *The Inter-American System of Human Rights* (Oxford University Press, 1998).

[40] Cogen, *An Introduction to European Intergovernmental Organizations* (n 33) 136.

[41] See, among others, JHH Weiler and UR Haltern, 'Constitutional or International? The Foundations of the Community Legal Order and the Question of Judicial Kompetenz-Kompetenz' in JHH Weiler, A-M Slaughter, and A Stone Sweet (eds), *The European Courts and National Courts* (Hart Publishing, 1998); and Pescatore, 'International Law and Community Law' (n 27).

[42] A Moravcsik, 'The European Constitutional Settlement' in S Meunier and K McNamara (eds), *Making History: European Integration and Institutional Change at Fifty* (Oxford University Press, 2007) 23.

[43] Case C-621/18 *Andy Wightman and others v Secretary of State for Exiting the European Union* ECLI:EU:C:2018:999 [2018], para 44; and Opinion 2/13, para 157.

[44] S Gardbaum, 'Human Rights as International Constitutional Rights' (2008) 19 *European Journal of International Law* 749, 759.

More specifically, it puts forward that the EU may provide certain added value to some aspects of the protection of fundamental rights in comparison with the Council of Europe, the organisation for the protection of fundamental rights in the European area par excellence.[45] While the primary focus of this book lies in examining the structure and functioning of the EU Fundamental Rights Law framework rather than adopting a comparative approach, the analysis will at certain points still draw upon comparisons with international human rights law, to illuminate the distinctive features of the EU system. In this context, the practice of the European Court of Human Rights (ECtHR) is an 'obvious comparator' when we want to study the practice of the CJEU in the field of fundamental rights protection, as it protects the same range of fundamental rights, and does so in overlapping geographical areas.[46] However, as recalled by Laurence Burgorgue-Larsen, the EU and the Council of Europe do not have the same raison d'être and are not based on the same premises either.[47] Contrary to the Council of Europe, the EU can only act in a limited way, because of the lack of general competence in the field of human rights protection. Moreover, the EU pursues other core objectives which can sometimes enter into conflict with these rights. On the other hand, the EU constitutes a supranational organisation with important integration tools and harmonisation powers, in contrast to the Council of Europe, which is an intergovernmental organisation dedicated to ensuring adherence to minimal human rights standards on a subsidiary basis. Although more limited in scope, the EU's capacity in the area of fundamental rights protection may, in some cases, be more vigorous than those at the disposal of other international human rights organisations of an intergovernmental nature.

Section III – A Common Area of Fundamental Rights Protection

Building on the EU's evolving role in the protection of fundamental rights, a 'common area of protection of fundamental rights' has gradually emerged at the EU level, particularly since the adoption of the Lisbon Treaty. This concept draws inspiration from the term proposed by Advocate General Ruiz-Jarabo Colomer in 2002, when he referred to a 'common market of fundamental rights' in his Opinion in the *Gözütok and Brügge* case concerning the principle of *ne bis in idem*.[48] Today, this expression takes on renewed significance, given advances in fundamental rights protection within the EU's legal framework, which in some

[45] Statute of the Council of Europe [1949], art 3.
[46] Beijer, *The Limits of Fundamental Rights Protection by the EU* (n 23) 3.
[47] Burgorgue-Larsen, *The 3 Regional Human Rights Courts* (n 37) 17.
[48] Joined Cases C-187/01 and C-385/01 *Criminal proceedings against Hüseyin Gözütok (C-187/01) and Klaus Brügge (C-385/01)* ECLI:EU:C:2003:87 [2003] ECR 2003 I-01345, Opinion of Advocate General Ruiz-Jarabo Colomer, para 124.

respects mirror the integration achieved in the Internal Market. Similarly, in 2008, Advocate General Poiares Maduro described a 'European area of protection of fundamental rights' in the *Elgafaji* case,[49] further underscoring this evolving integration.

Straddling these two concepts, it now seems appropriate to refer to the existence of a 'common area of protection of fundamental rights'. Integration in the field of fundamental rights protection aligns with the broader 'area' encompassed by European integration, notably within the framework of the Area of Freedom, Security and Justice (AFSJ). In this context, the term 'area' is preferred over 'territory', as the latter is often intrinsically tied to the notion of the state.[50] Yet, the unity pursued in the EU does not have the ambition to make either the states or their territories disappear: 'without implying the abolition of national territories, the area is superimposed on them in order to highlight their belonging to a common geographical whole, in which the borders … are becoming increasingly porous'.[51]

The common area of protection of fundamental rights co-exists with existing protection systems at the national and international levels. Therefore, the layer provided by EU law does not *replace* other sources of fundamental rights protection but, rather, *complements* them.

In this context, as underlined by Advocate General Poiares Maduro already, back in 2008,

> it is important, for each existing protection system, while maintaining its independence, to seek to understand how the other systems interpret and develop those same fundamental rights in order not only to minimise the risk of conflicts, but also to begin a process of informal construction of a European area of protection of fundamental rights.[52]

In order to avoid conflicts in building this common area of protection of fundamental freedoms, it is, therefore, essential to have a thorough understanding of the functioning of the fundamental rights protection system offered by the EU – and that is precisely what this book proposes.

The concept of 'area' also allows us to delimit our object of study, which will focus on the internal dimension of fundamental rights protection in the EU. As we have already emphasised, the main objective of this book is to analyse the particularities and added value of fundamental rights protection provided by EU law for individuals in Europe. The emphasis is, therefore, placed primarily on the beneficiaries of these rights rather than on the EU's influence over the protection

[49] Case C-465/07 *Meki Elgafaji and Noor Elgafaji v Staatssecretaris van Justitie* ECLI:EU:C:2009:94 [2009] ECR 2009 I-00921, Opinion of Advocate General Poiares Maduro, para 22.

[50] R Barents, 'De Nationalisering van Het Strafrecht' (2006) *Sociaal-economosiche wetgeving* 358.

[51] A Weyembergh, 'La cooperation pénale dans l'Union européenne: de mécanismes classiques marqués par le principe de la territorialité nationale à la mise sur pied d'un "territoire européen"' in L Potvin-Solis (ed), *L'Union européenne et les territoires* (Bruylant, 2022) 299 (own translation).

[52] Case C-465/07 *Elgafaji* [2009] Opinion of Advocate General Poiares Maduro, para 22.

of fundamental rights within legal systems outside its jurisdiction. Furthermore, the protection of fundamental rights in the context of the EU's external relations has already been the subject of extensive research.[53]

This is also why, throughout this book, the term 'fundamental rights' is generally preferred over 'human rights' when referring to the protection provided within the EU. Although it does not seem necessary to place undue emphasis on the distinction between these two concepts, both traditionally referring to 'the rights human beings have simply by virtue of being human',[54] most of the time EU legal texts refer to the notion of 'fundamental rights' when speaking about this protection in its *internal dimension*.[55] On the other hand, the notion of 'human rights' is most often used in EU law in reference to its external action,[56] or with reference to other international human rights treaties.[57] For example, Article 67 of the TFEU enshrines that 'the Union shall constitute an area of freedom, security and justice with respect for fundamental rights', while according to Article 3(5) of the TEU, the EU shall contribute to the protection of human rights in its relations with the wider world. Differentiating these two terms also allows us to distinguish between the action of the EU and that of traditional human rights protection organisations. While the term 'fundamental rights' permeates the discourse of EU institutions, it is more often the term 'human rights' that is found in the discourse of traditional international human rights protection organisations. This choice is, therefore, also justified by the hypothesis put forward in this book: while the EU has become an undisputed key player in the protection of *fundamental rights* in Europe, this does not make it a traditional *human rights* organisation. The term 'fundamental rights' is defined here by referencing the rights and freedoms deemed 'fundamental' in EU law, as enumerated in the EU Charter.[58] In this book, the expression *EU Fundamental Rights Law* is capitalised to denote this specific and distinct layer within the broader human rights framework.

[53] See, among others, C Hillion, 'External Action as Mandate to Uphold the Rule of Law Outside and Inside the Union' [2023] *Columbia Journal of European Law* 228–80; M Ovádek, 'Human Rights in EU External Action' in J Wouters and M Ovádek, The European Union and Human Rights (n 25); and A Nisson, The European Union, Emerging Global Business and Human Rights, 1st edn (Cambridge University Press, 2022).

[54] Besson, 'The European Union and Human Rights' (n 12) 330.

[55] This is the case of the EU's bill of rights, named 'the EU Charter of Fundamental Rights of the European Union'. In the Treaties, art 6 TEU also refers to 'fundamental rights'. See, for the adoption of the same distinction, Williams, *The Ethos of Europe* (n 13) 112; and Wouters and Ovádek, *The European Union and Human Rights* (n 25) 71. Nevertheless, this linguistic distinction between the internal and external level of protection is not always verified (see, for instance, art 2 of the TEU, which refers to 'human rights' as a founding value of the EU internal legal system).

[56] See, for instance, TEU, arts 3(5) and 21.

[57] In particular, the ECHR. See, for instance, TEU, art 6(3).

[58] In this context, I will not make an initial distinction between rights and principles, as specified in art 52(5) of the EU Charter. Despite the requirement for implementation through legislative and executive acts, and their ensuing limited justiciability, the 'principles' maintain their 'fundamental' status by being enshrined in the EU Charter.

While a common area of fundamental rights has now taken shape, the EU's contribution to the protection of such rights is not entirely positive. It must not be overlooked that this achievement coincides with other developments pursuing different objectives of the Union, which, as previously noted, is not an international human rights organisation. As an entity driven by multiple and sometimes competing objectives, and responsible for implementing wide-ranging public policies, the EU frequently impose restrictions on individual rights and freedoms. This duality highlights the need for a balanced analysis that considers both the added value the EU brings to rights protection and the limitations or constraints its actions may impose. Recognising these complexities is essential to understanding the EU's overall impact on fundamental rights. This book will, therefore, not shy away from addressing these limitations and difficulties, which are integral to a comprehensive understanding of the evolving EU Fundamental Rights Law.

Section IV – Relationship to Existing Literature

Unsurprisingly, this book is not in uncharted territory in academic scholarship – far from it – the legal doctrine has long been interested in the complex architecture of the protection of fundamental rights in the EU, and in its interactions with the other systems protecting these same rights in Europe. Indeed, an important strand of the literature focuses its attention on why and how the protection of fundamental rights emerged at EU level.[59] Following the development of this level of protection, another strand aims at analysing the substantive content of the protection of fundamental rights offered by the EU, as enshrined in the EU Charter,[60] but also in specific policy fields.[61] Experts have also worked on the multi-level architecture of the protection of fundamental rights in Europe,[62] including the relationship between the EU and the ECHR's protection of fundamental freedoms,[63] as well as on the interaction between the ECHR and national

[59] See, among others, G de Búrca, 'The Evolution of EU Human Rights Law' in P Craig and G de Búrca (eds), *The Evolution of EU Law* (Oxford University Press, 2021) 480 et seq; and E Spaventa, 'Fundamental Rights in the European Union' in C Barnard and S Peers (eds), *European Union Law*, 3rd edn (Oxford University Press, 2020) 243.

[60] See, among others, Peers et al (eds), *The EU Charter of Fundamental Rights* (n 18); and F Picod, C Rizcallah, and S Van Drooghenbroeck (eds), *La Charte des droits fondamentaux de l'Union européenne. Commentaire article par article* (Bruylant, 2023).

[61] See, among others, S Iglesias Sánchez and M González Pascual (eds), *Fundamental Rights in the EU Area of Freedom, Security and Justice*, 1st edn (Cambridge University Press, 2021); Muir, *EU Equality Law* (n 20); C Costello, *The Human Rights of Migrants and Refugees in European Law* (Oxford University Press, 2015); and O Lynskey, *The Foundations of EU Data Protection Law* (Oxford University Press, 2015).

[62] S Imamovic, *The Architecture of Fundamental Rights in the European Union* (Bloomsbury, 2022).

[63] See, among others, T Lock, *The European Court of Justice and International Courts* (Oxford University Press, 2015); J Callewaert, 'Do we still need Article 6(2) TEU? Considerations on the Absence of EU Accession to the ECHR and its Consequences' (2018) *Common Market Law Review* 1685; X Groussot and E Stavefeltd, 'Accession of the EU to the ECHR: A Legally Complex

legal orders.[64] The way fundamental rights are 'governed' or 'implemented' by EU institutions has also been at the centre of landmark doctrinal works.[65] The question of the relevance of developing a human rights policy at the EU level has also been widely debated for a long time.[66] Reference books have also been published to provide a comprehensive analysis of the protection of fundamental rights by the EU.[67]

Nevertheless, the structure, functioning, and singularities of the EU's contribution to the protection of fundamental rights have not yet been identified and studied from a cross-cutting perspective.[68] In order to fully understand the landscape of human rights in Europe today, it seems essential to fill this gap. To do this, the present work aims to provide an additional building block by relying on the aforementioned research. Drawing on a thorough examination of the protection of fundamental rights protection offered by the EU, this research will strive to identify the specific functioning of EU Fundamental Rights Law as an additional layer of protection within the Member States. The present work, therefore, seeks to engage with previous research and, by building bridges between these different strands, offer innovative results to the existing literature. After analysing the legal framework and its unique features, the book expands its scope to explore the legal challenges stemming from the creation of the common area of fundamental rights protection.

It should be clarified that the aim in this regard is not to assess whether the EU – or its Member States – provide sufficient protection of fundamental rights or not, from a substantive point of view. Consequently, this is not an attempt to make a comprehensive and definitive evaluation of the protection of fundamental rights

Situation' in J Nergelius and E Kristoffersson (eds), *Human Rights in Contemporary European Law* (Hart Publishing, 2015) 7; S O'Leary, 'A Tale of Two Cities – Fundamental Rights Protection in Strasbourg and in Luxembourg' (2018) *Cambridge Yearbook of European Legal Studies* 3; and B de Witte, 'The use of the ECHR and Convention Case Law by the European Court of Justice' in P Popelier, C Van de Heyning, and P Van Nuffel (eds), *Human Rights Protection in the European Legal Order: The Interaction between the European and the National Courts* (Intersentia, 2011) 17.

[64] See, among others, S Van Drooghenbroeck, *Le droit international et européen des droits de l'homme devant le juge national* (Larcier, 2014); H Keller and A Stone Sweet, *A Europe of Rights: The Impact of the ECHR on National Legal Systems* (Oxford University Press, 2009).

[65] See, among others, M Dawson, *The Governance of EU Fundamental Rights* (Cambridge University Press, 2017); J Wouters and others (eds), *The European Union and Human Rights: Law and Policy* (Oxford University Press, 2020); E Spaventa, 'Should we "harmonise" fundamental rights in the EU? Some reflections about minimum standards and fundamental rights protection in the EU composite constitutional system' (2018) *Common Market Law Review* 997; and G de Búrca, 'After the EU Charter of Fundamental Rights: The Court of Justice as a Human Rights Adjudicator' (2013) 20 *Maastricht Journal of European and Comparative Law* 168.

[66] See, among others, Alston and Weiler, 'An "Ever Closer Union"' (n 12); von Bogdandy, 'The European Union as a Human Rights Organization?' (n 32); and Cassese and others, *Leading By Example* (n 12).

[67] Tinière R and Vial C, *Droit de l'Union européenne des droits fondamentaux* (Bruylant, 2023) and Wouters and Ovádek, *The European Union and Human Rights* (n 25).

[68] See, however, some studies that analyse the possible consequences of transforming the EU into an international human rights organisation: Besson, 'The European Union and Human Rights' (n 12); and von Bogdandy, 'The European Union as a Human Rights Organization?' (n 32) 1307.

within the EU. The book also refrains from evaluating whether the EU institutions themselves adequately respect fundamental rights in the course of their activities. Rather, the objective is to examine what EU law offers, in terms of protection of fundamental rights, to its beneficiaries, and the unique features of this protection in relation to other sources of protection applicable within national legal orders in Europe. The EU is, indeed, a 'very powerful organisation' that could possibly 'fill in the gaps or complement the actions taken by other international organisations, such as the ECtHR'.[69]

Section V – Why Studying the Role of the EU in Protecting Fundamental Rights Matters Now

This research appears particularly timely for four key reasons.

Firstly, because it is clear that the protection of fundamental rights in the EU has now reached a certain level of maturity. This evolution calls for a 'reshuffling' of our understanding of fundamental rights law in Europe.[70] It is, thus, now time to question how the EU layer of protection is unfolding in the legal landscape of fundamental rights in Europe, rather than still focusing on the reasons which initially pushed its consecration, or on the manner in which it was initially developed.

Secondly, because the current context is one of increasing resistance to European integration and the protection of liberal values, including fundamental rights.[71] If the end of the 'permissive consensus' dates back a long time, recent years have seen a resurgence of challenges towards the EU, which question the way its action unfolds and can be accepted in the national legal orders.[72] Current times also appear to be more and more hostile towards the protection of fundamental rights.[73] It is not surprising that the EU's action in the area of fundamental rights protection is far from being universally embraced by national legal systems; on the contrary, it is often met with significant resistance.[74] This situation, of course, calls for urgent reflection on the EU's role to protect fundamental rights in the face of such challenges.

[69] Beijer, *The Limits of Fundamental Rights Protection* (n 23) 161.

[70] E Muir, 'Reshuffling Our Understanding of Fundamental Rights Law in Europe: An EU Lawyer's Research Agenda' (2021) 2 *European Human Rights Law Review* 142.

[71] See, among others, M Wind, *The Tribalization of Europe: A Defence of Our Liberal Values* (Polity, 2020); MA Graber, S Levinson, and MV Tushnet, *Constitutional Democracy in Crisis?* (Oxford University Press, 2018) and the Epilogue of this book.

[72] G Levi and D Preda (eds), *Euroscepticisms. Resistance and Opposition to the European Community/European Union* (Il Mulino, 2019).

[73] For an in-depth analysis, see J Lacroix and J-Y Pranchère, *Human Rights on Trial: A Genealogy of the Critique of Human Rights* (Cambridge University Press, 2018).

[74] On 'EU Human Rights Scepticism', see Dawson, *The Governance of EU Fundamental Rights* (n 65) 21–26.

Thirdly, and more substantively, it is crucial for the effectiveness of the protection of fundamental rights of both European and non-European citizens in Europe to understand the characteristics and functioning of this protection system. As highlighted above, the EU is increasingly active in the field of fundamental rights protection. To fully grasp the potential of this activity, it is essential to have the necessary tools to utilise this protection. In a context of growing resistance to human rights worldwide, and the rise of right-wing populism, ensuring the effectiveness of these rights has become an urgent priority.

Finally, as Elise Muir and Cécile Leconte have already emphasised,[75] understanding the EU system of fundamental rights protection is also essential for the rest of the world. Indeed, developments within the EU can provide valuable insights for other regions where regional organisations are seeking to enhance their own systems of fundamental rights protection. In a spirit of mutual learning, providing resources that facilitate the understanding of regional human rights protection systems aims to improve the protection of human rights on a global scale. For decades, there have been calls for the EU to assume a leadership role on the global stage in human rights, particularly by developing a coherent and comprehensive human rights policy.[76] This work provides an opportunity to examine whether such a policy exists within the EU's now mature fundamental rights framework, and to explore its potential strengths and limitations.

For human rights lawyers worldwide, this book is thus meant to constitute an essential resource, offering cross-cutting insights into a system that is often under-explored but increasingly influential. Despite the EU's expanding role as a key player in human rights protection, its legal framework remains largely unfamiliar to many in the international human rights community. This book addresses that gap, providing these professionals with the knowledge they need to fully engage with EU law and understand its significant impact on the protection of human rights globally.

Section VI Structure of the Book

The book will start by underlining the paradox deriving from the fact that, even though the EU has only a limited capacity, it can nevertheless be a particularly strong fundamental rights protector (chapter one). The 'distinctive features' of EU (Fundamental Rights) Law – notably in comparison to traditional international law – as well as the judicial apparatus supporting it, will then be analysed

[75] C Leconte and E Muir, 'Introduction to Special Issue "Understanding Resistance to the EU Fundamental Rights Policy"' (2014) 15 *Human Rights Review* 1, 22.

[76] Alston and Weiler, 'An "Ever Closer Union"' (n 12). See, for conflicting views, von Bogdandy, 'The European Union as a Human Rights Organization?' (n 32).

(chapter two). The EU's administrative and financial tools that exist to enforce the EU protection of fundamental rights will also be subject to discussion (chapter three). Finally, the concluding chapter (chapter four) will examine the EU's position within the broader architecture of human rights protection, while also exploring how human rights may, in turn, enrich the EU itself – by providing the contours of a political project capable of fostering an integrated European society.

1

A Simultaneously Strong and Limited Human Rights Protector

> The adoption of a catalogue of rights will make it possible to give a clear response to those who accuse the Union of employing one set of standards at external level and another internally.[1]

Introduction

The European Union (EU)'s current role in protecting fundamental rights was far from obvious at the time of its birth. However, it is now widely acknowledged to be a central actor that can safeguard these rights within the common area of fundamental rights in certain situations, and to a certain extent.

But its new role remains complex and is not easily defined. It cannot be equated with the fundamental rights role of a state or a traditional international organisation. The EU does not have full legal competence over the territory it covers in the way that a state does. The EU can only act within the limits of competences that were specifically conferred on it by the Member States, and it lacks a general and express legal competence to act in the field of fundamental rights protection. Unlike traditional international human rights organisations, the *primary* purpose of the EU is not to protect human rights. The EU is not a 'human rights organisation',[2] at least in the traditional understanding of the term.[3]

Given this perspective, what is the EU's contribution to the protection of individuals' fundamental rights? In this Introduction, I posit that, while the EU's capacity to protect fundamental rights is limited, it remains robust. Although the EU does not have *general* competence in the field of fundamental rights protection, its contribution can be *substantial* when circumstances allow. And this capacity has developed gradually over time.

[1] European Commission, Communication on the Charter of Fundamental Rights of the European Union [2000] COM (2000) 559, para 12.

[2] K Lenaerts and JA Gutiérrez-Fons, 'The Place of the Charter in the European Legal Space' in S Peers et al (eds), *The EU Charter of Fundamental Rights: A Commentary*, 2nd edn (Bloomsbury, 2021) 1712.

[3] See the Introduction for the definition of 'human rights organisation'.

Initially, the EU simply adhered to traditionally protected standards that already applied in the European arena via national constitutions and international protection instruments – especially the European Convention on Human Rights (ECHR). It was mainly a deferential 'norm-*taker*' in the field of fundamental rights. This was primarily to ensure that EU law complied with these standards (section I).

Gradually, however, the protection of fundamental rights was elevated and came to be recognised as a founding value of the EU legal order (section II). The need to ensure such protection at the EU level became increasingly indispensable as European integration both deepened and widened – deepened through the expansion of EU competences into areas inherently linked to fundamental rights, and widened through successive enlargements that required the articulation of shared political and value-based criteria to define a common EU identity, and to ensure that new Member States would commit to upholding it (section III).

But there was no parallel granting of a general competence to the EU in the field of human rights protection: its capacity remains limited in this respect (section IV). Additionally, certain voices have criticised the EU for its purportedly hypocritical approach in presenting the protection of fundamental rights as one of its priorities, especially given the EU's competing objectives (section V).

Despite the constitutional constraints, the EU has, nevertheless, gradually evolved into an active player in the field of fundamental rights protection. This development has been propelled by institutional and judicial innovation alike: on the one hand, through the selective exercise of harmonisation powers in specific policy areas; and, on the other, through the Court of Justice's dynamic interpretation of the thresholds and scope of certain fundamental rights. Notwithstanding these limitations and the criticisms that accompany them, the EU has today become, at least to some extent, a genuine 'norm-*maker*' in the field of protection of fundamental rights in Europe (section VI).

Section I – Deference: The European Communities as 'Norm-takers'

Fundamental rights protection was not a primary concern during the early stages of EU integration in the 1950s. The idea of safeguarding these rights was briefly considered during discussions on the proposed European Political Community, but the initiative failed and there was no reference to fundamental rights in the founding framework of the European Communities.[4] Although the European

[4] See, for an extensive analysis, G de Búrca 'The Evolution of EU Human Rights Law' in P Craig and G de Búrca (eds) *The Evolution of EU Law*, 3rd edn (Oxford University Press, 2021) 480–505; and E Spaventa, 'Fundamental Rights in the European Union' in C Barnard and S Peers (eds), *European Union Law*, 4th edn (Oxford University Press, 2023) 242–83.

Communities were established with the objective of maintaining peace and economic stability on the European continent,[5] the specific ambit was limited to the creation of a common market.[6]

The issue of human rights was left to national constitutional systems and the Council of Europe, which in the 1950s became the birthplace of the European Court of Human Rights (ECtHR).[7] The Council of Europe was created as a direct result of the willingness to avoid – at all costs – a repetition of the atrocities committed during the Second World War. It was deemed necessary to establish a third-party authority capable of acting as a backup option if national systems failed to prevent large-scale human rights violations.[8]

The issue of the protection of fundamental rights was, however, quickly reintroduced at the Community level. The story is very well known: the European Communities had no specific power to ensure the respect of fundamental rights, the primacy of Community law was soon challenged by a number of national constitutional courts in relation to their own catalogue of protection.[9] Accepting the primacy of EU law over national law, as proclaimed by the European Court of Justice (as it was then described) in its famous *Costa v Enel* judgment,[10] was indeed a threat to their national legal order governing the protection of human rights, especially since the creators and implementers of Community law were not themselves under an obligation to respect those rights. The German Constitutional Court famously opposed the acceptance of such primacy unless the EU had a legal basis providing it with an official fundamental rights protection role, namely until:

> the integration process has … progressed so far that Community law also receives a catalogue of fundamental rights decided on by a parliament and of settled validity, which is adequate in comparison with the catalogue of fundamental rights contained in the [German] Basic Law.[11]

Following this resistance, the European Court of Justice ruled in favour of there being a Community-law-level of fundamental rights protection, through the vehicle of 'general principles of law'.[12] This evolution was not, however, driven by a motivation to promote fundamental rights per se – that was not the role of the

[5] Notably in order to contribute to the Member States' political and economic interests. See AS Milward, *The European Rescue of the Nation-State*, 2nd edn (Routledge, 2000).

[6] de Búrca, 'The Evolution of EU Human Rights Law' (n 4) 487.

[7] DW Urwin, *The Community of Europe: A History of European Integration since 1945*, 2nd edn (Routledge, 1995) 38.

[8] L Burgorgue-Larsen, *The 3 Regional Human Rights Courts in Context. Justice That Cannot Be Taken for Granted* (Oxford University Press, 2024), 13.

[9] See, eg BVerfGE 37, 271 2 BvL 52/71 *Solange I-Beschluß*, 29 May 1974.

[10] Case 6/64 *Flaminio Costa v E.N.E.L.* ECLI:EU:C:1964:66 [1964] ECR 585.

[11] BVerfGE 37, 291, 29 May 1974 *(Solange I)*. On this issue, see, among others, KJ Alter, *Establishing the Supremacy of European Law: The Making of an International Rule of Law in Europe* (Oxford University Press, 2006) 90.

[12] Case 29/69 *Erich Stauder v Ville d'Ulm – Sozialamt* ECLI:EU:C:1969:57 [1969] ECR 419.

Communities – but, rather, aimed at preserving the hierarchy of the EU legal order. As stressed by Gráinne de Búrca,

> the reason for the volte-face of the Court is widely accepted to be its concern to maintain the autonomy and supremacy of EC law, and to avoid domestic court and domestic litigant claims that Community law must be subordinate to national constitutional rights.[13]

Over the years, the Court of Justice of the European Union (CJEU), as it has been known since 2009, thus developed a catalogue of fundamental rights through its case law, the content of which was inspired by the common constitutional traditions of the Member States,[14] and those international instruments for the protection of fundamental rights ratified by the Member States, in particular the European Convention on Human Rights (ECHR).[15] This development was duly taken into account by those resistant constitutional courts. They finally accepted that they would no longer review the validity of Community law against their *national* rules on the protection of fundamental rights, because equivalent protection was now guaranteed at the Community level.[16]

While fundamental rights thus made their way into the legal order of the Communities, the latter positioned themselves in this context more as 'norm-takers', replicating relevant national and international standards. For example, the CJEU has regularly referred to the case law of the ECtHR[17] to offer strong legitimising support for the general principles of law that it has 'unveiled'. The protection of fundamental rights was primarily upheld in a negative sense – serving as a constraint that both European institutions and Member States were required to observe when acting within the framework of EU law.[18] The traditional function of fundamental rights, in the way the CJEU designed it, was thus as a defensive 'shield' for individuals vis-à-vis public authorities.

Section II – Consolidation: Elevating Fundamental Rights

Alongside these judicial developments, the protection of fundamental rights also became more prominent in the political sphere. A series of political stances in the 1970s firmly established fundamental rights protection as a core objective of

[13] de Búrca, 'The Evolution of EU Human Rights Law' (n 4).

[14] Case 11/70 *Internationale Handelsgesellschaft mbH v Einfuhr- und Vorratsstelle für Getreide und Futtermittel* ECLI:EU:C:1970:114 [1970] ECR 1125, para 4.

[15] Case 4/73 *J Nold, Kohlen- und Baustoffgrosshandlung v Commission of the European Communities* ECLI:EU:C:1974:51 [1974] ECR 491, para 13.

[16] BverfGE 73, 339, 22 October 1986 *(Solange II)*.

[17] See, for instance, Case C-128/18 *Dorobantu* ECLI:EU:C:2019:857 [2019], paras 56–57.

[18] E Muir, 'Fundamental Rights: An Unsettling EU Competence' (2014) 15 *Human Rights Review* 26.

the European project;[19] respect for fundamental rights became a prerequisite for accession.[20] In a Declaration adopted in 1973, the Member States underlined that they were 'determined to defend the principles of representative democracy, of the rule of law, of social justice – which is the ultimate goal of economic progress – and of respect for human rights' and described them as 'fundamental elements of the European Identity'.[21]

In 1977, the European Parliament, the Council of the European Union, and the European Commission adopted a Joint Declaration stressing 'the prime importance' of the protection of fundamental rights, 'as derived in particular from the constitutions of the Member States and the European Convention for the Protection of Human Rights and Fundamental Freedoms', and that, 'in the exercise of their powers and in pursuance of the aims of the European Communities they respect and will continue to respect these rights'.[22]

Fundamental rights were formally incorporated into the Treaties with the adoption of the Single European Act, in 1986, and the Maastricht Treaty, in 1992, which signalled the transition to a fully political European Union.[23] Protection of them was an objective to be promoted, as stated in the preamble to the Single European Act; then, later, as rules that the EU must respect, as per the wording of Article F of the Maastricht Treaty.[24] The Treaty of Amsterdam amended the latter provision to state that 'the European Union is founded on the principles of liberty, democracy, respect for human rights and fundamental freedoms, and the rule of law, principles which are common to the Member States'.[25] During this period, academic literature increasingly advocated for the EU to take a more proactive role in the protection of fundamental rights.[26]

A few years later, an actual EU 'Bill of Rights' emerged. The Charter of Fundamental Rights of the European Union (EU Charter) was formally proclaimed in Nice in 2000. This marked a turning point in the EU's protection of fundamental rights. Drafted at a Convention composed mainly of representatives of Member States, national parliaments, the European Parliament, and the European Commission, this text intended to affirm the importance of the protection of fundamental rights for the European project. To do this, it aimed to make

[19] See, among others, Declaration on European Identity of 14 December 1973 [1973]; Joint Declaration of the European Parliament, Council of the European Union, and the European Commission concerning the protection of fundamental rights and the European Convention for the Protection of Human Rights and Fundamental Freedoms [1977] OJ C103/01 (Joint Declaration concerning the protection of fundamental rights and the ECHR).

[20] Declaration on Democracy at the Copenhagen European Council of 7 and 8 April 1978 [1978].

[21] Declaration on European Identity of 14 December 1973 [1973].

[22] Joint Declaration concerning the Protection of Fundamental Rights and the ECHR.

[23] JHH Weiler, 'The Transformation of Europe' (1991) 100 *The Yale Law Journal* 2403.

[24] Treaty on European Union [1992] OJ C 191/91, art F.

[25] Consolidated version of the Treaty on European Union [1997] OJ C 340/02, art 6.

[26] See, among others, P Alston and JHH Weiler, 'An "Ever Closer Union" in Need of a Human Rights Policy' (1998) *European Journal of International Law* 658; and A Cassese and others, *Leading By Example: A Human Rights Agenda for the European Union for the Year 2000* (Academy of European Law, 1998).

the protection that already existed through the general principles of law more 'visible', as well as to reinforce this protection 'in the light of changes in society, social progress and scientific and technological developments'.[27]

Three main arguments were advanced to justify the inclusion of such a text within the EU's legal framework.[28] First, it aimed to enhance legal certainty by making the protection provided through jurisprudence and general principles of law more transparent.[29] Second, it sought to improve the effectiveness of this protection by enshrining fundamental rights in a formal text.[30] Finally, adoption of the text was driven by the ambition to bolster the EU's legitimacy in the eyes of its citizens.[31] At the time, however, the EU Charter only had political significance, leaving the legal protection of fundamental rights to be governed by the EU's general principles of law. Nine years later, when the Lisbon Treaty was adopted, the Charter was granted the status of primary law.[32] As underlined by Koen Lenaerts and José Gutiérrez-Fons, it is now safe to say 'that the Charter is one of the most important achievements in the history of European integration'.[33] This instrument has indeed 'given far greater visibility and prominence' to human rights that were initially protected by the EU's general principles in the EU's legal order.[34]

In terms of content, the EU Charter draws heavily on inspiration from the ECHR and the case law of the ECtHR. It contains all the rights traditionally protected by international human rights instruments, as well as more 'modern' provisions, including social, economic, and cultural rights. Article 52 of the EU Charter, however, makes a distinction between rights and principles contained within it – the latter do not have direct effect. Article 52(3) of the EU Charter provides that rights similarly enshrined in the EU Charter and the ECHR should be subject to the same interpretation as in the ECHR (as developed by the ECtHR), unless the EU decides to offer a higher level of protection.

The Lisbon Treaty brought about a major change by granting the EU Charter the same legal value as the Treaties.[35] It also elevated the protection of fundamental rights to the highest rank among the founding values of the EU, alongside the rule of law and democracy.[36] Additionally, it stipulated that it was an EU objective to

[27] Preamble of the Charter of Fundamental Rights of the European Union, OJ C 83/2010.

[28] S Van Drooghenbroeck, E Bribosia, and C Rizcallah, 'La Charte a vingt ans. Regards croisés pour un anniversaire' (2021) *Cahiers de droit européen* 23.

[29] J-P Jacqué, 'La démarche initiée par le Conseil européen de Cologne' (2000) 12 *Revue Universelle des droits de l'homme* 4.

[30] E Bribosia, 'La protection des droits fondamentaux' in P Magnette (ed), *La constitution de l'Europe* (Éditions de l'Université de Bruxelles, 2000) 107–27.

[31] Communication of the European Commission on the Charter of Fundamental Rights of the European Union, 13 September 2000, COM(2000) 559 final, point 8.

[32] TEU, art 6.

[33] Lenaerts and Gutiérrez-Fons, 'The Place of the Charter in the EU Legal Space' (n 2) 1712.

[34] ibid.

[35] TEU, art 6(1).

[36] TEU, art 2.

promote these rights.[37] The EU's accession to the ECHR was also provided for by the Lisbon Treaty. Following the addition of this obligation in the EU Treaties, negotiations with the Council of Europe took place until a draft agreement was achieved. It was presented to the Court of Justice of the European Union (CJEU) for a formal Opinion, and in its famous *Opinion 2/13*,[38] the CJEU considered that the draft agreement was not compatible with the EU Treaties. Since then, negotiations have resumed, and finding a new agreement is considered a priority.[39]

The official stance now underscores the inclusion of fundamental rights in the identity and foundational values of the EU, and is promoted by all of its institutions.[40] However, there are certain obstacles, in practice, that still curtail their actual effectiveness, as discussed below.

Section III – Indispensability: EU Fundamental Rights Protection, an Essential Condition for EU Integration

There was a clear intention to define the EU's identity as intrinsically tied to the protection of fundamental rights, but the development of such protection at the EU level was also justified by more instrumental considerations. It soon became evident that this protection was essential for the effective functioning of EU integration, driven in particular by two key phenomena: the deepening of integration between existing Member States, and the territorial expansion of the EU.

Over time, EU integration has deepened significantly. The history is well documented, and we will not explore it in depth here.

Initially confined to economic integration, the scope of European integration gradually expanded, encompassing areas closely linked to the protection of fundamental rights. The EU acquired new competences in areas such as judicial and police co-operation in criminal and civil matters, and migration policy. These

[37] TEU, art 3.

[38] Opinion 2/13 of the Court pursuant to Article 218(11) TFEU *Accession of the European Union to the European Convention for the Protection of Human Rights and Fundamental Freedoms* ECLI:EU:C:2014:2454 [2014].

[39] Statement of the European Commission, 'The EU's Accession to the European Convention on Human Rights: Joint statement on behalf of the Council of Europe and the European Commission' [2020] 20/1748.

[40] See, among others, Case C-156/21 *Hungary v European Parliament and Council* ECLI:EU:C:2022:97 [2022], para 12; Communication from the Commission to the European Parliament, the Council of the European Union, the European Economic and Social Committee and the Committee of the Regions, 'Strategy to strengthen the application of the Charter of Fundamental Rights in the EU' [2020] COM(2020) 711 final, 19; Council conclusions on strengthening the application of the Charter of Fundamental Rights in the European Union [2021] 6795/12; European Parliament Resolution of 26 November 2020 on the situation of Fundamental Rights in the European Union [2019] (2019/2199(INI)).

domains, which now fall under the ambit of the Area of Freedom, Security, and Justice (AFSJ), are intricately connected to the question of fundamental rights. After all, how can the EU justify action in these areas if it does not protect these rights?

The instruments adopted in these domains often rely on the 'principle of mutual trust' among Member States.[41] This principle encapsulates a presumption by a Member State that all other Member States respect fundamental rights, the aim being to rely on a relationship of mutual recognition of decisions and trust between national authorities when they co-operate in cross-border civil and criminal matters.

To support this principle, the EU has had to be proactive, such as by adopting measures for the minimum harmonisation of related rights, to ensure a common level of protection among Member States collaborating under the auspices of EU law instruments (for an extended analysis, see section VI below). In this context, the EU must *actively* ensure that fundamental rights are respected by its Member States; it is a *prerequisite* for its proper internal functioning.

One notable example is the Framework Decision setting out the European Arrest Warrant system, which is one of the most effective mechanisms for intergovernmental co-operation in criminal matters worldwide.[42] This system enables the quasi-automatic surrender of individuals sought by one Member State, to another. If Member State A requests the arrest and surrender of a person present in Member State B, the latter is obliged to carry out these operations. Exceptions justifying a refusal by Member State B to surrender a person to Member State A are limited. It is important to note that there is no general exception based on the protection of fundamental rights, precisely due to the presumption that human rights are already safeguarded under the principle of mutual trust.[43] For the smooth functioning of the AFSJ, it is therefore crucial that all Member States uphold fundamental rights, to live up to the presumption. What was initially a matter of national concern has gradually, in line with the deepening of EU integration, become an issue of direct interest to the EU itself. The need to develop the protection of fundamental rights at EU level has thus also resulted from these new fields of EU competences.

Secondly, the consolidation of fundamental rights protection within the EU has also emerged as a vital prerequisite for the continued territorial expansion of

[41] C Rizcallah, *The Principle of Mutual Trust in European Union Law. An essential principle facing a crisis of values* (Bruylant, 2022).

[42] Consolidated version of Council Framework Decision 2002/584/JHA of 13 June 2002 on the European Arrest Warrant and the Surrender Procedures between Member States [2002] OJ L190/01.

[43] A two-step approach was nevertheless developed by the Court of Justice in order to prevent serious violations of fundamental rights. However, given the particularly stringent nature of the conditions set out in this test, it is arguable whether it truly results in effective protection of fundamental rights. On this issue, see Rizcallah, *The Principle of Mutual Trust in EU Law* (n 41); and C Rizcallah, 'The Principle of Mutual Trust and the Protection of Fundamental Rights in the Area of Freedom, Security and Justice: A critical look at the Court of Justice's stone-by-stone approach' [2023] *Maastricht Journal of European and Comparative Law* 255.

the EU. In particular, as the decision was taken to embrace and build closer relationships with countries in Central and Eastern Europe after the fall of Communism, it became imperative to establish precise criteria to uphold the rule of law and safeguard fundamental rights.[44] The 'turning point'[45] of this undertaking was the Copenhagen Summit of 1993, which set a political condition for would-be new members of the EU: the 'stability of institutions guaranteeing democracy, the rule of law, human rights and respect for and protection of minorities'.[46]

Yet, as underlined by Bruno de Witte, the enshrinement of such political conditionality for new Member States also stimulated 'the debate on whether the European Union itself should take these basic constitutional values more seriously by entrenching them more firmly in its own legal order'.[47] This was followed by important treaty changes, in particular the insertion, by the Treaty of Amsterdam, of Article 6(1) into the Treaty on European Union (TEU), which enshrined the 'fundamental values' of the EU, including fundamental rights, in a context of preparing the EU for the following wave of accession.[48]

From the outset, however, the presence of differing standards when it came to existing Member States and new entrants was a cause for concern. The fact that, at that time, there was no genuine EU Fundamental Rights catalogue was among other aspects specifically invoked to exemplify the disparate treatment experienced by candidate states.[49] Indeed, these states were to be scrutinised for their adherence to values, including the protection of fundamental rights, with a view to accession to the EU. Wojciech Sadurski explained this approach not as being influenced by human rights concerns, but rather by political factors:

> The causes of this contrast are not difficult to guess: there is a natural, and largely understandable, suspicion in the Western part of Europe concerning the depth and sincerity of democratic transformations in the Central and Eastern parts of the continent … For reasons of geographic and cultural proximity, this suspicion was not felt within the then member states when Spain, Portugal, and Greece were to join the European Community after their own abandonment of authoritarian rule. But this is not the only reason, and to the question raised by Williams – 'why have the European Union institutions embraced a human rights policy of distinction [between the current members and applicant countries] rather than rely upon the highly developed human rights system established under the Council of Europe?' – I offer an answer in terms of Realpolitik.

[44] A Albi, 'Ironies in Human Rights Protection in the EU: Pre-Accession Conditionality and Post-Accession Conundrums' (2009) 15 *European Law Journal* 46.

[45] W Sadurski, 'Accession's Democracy Dividend: The Impact of the EU Enlargement upon Democracy in the New Member States of Central and Eastern Europe' (2004) 10 *European Law Journal* 371–74.

[46] Copenhagen European Council of 21–22 June 1993 [1993].

[47] B de Witte, 'The Impact of Enlargement on the Constitution of the European Union' in M Cremona (ed), *The Enlargement of the European Union*, 1st edn (Oxford University Press, 2003) 209.

[48] ibid, 218.

[49] ibid, 233; A Williams, 'Enlargement of the Union and Human Rights Conditionality: A Policy of Distinction?' [2000] *European Law Review* 601; W Sadurski, 'Charter and Enlargement' (2002) 8 *European Law Journal* 340.

> These double standards were developed, partly, in order to provide the current Member States with a convenient excuse for not admitting a particular applicant country, even if that country fulfils all the acquis criteria, if in future there is insufficient 'political will' or societal support within the Union to enlarge. The human rights criteria are so malleable and vague that they can serve as a very handy device for refusing entry.[50]

Later on, the adoption of the EU Charter was presented – notably by the European Commission – as a remedy to this problem: 'a step taken in order to close the gap between external requirements and the internal human rights policy'.[51] The European Commission, in this regard, explicitly stated that 'the adoption of a catalogue of rights will make it possible to give a clear response to those who accuse the Union of employing one set of standards at external level and another internally'.[52]

The prospect of enlargement, along with the deepening of European integration, thus served as catalysts for an EU-designed protection of fundamental rights.

Section IV – Limitation: A Paradoxically Restricted Mandate

Although the protection of fundamental rights is now explicitly recognised as part of the EU's objectives and identity, the EU still does not have a general mandate in this area. In fact, the EU, the powers of which are limited by the principle of attributed competences, has not been given a general competence to legislate or act in order to protect fundamental rights in the EU. It is unlike the Council of Europe, the objective of which is the protection of human rights; that is not the EU's main mission. Nor is there a general competence for such protection (section IV.1). Consequently, the EU Charter of Fundamental Rights only has a limited scope of application (section IV.2). Moreover, even where the EU has received certain competences in the field of fundamental rights protection, it must respect various principles constraining how it exercises them (section IV.3).

IV.1. The Absence of a General Mandate for Fundamental Rights Protection

As underlined by the CJEU itself, the EU is 'precluded by its very nature from being considered as a State'. Even though its structure has very specific characteristics, the very nature of the EU remains regulated by international law. The EU, indeed, 'came into being as [a creature] of international law, as [it was] established by means of international treaties concluded by States'.[53] These Treaties still form the

[50] Sadurski, 'Charter and Enlargement' (n 49) 344.
[51] ibid.
[52] European Commission Communication on the Charter of Fundamental Rights of the EU, para 12.
[53] B de Witte, 'EU Law: Is It International Law?' in C Barnard and S Peers (eds), *European Union Law* (n 4) 210.

foundation of the EU legal order, and the validity of EU secondary legislation is directly dependent on them. Moreover, international law does not limit the scope of the competences that can be conferred on an international organisation;[54] and the EU is still considered to be an international organisation under the constitutional law of most of the Member States.[55]

Like any other international organisation, the EU is governed by the 'principle of specialty'. This means that it can only act within the competences that have been conferred on it, unlike states, which enjoy plenary jurisdiction. In EU law, it is the principle of conferral that reflects this limit; it is contained in Article 5 of the TEU, which states that 'the limits of Union competences are governed by the principle of conferral'. It moreover specifies that 'the use of Union competences is governed by the principles of subsidiarity and proportionality'.

The EU has never been granted a general competence in the field of fundamental rights protection.[56] This was clearly affirmed by the CJEU in its *Opinion 2/94* concerning the first attempt at EU accession to the ECHR. The CJEU indeed noted that 'no Treaty provision confers on the Community institutions any general power to enact rules on human rights or to conclude international conventions in this field'.[57] Therefore, the draft accession agreement was considered, at that time, as breaching the principle of conferral.

In the meantime, the Treaties have been amended in order to allow for accession. The Treaty of Lisbon added Article 6(2) to the TEU, which now states that 'the Union shall accede to the European Convention for the Protection of Human Rights and Fundamental Freedoms', thereby providing a legal basis for this accession. Nevertheless, this same provision stresses that 'such accession shall not affect the Union's competences as defined in the Treaties'. Thus, despite the modification of the Treaties, the EU remains deprived of a general competence in the field of fundamental rights protection. The same conclusion applies with regard to the adoption of the EU Charter. Indeed, Article 6(1) TEU unequivocally enshrines that 'the provisions of the Charter shall not extend in any way the competences of the Union as defined in the Treaties'. This principle is even recalled in the EU Charter itself, in its Article 51(2):

> the Charter does not extend the field of application of Union law beyond the powers of the Union or establish any new power or task for the Union, or modify powers and tasks as defined in the Treaties.

[54] ibid, 192.

[55] ibid, 196.

[56] See, however, Robin CA White, who argues that the 'Union is moving inexorably towards a general human rights competence', and has been since the Treaty of Lisbon, because of the elevation of the Charter at the rank of primary law and the foreseen accession to the ECHR: RCA White, 'Reshaping the Human Rights Landscape of the European Union' in N Nic Shuibhne and LW Gormley (eds), *From Single Market to Economic Union* (Oxford University Press, 2012).

[57] Opinion 2/94 of the Court *Accession by the Community to the European Convention for the Protection of Human Rights and Fundamental Freedoms* ECLI:EU:C:1996:140 [1996] ECR I-01759, para 27.

The EU's capacity in the field of fundamental rights protection is, therefore, clearly limited. The EU can only actively act in the field of fundamental rights protection – for example, by adopting harmonisation measures – within the limits of the powers that have been conferred upon it. This principle has important consequences for the protection of fundamental rights. As stressed by Gráinne de Búrca, 'the field of human rights protection and promotion is a very different one, in the European Union context, from that of a state, and it is one in which the competences problem looms large'.[58]

This situation heavily impacts on the scope of application of the EU Charter, which will be analysed below. It is also one of the main differences between the EU and traditional international human rights organisations. As underlined by Samantha Besson, 'only an institution which can place human rights at the core of its internal and external governance can be deemed a human rights institution'.[59]

IV.2. Limits to the Scope of the EU Charter and the General Principles of EU Law

The existence of the EU Charter of Fundamental Rights, and its subsequent attainment of legally binding value, has had no impact on the absence of general competence of the EU in the field of fundamental rights protection. As the EU does not have overarching competence in the area of fundamental rights, this instrument is, naturally, not designed to apply universally. This restriction also applies to the general principles of EU law. According to Article 51 of the EU Charter, its provisions are, indeed,

> addressed to the institutions, bodies, offices and agencies of the Union with due regard for the principle of subsidiarity and to the Member States only when they are implementing Union law.

Therefore, compliance with the EU Charter (and the general principles) is binding on the EU's institutions and bodies,[60] and on Member States, but only when they implement EU law. This notion has been construed by the CJEU

[58] G de Búrca, 'New Modes of Governance and the Protection of Human Rights' in P Alston and O de Schutter (eds), *Monitoring Fundamental Rights in the EU: the Contribution of the Fundamental Rights Agency* (Hart, 2005) 29.

[59] S Besson, 'The European Union and Human Rights: Towards A Post-National Human Rights Institution?' (2006) 6 *Human Rights Law Review* 342.

[60] It is worth noting that they are bound not only when acting within the EU's competences but also when operating beyond the strict confines of its legal framework. This principle was affirmed by the CJEU in relation to the powers conferred upon the European Commission by the Treaty establishing the European Stability Mechanism, which, although concluded outside the institutional framework of the EU's legal order, entrusted certain responsibilities to its institutions: Joined Cases C-8/15 P to C-10/15 P, *Ledra Advertising Ltd v European Commission* ECLI:EU:C:2016:701 [2016], para 67.

as encompassing 'all the situations governed by European Union law'.[61] This broadly includes situations where Member States implement EU law, exercise a discretionary power offered by EU law, or use exceptions or derogations provided by EU law.[62] Acts that exhibit 'a certain degree of connection' with EU law, 'above and beyond the matters covered being closely related or one of those matters having an indirect impact on the other',[63] should be added to the list. To assess this connection, the CJEU, notably, considers the existence or lack of a 'specific obligation' arising from EU law in relation to the national act in question.[64]

It is, therefore, clear that it was not intended that the EU Charter should apply to all situations that take place within the territory of the EU; it should apply only to the ones falling within the material scope of EU law. To quote Koen Lenaerts and José Gutiérrez-Fons, 'the Charter is the "shadow" of EU law. Just as an object defines the contours of its shadow, the scope of EU law determines that of the Charter'.[65] However, one cannot fail to highlight the uncertainties underlying the determination of this scope of application. This determination is notoriously complex – a point to which we shall return at the end of this chapter.[66] The notion of 'implementing EU law' remains open to interpretation and continues to evolve. Similarly, what constitutes a 'certain degree of connection' with EU law is far from a fixed concept.

It should already be underlined, however, that this feature marks a significant distinction between the EU Charter and traditional international human rights treaties. In international law, instruments safeguarding human rights typically have a primarily territorial scope, applying uniformly across the entire territory of the contracting parties. In exceptional cases, they may also have extraterritorial consequences. They are generally not subject to material limitations in their scope of application, as their core purpose is to ensure the protection of human rights, imposing binding obligations on states across all their activities.

Article 1 of the ECHR reads as follows:

> The High Contracting Parties shall secure to everyone within their jurisdiction the rights and freedoms defined in Section I of this Convention.

[61] Case C-617/10 *Åklagaren v Hans Åkerberg Fransson* ECLI:EU:C:2013:105 [2013], para 19.

[62] A Ward, 'Article 51' in S Peers and others (eds), *The EU Charter of Fundamental Rights* (n 2) 1576. Determining the scope of application is not an easy matter, and many areas of uncertainty remain. However, a comprehensive and in-depth analysis of this issue would go beyond the scope of my analysis. In this regard, I refer to Ward's contribution and, among others, A Bailleux, 'Les contours du champ d'application de la Charte – Une tentative de recadrage' in A Iliopoulou-Penot and L Xenou (eds), *La Charte des droits fondamentaux, source de renouveau constitutionnel européen?* (Bruylant, 2020) 201–18.

[63] Case C-206/13 *Siragusa* ECLI:EU:C:2014:126 [2014], para 24.

[64] ibid, para 27.

[65] Lenaerts and Gutiérrez-Fons 'The Place of the Charter in the EU Constitutional Edifice' (n 2) 1568.

[66] *cf* ch 1, s VI.3, 'A Constitutional Balance under Tension'; and ch 4, s II.1, 'A Fragmented Layer of Protection with Blurred Boundaries'.

Consequently, it is the notion of 'jurisdiction' that defines the scope of its application, and states are required to ensure compliance strictly within these boundaries. The notion of jurisdiction is, nonetheless, cross-cutting, unlike the notion of 'implementation of Union law' found in Article 51 of the EU Charter. The notion of jurisdiction does not refer to particular matters, domains, or competences of the state, but rather to the issue of 'imputability'. According to the ECtHR, which relies on general international law, the notion of jurisdiction is 'primarily territorial'.[67] The extraterritorial jurisdiction of a high contracting party may be recognised exceptionally and requires 'special justification in the particular circumstances of each case'.[68] Therefore, the principle is that the territorial criterion should be central to determining the scope of the ECHR's application. The reasoning behind this approach diverges fundamentally from the principles underpinning the EU Charter.

This difference aligns with the reality that the EU is not a traditional international organisation created exclusively to safeguard human rights. Although the protection of fundamental rights is one of its core founding values, the EU's capacity to act in this area remains significantly constrained. I will return below to the ambiguities of the scope of EU law, in connection with the EU's legislative capacity in this area and the elusive constitutional balance it entails.[69]

IV.3. The Constraints Limiting the Exercise of EU Competences

In certain areas, the EU holds only *specific* competences that empower it to take active measures in safeguarding fundamental rights. Over time, various legal bases conferring these specific competences on the EU in this field have been integrated into the Treaties. These legal bases provide the foundation for the EU to adopt binding acts, which may require the harmonisation of national fundamental rights standards. Section VI below will explore the EU's harmonisation powers within this domain in greater detail.

It is important, however, to note additional limits to the exercise of these specific EU competences in the area of fundamental rights protection. In addition to the principle of conferral that defines the scope of EU competences, other principles also regulate the way in which the EU can exercise its competences, and these are applicable in the domain of fundamental rights. I will briefly review these constraints.

The first constraint derives from the principle of subsidiarity. This principle requires that the EU only take action if and to the extent that it can bring added

[67] The ECtHR's Decision as to the Admissibility of *Banković and Others v Belgium and Others* App no 52207/99 ECLI:CE:ECHR:2001:1212DEC005220799 (ECtHR, 12 December 2001), para 59.

[68] ibid, para 60.

[69] See ss VI.1 and VI.3 of this chapter.

value compared to the action of the Member States.[70] It therefore acts as a brake 'on the exercise of competence which has indubitably been conferred on the Union'.[71] As underlined by Mariane Dony, 'even if the EU has competence in a certain matter, it cannot automatically make use of all the necessary powers to exercise that competence'.[72] This principle applies to all EU competences except the exclusive ones, because by definition only the EU is authorised to act in these areas. The underlying rationale of the principle is the fact that action should be taken as closely as possible to the citizen. In the realm of fundamental rights protection, the principle of subsidiarity in EU law reflects the spirit of the ECHR. It establishes that the primary responsibility for safeguarding fundamental rights lies with national authorities. International bodies are to step in only as a supporting safeguard in cases of national failure.[73]

The catalogue of competences contained in Articles 3 to 6 of the Treaty on the Functioning of the European Union (TFEU) does not indicate the nature of the EU's competences in the field of fundamental rights protection. The competences the EU has been given in this area should, nevertheless, be considered as being competences that are shared, as described in Article 4 TFEU, with the Member States.[74] Indeed, Member States can, logically, continue to take action in the field of fundamental rights protection to the extent that the EU has not exercised its competence. In principle, therefore, the exercise by the EU of its specific competences in the area of fundamental rights protection must respect the principle of subsidiarity.

This means that the EU should only act if: (i) 'the objectives of the proposed action cannot be sufficiently achieved by the Member States, either at central level or at regional and local level'; and (ii) 'by reason of the scale or effects of the proposed action [the Union objectives can] be better achieved at Union level'.[75]

In other words, two conditions must be met. First, the EU should not act if Member States can achieve the objectives either at central or local level. Second, EU action should offer added value to a Member State's actions when it is acting individually.[76]

The carrying out of this test is not an easy task, due to its forward-looking nature and the uncertainties that surround public action.[77] These difficulties can

[70] TEU, art 5(3).

[71] K Bradley, 'Legislating in the European Union' in Barnard and Peers (n 4), 117.

[72] M Dony, *Droit de l'Union européenne*, 5th edn (Éditions de l'Université de Bruxelles, 2014) 179.

[73] M Beijer, *The Limits of Fundamental Rights Protection by the EU: The Scope for the Development of Positive Obligations* (Intersentia, 2017) 206.

[74] E Muir, *EU Equality Law: The First Fundamental Rights Policy of the EU*, 1st edn (Oxford University Press, 2018) 47.

[75] Consolidated version of the Treaty on the Functioning of the European Union [2012] OJ C326/47 (TEU), art 5.

[76] Bradley, 'Legislating in the European Union' (n 71) 118.

[77] É Dubout, *Droit constitutionnel de l'Union européenne*, 1st edn (Bruylant, 2021) 150. See, on these difficulties, G Davies, 'Subsidiarity: The Wrong Idea, in the Wrong Place, at the Wrong Time' [2006] *Common Market Law Review* 63; P Craig, 'Subsidiarity: A Political and Legal Analysis' (2012) 50 *Journal of Common Market Studies* 72.

be even greater in the field of fundamental rights protection, in particular when the competence of the EU is not linked to a cross-border component.[78]

The EU has, indeed, been given specific competences in the field, enabling it to regulate internal situations within Member States, and not their interrelationships. This is, notably, the case for the EU's competence to take actions combating discrimination, laid down in Article 19 TFEU. It is not at all linked to Member States' transnational relationships, but rather is intended to 'represent a contribution to the ideal of a "Europe of Rights"'.[79] In these situations, the principle of subsidiarity might thus prove to be inoperative.

Moreover, the choice of fundamental rights standards is not usually the result of a comparative efficiency test, but rather of prioritising certain values.[80] Therefore, as stated by Elise Muir, 'although the principle [of subsidiarity] is thus doctrinally relevant, its practical implications in the context of fundamental rights protection are most unclear'.[81] Although the 'comparative efficiency test' can thus hardly be achieved in this field, the principle of subsidiarity can nevertheless help to determine the level of precision with which EU legislation will regulate fundamental rights matters, and, conversely, the margin of manoeuvre left to the Member States in this field.[82]

Despite its challenging practicalities, the principle of subsidiarity has, nevertheless, served as a benchmark in several proposals concerning the harmonisation of fundamental rights within the EU.[83] For example, justification for the adoption of the General Data Protection Regulation is cited, in the explanatory memorandum to its legislative proposal, as being the increasing cross-border flow of personal data.[84] Similarly, the need to harmonise certain rights in the area of criminal procedure has been supported by an increase in the cross-border movement of individuals.[85] The cross-border judicial element, indeed, highlights the need for EU-level action.

[78] Muir, *EU Equality Law* (n 74) 48.

[79] FW Scharpf, 'Perpetual Momentum: Directed and Unconstrained?' (2012) 19 *Journal of European Public Policy* 127–33.

[80] Muir, *EU Equality Law* (n 74) 49.

[81] E Muir, 'The Fundamental Rights Implications of EU Legislation: Some Constitutional Challenges' (2014) 51 *Common Market Law Review*, 240.

[82] V Kosta, 'Investigating Lessons for the EU's Fundamental Rights Policies' (2023) 19 *European Constitutional Law Review* 10.

[83] Beijer, *The Limits of Fundamental Rights Protection by the EU* (n 73) 208.

[84] Proposal for a Regulation of the European Parliament and of the Council on the protection of individuals with regard to the processing of personal data and on the free movement of such data (General Data Protection Directive) [2012] COM(2012) 011, preamble 4.

[85] Impact Assessment for a Commission Proposal for a Directive on procedural safeguards for children suspected or accused in criminal proceedings [2013] SWD(2013) 480 final, 32: 'In the EU people are constantly travelling and moving across borders. Around 11.3 million Europeans reside permanently outside their home country, 10% of Europeans have lived and worked abroad during a period of their lives and 13% have gone abroad for education and training. These numbers show the importance of ensuring proper, effective action on the rights of those who get involved in criminal proceedings, in their own country while travelling or living abroad. The EU must ensure that suspects and accused persons, although they may not be fully aware of various specific aspects of the procedure, should be protected by minimum safeguards across the EU.'

The second principle limiting the EU from exercising its competences is the 'principle of proportionality', also enshrined in Article 5 TFEU. This provision states that 'the content and form of Union action shall not exceed what is necessary to achieve the objectives of the Treaties'. This principle thus requires

> that measures adopted by Community institutions do not exceed the limits of what is appropriate and necessary in order to attain the objectives legitimately pursued by the legislation in question; when there is a choice between several appropriate measures recourse must be had to the least onerous, and the disadvantages caused must not be disproportionate to the aims pursued.[86]

Application of the principle of proportionality means that the extent to which EU action is allowed in a specific field can be controlled. It can justify the preference for minimum harmonisation, or the granting of a margin of appreciation to the Member States when they are implementing a harmonisation measure.[87] This principle can also prove useful in fundamental rights conflicts, for example the rights conflict in prohibiting the wearing of religious symbols in the workplace, which may pit the fundamental freedom of religion against that of conducting a business.[88]

Enforcement of these two principles is possible through political and judicial means. For example, national parliaments can oppose the adoption of a norm if they consider that the principle of subsidiarity has been breached.[89] And respect for the principle may be subject to judicial oversight. But judicial review to ensure that the subsidiarity principle is respected remains marginal in practice. From a procedural perspective, the CJEU ensures that the European Commission has properly fulfilled its information obligations, especially those owed to national parliaments. In terms of substance, as pointed out by Edouard Dubout, the CJEU generally limits itself to referring to the existence of significant disparities in legislation among the Member States.[90] To date, it has never annulled an EU act for violation of the subsidiarity principle.

The CJEU's scrutiny of an EU act's compliance with the principle of proportionality is also relatively limited, except if there is a fundamental rights restriction at stake.[91] Indeed, the Court has established that

> with regard to judicial review of compliance with [the conditions flowing from the principle of proportionality], where interferences with fundamental rights are at issue,

[86] Joined Cases C-133/93, C-300/93 and C-326/93 *Antonio Crispoltoni v Fattoria Autonoma Tabacchi and Giuseppe Natale and Antonio Pontillo v Donatab Srl* ECLI:EU:C:1994:364 [1994] ECR I-04863, para 41.

[87] On the margin of appreciation/discretion, see s VI.3.a of this chapter, 'The Ambit of European Fundamental Rights Law in the Absence of EU Harmonisation'.

[88] See, for instance, Joined Cases C-804/18 and C-341/19 *IX v WABE eV and MH Müller Handels GmbH v MJ* ECLI:EU:C:2021:594 [2021].

[89] Protocol (No 2) to the Treaty on the Application of the Principles of Subsidiarity and Proportionality annexed to the Treaty on European Union and the Treaty on the Functioning of the European Union by the Treaty of Lisbon [2007] OJ C 83/206.

[90] Dubout, *Droit constitutionnel de l'Union européenne* (n 77) 146.

[91] T Ronse, *Les compétences de l'Union européenne* (Édition de l'Université de Bruxelles, 2017) 186.

> the extent of the EU legislature's discretion may prove to be limited, depending on a number of factors, including, in particular, the area concerned, the nature of the right at issue guaranteed by the Charter, the nature and seriousness of the interference and the object pursued by the interference.[92]

In my view, this limitation should also apply when the EU's legislature gives specific expression to a fundamental right through legislation. This is because, once a fundamental right has been implemented by legislative action, it is inherently defined and subject to certain restrictions.

In summary, the EU has limited competences in the field of fundamental rights. And in the areas where it does have such competences, they are limited by the principles of subsidiarity and proportionality.

Section V – In Search of a Human Rights Telos?

Although the EU has been quite active within the limits of its competences in the field of fundamental rights protection, this is not its sole or primary objective. This is another characteristic that significantly sets it apart from traditional international human rights organisations. In fact, the EU pursues other competing objectives (section V.2), and some even question the sincerity of its objective to protect fundamental rights (section V.1). While the criticisms of the EU's role in fundamental rights protection are not without foundation, it is also clear that progress has been made in this area. The EU's contribution to fundamental rights can no longer be viewed solely in negative terms. Taking into account the various measures it has implemented to safeguard these rights, it may be more appropriate to adopt a balanced perspective – one that sees the EU not as a dedicated 'international human rights organisation', but as an international organisation that plays a non-negligible role, within its limits and imperfectly, in protecting fundamental rights (section V.3).

V.1. The EU's Human Rights Commitment: A Fake Narrative?

The EU has often been criticised for its perceived shortcomings in enforcing human rights. Some scholars even question the authenticity of its commitment to protecting them. There is broad agreement that the initial development of a fundamental rights framework within the EU legal order was, at least in part, driven

[92] Joined Cases C-293/12 and C-594/12 *Digital Rights Ireland Ltd v Minister for Communications, Marine and Natural Resources and Others and Kärntner Landesregierung and Others* ECLI:EU:C:2014:238 [2014], para 47.

by the instrumental need to safeguard the principle of primacy of EU law.[93] But opinions in the literature diverge regarding the extent to which this framework has evolved to reflect a more autonomous logic genuinely dedicated to the protection of fundamental rights within the EU.[94]

Andrew Williams' work, for instance, asserts that the EU's declared commitment to fundamental rights protection is undermined by a lack of consistent action, and incoherent policy implementation. While the EU projects strong rhetoric and a robust legal framework for safeguarding human rights, Williams highlights significant deficiencies in how these standards are applied and enforced. He further suggests that this gap may stem from the EU's decisions being driven less by a genuine commitment to human rights and more by other, perhaps instrumental, priorities. His work considers it a myth that the European construct is based on a common ambition to protect fundamental rights.[95] According to him, the establishment of the European Communities had absolutely no connection to the issue of human rights, despite the language of Article 2 TEU, as its focus was purely economic. Moreover, at the beginning of EU integration, any risk of these rights being jeopardised by the process of integration was considered entirely remote.[96] According to Williams, if a human rights discourse emerged later in the European Communities, it was, in fact, to legitimise the Community as a source of governance. In his view, it is solely because the European Communities were searching for an identity – an 'ethos' – that 'the discourse of human rights has become of particular constitutional importance'.[97] Furthermore, Williams argues that current EU policies and practices, both internally and externally, do not reflect a genuine commitment to human rights, despite the rhetoric of official discourse.[98] Williams contends that the EU's reluctance to develop a comprehensive human rights policy is partly due to the constraints of its institutional framework and design.[99] The EU's institutional design, he argues, prioritises economic and security objectives

[93] C Rizcallah, 'La protection des droits fondamentaux dans l'Union européenne: l'immuable poids des origines?' (2015) *Cahiers de droit européen* 399; N Türküler Isiksel, 'Fundamental Rights in the EU after Kadi and Al Barakaat' (2010) 16 *European Law Journal* 554.

[94] On the development of a political 'foundational' myth around fundamental rights in the EU, and the fact that this narrative is used both to legitimise the European polity and to stir to action in the defence of fundamental rights, see S Smismans, 'Fundamental rights as a political myth of the EU: can the myth survive?' in S Douglas-Scott and N Hatzis, *Research Handbook on EU Law* (Edward Elgar Publishing, 2017) 13–34; and S Smismans, 'The European Union's Fundamental Rights Myth' (2010) 48 *Journal of Common Market Studies* 45.

[95] A Williams, *EU Human Rights Policies: A Study in Irony* (Oxford University Press, 2004) 129. See, for a comparable and more recent stance, S Ganty and D Kochenov, 'EU Lawlessness Law' (2024) 30(1) *Columbia Journal of European Law* 78–156.

[96] P Twomey, 'The European Union: Three Pillars without a Human Rights Foundation' in D O'Keefe and P Twomey (eds), *Legal Issues of the Maastricht Treaty* (Wiley Chancery Law, 1994) 121–22.

[97] Williams, *EU Human Rights Policies* (n 95) 133.

[98] A Williams, *The Ethos of Europe: Values, Law and Justice in the EU*, 1st edn (Cambridge University Press, 2010) 153.

[99] A Williams, 'Human Rights in the EU' in D Chalmers and A Arnull (eds), *The Oxford Handbook of European Union Law* (Oxford University Press, 2015) 250.

over human rights concerns, resulting in a situation where human rights considerations are often subordinate to other policy goals.

In the same vein, some scholars argue that the CJEU's decision to integrate fundamental rights into its case law was driven not by philosophical or humanitarian considerations, but solely by concerns over safeguarding the principle of primacy of EU law.[100] Coppel and O'Neill took this critique even further in their well-known 1992 article, published in the *Common Market Law Review*, entitled 'The European Court of Justice: Taking Rights Seriously?'.[101] In this particularly critical piece, they argued that the CJEU was, in fact, not seeking to protect fundamental rights at all, but was actively using them as a tool to expand its jurisdiction into areas traditionally reserved for Member States. According to these authors, 'the Court has employed fundamental rights instrumentally, so as to accelerate the process of legal integration in the Community. It has not protected these fundamental rights for their own sake. It has not taken these rights seriously.'[102] The criticism is severe and was notably addressed in a rebuttal published by Joseph HH Weiler and Nicolas JS Lockhart.[103]

While I do not endorse the intensity of the harshest critiques, it is important to recognise that some of these observations are rooted in undeniable past and present realities. First, it is clear that the protection of fundamental rights was not an original objective of the EU, despite being labelled a 'foundational value'. This issue only gained prominence well after the EU's creation, with history showing that it was entirely missing in the priorities of the early European Communities.[104] Furthermore, the EU's track record on fundamental rights protection is far from impeccable. It is also fair to question the extent to which this value is genuinely shared among the Member States.[105]

It is equally crucial to emphasise that the purpose of this book is not, in any way, to act as a 'defender' or 'apologist' for the EU in the field of fundamental rights protection – borrowing the words of JHH Weiler.[106] Instead, I am convinced that EU law, within certain limits and in specific circumstances, can provide meaningful added value to the protection of human rights in Europe. The aim of this book is to equip rights beneficiaries with the tools necessary to recognise and harness these potential benefits. However, it is not intended to vindicate the EU of all criticism, or to gloss over its shortcomings in the field of fundamental rights, some of

[100] L Bondo Krogsgaard, 'Fundamental Rights in the European Community after Maastricht' (1993) 20 *Legal Issues of European Integration* 101.

[101] J Coppel and A O'Neill, 'The European Court of Justice: Taking Rights Seriously?' [1992] *Common Market Law Review* 669–92.

[102] ibid, 670.

[103] JHH Weiler and NJS Lockhart, '« Taking Rights Seriously? » Seriously: The European Court and Its Fundamental Rights Jurisprudence', published in two parts in the *Common Market Law Review* [1995], 51–94 and 579–627.

[104] Smismans, 'Fundamental rights as a political myth of the EU' (n 94) 21, 26.

[105] ibid, 26.

[106] Weiler and Lockhart, 'Taking Rights Seriously?' (n 103), pt I, 57.

which, in certain cases, can be judged quite severely. The way the EU has managed recent crises highlights some of its failings in this area.

A particularly stark example is the EU's handling of the economic crisis, where the implementation of austerity measures seriously threatened the protection of fundamental social rights.[107] The EU's stringent fiscal policies prioritised deficit reduction and debt control over social welfare, and exacerbated poverty, inequality, and social exclusion. These measures undermined a range of fundamental rights, including access to health, education, and adequate housing.[108]

The EU's approach to managing the influx of refugees and migrants in Europe is another example of deeply problematic policies which have undeniably led to numerous very serious human rights violations. While certain measures have been implemented to address the challenges posed by these arrivals, the actions of both the EU and its Member States in this domain have been highly questionable. For instance, the reliance on external border controls and the outsourcing of refugee processing to non-EU countries have directly contributed to severe abuses, including detention, deportation, and violence against asylum seekers. These practices manifestly contravene the fundamental rights the EU professes to protect.[109]

In a related area, the EU can also be criticised for a certain leniency towards Member States that have adopted measures systematically undermining fundamental rights and the principles of the rule of law. Such actions, which threaten essential democratic institutions like the judiciary, the media, and civil society, have prompted significant condemnation and legal challenges. Nevertheless, EU institutions have shown reluctance to fully deploy the available tools and sanction mechanisms to address these violations effectively. This hesitancy has raised broader concerns about the EU's ability to enforce the rule of law consistently and its resolve in upholding the democratic values at the heart of its foundation.[110]

These non-exhaustive examples highlight the significant challenges to the protection of fundamental rights that can arise from European integration. However, I must emphasise that these issues cannot be attributed solely to the EU as an abstract entity. Responsibility also lies with the actors and individuals making up its institutions, including the Member States themselves, which play a

[107] On this issue, see J Fraczyk, 'EU Fundamental Rights and the Financial Crisis' in Douglas-Scott and Hatzis, *Research Handbook on EU Law Human Rights* (n 94) 468–91.

[108] See, among others, L Fromont, *La gouvernance économique européenne: les conséquences constitutionnelles d'une décennie de crises* (Larcier, 2022); A Kornezov, 'Social Rights, the Charter, and the ECHR: Caveats, Austerity, and Other Disasters' in F Vandenbroucke, C Barnard, and G De Baere (eds), *A European Social Union after the Crisis*, 1st edn (Cambridge University Press, 2017).

[109] See, among others, V Moreno Lax, Accessing Asylum in Europe: Extraterritorial Border Controls and Refugee Rights under EU Law (Oxford University Press, 2017); and P Cuttitta, 'Delocalization, Humanitarianism, and Human Rights: The Mediterranean Border Between Exclusion and Inclusion' (2018) 50 *Antipode* 783.

[110] See, among others, K Lane Scheppele, D Vladimirovich Kochenov, and B Grabowska-Moroz, 'EU Values Are Law, After All: Enforcing EU Values through Systemic Infringement Actions by the European Commission and the Member States of the European Union' (2021) 39 *Yearbook of European Law* 3–121; and L Pech and K Lane Scheppele, 'Illiberalism Within: Rule of Law Backsliding in the EU' (2017) 19 *Cambridge Yearbook of European Legal Studies* 3–47.

decisive role in shaping the policies pursued at the EU level through their participation in various bodies. Many of these challenges are, indeed, deeply rooted in the political and social contexts of the Member States.

This situation further highlights the inherent limitations of the EU as an active player in the field of fundamental rights protection, a role it undertakes while simultaneously pursuing objectives that can, at times, conflict with the safeguarding of these rights.

V.2. The EU's Competing Objectives and the Specific Characteristics of EU Law

While criticism can be levelled at both the rationale and implementation of fundamental rights protection in the EU, one of the key reasons for this weakness lies in the fact that the EU pursues objectives other than the safeguarding of fundamental rights. Unlike traditional international human rights organisations, the EU is guided by a multitude of other aims, which can sometimes compete with or undermine its commitment to protecting these rights. Whether it is the establishment of a 'single market' or an area of 'freedom, security, and justice', many policies implemented by the EU may run counter to the protection of individuals' rights and freedoms. In this context, the EU's position is more akin to that of a state, which in addition to protecting fundamental rights, must implement all kinds of other objectives. This situation certainly influences how fundamental rights are construed in the EU legal order. The CJEU, in this sense, explicitly acknowledged that

> the autonomy enjoyed by EU law in relation to the laws of the Member States and in relation to international law requires that the interpretation of those fundamental rights be ensured within the framework of the structure and objectives of the EU.[111]

Without delving into excessive detail, several examples can be offered to illustrate this point.

Firstly, within the Internal Market, and more broadly within the framework of EU economic integration, there are numerous instances where the protection of fundamental social rights has been undermined to prioritise economic imperatives. As already highlighted, tensions between economic integration and social rights became evident during the sovereign debt crisis. Member States were compelled to reform their social security systems as a condition for financial assistance from the European Commission, the European Central Bank, and the International Monetary Fund – commonly referred to as the Troika.[112] Fundamental social

[111] Opinion 2/13 of the Court, para 170.

[112] E De Becker, 'The (Possible) Role of the Right to Social Security in the EU Economic Monitoring Process' (2016) 17(3) *German Law Journal* 277–314.

rights were heavily restricted in favour of the objective of restoring the public finances of Member States.[113]

Similarly, within the CJEU's case law, the *Viking* and *Laval* cases are quintessential examples of this dynamic.[114] While the CJEU acknowledged in these cases that the right to collective action,[115] including the right to strike, was a fundamental right forming part of the general principles of EU law,[116] it significantly limited their scope in favour of the freedoms of movement, applying strict proportionality controls.

In the *Viking* judgment, the CJEU established that the use of collective action hindering the freedom of establishment should be a mechanism of last resort, to be used only when no less restrictive means are available to address the infringements on employees' rights.[117] In the *Laval* case, the CJEU ruled that a Swedish trade union could not require a Latvian construction company to sign a collective agreement in accordance with Swedish law before being allowed to operate in Sweden. According to the CJEU, the right to strike could not be used to prevent a company from temporarily relocating its activities to another Member State to provide services.[118] With these cases, the CJEU implicitly enshrined the principle according to which cross-national differences in labour standards distorted the operation of the Internal Market.[119] They highlight how the drive for economic freedoms can, at times, overshadow social fundamental rights. This phenomenon was heavily criticised in part of the literature.[120]

Similar dynamics play out in the AFSJ, where the principle of mutual trust that is central to its framework has, at times, placed significant limits on the protection of fundamental rights. This principle underpins the removal of internal physical, judicial, and legal borders within the EU by encouraging close co-operation

[113] On this phenomenon, see, among others, E De Becker, 'The Constraints of Fundamental Social Rights on EU Economic Monitoring: collective complaints: no. 76-80/2012, IKA-ETAM, Panhellenic Federation of Public Service Pensions, ISAP, POS-DEI, ATE v. Greece' (2015) 17 *European Journal of Social Security* 123–34.

[114] On this topic, see, among others, S Weatherill, 'The Internal Market and EU Fundamental Rights' in Douglas-Scott and Hatzis, *Research Handbook on EU Law* (n 107), 364–78.

[115] Case C-438/05 *International Transport Workers' Federation and Finnish Seamen's Union v Viking Line ABP and OÜ Viking Line Eesti* ECLI:EU:C:2007:772 [2007] ECR I-10779 *('Viking')*, para 44; Case C-341/05 *Laval un Partneri Ltd v Svenska Byggnadsarbetareförbundet, Svenska Byggnadsarbetareförbundets avdelning 1, Byggettan and Svenska Elektrikerförbundet* ECLI:EU:C:2007:809 [2007] ECR I-11767 *('Laval')*, para 91.

[116] On these judgments, see, among others, S Feenstra, 'How Can the Viking/Laval Conundrum Be Resolved? Balancing the Economic and the Social: One Bed for Two Dreams?' in Vandenbroucke, Barnard and De Baere, *A European Social Union after the Crisis* (n 108) 308–43.

[117] *Viking*, para 87.

[118] *Laval*, para 111.

[119] S Deakin, 'What Follows Austerity? From Social Pillar to New Deal' in Vandenbroucke, Barnard, and De Baere, *A European Social Union after the Crisis* (n 108), 198.

[120] See, among others, C Barnard, 'Social Dumping or Dumping Socialism' (2008) *Cambridge Law Journal* 262–64; and J Malmberg and T Sigeman, 'Industrial action and EU economic freedoms: the autonomous collective bargaining model curtailed by the European Court of Justice' (2008) *Common Market Law Review* 1115–46.

between Member States. It allows national legal decisions to be recognised in other jurisdictions by establishing an obligation of trust among Member States, creating a sense of unity despite the diversity of their legal systems.[121] It serves as the foundation for the establishment of the principle of mutual recognition, especially with regard to judgments.

The principle of mutual trust also underpins the Dublin Regulation,[122] which facilitates the transfer of asylum seekers between EU Member States. Although this principle is of fundamental importance, it carries significant risks for fundamental rights. It prevents Member States from: (i) demanding a higher level of protection of fundamental rights than that provided for by the EU Charter in the context of their inter-state cooperation; and (ii) monitoring the effective respect of these fundamental rights by their peers.[123] In other words, when Member State A is called upon to co-operate with Member State B (for example, to execute a European Arrest Warrant or a Dublin (asylum seeker) transfer), it must presume that Member State B respects the minimum guarantees offered by the EU Charter. It cannot demand a more protective standard, for example one that is guaranteed by its national constitution. Moreover, it cannot carry out a review to verify whether that standard is actually respected by the other Member States. Member States must 'trust' each other. Thanks to this principle, co-operation in civil and criminal cases is much faster and easier, but it involves serious risks for the protection of fundamental rights. It allows fundamental rights breaches to 'spread' from one Member State to another. For instance, a Member State could be called upon to recognise and enforce a judgment rendered by another Member State's judicial authorities in violation of the right to a fair trial as protected by Article 47 of the EU Charter. Similarly, asylum seekers could be transferred to a Member State from another without protecting some of their fundamental rights.

However, exceptions are enshrined in both EU legislation and the case law. Notably, the CJEU has established that, in exceptional circumstances – such as when there are serious risks of breach of fundamental rights – the principle of mutual trust can be set aside.[124] An analysis of the case law reveals an evolving and complex process of assessing whether there is a fundamental rights breach. The resulting legal tests set a very high bar, and ultimately mean that it is, in practice, quite difficult to justify the setting aside of the principle of mutual trust, due to a risk of a fundamental rights breach. Only the most serious violations, which

[121] See, on this principle, Rizcallah, *The Principle of Mutual Trust in EU Law* (n 41).

[122] Regulation (EU) No 604/2013 of the European Parliament and of the Council of 26 June 2013 establishing the criteria and mechanisms for determining the Member State responsible for examining an application for international protection lodged in one of the Member States by a third-country national or a stateless person (recast) [2013] OJ L180/31, now replaced by Regulation (EU) 2024/1351 of the European Parliament and of the Council of 14 May 2024 on asylum and migration management [2024] OJ L2024/1351.

[123] Opinion 2/13 of the Court.

[124] ibid, para 191.

threaten absolute fundamental rights or the essential content of rights, seem to warrant an exception to the principle of mutual trust.[125] Once again, the protection of fundamental rights is balanced with – and sometimes undermined by – other objectives pursued by the EU, such as the establishment of the AFSJ.

A third example can be drawn from *Opinion 2/13*, which concerned the proposed accession of the EU to the ECHR.[126] While this Opinion has already been extensively analysed,[127] it is worth noting that the CJEU held that the proposed accession agreement could not proceed in its current form, as it threatened the autonomy and the specific characteristics of the EU legal order. In this instance, accession to the ECHR – which may have potentially strengthened the protection of fundamental rights within the EU – had to be put aside in order to protect other imperatives of European integration, namely the autonomy of its legal order. As noted by Jean-Paul Jacqué about the Opinion,

> [o]ne important element that guides the reasoning of the Court is the fact that it ensures the respect of fundamental rights, but in line with the EU's objectives for the achievement of the integration process. This is what distinguishes the Court of Justice from the European Court of Human Rights. The Court of Justice is not a human rights court. The respect for human rights is ensured while taking into account the Union's objectives. In its task, the Court strives to strike a balance between the constraints arising from the Union's objectives on one hand, and the respect for fundamental rights on the other hand. On the contrary, the European Court of Human Rights is a specialized jurisdiction whose sole mission, within the framework of subsidiarity, is to ensure respect for the Convention. This means that the EU's objectives are not at the core of its approach, but rather serve as justifications for restrictions imposed on a right. It is from the tension between these different functions that arguments of incompatibility may arise.[128]

The pursuit of these concurrent objectives is, moreover, shaped by the specific characteristics of EU law, notably the principles of primacy, direct effect, and effectiveness. Yet, the quest for the effectiveness of EU law rules that compete with fundamental rights can result in the severe limitation of these rights. Going back to our example of mutual trust, the CJEU held in the landmark judgment *Melloni* that the execution of a European Arrest Warrant (EAW) could not be refused based on national standards of fundamental rights protection if that could compromise 'the primacy, unity, and effectiveness of EU law'.[129] Preserving the effectiveness of the EAW mechanism may thus justify setting aside a higher national standard of

[125] Rizcallah, *The Principle of Mutual Trust in EU Law* (n 41).

[126] Opinion 2/13 of the Court, para 174.

[127] See, among others, D Halberstam, '"It's the Autonomy, Stupid!" A Modest Defense of Opinion 2/13 on EU Accession to the ECHR, and the Way Forward' (2015) 16 *German Law Journal* 105–46; and P Eeckout, 'Opinion 2/13 on EU Accession to the ECHR and Judicial Dialogue: Autonomy or Autarky' (2015) 38 *Fordham International Law Journal* 955–92.

[128] J-P Jacqué, 'Pride and/or prejudice? Les lectures possibles de l'avis 2/13 de la cour de justice' (2015) 1 *Cahiers de droit européen* 32 (own translation).

[129] Case C-399/11 *Stefano Melloni v Ministerio Fiscal* ECLI:EU:C:2013:107 [2013].

fundamental rights protection than that offered by EU law, thereby contributing to a lowering of the overall level of protection.

A similar dynamic is at play in the field of protecting the EU's financial interests and the obligation for Member States to impose sanctions that have a sufficiently deterrent effect. Without delving into the entire *Tarrico* saga,[130] the judgment delivered in the *Lin* case perfectly illustrates the tension that can exist between the need to ensure the effectiveness of protecting both the EU's financial interests and fundamental rights. Indeed, the CJEU considered that the need to avoid a systemic risk of impunity in the field of the protection of the EU's financial interests could mean that national judges have to disapply a national standard of protection relating to the principle of the retroactive application of the more lenient criminal law (*lex mitior*) which would result in such a risk.[131]

On the other hand, as will be demonstrated in depth in the following parts of this book, the broader principle of effectiveness *supports* the EU protection of fundamental rights and, more generally, EU values, in particular the rule of law, through the connected 'principle of effective judicial protection'.[132] In view of this, as stressed by Giulia Gentile, 'the effectiveness of EU law has two sides: it is concerned with the effective enforcement of individual EU rights, as well as the protection of EU constitutional features and policy goals'.[133] The dichotomy between fundamental rights, on the one hand, and the principle of effectiveness, on the other, can thus be nuanced, with the latter serving as a double-edged sword in this context.[134]

V.3. Not a Traditional 'International Human Rights Organisation'

The two preceding sections have highlighted the main reasons why the EU cannot be considered a traditional international organisation dedicated to the protection of human rights: it was not established with the primary purpose of protecting these rights; it is also driven by other objectives, which may sometimes conflict with fundamental rights. However, these elements do not undermine my argument that

[130] See, among others, G Piccirilli, 'The "*Taricco* Saga": The Italian Constitutional Court Continues Its European Journey: Italian Constitutional Court, Order of 23 November 2016 No. 24/2017; Judgment of 10 April 2018 No. 115/2018 ECJ 8 September 2015, Case C-105/14, *Ivo Taricco and Others*; 5 December 2017, Case C-42/17, *M.A.S. and M.B.*' (2018) 14 *European Constitutional Law Review* 814.

[131] For an extensive analysis these judgments, see ch 1, s VI.3.a, 'The Ambit of EU Fundamental Rights Law in the Absence of EU Harmonisation'.

[132] See ch 2, ss I.1.c and I.4 of this book, 'The Principle of Effectiveness'; and 'An Effective Fundamental Rights Law System'; G Gentile, 'One, No One, One Hundred Thousand: The Multi-Faceted Effectiveness of EU Law' (2022) 34(3) *European Review of Public Law* 613– 40.

[133] Gentile, 'One, No One, One Hundred Thousand' (n 132) 637.

[134] For an illustration, see R Sicurella, 'Effectiveness of EU Law and Protection of Fundamental Rights: The Questions Settled and the New Challenges after the ECJ Decision in the M.A.S. and M.B. Case (C-42/17)' (2018) 9 *New Journal of European Criminal Law* 24.

the EU has evolved into a genuine protector of fundamental rights, alongside the other responsibilities it shoulders. The fact that this was not its original purpose, nor its sole focus today, does not preclude the EU from playing an active, albeit partial, role in safeguarding these rights across Europe.

Its role remains nevertheless quite distinctive. In contrast to traditional international organisations dedicated to protecting human rights, the EU must navigate a delicate equilibrium between fundamental rights and other objectives it seeks to achieve. This intricate balancing act shapes the role that the EU assumes in this domain. In this context, ensuring a uniform level of protection of fundamental rights within the EU could support integration in other areas. For instance, the establishment of a common level of fundamental rights protection in criminal procedure makes it easier for the judicial authorities of one Member State to apply mutual recognition of national criminal law judgments from another Member State. On the other hand, if each state could rely on its own national standard of protection to refuse to implement EU legal mechanisms, it would compromise their effectiveness.

The CJEU has confirmed that one of the objectives of the EU's protection of fundamental rights is precisely 'to avoid a situation [in] which the level of protection of fundamental rights varies according to national law … in such a way as to undermine the unity, primacy and effectiveness of EU law'.[135] Recent case law, moreover, demonstrates that safeguarding the principles of primacy, uniformity, and effectiveness of EU law remain 'important rationales' for the protection of human rights by the EU.[136]

However, supporting the overall effectiveness of EU integration is not – or at least is no longer – the sole motivation behind the EU's active involvement in protecting fundamental rights. A genuine 'autonomous' logic has been added to this instrumental logic, where protection is sought because it is now genuinely part of the EU's identity.[137] Even though the creation of a Single Market was central to the European integration project, issues related to justice, welfare, living standards, and social progress were by no means insignificant. On the contrary, the establishment of the Single Market was actually perceived as a means to achieve these objectives. The narrative of market integration was, in fact, seen as a 'tool for democratization and development'.[138] Although their primary focus was economic, the European Communities were nevertheless driven by 'ultimate goals

[135] Case C-198/13 *Víctor Manuel Julian Hernández and Others v Reino de España (Subdelegación del Gobierno de España en Alicante) and Others* ECLI:EU:C:2014:2055 [2014], para 47; Case C-206/13 *Cruciano Siragusa v Regione Sicilia – Soprintendenza Beni Culturali e Ambientali di Palermo* ECLI:EU:C:2014:126 [2014], paras 31–32.

[136] Beijer, *The Limits of Fundamental Rights Protection by the EU* (n 73) 114.

[137] E Bribosia, 'La protection des droits fondamentaux dans l'ordre juridique communautaire: le poids respectif des logiques fonctionnelle et autonome dans le cadre normatif et jurisprudentiel' (PhD in law submitted at the Université libre de Bruxelles, 2001).

[138] E Frantziou, *The Horizontal Effect of Fundamental Rights in the European Union: A Constitutional Analysis* (Oxford University Press, 2019) 59.

(*finalités lointaines*)' that were more political in nature.[139] Today, the safeguarding of fundamental rights also stands out as an autonomous imperative, prominently invoked to justify specific actions undertaken by the EU. In this context, as we will see throughout this book, EU law can now provide limited yet tangible added value to the protection of fundamental rights in Europe from the perspective of their beneficiaries.

Acknowledging the positive contribution, in certain circumstances, to the protection of fundamental rights by the EU does not, however, imply that the EU's actions in this regard are without flaws. As highlighted below, numerous criticisms can be directed at the EU regarding its respect for human rights.

As previously highlighted, the EU is not solely responsible for safeguarding fundamental rights in Europe. That is a shared responsibility, especially with the Member States. Addressing these challenges, therefore, requires not only stronger EU policies in support of fundamental rights, but also a steadfast commitment from Member States to uphold and promote human rights and democratic values. In this context, it is insufficient to simply declare in legal texts that the EU is founded on values, including fundamental rights. While Article 2 TEU affirms that fundamental rights are integral to the EU's shared identity with its Member States, this alone is not enough to ensure they are effectively respected and enforced. As underlined by Jürgen Habermas, European identity 'is not produced in the same way as goods and capital are circulated'.[140] Although the assertion that the EU is based on these common values might contribute to their effectiveness, that is not enough to guarantee their implementation in practice. Indeed, the performative capacity of legal discourses is limited.[141] In many ways, legal institutionalisation is still dependent on the primary normativity from which it emerged.[142] The capacity of law to produce tangible effects thus forms part of a push-and-pull dynamic between the project it enshrines and its realisation by the established social order. Thus, if the law is an 'instrument of change',[143] capable of influencing the situations it regulates, it is nonetheless dependent on its implementation.

To give practical effect to the principle enshrined in Article 2 TEU, it is essential for both the EU and its Member States to actively respect and protect fundamental rights. The aim of this book, however, is not to present a normative argument on the matter but, rather, to explore how EU law can offer added value to the protection of fundamental rights in Europe. In light of this, the following section will

[139] P Pescatore, *Le droit de l'intégration: émergence d'un phénomène nouveau dans les relations internationales selon l'expérience des Communautés européennes* (Bruylant, 2005) 28.

[140] J Habermas, *Sur l'Europe* (Bayard, 2006) 65 (own translation).

[141] See, in this regard, JL Austin, *How to Do Things with Words: The William James Lectures Delivered at Harvard University in 1955* (Oxford University Press, 1973). See also N Fairclough, Language and Power, 3rd edn (Routledge, 2015).

[142] F Ost, *A quoi sert le droit? Usages, fonctions, finalités* (Bruylant, 2016) 160.

[143] F Ost, 'L'instantané Ou l'institué? L'institué Ou l'instituant? Le Droit a-t-Il Pour Vocation de Durer?' in F Ost and M Van Hoecke (eds), *Temps et droit. Le droit a-t-il pour vocation de durer* (Bruylant, 1998) 7.

demonstrate how the EU contributes to this field – particularly by establishing new standards of protection.

Section VI – Emancipation: A New 'Norm-maker'

While criticism and limitations persist regarding the EU's role in protecting fundamental rights, it is undeniable that the EU has evolved into a proactive 'norm-maker' in this domain. Initially acting as a 'passive' user of protection standards shaped by others, the EU has now emerged as a genuine standard-setter.

What began as a mechanism to ensure that fundamental rights as defined in the constitutions of Member States were respected by EU institutions has since transformed into a more ambitious effort. The EU now plays a leading role in defining new standards of protection, often requiring Member States to adopt and implement them. As underlined by Elise Muir, we progressively moved 'from an era in which the protection of fundamental rights in the EU was primarily "passive", to a new stage marked by a strong "pro-active" role of EU institutions in this field'.[144] This evolution is noticeable both at the level of the political institutions of the EU, through their power of harmonisation (section VI.1), and at the level of the CJEU, which is adopting an increasingly autonomous interpretation of EU standards in the field of fundamental rights protection (section VI.2). Nevertheless, this new EU capacity does not come without challenges, particularly regarding the constitutional balance between the EU and the Member States (section VI.3).

VI.1. The EU's Harmonisation Power

The first aspect that reveals the EU's emancipation in the field of fundamental rights protection results from the specific competences it has been given, which have allowed positive integration in this domain. Treaty revisions have meant that the EU now has a range of competences allowing for the harmonisation of various protection standards in the realm of fundamental rights.

This element constitutes a crucial aspect of the EU's distinctiveness as an international organisation safeguarding fundamental rights: other international organisations active in this field do not have such a power to approximate national laws. As observed by Eva J Lohse, the technique of harmonisation is a specific feature of the EU construct, which comes into play 'within a unique institutional framework, where institutions, entitled by the "signatories" to enact unifying law, issue harmonising measures independently from the "signatories"'.[145]

[144] Muir, 'Fundamental Rights: An Unsettling EU Competence' (n 18) 26.

[145] E Lohse, 'The Meaning of Harmonisation in the Context of European Union Law – a Process in Need of Definition' in M Andenas and C Andersen (eds), *Theory and Practice of Harmonisation* (Edward Elgar Publishing, 2012) 286.

EU harmonisation measures are thus binding for the Member States without further action, and can, in certain circumstances, be directly relied upon by individuals before national authorities and courts. In this context, while the traditional international instruments for the protection of fundamental rights usually define minimum standards that must be respected by the Member States, full and maximum harmonisation measures may, in certain cases, be adopted at EU level. EU action can, thus, in certain circumstances, be far more intrusive vis-à-vis national legal orders than traditional international rules.

The process of harmonisation also leads to a politicisation of fundamental rights. This constitutes an original characteristic of EU law compared with international human rights law, the interpretation of which is often in the hands of international jurisdictions or advisory committees, as there is no proper international legislative power within the realm of international human rights law. I will delve more deeply into the politicisation of EU Fundamental Rights Law in chapter four of this book.[146]

The framework within which these specific EU competences can be exercised is fragmented. Indeed, it is governed by different legal bases which do not follow the same logic or apply the same conditions for the adoption of harmonisation measures.

The EU was given two self-standing competences in the field of fundamental rights protection in the areas of combating discrimination and protection of personal data (see section VI.1.a below). These competences reflect a growing recognition of the importance of fundamental rights within the legal framework of the EU and implement the willingness to ensure that such rights are given the appropriate level of protection. In addition to these self-standing fundamental rights legal bases, the EU also takes action in the field of fundamental rights protection based on other 'functional' legal bases, as measures flanking other policies, in particular the establishment of the Internal Market (VI.I.b) and the development of the AFSJ (VI.1.c). Here, the harmonisation of fundamental rights pursues a dual objective: protection of such rights, but also the proper functioning of the freedoms of movement within the European area without internal borders. Finally, the EU has also established itself as a guarantor of certain social fundamental rights by fleshing out some of them through legislation (VI.1.d). After analysing these different types of EU harmonisation measures for fundamental rights, I will draw on some broader considerations on the impact of harmonisation on the protection of fundamental rights in the EU (VI.1.e).

Within the scope of the analysis, I do not purport to provide an exhaustive account. I have selected specific examples to bolster my argument, yet it is clear that numerous other legislative measures, which I will not list here, also contribute, at least partially, to the definition of fundamental rights' standards. Indeed,

[146] Ch 4, s III.

the exercise of various competences by the EU means that a delicate balance with the protection of fundamental rights must be found, and thereby implies regulating them.[147]

VI.1.a. EU 'Self-standing' Fundamental Rights Competences: Non-discrimination and the Protection of Personal Data

The EU was given two specific self-standing fundamental rights competences. The first is found in the field of equality and non-discrimination, for which the EU can adopt harmonisation measures on the basis of Articles 19 and 157 TFEU. The second concerns the protection of personal data, on the basis of Article 16 TFEU.

The area of combating discrimination is undoubtedly the domain in which the EU is most 'positively' active in the field of protecting fundamental rights. This is not surprising, as the principles of equality and non-discrimination have been cornerstones of the European construct since its inception. Very quickly, these principles were elevated to the rank of general principles of EU law.[148] The principle of gender-equal pay was already enshrined in primary law by the Treaty of Rome.[149] This inclusion was initially driven by France, which advocated for the principle's incorporation in order to safeguard a core element of its domestic legal order and to prevent distortions of competition. In the absence of such a principle in other Member States, disparities could have rendered certain jurisdictions more attractive to businesses. The principle was therefore enshrined in the Treaties with the aim of ensuring a level playing field among the Member States.

While the principle of equal pay was originally enshrined with the purpose of serving the Internal Market, its importance as a fundamental social right has only grown over time. In 1978, the European Court of Justice even went as far as recognising the horizontal direct effect of this provision, in the landmark *Defrenne* judgment.[150] Later on, the EU decided to use the competence enshrined in Article 157(3) TFEU to adopt EU legislation in the form of a Directive aiming to implement the principle of equal opportunities and equal treatment of men and women in matters of employment and occupation.[151] More recently, a new Directive strengthening the application of the principle of equal pay for equal work or work of equal value between men and women, through pay transparency

[147] Muir, *EU Equality Law* (n 74) 142.

[148] M Bell, 'EU Anti-Discrimination Law: Navigating Sameness and Difference' in Craig and de Búrca, *The Evolution of EU Law* (n 4), 667.

[149] Treaty of Rome, art 119; D Beck, 'Equal Pay and the Implementation of Article 119 of the Treaty of Rome' (1978) 13 *Irish Jurist* 112.

[150] Case 149/77 *Gabrielle Defrenne v Société anonyme belge de navigation aérienne Sabena* ECLI:EU:C:1978:130 [1978] ECR 1365.

[151] Directive 2006/54/EC of the European Parliament and of the Council of 5 July 2006 on the implementation of the principle of equal opportunities and equal treatment of men and women in matters of employment and occupation [2006] OJ L 204/23.

and enforcement mechanisms, was adopted on the same legal basis.[152] In essence, it requires employers to make 'a description of the criteria used to determine pay levels and career progression for workers' easily accessible.[153] The aim of this measure is to facilitate the detection and proof of possible discrimination based on gender. It also requires companies with more than 250 employees to make certain information publicly available and accessible, such as the pay gap between female and male workers in their organisation, also in complementary or variable components, beyond the ordinary basic salary.[154] This Directive also strengthens remedies, including by ensuring a right to compensation for victims of discrimination,[155] allowing competent authorities to issue injunction orders to put an end to violations of the principle of equal pay,[156] and shifting the burden of proof in favour of victims.[157] The Directive, therefore, goes a long way in implementing the principle of equal pay by specifying exactly how it should be implemented at the national level. The EU also adopted various anti-discrimination measures in relation to the establishment of the Internal Market and EU citizenship.[158]

With the Treaty of Amsterdam, the EU gained a new and cross-cutting fundamental right competence in the field of non-discrimination: Article 13 of the then TEU granted the EU the authority to adopt measures aimed at combating discrimination on various grounds, independently of its objective to establish an Internal Market. This legal basis required the use of a special legislative procedure, where the Council of the European Union as legislator acts unanimously after consulting the European Parliament. Today, the same procedure applies according to Article 19 TFEU, with the exception that the consent of the European Parliament is now *required*.[159] Despite the stringent requirements laid down in this legal basis, the Racial Equality Directive 2000/43 was adopted quickly,[160] as was the Employment Equality Directive 2000/78,[161] thereby founding a genuine EU policy in the field of equality and non-discrimination.[162]

[152] Proposal for a Directive of the European Parliament and of the Council to strengthen the application of the principle of equal pay for equal work or work of equal value between men and women through pay transparency and enforcement mechanisms [2021] COM/2021/93 final.

[153] Directive (EU) 2023/970 of the European Parliament and of the Council of 10 May 2023 to strengthen the application of the principle of equal pay for equal work or work of equal value between men and women through pay transparency and enforcement mechanisms [2023] OJ L132/21 (Directive 2023/970), art 6.

[154] ibid, art 8.

[155] ibid, art 14.

[156] ibid, art 15.

[157] ibid, art 16.

[158] Muir, *EU Equality Law* (n 74) 71. In particular, TFEU, arts 18, 21, 46, 50, 59, and 157.

[159] At the time of the Amsterdam Treaty, the European Parliament only had a right of consultation.

[160] Council Directive 2000/43/EC of 29 June 2000 implementing the principle of equal treatment between persons irrespective of racial or ethnic origin [2000] OJ 180/22.

[161] Council Directive 2000/78/EC of 27 November 2000 establishing a general framework for equal treatment in employment and occupation [2000] OJ L303/16.

[162] On these Directives, see, among others, U Belavusau and K Henrard (eds), *EU Anti-Discrimination Law beyond Gender* (Hart, 2019); TE Givens and R Evans Case, *Legislating Equality: The Politics of Antidiscrimination Policy in Europe*, 1st edn (Oxford University Press, 2014).

As noted by Elise Muir, these Directives are 'remarkable in scope'.[163] The first one, indeed, prohibits discrimination on grounds of race and ethnic origin in the fields of employment and occupation, vocational training, membership of employer and employee organisations, social protection, including social security and health care, education, and access to goods and services which are available to the public, including housing.[164] Yet the EU has very limited, if any, competence in these fields; and it has no competence at all in the field of housing – or is explicitly prevented from pursuing harmonisation, in fields such as education or health care.[165]

Directive 2000/78 establishes a general framework for combating discrimination on the grounds of religion or belief, disability, age, or sexual orientation in the field of employment and occupation.[166] It applies to both public and private sectors, in relation to:

- conditions for access to employment, to self-employment or to occupation, including selection criteria and recruitment conditions, including promotion;
- access to all types and to all levels of vocational guidance, vocational training, advanced vocational training and retraining, including practical work experience;
- employment and working conditions, including dismissals and pay; and
- membership of, and involvement in, an organisation of workers or employers, or any organisation whose members carry on a particular profession, including the benefits provided for by such organisations.[167]

As observed by Mark Bell,[168] common features can be identified in both Directives, including the fact that both direct and indirect discrimination are prohibited, as well as giving instructions to discriminate, and harassment.[169] Other common features are that positive action may be permitted by Member States;[170] there is a precise requirement of effectiveness of national judicial and administrative procedures;[171] and a shift of the burden of proof from the alleged victim to the respondent is foreseen.[172] In summary, a common well-developed legal arsenal is enshrined in the area of equality and non-discrimination by these two Directives.

[163] Muir, *EU Equality Law* (n 74) 74.

[164] Council Directive 2000/43/EC of 29 June 2000 implementing the principle of equal treatment between persons irrespective of racial or ethnic origin [2000] OJ L180/22 (Directive 2000/43/EC), art 3.

[165] Beijer, *The Limits of Fundamental Rights Protection by the EU* (n 73) 198.

[166] Council Directive 2000/78/EC of 27 November 2000 establishing a general framework for equal treatment in employment and occupation [2000] OJ L303/16 (Directive 2000/78/EC), art 1.

[167] ibid, art 3.

[168] Bell, 'EU Anti-Discrimination Law' (n 148) 661.

[169] Directive 2000/43/EC, art 2; Directive 2000/78/EC, art 2.

[170] Directive 2000/43/EC, art 5; Directive 2000/78/EC, art 7.

[171] Directive 2000/43/EC, art 7(1); Directive 2000/78/EC, art 9(1).

[172] Directive 2000/43/EC, art 8; Directive 2000/78/EC, art 10.

In addition to this genuine equality policy, a specific legal basis was introduced by the Lisbon Treaty, for the protection of personal data, in Article 16(2) TFEU. Before this legal basis was enshrined in that provision, the EU was already active in the field of data protection, but in relation to the establishment of the Internal Market.[173] With this evolution, the EU now has a specific legal basis to adopt an active policy in the field of data protection.[174] Indeed, as underlined by Orla Lynskey, even if data protection continues to serve its integrationist purpose, 'its fundamental rights objective is no longer overlooked'.[175] Thanks to this legal basis, a uniform regulatory environment for data processing in the EU was established through the General Data Protection Regulation (GDPR).[176] In addition to the choice itself of the legal instrument used in this framework (a Regulation), several mechanisms were put in place in order to contribute to the uniform application of a common data protection framework among the Member States.[177] The GDPR requires 'effective, proportionate and dissuasive penalties'.[178] There is still room for limited diversity, however, given the fact that national law should still give effect to this Regulation, 'subject to the principle of national procedural autonomy'.[179]

An independent European Data Protection Supervisor (EDPS) has also been established in order to monitor and ensure the protection of personal data and privacy by EU institutions and bodies and advise them in this area.[180] In this context, the EDPS has notably used its powers to influence the evolution of EU data protection law.[181]

As observed by Thomas Streinz, the fundamental rights rationale has, little by little, taken precedence over the initial market-integration objective in the field of data protection, also because of the enshrinement of a fundamental right to data protection in the EU Charter,[182] and the case law of the CJEU being influenced by the ECtHR.[183]

[173] T Streinz, 'The Evolution of European Data Law' in Craig and de Búrca, *The Evolution of EU Law* (n 4), 908.

[174] On the problems of implementation of this system, see, ch 4, s II of this book, 'A Field of Tensions and Contradictions'.

[175] O Lynskey, *The Foundations of EU Data Protection Law* (Oxford University Press, 2015) 47.

[176] Regulation (EU) 2016/679 of the European Parliament and of the Council of 27 April 2016 on the protection of natural persons with regard to the processing of personal data and on the free movement of such data, and repealing Directive 95/46/EC (General Data Protection Regulation) [2016] OJ L 119/1 ('GDPR').

[177] Lynskey, *The Foundations of EU Data Protection Law* (n 175) 66 ff.

[178] GDPR, arts 83–84.

[179] Lynskey, *The Foundations of EU Data Protection Law* (n 175) 72.

[180] Regulation (EU) 2018/1725 of the European Parliament and of the Council of 23 October 2018 on the protection of natural persons with regard to the processing of personal data by the Union institutions, bodies, offices and agencies and on the free movement of such data and repealing Regulation (EC) No 45/2001 and Decision No 1247/2002/EC [2018] OJ L 295/39, art 52.

[181] Streinz, 'The Evolution of European Data Law' (n 173) 913.

[182] Charter of Fundamental Rights of the European Union, art 8.

[183] Streinz, 'The Evolution of European Data Law' (n 173) 912.

Thanks to these two legal bases enabling the EU to adopt harmonisation measures in the areas of non-discrimination and the protection of personal data, two genuine policies have been developed to safeguard these two fundamental rights. The EU clearly positions itself as a 'norm-*maker*' in these two fields.

These new policies has also given rise to abundant case law from the CJEU, which has become a true norm-setter in these areas, as will be further developed below. One illustrative example is the *Deldits* case,[184] in which the CJEU held that Article 16 GDPR obliges national authorities to rectify the registered gender of a transgender person when the information is inaccurate. The CJEU further clarified that, while it is legitimate for authorities to request supporting evidence, requiring proof of gender reassignment surgery constitutes a violation of EU Fundamental Rights Law.

VI.1.b. Fundamental Rights Harmonisation and the Development of the Internal Market

In addition to these two legal bases enabling direct action in the field of fundamental rights protection, the EU is also active on the basis of other legal bases, the primary purpose of which is not the protection of these rights.

Article 114 TFEU, which serves as the primary legal basis for implementing essential Internal Market measures, has regularly been used to establish common standards safeguarding fundamental rights. This provision enables the EU to enact measures for the approximation of the provisions laid down by law, regulation, or administrative action across Member States, specifically designed to establish and facilitate the Internal Market. As observed by Catherine Barnard, the CJEU acknowledged

> that even in a policy field where the EU has no competence to adopt legislative measures, the internal market provision may be used to achieve the protection of public values, provided that the measure also serves the internal market; a threshold that is easily met.[185]

As underlined by Bruno de Witte, the achievement of non-economic common objectives has thus justified the adoption of many EU legislative texts, on the basis of Article 114 TFEU, where market concerns were often only ancillary.[186] Some of these legislative texts, unsurprisingly, concern the protection of fundamental rights.

[184] C-247/23 *Deldits* ECLI:EU:C:2025:172 [2025].

[185] C Barnard, 'EU "Social" Policy: From Employment Law to Labour Market Reform' in Craig and de Búrca, *The Evolution of EU Law* (n 4), 720; citing Case C-376/98 *Federal Republic of Germany v European Parliament and Council of the European Union* ECLI:EU:C:2000:544 [2000] ECR I-8419.

[186] On this phenomenon, see, among others, B de Witte, 'Non-Market Values in Internal Market Legislation' in N Nic Shuibhne (ed), *Regulating the Internal Market* (Edward Elgar Publishing, 2006) 62; and G Davies, 'The Competence to Create an Internal Market: Conceptual Poverty and Unbalanced Interests' in S Garben and I Govaere (eds), *The Division of Competences between the EU and the Member States: Reflections on the Past, the Present and the Future* (Hart Publishing, 2017).

I will rely on a selection of three examples to illustrate this phenomenon:[187] the Patient's Rights Directive, the European Accessibility Act, and the European Media Freedom Act. They all aim, to a certain extent, to protect fundamental rights enshrined in the EU Charter: the right to health;[188] the integration of persons with disabilities;[189] and the freedom of expression and information.[190] These examples have been chosen because they cover different types of rights – civil and political rights, and economic and social rights – which can be considered as having a direct impact on human life, as opposed to more traditional economic activity,[191] and because they have been adopted at different periods of time, showing different phases of fundamental rights policy in the development of the Internal Market.

With regard to the fundamental right to health, the EU legislature has adopted several pieces of legislation on the basis of Article 114 TFEU.[192] Article 114(3) TFEU requires the European Commission to take 'as a base a high level of protection, taking account in particular of any new development based on scientific facts' in its legislative proposals concerning health, safety, environmental protection, and consumer protection. The CJEU considered, in view of this, that even though Article 168(5) TFEU expressly excludes harmonisation in the field of human health, this did not prevent the adoption of harmonisation measures having an impact on the protection of human health based on other provisions of the Treaty.[193] In this context, the Patients' Rights Directive[194] was adopted in 2011. As underlined by Vincent Delhomme, this piece of legislation pursues a dual objective: the establishment and the functioning of the Internal Market, but also, to no lesser extent, the protection of human health.[195] In the present case, the preamble of the Directive clearly relies upon Article 168(1) TFEU, which states that a high level of human health protection is to be ensured in the definition and implementation of all EU policies and activities. Its stated aim is to facilitate 'access to safe and high-quality cross-border healthcare in the Union'.[196] Even if the link with

[187] Many other examples of measures based on art 114 TFEU and driven by non-economic objectives could be cited, but I chose to limit my analysis to three recent and telling examples in the field of fundamental rights protection (see, for an in-depth study, V Kosta, *Fundamental Rights in EU Internal Market Legislation* (Hart Publishing, 2015)).

[188] Charter of Fundamental Rights, art 35.

[189] ibid, art 26.

[190] ibid, art 11.

[191] For a similar approach, see Kosta, *Fundamental Rights in EU Internal Market Legislation* (n 187). I could also have cited the legislation adopted in the field of consumer protection, but, as underlined by Bruno de Witte, this objective can be considered to be a market concern (de Witte, 'Non-Market Values in Internal Market Legislation' (n 186) 63). The same holds true for the protection of intellectual property, even if both objectives have been elevated to the rank of fundamental rights by the EU Charter.

[192] V Delhomme, 'Emancipating Health from the Internal Market: For a Stronger EU (Legislative) Competence in Public Health' (2020) 11 *European Journal of Risk Regulation* 747.

[193] Case C-376/98 *Federal Republic of Germany v European Parliament and Council of the European Union* ECLI:EU:C:2000:544 [2000] ECR I-8419, para 88.

[194] Directive 2011/24/EU of the European Parliament and of the Council of 9 March 2011 on the application of patients' rights in cross-border healthcare [2011] OJ L88/45 (Directive 2011/24/EU).

[195] Delhomme, 'Emancipating Health from the Internal Market' (n 192) 749.

[196] Directive 2011/24/EU, recital 10.

the fundamental right to health was not explicitly made in the Directive, it is clear that it enhances this right, at least in cross-border situations,[197] in particular with regard to the quality of care. Notably, the Directive requires the establishment of complaint procedures and systems of professional liability in case of harm arising from the health care received;[198] respect of the fundamental right to privacy in the context of health care;[199] and the patient's right to information.

Recently, there has been a more explicit emphasis on the fundamental rights justification for acts adopted under Article 114 TFEU. This shift is likely linked to the growing prominence of fundamental rights within the framework of the EU, as previously emphasised.

The evolution can be exemplified by the adoption of the EU Accessibility Act, through Directive 2019/882 on the accessibility requirements for products and services.[200] This Act followed the EU's ratification of the UN Convention on the Rights of Persons with Disabilities (CRPD) 2010 on the basis of Article 114 TFEU. This was the first time that the EU became a full member of an international agreement focusing purely on the protection of human rights. Along with the announcement of the Disability Strategy 2010–2020, implementation of the CRPD in the EU was identified as a priority by the European Commission.[201] It decided to use Article 114 TFEU as a legal basis in that framework, drawing on Declaration No 22 annexed to the Treaty of Amsterdam, which states that the EU's institutions shall take account of the needs of persons with a disability when relying on this provision. Access to goods and services for persons with disabilities was, indeed, presented as 'a constituent part of the creation of a "deeper and fairer" internal market'.[202]

While a dual legal basis could have been envisaged, namely the combination of Articles 19 and 114 TFEU, the European Commission decided to rely only upon the Internal Market provision, probably to avoid the Article 19 TFEU requirement of unanimity in the Council of the European Union.[203]

It was thus necessary to highlight the link between the EU Accessibility Act and the removal of obstacles in the Internal Market and the gain in competitiveness.[204] Nevertheless, the human rights rationale is also clearly

[197] Kosta, *Fundamental Rights in EU Internal Market Legislation* (n 187) 286.

[198] Directive 2011/24/EU, art 4(2)(c)–(d).

[199] ibid, art 4(2)(e).

[200] Directive (EU) 2019/882 of the European Parliament and of the Council of 17 April 2019 on the accessibility requirements for products and services [2019] OJ L151/70 (Directive 2019/882).

[201] Communication from the European Commission to the European Parliament, the Council of the European Union, the European Economic and Social Committee and the Committee of the Regions, 'European Disability Strategy 2010–2020: A Renewed Commitment to a BarrierFree Europe' [2010] COM(2010) 636 final.

[202] D Ferri, 'The European Accessibility Act and the Shadow of the "Social Market Economy"' [2020] *European Law Review* 660, 669, quoting the roadmap presented by the Juncker Commission in 2015. See the Press Release at https://ec.europa.eu/commission/presscorner/detail/en/IP_15_5909.

[203] Ferri, The European Accessibility Act' (n 202) 670.

[204] See, among others, Directive 2019/882, recitals 1, 5, 6, 28, 50, 72.

presented as being at the core of the Directive: its third recital indeed stresses that

> this Directive promotes full and effective equal participation by improving access to mainstream products and services that, through their initial design or subsequent adaptation, address the particular needs of persons with disabilities.[205]

The directive also expressly states that

> this Directive seeks to ensure full respect for the rights of persons with disabilities to benefit from measures designed to ensure their independence, social and occupational integration and participation in the life of the community and to promote the application of Articles 21, 25 and 26 of the Charter.[206]

The Directive has a very large scope, covering a wide range of consumer goods (smartphones, e-readers, computers, and so on) and services (e-commerce services, online maps and mapping services, consumer banking services, some elements of transport services, and so on).[207] Its beneficiaries include people with disabilities, but also 'persons with functional limitations', such as the elderly, pregnant women, or any person who has physical, mental, intellectual, or sensory impairments.[208] The Directive enshrines many obligations for both public and private manufacturers, importers, distributors, and service providers. In substance, they must make sure that products and services are accessible. This requirement concerns, notably, information on the use of the product that shall be made available via more than one sensory channel; the user interface and functionality design; the presence of subtitles for instructions, videos, and so on.[209] Member States are also required to establish adequate and effective means to ensure compliance with the Directive,[210] including effective, dissuasive, and proportionate rules on penalties.[211]

The third example can be drawn from the European Media Freedom Act (EMFA).[212] The legal basis of the proposed EU Regulation is Article 114 TEU, as it aims to 'address the fragmented national regulatory approaches related to media freedom and pluralism and editorial independence' and 'foster a common approach and coordination at EU level, ensure the optimal functioning of the internal market for media services, and prevent the emergence of future obstacles

[205] On this rationale, see also AK Drabarz, 'Harmonising Accessibility in the EU Single Market: Challenges for Making the European Accessibility Act Work' (2020) 43 *Review of European and Comparative Law* 83.

[206] Directive (EU) 2019/882 of the European Parliament and of the Council of 17 April 2019 on the accessibility requirements for products and services [2019] OJ L151/70 (Directive 2019/882), recital 103.

[207] ibid, art 2.

[208] ibid, recital 4.

[209] See Annexes attached to Directive 2019/882.

[210] Directive 2019/882, art 29.

[211] ibid, art 30.

[212] Regulation (EU) 2024/1083 of the European Parliament and of the Council of 11 April 2024 establishing a common framework for media services in the internal market [2024] OJ L 2024/1083.

to the operation of media service providers across the EU'. Yet this text undoubtedly harmonises certain standards of protection concerning freedom of the press, freedom of expression, and the right to information. The Regulation is openly presented as having the potential to safeguard media independence and pluralism, thereby contributing to the protection of the freedom of expression protected by Article 11 of the EU Charter.[213] Harmonisation notably concerns the minimum safeguards required with regard to the appointment and dismissal of the people managing public service media providers,[214] the allocation of public funds to media service providers,[215] and transparency obligations owed by media service providers.[216] If it is, indeed, on the basis of the Internal Market that this measure has been adopted, it is clear that it has a direct impact on the protection of fundamental rights within the EU, and, more generally, its founding values.

These examples show how supporting the functioning of the Internal Market can go hand in hand with strengthening the protection of fundamental rights. As put forward by Olivier De Schutter, these measures indeed serve a dual function, ensuring

> that this conflict will not result in the creation of barriers within the internal market – which the EU Member States may be tempted to justify by the need to ensure a certain level of protection of fundamental rights within their territory; [and]
>
> that the high level of protection of fundamental rights certain Member States may be seeking to ensure will not be threatened by the need to recognise the primacy of economic freedoms of movement.[217]

VI.1.c. Fundamental Rights Harmonisation as a Key to Unlocking the Area of Freedom, Security and Justice

In the AFSJ, a similar dynamic can be observed, as measures addressing fundamental rights were essential to ensure its proper functioning. The name itself highlights the broad objectives it aims to achieve: freedom, security, and justice – concepts that have been described as a 'highly abstract triumvirate of values'.[218]

Harmonisation of fundamental rights emerged early on as necessary to ensure the proper functioning of the AFSJ. It was developed in both the fields of civil and criminal judicial co-operation with this in mind. The primary objective here was to facilitate mutual recognition of judgments, and therefore their free circulation

[213] ibid, 13. See also Proposal of the European Media Freedom Act, recital 6.
[214] Proposal of the European Media Freedom Act, art 5(2).
[215] ibid, art 24.
[216] ibid, art 6.
[217] O De Schutter, 'Fundamental Rights and the Transformation of Governance in the European Union' (2007) 9 *Cambridge Yearbook of European Legal Studies* 133, 152.
[218] N Walker, 'In Search of the Area of Freedom, Security and Justice: A Constitutional Odyssey' in N Walker (ed), *Europe's Area of Freedom, Security and Justice* (Oxford University Press, 2004) 5.

within the common area. Harmonisation of fundamental rights for migrants and asylum seekers has also been developed, in particular to prevent secondary movements within the EU, which were made much easier by the abolition of frontiers between Member States. The adoption of a common minimum standard on national procedures for granting and withdrawing refugee status was, indeed, justified by the fact that it will contribute to reducing the willingness of asylum applicants to move from one Member State to another because of disparities in procedures among them. The idea was that harmonisation would mean 'applicants for asylum will decide on their country of destination less on the basis of the procedural rules and practices in places than before'.[219]

Alongside this instrumental logic, a distinct and autonomous logic gradually emerged within the AFSJ, driven by the primary goal of safeguarding fundamental rights. The balance struck between the autonomous logic and the functional logic depends on the domains and instruments involved. In contrast to the general legal basis enabling the adoption of legislation in the field of the Internal Market (Article 114 TFEU), the landscape is fragmented here, as there is no single general legal basis, but various specific ones enabling the EU to legislate. The legal frameworks for judicial co-operation in civil and criminal matters – as well as for immigration and asylum – differ significantly.

I will briefly revisit each of these domains below. As a reminder, the objective is not to provide an exhaustive list of legislation with aspects related to the protection of fundamental rights. Such a list would far exceed the space allocated because, as previously emphasised, it is quite common for the EU to strike a balance in its secondary legislation between integration objectives and fundamental rights protection. A set of examples illustrate the argument that has been chosen.

Regarding judicial co-operation in civil matters, the relevant legal basis is Article 81(1) and (2) TFEU, which empowers the EU to adopt 'approximation measures' to 'develop judicial cooperation in civil matters that have cross-border implications'. As observed by Agnieszka Frąckowiak-Adamska, the cross-border requirement has been construed restrictively by the CJEU, implying that EU legislation adopted on the basis of Article 81(1) and (2) TFEU could be applied exclusively in cross-border cases.[220] Furthermore, the EU has demonstrated 'self-restraint' in protecting fundamental rights in the context of civil judicial co-operation.

[219] Proposal for a Council Directive on minimum standards on procedures in Member States for granting and withdrawing refugee status [2000] COM(2000) 578 final, OJ C62 E 231. The Directive has now been adopted: Council Directive 2005/85/EC on minimum standards on procedures in Member States for granting and withdrawing refugee status [2005] OJ L 326/13 (Directive 2005/85/EC).

[220] A Frąckowiak-Adamska, 'Procedural Rights (and Obligations) of Parties to Civil Proceedings' in M González Pascual and S Iglesias Sánchez (eds), *Fundamental Rights in the EU Area of Freedom, Security and Justice* (Cambridge University Press, 2021) 238, citing Case C-170/11 *Maurice Robert Josse Marie Ghislain Lippens and Others v Hendrikus Cornelis Kortekaas and Others* ECLI:EU:C:2012:540 [2012], para 28; Case C-332/11 *ProRail BV v Xpedys NV and Others* ECLI:EU:C:2013:87 [2013], para 42. See also R Mańko, 'Europeanisation of Civil Procedure: Towards Common Minimum Standards?' (2015) *European Parliamentary Research Service In-Depth Analysis* 13. This contrasts with the conditions required to use the internal market legal basis (TFEU, art 144), where harmonisation

To date, the EU has only adopted two Directives protecting procedural rights, the scope of application of which is limited to cross-border cases, and which provide a relatively low level of protection.[221] These are the Directive establishing minimum common rules relating to legal aid[222] and the Directive on certain aspects of mediation in civil and commercial matters.[223] The instrumental approach of supporting free movement is still very much present in these instruments.

Nevertheless, it should be noted that certain elements of protection of fundamental rights can also be found in acts implementing the mutual recognition of judgments in civil matters. As an example, the Brussels IIb Regulation on jurisdiction, the recognition and enforcement of decisions in matrimonial matters and matters of parental responsibility, and on international child abduction, protects the fundamental right of the child to have their best interests safeguarded, through several of its provisions.[224]

It is also worth adding the recently adopted "anti-SLAPP Directive," which aims to protect individuals who engage in public participation from manifestly unfounded claims or abusive court proceedings.[225] In other words, the directive seeks to prevent the misuse of judicial procedures to silence public voices, including journalists, publishers, media organisations, whistleblowers, and human rights defenders, as well as civil society organisations, NGOs, trade unions, artists, researchers, and academics, through proceedings initiated to deter them from engaging in public debate. Although the directive was adopted on the basis of Article 81(2) TFEU, it clearly pursues a human rights objective, in particular the protection of freedom of expression. While its scope remains limited, as it applies only to cross-border cases, it must nonetheless be acknowledged that, in certain circumstances, it can provide genuine and meaningful protection of human rights.

The picture is somewhat different with regard to judicial co-operation in criminal matters. The entry into force of the Lisbon Treaty marked a new paradigm

may be adopted even with regard to purely national situations, as long as this harmonisation is needed for the well-functioning of the internal market (S Peers, *EU Justice and Home Affairs Law*, 3rd edn (Oxford University Press, 2011) 611, Joined Cases C-465/00, C-138/01, and C-139/01 *Rechnungshof v Österreichischer Rundfunk and Others and Christa Neukomm and Joseph Lauermann v Österreichischer Rundfunk* ECLI:EU:C:2003:294 [2003] ECR I-4989, para 41.

[221] Frąckowiak-Adamska, 'Procedural Rights (and Obligations) of Parties to Civil Proceedings' (n 220) 238.

[222] Council Directive 2002/8/EC of 27 January 2003 to improve access to justice in cross-border disputes by establishing minimum common rules relating to legal aid for such disputes [2003] OJ L 26/41.

[223] Directive 2008/52/EC of the European Parliament and of the Council of 21 May 2008 on certain aspects of mediation in civil and commercial matters [2008] OJ L 136/3.

[224] Council Regulation (EU) 2019/1111 of 25 June 2019 on jurisdiction, the recognition and enforcement of decisions in matrimonial matters and the matters of parental responsibility, and on international child abduction (recast).

[225] Directive (EU) 2024/1069 of the European Parliament and of the Council of 11 April 2024 on protecting persons who engage in public participation from manifestly unfounded claims or abusive court proceedings ('Strategic lawsuits against public participation') [2024] OJ L 2024/1069.

for European co-operation in criminal matters by placing increased emphasis on the protection of individuals,[226] even though the movement had already been set in motion beforehand.[227] The EU acquired the competence, on the legal basis of Article 82(2) TFEU, to adopt minimum standards, particularly with regard to the rights of individuals in criminal proceedings and victims of crime.

Several Directives have been adopted on this legal basis, which protect various fundamental rights in the context of criminal proceedings: on the right to interpretation and translation, the right to information,[228] the right of access to a lawyer,[229] the presumption of innocence,[230] the rights of children in criminal proceedings,[231] the right to legal aid, and the rights of victims.[232] These Directives crystallise and flesh out several fundamental rights guaranteed by the EU Charter, including the right to an effective remedy (Article 47) and the presumption of innocence (Article 48). In this context, they aim to strengthen the minimum protection offered by the EU Charter and the ECHR.[233] The Directive on access to a lawyer, for example, states that

> strengthening mutual trust requires *detailed rules* on the protection of the procedural rights [and] *further development* within the Union of the minimum standards set out in the Charter and in the ECHR (emphasis added).[234]

As several authors have pointed out, the protection of fundamental rights in the context of criminal proceedings has now become a genuine autonomous project of the EU,[235] and the rules apply not only in cross-border situations but also in purely

[226] F Catteau, 'Les droits procéduraux des personnes poursuivies et des victimes de criminalité devant la Cour de justice de l'Union européenne. Vers un droit européen de la procédure pénale ?' (2020) *Cahiers de droit européen* 485–88.

[227] Conclusions of the Tampere Council of 15 and 16 October 1999 [1999], para 32; and Communication from the European Commission to the Council of the EU and the European Parliament of 10 May 2005, 'The Hague Programme: ten priorities for the next five years. The Partnership for European renewal in the field of Freedom, Security and Justice' [2005] COM(2005) 184 final.

[228] Directive 2012/13/EU of the European Parliament and of the Council of 22 May 2012 on the right to information in criminal proceedings [2012] OJ L 142/1.

[229] Directive 2013/48/EU of the European Parliament and of the Council of 22 October 2013 on the right of access to a lawyer in criminal proceedings and in European arrest warrant proceedings, and on the right to have a third party informed upon deprivation of liberty and to communicate with third persons and with consular authorities while deprived of liberty [2013] OJ L 294/1 (Directive 2013/48).

[230] Directive 2016/343 of the European Parliament and of the Council of 9 March 2016 on the strengthening of certain aspects of the presumption of innocence and of the right to be present at the trial in criminal proceedings [2016] OJ L 66/1.

[231] Directive 2016/800 of the European Parliament and of the Council of 11 May 2016 on procedural safeguards for children who are suspects or accused persons in criminal proceedings [2016] OJ L 132/1.

[232] Directive 2016/1919 of the European Parliament and of the Council of 26 October 2016 on legal aid for suspects and accused persons in criminal proceedings and for requested persons in European arrest warrant proceedings [2016] OJ L 297/1.

[233] As allowed by art 52(3) of the Charter of Fundamental Rights of the European Union, which authorises the EU to go beyond the protection offered by the ECHR.

[234] Directive 2013/48, recital 6.

[235] J Ouwerkerk, 'EU Competence in the Area of Procedural Criminal Law: Functional vs. Self-Standing Approximation of Procedural Rights and Their Progressive Effect on the Charter's Scope

internal ones.[236] Indeed, despite the wording of Article 82(2) TFEU, which, similarly to Article 81 TFEU, refers to 'criminal matters having a cross-border dimension', the Directives are applicable to domestic situations as well. The CJEU indeed considered, in relation to the Directive on the right to be informed of the charge, that it

> contributes to establishing minimal harmonisation of criminal proceedings in the European Union, and the application, in a Member State, of the rules laid down by that directive is independent of the existence of any cross-border situation in the context of a dispute arising in that Member State.[237]

According to Irène Wieczorek, given the fact that the other Directives on procedural rights similarly define their scope of application, it is fair to assume that they should benefit from the same wide interpretation.[238] She goes as far as to conclude that, 'through secondary law, the EU has created a "national" area of justice as far as the enjoyment of individuals' rights in criminal proceedings are concerned', and that it constitutes a 'common space where every individual enjoys the same rights regardless of their involvement in domestic or cross-border proceedings'.[239] Moreover, several Directives expressly refer to the objective of protecting fundamental rights in themselves, alongside that of improving the effectiveness of cross-border co-operation. For instance, the preamble of the Directive on access to a lawyer states that

> common minimum rules should lead to increased confidence in the criminal justice systems of all Member States, which, in turn, should lead to more efficient judicial cooperation in a climate of mutual trust and to the promotion of a fundamental rights culture in the Union.[240]

The generous interpretation of the scope of these Directives, moreover, significantly broadens the scope of application of the EU Charter, since it brings the matters it regulates under the scope of EU law.[241] We will return to examine the relationship between EU legislation and the direct effect of EU Charter provisions in chapter two of the book.[242]

of Application' (2019) 27 *European Journal of Crime, Criminal Law and Criminal Justice* 89–93, and references cited.

[236] Catteau, 'Les droits procéduraux' (n 226) 491.

[237] Case C-646/17, *Criminal proceedings against Gianluca Moro* ECLI:EU:C:2019:489 [2019], para 36.

[238] I Wieczorek, 'The Emerging Role of the EU as a Primary Normative Actor in the EU Area of Criminal Justice' (2021) 27 *European Law Journal* 394.

[239] ibid, 395.

[240] Directive 2013/48/EU of the European Parliament and of the Council of 22 October 2013 on the right of access to a lawyer in criminal proceedings and in European arrest warrant proceedings, and on the right to have a third party informed upon deprivation of liberty and to communicate with third persons and with consular authorities while deprived of liberty [2013] OJ L 294/1, recital 8.

[241] See art 51 of the Charter of Fundamental Rights; Case C-646/17 *Criminal proceedings against Gianluca Moro* ECLI:EU:C:2019:489 [2019] para 68; Catteau, 'Les droits procéduraux' (n 226) 495; and Ouwerkerk, 'EU Competence in the Area of Procedural Criminal Law' (n 234) 95. The limit of the Charter's scope of application in relation to these Directives and the protection of procedural rights in criminal matters is, however, not easy to define. See, for instance, Case C-467/19 PPU *Criminal proceedings against QR* ECLI:EU:C:2019:776 [2019], and Case C-377/18 *Criminal proceedings against AH and others (Presumption of Innocence)* ECLI:EU:C:2019:670 [2019].

[242] See ch 2, s I.3. of this book, 'The Individual-rights-based EU Fundamental Rights Law'.

A genuine policy for protecting fundamental rights in the context of criminal proceedings has thus been developed at the EU level, which establishes precise common minimum standards for Member States. Advocate General Bot underlined that, even if these Directives were referred to as a 'minimum', they 'actually relate to major principles governing, inter alia, the rights of the defence and respect for the right to a fair hearing, from which the Member States may not derogate'.[243] He therefore preferred to speak about 'non-derogable rules' instead of minimum rules, in order to mark their 'foundational' importance.[244]

However, one can still regret that the wording of Article 82(2) TFEU is too restrictive to legitimise such a development. As Jannemieke Ouwerkerk points out, 'the provision is not fit for today's European Union which in matters of criminal justice currently presents itself as a values-based actor, leading to both repressive and – to an increasing extent – protective criminal law measures'.[245] A similar critique could also be formulated with regard to the anti-discrimination legal basis – Article 19 TFEU – which confines the EU's competence in this field to 'the limits of the powers conferred by [the treaties] upon the Union'.

However, these textual limitations did not prevent the EU from developing robust protection for both procedural rights in criminal matters, and against discrimination. It also appears that the fact that these rights have been fleshed out at the level of EU law has had an influence on the jurisprudence of the ECtHR in this area.[246]

A 'made in the EU' protection of fundamental rights has also been developed in the areas of asylum and migration.[247] Since the Treaty of Amsterdam, the EU has been given the objective of establishing a Common European Asylum System (CEAS).[248] Various harmonisation measures have been adopted within this framework, including minimum standards protecting asylum seekers' fundamental rights. The objective of these harmonising laws was twofold: on the one hand – and probably most importantly, at the beginning – to prevent secondary movements towards Member States offering the most generous conditions; and, on the other hand, to ensure that the fundamental rights of applicants were protected.[249]

[243] Opinion of Advocate General Bot, Case C-216/14 *Criminal proceedings against Gavril Covaci* ECLI:EU:C:2015:305 [2015], para 30.

[244] ibid, para 32.

[245] Ouwerkerk, 'EU Competence in the Area of Procedural Criminal Law' (n 235) 94.

[246] N Daminova, 'The European Court of Human Rights on the "Stockholm's Roadmap Directives": the quest for a coherent application of "due process" rights in Europe?' (2023) Weekend Edition no 156, *EU Law Live*, at www.eulawlive.com.

[247] On this policy and the Charter, see S Peers, 'Immigration, asylum and human rights in the European Union' in Douglas-Scott and Hatzis, *Research Handbook on EU Law* (n 107) 439–50.

[248] Now enshrined in arts 78(1) and 78(2) of the TFEU.

[249] Communication from the European Commission to the Council of the EU and the European Parliament on the right of asylum [1991] SEC(91)1857 final, 7, which states, among others, that 'the measures to be taken jointly in respect of the right of asylum would be aimed primarily at eliminating abuse of that right, while at the same time protecting the rights of asylum seekers'.

The legislative framework of the CEAS has recently been reformed by the New Pact on Asylum and Migration.[250] The reform does not significantly challenge the fundamental rights dimension of this policy, apart from it relying more on EU Regulations than on EU Directives, which will naturally affect the degree of harmonisation within the EU across national legal systems.

Among these measures, there is a Directive that harmonises reception conditions for asylum seekers or persons granted subsidiary protection. Under this framework, the Reception Conditions Directive[251] provides a subjective right to minimum subsistence means for asylum seekers, including housing, food, clothing, and daily expenses.[252] It applies to

> all third-country nationals and stateless persons who make an application for international protection on the territory, including at the external border, in the territorial sea or in the transit zones of the Member States, provided that those third-country nationals and stateless persons are allowed to remain on the territory as applicants.[253]

The Directive lays down the right to schooling for minor applicants,[254] access to employment,[255] access to an adequate standard of living and protection of physical and mental health,[256] housing,[257] and so on. All these rights are fleshed out by the Directive, which defines particular minimum standards that have to be respected by the Member States. The Directive also prevents the detention of asylum seekers, save in exceptional circumstances, with certain guarantees and under certain strict conditions.[258]

While there may be criticism with respect to the leeway granted in certain respects to Member States in the implementation of this Directive, it is nevertheless undeniable that it contributes significantly to the protection of the fundamental rights of asylum seekers. In this regard, the CJEU plays an important role in facilitating an extensive interpretation of the obligations of Member States that are based on fundamental rights requirements. As noted by Lieneke Slingenberg, the CJEU confirms that Member States have important 'result-oriented obligations to

[250] Communication from the European Commission to the European Parliament, the Council of the EU, the European Economic and Social Committee and the Committee of the Regions on a New Pact on Migration and Asylum [2020] COM(2020) 609 final.

[251] Council Directive 2003/9/EC of 27 January 2003 laying down minimum standards for the reception of asylum seekers [2003] OJ L 31/18 (Directive 2003/9/EC), now replaced by Directive 2024/1346/EU of the European Parliament and of the Council of 14 May 2024 laying down standards for the reception of applicants for international protection OJ L 2024/1346 (Directive 2024/1346/EU).

[252] L Slingenberg, 'Reception Conditions for Asylum Seekers: Inherent Duality' in E Tsourdi and P De Buycker (eds), *Research Handbook on EU Migration and Asylum Law* (Edward Elgar Publishing, 2022) 206.

[253] Directive 2024/1346/EU, art 3(1).

[254] ibid, art 16.

[255] ibid, art 17.

[256] ibid, art 19.

[257] ibid, art 20.

[258] ibid, arts 10–13.

provide housing for all asylum seekers on their territory'.[259] Therefore, it seems that, in this respect, 'the Directive appears to require more from Member States than what they are obligated to provide to their nationals under human rights law'.[260] The CJEU has also shown great protectiveness of asylum seekers' right to liberty, by interpreting the conditions under which they may be detained very restrictively, a matter which I will elaborate upon in the following section.

A Directive harmonising national asylum procedures was also adopted in 2005,[261] recast in 2013,[262] and transformed into a Regulation in 2024,[263] notably to ensure that international protection requests are examined and decisions concerning them are made in an objective and impartial manner.[264] Although the Geneva Convention does not provide specific standards for the procedure determining the refugee status,[265] the EU legal framework defines precise common standards to which all Member States must adhere in implementing their asylum policies. The Regulation specifies obligations such as general guarantees for applicants;[266] deadlines that must be respected;[267] requirements on providing information and counselling;[268] the right to remain in the Member State pending the examination of the application;[269] and requirements for asylum-related interviews.[270] The Regulation also enshrines guarantees that must be provided if the asylum seeker undergoes a medical examination to verify the existence of serious harm or persecution.[271] The Regulation also specifies a number of guarantees that must be respected in order to ensure the right to an effective remedy. Issues related to the right of appeal before a court or tribunal and its scope, as well as its suspensive effect, are regulated by the Directive.[272]

Finally, the EU has also taken action to harmonise the conditions under which one can benefit from the right of asylum in the EU. Known as the 'Qualification

[259] Slingenberg, 'Reception Conditions for Asylum Seekers' (n 251) 223.
[260] ibid.
[261] Directive 2005/85/EC.
[262] Directive 2013/32/EU of the European Parliament and of the Council of 26 June 2013 on common procedures for granting and withdrawing international protection (recast) [2013] OJ L 180/60 (Directive 2013/32/EU).
[263] Regulation 2024/1348/EU of the European Parliament and of the Council of 14 May 2024 establishing a common procedure for international protection in the Union and repealing Directive 2013/32/EU, OJ L 2024/1348 (Regulation 2024/1348/EU).
[264] Directive 2013/32/EU, recital 17. On the content of the amending Regulation, see ch 2, section I.1.4(a) of this book, 'Effectiveness through Legislation'.
[265] J Vedsted-Hansen, 'Asylum Procedures: Seeking Coherence within Disparate Standards' in Tsourdi and De Buycker, *Research Handbook on EU Migration and Asylum Law* (n 251) 246.
[266] Regulation 2024/1348/EU, art 8.
[267] ibid, art 35.
[268] ibid, art 15.
[269] ibid, art 10.
[270] ibid, arts 11–14.
[271] ibid, art 24.
[272] ibid, art 67.

Directive', it was first adopted in 2005,[273] and recast in 2011,[274] and has been amended by the 'Qualification Regulation'.[275] It grants two protection statuses: asylum and subsidiary protection. The refugee status coincides with the protection offered by the Geneva Convention,[276] while subsidiary protection is a specific EU category deriving from other regional and national systems.[277] The latter should be granted to those who do not qualify as a refugee, namely a

> third-country national or a stateless person who does not qualify as a refugee but in respect of whom substantial grounds have been shown for believing that that person, if returned to his or her country of origin or, in the case of a stateless person, to his or her country of former habitual residence, would face a real risk of suffering serious harm.[278]

That includes protection against the death penalty, torture, or inhuman and degrading treatment or punishment, or serious and individual threat to a civilian's life or person by reason of indiscriminate violence in situations of international or internal armed conflict.[279] By specifying the conditions for acquiring these statuses, the Directive contributes to predictability in this field. Moreover, the interpretation given by the CJEU contributes to strengthening human rights and the individualisation of cases.[280] Furthermore, as it embeds minimum standards, the Directive does not prevent Member States from granting more protection.[281]

There is no doubt that these sets of standards flesh out the fundamental rights of international protection seekers within the EU, including the fundamental right to asylum,[282] the right to an effective remedy,[283] the right to respect for privacy and family life,[284] the right to liberty,[285] and so on. These pieces of legislation have,

[273] Council Directive 2004/83/EC on minimum standards for the qualification and status of third country nationals or stateless persons as refugees or as persons who otherwise need international protection and the content of the protection granted [2004] OJ L 304/12.

[274] Directive 2011/95/EU of the European Parliament and of the Council on standards for the qualification of third-country nationals or stateless persons as beneficiaries of international protection, for a uniform status for refugees or for persons eligible for subsidiary protection, and for the content of the protection granted [2011] OJ L 337/9. Note that 25 Member States are currently bound by it. Denmark benefits from an opt-out, and Ireland is still bound by the first Directive, of 2004.

[275] Regulation 2024/1347/EU of the European Parliament and of the Council of 14 May 2024 on standards for the qualification of third-country nationals or stateless persons as beneficiaries of international protection, for a uniform status for refugees or for persons eligible for subsidiary protection and for the content of the protection granted [2004] OJ L 2024/1347 (Regulation 2024/1347/EU).

[276] Case C-369/17 *Shajin Ahmed v Bevándorlási és Menekültügyi Hivatal* ECLI:EU:C:2018:713 [2018], para 40, with reference to earlier case law.

[277] B Nagy, 'Qualifying for International Protection in the EU' in Tsourdi and De Buycker, *Research Handbook on EU Migration and Asylum Law* (n 252) 170.

[278] Regulation 2024/1347/EU, art 3(6).

[279] ibid, art 15.

[280] Nagy, 'Qualifying for International Protection in the EU' (n 280) 192.

[281] C Costello, *The Human Rights of Migrants and Refugees in European Law* (Oxford University Press, 2015) 200.

[282] Charter of Fundamental Rights, art 18.

[283] ibid, art 47.

[284] ibid, art 7.

[285] ibid, art 6.

moreover, led to numerous judgments from the CJEU proposing an autonomous interpretation of the rights they confer, which is applicable throughout the EU.

For instance, in connection with methods of assessment of previous harm or persecution, the CJEU has handed down various judgments recalling that such assessment must be carried out in accordance with the EU Charter of Fundamental Rights.[286] In the *F* judgment, the CJEU opposed the use of a psychologist's expert report based on Rorschach and Szondi tests to assess the veracity of a claim made by an applicant for international protection concerning his sexual orientation.[287] Many judgments have been issued regarding the guarantees required for the principle of effective remedy in the asylum field. I delve deeper into them in chapter two, which focuses on the specific features of EU Fundamental Rights Law. It is already worth noting, however, that due to the existence of a common regulatory framework from a substantive and a procedural point of view, the CJEU has been very proactive in enforcing the requirements of these Directives.[288]

The Family Reunification Directive[289] is another example of harmonisation of the fundamental rights of persons from third countries. Although it is an instrument of EU migration policy,[290] this Directive actually implements the fundamental right to family life.[291] Recital 6 of the preamble explicitly states that the Directive aims 'to protect the family and establish or preserve family life'. In this regard, it imposes an obligation on Member States to enshrine the directly applicable right of family reunification for third-country nationals fulfilling certain conditions. The Court of Justice underlined in this regard that

> the Directive imposes precise positive obligations, with corresponding clearly defined individual rights, on the Member States, since it requires them, in the cases determined by the Directive, to authorise family reunification of certain members of the sponsor's family, without being left a margin of appreciation.[292]

With such an individual-rights-based interpretation, the CJEU paved the way for domestic-level disputes against possible restrictions that would contravene the Directive, and also implied a narrow interpretation of possible derogations from the right to family reunification.[293]

As observed by Cathryn Costello, the approach of the Directive is thus very different from that of the ECtHR, as it creates a genuine 'right to family reunification'.[294]

[286] See Joined Cases C-148/13 to C-150/13 *A and Others v Staatssecretaris van Veiligheid en Justitie* ECLI:EU:C:2014:2406 [2014].

[287] Case C-473/16 *F v Bevándorlási és Állampolgársági Hivatal* ECLI:EU:C:2018:36 [2018].

[288] See, among others, Joined Cases C-704/20 and C-39/21 *Staatssecretaris van Justitie en Veiligheid (Examen d'office de la retention)* ECLI:EU:C:2022:858 [2022], para 86.

[289] Council Directive 2003/86/EC of 22 September 2003 on the right to family reunification [2003] OJ L 251/12.

[290] Adopted on the basis of the Treaty establishing the European Community (Consolidated version 2002) [2002] OJ C325/33, art 63(3)(a); now replaced by art 79(3)(a) of the TFEU.

[291] As protected by art 7 of the Charter of Fundamental Rights.

[292] Case C-540/03 *European Parliament v Council of the European Union* ECLI:EU:C:2006:429 [2006] ECR I-5769, para 60.

[293] Costello, *The Human Rights of Migrants and Refugees in European Law* (n 281) 149.

[294] ibid, 139.

While the ECtHR is often called upon to decide upon individual cases related to family reunification on the basis of Article 8 of the ECHR, the 'Community' method has shifted the issue to the political arena at the EU level, resulting in the adoption of a harmonisation text.[295] However, the political sensitivity of the issue did not do any favours for the quality and readability of the Directive. Henri Labyle noted in this regard that it was 'written in a deplorable manner because it was negotiated reluctantly, the text is undoubtedly the counter-example of what Community legislation should be'.[296] Nevertheless, this legislative text significantly contributes to the protection of the fundamental right to family life of third-country nationals. As underlined by Kees Groenendijk and Tineke Strik, who analysed the implementation of the Directive about 20 years after its adoption, 'the establishment of a subjective right to family reunification and the obligations that right involves for Member States go far beyond the right to family life of Article 8 ECHR'.[297]

On the external level, the EU ratified the Council of Europe's Convention on Preventing and Combating Violence Against Women and Domestic Violence, also known as the Istanbul Convention. The process was long, and was a matter of debate for the different Member States. Nevertheless, the CJEU confirmed the EU's competence in this area. The conclusion of this agreement was based, among others, on Article 82(2) TFEU in relation to minimum standards applicable in criminal proceedings, and on Article 78(2) TFEU, which gives the EU competence to establish a common asylum policy.[298] Only a qualified majority in the Council of the European Union,[299] and the approval of the European Parliament,[300] was thus needed to conclude this treaty. It was the second international fundamental rights instrument ratified by the EU, after the UN Convention on the Rights of Persons with Disabilities. As the focus of this work is an analysis of the internal dimension of the EU's protection of fundamental rights, I will not go further into the analysis of that instrument.

Nevertheless, it is worth noting that the CJEU has recently clarified that the Istanbul Convention must be respected by the Member States – even those that have not ratified that Convention – when they operate within the scope of EU law. Consequently, in the *WS* judgment, the CJEU confirmed that the Qualification Directive,[301] in the context of the CEAS, should be construed (by Bulgaria, in that case) in accordance with the Istanbul Convention. This was despite Bulgaria not having ratified that

[295] R Lawson, 'Family Reunification Directive – Court of Justice of the European Communities: Family Reunification and the Union's Charter of Fundamental Rights, Judgment of 27 June 2006, Case C-540/03, Parliament v. Council' (2007) 3 *European Constitutional Law Review* 324, 328.

[296] H Labayle, 'Architecte ou spectatrice? La Cour de Justice de l'Union dans l'Espace de liberté, sécurité et justice' (2006) *Revue Trimestrielle de Droit Européen* 1 (own translation).

[297] K Groenendijk and T Strik, 'Directive 2003/86 on the Right to Family Reunification: A Surprising Anchor in a Sensitive Field' in E Tsourdi and P De Buycker (eds), *Research Handbook on EU Migration and Asylum Law* (n 252) 326.

[298] See Opinion 1/19 of the Court, *Istanbul Convention* ECLI:EU:C:2021:198 [2021], paras 294 and 304.

[299] TFEU, art 218(8).

[300] TFEU, art 218(6)(a), (v).

[301] Directive 2011/95/EU, now replaced by Regulation (EU) 2024/1347.

Convention.[302] Through its exercise of external competence, the EU also has an influence on the protection of fundamental rights within the Member States.

VI.1.d. The Slow Development of a Social Policy Shaping the Emergence of EU Fundamental Social Rights[303]

The appearance of fundamental social rights in the EU was a slow process.[304] The development of labour and social law emerged only gradually, and as a corollary of the free movement of workers.[305] Initially, the main aim was to avoid unfair competition among the various Member States based on their social law, and to ensure free movement of workers through the co-ordination of national social security schemes. The architects of European integration believed that social progress would naturally flow along with economic integration. Consequently, they initially decided not to interfere with social security policies. This did not, however, occur in practice. Instead, the Internal Market led to additional pressure on national social security systems. Given these detrimental effects, social objectives were gradually incorporated into the European agenda over time.[306] Nowadays, 'social progress'[307] and 'the protection of fundamental social rights'[308] have been defined as EU objectives. According to Article 3 of the TEU, the EU shall establish an Internal Market based on a 'social market economy, aiming at full employment and social progress', which should 'combat social exclusion and discrimination and promote social justice and protection'.[309] Article 151 TFEU adds that the

> Union and the Member States, having in mind fundamental social rights such as those set out in the European Social Charter signed at Turin on 18 October 1961 and in the 1989 Community Charter of the Fundamental Social Rights of Workers, shall have as their objectives the promotion of employment, improved living and working conditions, so as to make possible their harmonisation while the improvement is being maintained, proper social protection, dialogue between management and labour, the development of human resources with a view to lasting high employment and the combating of exclusion.

Nevertheless, the economic rationale has not disappeared, as the EU Treaties still make reference to the objective of ensuring the functioning of the Internal Market.[310]

[302] Case C-621/21 *WS v Intervyuirasht organ na Darzhavna agentsia za bezhantsite pri Ministerskia savet* ECLI:EU:C:2024:47 [2024], para 46.

[303] I am grateful to Professor Eleni De Becker for reviewing this section, and for her insightful advice. Any remaining errors or inaccuracies are my own.

[304] On this process, see S Douglas-Scott and N Hatzis, 'EU Law and Social Rights' in Douglas-Scott and Hatzis, *Research Handbook on EU Law* (n 107), 492–515.

[305] R White, 'Social Security' in S Peers and A Ward (eds), *The EU Charter of Fundamental Rights: Politics, Law and Policy* (Hart, 2004) 310.

[306] On this evolution, see A Aranguiz, *Combating Poverty and Social Exclusion in European Union Law* (Routledge, 2022) 2.

[307] TFEU, preamble.

[308] TEU, preamble.

[309] See also art 9 of the TFEU.

[310] ibid, art 151(3).

In this context, the EU has been granted a few competences[311] which enable it to legislate in order to promote 'employment, improved living and working conditions … proper social protection, dialogue between management and labour' and 'the development of human resources with a view to lasting high employment and the combating of exclusion'.[312]

Article 153 TFEU provides a competence to the EU to 'support and complement' Member States' actions in the field, among other fields, to protect workers' health and safety, working conditions, and social security, as well as for the social protection of workers, equality between men and women with regard to labour market opportunities and treatment at work, and so on. To this end, the EU may adopt Directives imposing 'minimum requirements for gradual implementation, having regard to the conditions and technical rules obtaining in each of the Member States'.[313] As underlined by Sacha Garben, EU social policy is thus 'necessary to ensure a "level playing field" for economic actors', as,

> without certain minimum common labour rules, for instance, (companies in) countries with high levels of social protection could suffer a competitive disadvantage and these countries would thereby be incentivised to lower their standards to prevent the loss of competitiveness of domestic companies and to attract foreign business.[314]

The economic dimension of these competences is, therefore, strongly evident. Even so, a set of Directives concerning aspects of labour law and gender equality has been adopted on this foundation, establishing 'an important floor of social rights protecting EU citizens against some of the most important vicissitudes of working life'.[315]

One of the most noteworthy is the Working Time Directive,[316] which constitutes a highly important acquis for the EU in both 'symbolic and practical terms'.[317] This Directive was adopted on the basis of Article 153(1)(b) TFEU. It contributes to the protection of all workers' health and safety across Europe, by providing a maximum weekly working time of 48 hours on average, and determining a minimum for rest periods and paid holidays. In this way, it can now be acknowledged that the Directive implements fundamental social rights guaranteed by the EU Charter, particularly the right to fair and just working conditions. The Explanations to the EU Charter related to its Article 31(2) expressly refer to the Working Time

[311] From the outset, by the agreement on social policy concluded between the Member States of the European Community, with the exception of the United Kingdom of Great Britain and Northern Ireland, adopted along with the conclusion of the Treaty of Maastricht.

[312] TFEU, art 151.

[313] ibid, art 153(2)(b), (former art 118a of the EC Treaty).

[314] S Garben, 'Title X Social Policy' in M Kellerbauer, M Klamert and J Tomkin (eds), *The EU Treaties and the Charter of Fundamental Rights: A Commentary* (Oxford University Press, 2019) 1359.

[315] S Garben, E Muir, and C Kilpatrick, 'Towards a European Pillar of Social Rights: Upgrading the EU Social Acquis' (2017) *College of Europe Policy Brief* 2.

[316] Council Directive 93/104/EC of 23 November 1993 concerning certain aspects of the organization of working time [1993] OJ L 307/18, replaced by Directive 2003/88/EC of the European Parliament and of the Council of 4 November 2003 concerning certain aspects of the organisation of working time [2003] OJ L 299/9.

[317] Garben, 'Title X Social Policy' (n 313) 1371.

Directive.[318] By implementing this right, this harmonisation measure undoubtedly contributes to its protection. First, the Directive lays out the content of this right by determining specific rights and obligations that flow from it. Second, in landmark jurisprudence which will be discussed in more depth in chapter two of this book, the CJEU has also recognised that the combination of the protection offered by the EU Charter and such legislation allows for the recognition of the horizontal direct effect of Article 31(2) of the EU Charter.[319] This provides a very robust legal framework to protect the right to annual paid leave in the EU.

However, it should be noted that there are important limitations on the adoption of legislation on the basis of Article 153(1)(b) TFEU. The use of this legal basis only allows for the adoption of Directives establishing 'minimum requirements for gradual implementation'. The CJEU has further determined that any potentially more protective standards established by Member States should not be considered as falling within the scope of the Directive, nor within the application of the EU Charter.[320]

This example, among others, demonstrates that the scope of EU legislative action in the field of fundamental social rights exists, even if it remains limited.[321] As stressed by Ane Aranguiz, the contribution of EU law in the field of social rights has been limited, despite the fact that the EU's competences in this field have been broadened over time.[322] However, it is important to emphasise the difficulty Member States have in reaching a consensus on this matter, largely due to differing national approaches. In response, the EU has increasingly turned to soft-law instruments, aiming to foster gradual progress in the development of social rights. One example of this approach is the adoption of reports on the implementation of the recommendation on access to social protection, as a tool of monitoring, by the European Commission.

In 2017 the European Commission also launched the 'European Pillar of Social Rights'. It consists of a package of 20 social principles accompanied by various soft-law and hard-law proposals – including, among others, the right to education and lifelong learning, gender equality, equal opportunities, secure and adaptable employment, work–life balance, social protection, minimum income, long-term care, and so on. The establishment of this pillar was signed off on by the European Commission, the European Parliament, and the Council of the European Union in Gothenburg on 17 November 2017. Although this political initiative is ambitious and symbolic, it is still only soft law. It has, nevertheless, been used as if it were a

[318] Explanations relating to the Charter of Fundamental Rights OJ C 303/02. Available at https://eur-lex.europa.eu/legal-content/EN/TXT/?uri=oj:JOC_2007_303_R_0017_01.

[319] Joined Cases C-569/16 and C-570/16 *Stadt Wuppertal v Maria Elisabeth Bauer and Volker Willmeroth v Martina Broßonn* ECLI:EU:C:2018:871 [2018]; Case C-684/16 *Max-Planck-Gesellschaft zur Förderung der Wissenschaften eV v Tetsuji Shimizu* ECLI:EU:C:2018:874 [2018]. See ch 2, s I.3.b (ii) of this book, 'Horizontal Effects through the CJEU's Case Law'.

[320] Joined Cases C-609/17 and C-610/17 *Terveys- ja sosiaalialan neuvottelujärjestö (TSN) ry v Hyvinvointialan liitto ry and Auto- ja Kuljetusalan Työntekijäliitto AKT ry v Satamaoperaattorit ry* ECLI:EU:C:2019:981 [2019], para 54.

[321] Garben, 'Title X Social Policy' (n 314) 1351.

[322] Aranguiz, *Combating Poverty and Social Exclusion in European Union Law* (n 305) 4.

policy agenda, setting out new steps for EU action and legislation. Notably, it led to the adoption of the new Directive on work–life balance for parents and carers,[323] giving flesh to several provisions of the EU Charter, including Article 23 on gender equality and Article 33 on the right to reconcile family and professional life. Several studies have explored the implications of adopting this pillar and the measures it has prompted.[324] The pillar is positioned within a broader context where the EU seeks to balance its objectives of establishing the Internal Market with its commitment to social protection. However, as stressed by Sacha Garben, 'the Pillar does not (and cannot) in itself resolve the constitutional imbalance between "the market" and "the social" in the EU'.[325] Moreover, this may have led to uncertainty about the status of fundamental social rights within the EU legal order, especially considering the recognition of rights or principles mirroring those found in the EU Charter.[326] It is, therefore, essential to temper expectations regarding the impact of this pillar. As previously highlighted, several EU measures, particularly those enacted during the financial crisis, have had a detrimental impact on social rights within the EU.

While EU law, through its social policies, can occasionally act as a supporter of fundamental social rights, it often produces the opposite effect. Moreover, a distinction should be made between labour law and social security law within the EU framework. Over the past years, the EU has made significant strides in labour law, establishing a body of legislation addressing various aspects, such as working hours,[327] equal treatment for part-time and temporary workers[328] and workers with fixed-term contracts,[329] gender equality,[330] and collective dismissals.[331] While it could always be argued that more needs to be done, these developments represent considerable progress. The CJEU plays a key role in interpreting these Directives, often referencing the EU Charter and emphasising its importance, particularly in areas like working time. However, there is a notable contrast when it comes to social security. In this field, the EU has mainly focused on co-ordination frameworks to ensure free movement, alongside a Directive on gender equality and a few

[323] Directive (EU) 2019/1158 of the European Parliament and of the Council of 20 June 2019 on work–life balance for parents and careers and repealing Council Directive 2010/18/EU [2019] OJ L 188/79.

[324] See, among others, E De Becker, 'The principle of adequate social protection in the European Pillar of Social Rights: Assessing the instruments used to realise its potential' (2024) 26(2) *European Journal of Social Security* 284–304.

[325] S Garben, 'The European Pillar of Social Rights: An Assessment of its Meaning and Significance' (2017) 21 *Cambridge Yearbook of European Legal Studies* 101, 125.

[326] I am grateful to Professor Eleni De Becker for recommending the inclusion of this element.

[327] Directive 2003/88/EC on Working Time.

[328] Directive 2008/104/EC on Temporary Agency Work.

[329] Directive 1999/70/EC on Fixed-Term Work.

[330] Directive 2006/54/EC on Equal Treatment of Men and Women in Employment and Occupation. See also Council Directive 92/85/EEC of 19 October 1992 on the introduction of measures to encourage improvements in the safety and health at work of pregnant workers and workers who have recently given birth or are breastfeeding (tenth individual Directive within the meaning of Article 16 (1) of Directive 89/391/EEC).

[331] Council Directive 98/59/EC of 20 July 1998 on the approximation of the laws of the Member States relating to collective redundancies.

Recommendations highlighting the need for adequate social protection and minimum safeguards. The references to the right to social security or social assistance in the EU Charter are relatively limited, even within the context of free movement. Furthermore, the impact of EU economic surveillance is also evident in this area, as I have already underlined.[332]

As is frequently the case within the EU's system of fundamental rights protection, the situation is not black and white; rather, it presents a nuanced picture, with outcomes that are variably positive or negative depending on the specific area in question.

VI.2. The Emancipatory Interpretation of the CJEU

The EU has gradually established itself as a key norm-setter in the field of fundamental rights, achieving this not only through its legislative initiatives but also via the increasingly assertive and independent jurisprudence of the CJEU.

As the 'authentic' interpreter of EU law, the CJEU has, at times, departed from national and international approaches to carve out its own path in the protection of fundamental rights. While it may once have been argued that the CJEU had limited experience in adjudicating human rights matters, its role in this area has evolved significantly. Over time, the CJEU has developed a substantial body of case law dedicated to the protection of fundamental rights, positioning itself as a central actor in shaping the standards applied across Europe. Within this framework, it maintains a close relationship with international human rights law, particularly the ECHR. In this regard, Article 52(3) of the EU Charter explicitly provides that, where rights in the EU Charter correspond to those in the ECHR, their meaning and scope must be the same as those in the ECHR. However, it also makes clear that 'this provision shall not prevent Union law providing more extensive protection', reiterating the EU's capacity to establish higher standards of fundamental rights protection where applicable. The Explanations attached to the EU Charter, moreover, add that

> this means in particular that the legislator, in laying down limitations to those rights, must comply with the same standards as are fixed by the detailed limitation arrangements laid down in the ECHR, which are thus made applicable for the rights covered by this paragraph, *without thereby adversely affecting the autonomy of Union law and of that of the Court of Justice of the European Union.*[333]

According to a study published in 2024, 24 of the CJEU's cases since 2016 have made reference to the autonomy of EU law when applying Article 52(3) of the

[332] I am also thankful to Professor Eleni De Becker for suggesting the addition of a paragraph on the distinction between milestones in labour law and in social security law.

[333] Emphasis added.

EU Charter.[334] This non-negligible number vividly reflects the CJEU's increasingly emancipatory approach.

Koen Lenaerts and José Antonio Gutiérrez-Fons emphasise that 'the relationship between international law and EU law is characterised by a dialectic of so-called "filiation/emancipation", which permeates the case law of the Court'.[335] While the CJEU is bound to uphold the unity of the international legal order, it is equally tasked with safeguarding the specificity and autonomy of the EU legal order, which occasionally means that there have to be divergent interpretations. The relationship between EU and international law thus induces a situation of 'selective permeability of the Union's internal legal system for external norms, with the ECJ as a gatekeeper'.[336] This is particularly evident in the domain of human rights protection.

Although the CJEU frequently draws on the jurisprudence of its Strasbourg counterpart, there are notable areas where it chooses to diverge and assert its independence. A similar observation can be made regarding the role of common constitutional traditions in shaping the interpretation of EU law. Although Article 6(3) TEU explicitly identifies these traditions as a source of the general principles of EU law, it does not require the CJEU to align its interpretations with every national constitution. In other words, the CJEU is not bound to settle for the lowest common denominator. Rather, this approach grants the CJEU the flexibility to consider multiple interpretive pathways and to adopt the one that best serves the overarching objectives of the EU.[337]

The first time the CJEU explicitly addressed the need to safeguard the autonomy of EU law in relation to Article 52(3) of the EU Charter was in the Grand Chamber *N.* judgment, which concerned the detention of an asylum seeker. The case raised the question of whether the detention of an asylum seeker carried out under the Reception Conditions Directive[338] was compatible with the EU Charter, read in the light of the case law of the ECtHR. In its ruling, the CJEU emphasised that the EU is not a party to the ECHR and that the validity of the provision in question 'must be examined solely in the light of the fundamental rights guaranteed by the Charter'.[339] While acknowledging the importance of ensuring

[334] On 113 cases referring to art 52.3 (the case law has been considered until 29/09/23), see C Langenfeld, 'The 'autonomization' of EU fundamental rights protection: Insights into the recent ECJ case law on Article 52(3) CFR' (2024) 31(2) *Maastricht Journal of European and Comparative Law* 188.

[335] K Lenaerts and JA Gutiérrez-Fons, *Les méthodes d'interprétation de la Cour de justice de l'Union européenne* (Bruylant, 2020) 75 (own translation).

[336] Editorial Comments, 'Keeping Europeanism at Bay? Strategic Autonomy as a Constitutional Problem' (2022) 59 *Common Market Law Review* 313, 322.

[337] Lenaerts and Gutiérrez-Fons, *Les méthodes d'interprétation de la Cour de justice* (n 334) 104 (own translation).

[338] Directive 2013/33/EU.

[339] Case C-601/15 PPU, *J. N. v Staatssecretaris van Veiligheid en Justitie* ECLI:EU:C:2016:84 [2016], para 46.

consistency between the two legal instruments, the CJEU underlined that this must not 'adversely affect the autonomy of Union law and … that of the Court of Justice of the European Union'.[340] In this instance, the CJEU concluded that the detention did not violate the EU Charter of Fundamental Rights. This is not the only case where the CJEU's jurisprudence reveals a somewhat regressive dynamic in the protection of fundamental rights, often due to competing objectives within the EU framework.[341] However, in the event of the EU's accession to the ECHR, one could hope that such situations will no longer arise.

Conversely, there are instances where the CJEU has adopted a more robust approach to protecting fundamental rights than its Strasbourg counterpart, positioning itself as a leader in this area. This dynamic could continue post-accession, as the spirit of the ECHR allows for the adoption of more protective standards when deemed necessary. To illustrate this point, I will draw on three examples.

The first, highlighted by Koen Lenaerts and José Antonio Gutiérrez-Fons, has been described as a significant advancement of EU law compared with the protection offered by the ECHR and the ECtHR's case law.[342] They noted that the CJEU's judgment in *Commission v Hungary (Higher Education)*[343] provided broader protection for academic freedom than the ECtHR jurisprudence had established thus far. In this ruling, the CJEU found that Hungary had violated its obligations under EU law – specifically, the principles of academic freedom and the freedom to provide services – by passing legislation requiring foreign universities to maintain a campus in their home country in order to operate in Hungary. This legislation effectively forced the Central European University (CEU) to leave the country. However, as Sébastien Van Drooghenbroeck observes, this case is more about 'anticipation' than outright 'exceeding'.[344] The ECtHR has not yet been faced with a similar question, and, as such, it remains uncertain how it would rule if presented with such a case.

Another compelling example, where both courts have already issued judgments, concerns the protection of the right to liberty for asylum seekers. In this context, the CJEU has taken a distinct stance on the detention of asylum seekers,

[340] ibid, para 47.

[341] See, among others, the case law of both courts on the *ne bis in idem* principle. On this issue, see, among others, J Callewaert, 'A different "ne bis in idem" in Luxembourg? Judgment of the CJEU in Generalstaatsanwaltschaft Bamberg', available at https://johan-callewaert.eu/a-different-ne-bis-in-idem-in-luxembourg-judgment-of-the-cjeu-in-generalstaatsanwaltschaft-bamberg/. See also J Callewaert, 'Convention Control Over the Application of Union Law by National Judges: The Case for a Wholistic Approach to Fundamental Rights' (2023) 8 *European Papers – A Journal on Law and Integration* 331.

[342] Lenaerts and Gutiérrez-Fons, *Les méthodes d'interprétation de la Cour de justice* (n 335) 46.

[343] Case C-66/18 *Commission/Hongrie* (*Enseignement supérieur*) ECLI:EU:C:2020:792 [2020], para 226 ff.

[344] S Drooghenbroeck, 'Vérité à Luxembourg, erreur à Strasbourg. A propos de certaines plus-values discrètes de la Charte des droits fondamentaux de l'Union européenne' in F Picod and C Blumann, *Annuaire de droit de l'Union européenne* (Editions Panthéon Assas, 2021) 173–92.

diverging from the approach of the ECtHR and, in doing so, potentially offering a stronger form of protection.[345]

In the case of *Ilias and Ahmed v Hungary*, the ECtHR addressed the legality of Hungary's transit zones for asylum seekers, located at its external borders. These zones, enclosed by four-metre-high fences and guarded by armed officers, serve as detention facilities where asylum seekers are held during the processing of their claims. Initially, the Fourth Section of the ECtHR ruled that this practice violated Article 5 ECHR, which guarantees the right to liberty.[346] However, this position was overturned by the Grand Chamber, which instead concluded that this practice did not fall under Article 5 ECHR. According to the Grand Chamber, several arguments justified considering that it did not constitute an infringement of the freedom of asylum seekers: (i) they enter these zones of their own free will;[347] (ii) the objective of establishing these zones is simply to control the entry of foreigners into Hungarian territory;[348] (iii) the duration of detention (23 days in this case) to respond to the asylum application is reasonable;[349] (iv) asylum seekers had an actual, specific, and effective possibility of leaving these transit zones to return to Serbia, from where they had come.[350]

Shortly thereafter, a similar question had to be settled by the CJEU in the *F.M.S ea c. Országos Idegenrendészeti Főigazgatóság Dél-alföldi Regionális Igazgatóság* case. Sitting in Grand Chamber formation, it adopted a different approach from that of the ECtHR. Drawing on the Reception Conditions Directive 2013/33,[351] and on the Opinion of the Advocate General,[352] the CJEU considered that the detention of these asylum seekers in these transit zones constituted detention, in the sense of a 'coercive measure that deprives the applicant of his or her freedom of movement and isolates him or her from the rest of the population, by requiring him or her to remain permanently within a restricted and closed perimeter'.[353] The CJEU quickly rejected the argument that asylum seekers could freely leave the transit zone, as, in fact, their entry into Serbia would have been illegal,[354] and leaving Hungary meant that they would lose the chance to obtain refugee status in

[345] V Davio, 'Detention in the Hungarian Transit Zones: A Case of Higher Fundamental Rights Protection by EU Law Vis-a-Vis the ECHR' (2022) 47(3) *European Law Review* 393.

[346] *Ilias and Ahmed v Hungary* App no 47287/15 ECLI:CE:ECHR:2017:0314JUD004728715 (ECtHR, 14 March 2017).

[347] *Ilias and Ahmed v Hungary* App no 47287/15 ECLI:CE:ECHR:2019:1121JUD004728715 (ECtHR, 21 November 2019), para 220.

[348] ibid, 224–25.

[349] ibid, 226–27.

[350] ibid, 234–48.

[351] Directive 2013/33/EU.

[352] Opinion of Advocate General Pikamäe in Joined Cases C-924/19 PPU and C-925/19 PPU, *FMS and Others v Országos Idegenrendészeti Főigazgatóság Dél-alföldi Regionális Igazgatóság and Országos Idegenrendészeti Főigazgatóság* ECLI:EU:C:2020:294 [2020].

[353] Joined Cases C-924/19 PPU and C-925/19 PPU *FMS and Others v Országos Idegenrendészeti Főigazgatóság Dél-alföldi Regionális Igazgatóság and Országos Idegenrendészeti Főigazgatóság* ECLI:EU:C:2020: 367 [2020], para 223.

[354] ibid, 229.

Hungary.[355] This practice had to be considered as detention within the meaning of Article 2(h) of the Reception Conditions Directive. However, the detention in question did not comply with the provisions of the Directive, because it opposes the placement of an international protection applicant in detention solely on the grounds that he or she is unable to provide for his or her own needs. Secondly, this detention takes place without the prior adoption of a reasoned decision ordering detention, and without an examination of the necessity and proportionality of such a measure. And, thirdly, there is no judicial control over the legality of the administrative decision ordering the detention of the applicant.[356]

The contrasting approaches of the ECtHR and the CJEU concerning the detention of asylum seekers in transit zones reveal the varying degrees of protection provided by EU law in comparison with the ECHR, in this particular case.

A third illustration of the added value provided by the EU's system of fundamental rights protection concerns legal entities of public law. A long-standing debate has revolved around whether such entities can claim the protection of rights and freedoms on an equal footing with natural persons or private-law entities.

The ECtHR has long held the position that 'governmental organisations', which are 'legal entities participating in the exercise of public power or managing a public service under the control of the authorities',[357] do not have *locus standi* to bring a claim before it. The ECtHR derives this conclusion from a literal and strict reading of Article 34 ECHR, which only refers to natural persons and non-governmental organisations as potential applicants. However, as demonstrated by Sébastien Van Drooghenbroek,[358] a teleological interpretation of this provision could have been preferred, which would have taken into account the rationale of the formulation of Article 34 ECHR. The aim of this principle is to 'prevent a Contracting Party from acting as both an applicant and a respondent before the Court'.[359] In other words, it seeks to prevent a component of a state from challenging its own state, thereby safeguarding the principle of unity of responsibility in international law.

However, this raises the question, why should a governmental organisational entity that is not subordinate to the respondent state – for instance, a third state – be barred from lodging a complaint with the ECtHR regarding violations of rights guaranteed to it under the ECHR? Despite this reasoning, the ECtHR has firmly rejected such a possibility, among others in a case in which

[355] ibid, 230.

[356] ibid, 266.

[357] *Democratic Republic of the Congo v Belgium* App no 16554/19 ECLI:CE:ECHR:2020:1006DEC001655419 (ECtHR, 6 October 2020). See, on this judgment, S Van Drooghenbroeck, 'Les droits de l'Homme de l'État: au-delà des évidences' (2021) 6 *Journal des Tribunaux* 113.

[358] Van Drooghenbroeck, 'Vérité à Luxembourg, erreur à Strasbourg' (n 343) 173–92.

[359] *Islamic Republic of Iran Shipping Lines v Turkey* App no 40998/98 ECLI:CE:ECHR:2007:1213JUD004099898 (ECtHR, 13 December 2007), para 81.

the Democratic Republic of the Congo sought to bring a case against Belgium for alleged violations of the ECHR.[360] The ECtHR also stated very explicitly in *Slovenia v Croatia* that,

> according to the very nature of the Convention, even in an inter-State case it is always the individual, and not the State, who is directly or indirectly harmed and primarily 'injured' by a violation of one or several Convention rights … In other words, only individuals, groups of individuals and legal entities which qualify as 'non-governmental organisations' within the meaning of Article 34 can be bearers of rights under the Convention, but not a Contracting State or any legal entity, which has to be regarded as a governmental organisation.[361]

On the other hand, the CJEU adopts a completely different position. Indeed, it readily recognises that a legal entity of public law, like a governmental entity emanating from a non-EU state, may not only be recognised as a holder of fundamental rights but also claim the right to a legal remedy before the CJEU. In the *Bank of Industry and Mine* judgment, the CJEU unambiguously stated that,

> according to the case-law, neither in the Charter of Fundamental Rights of the European Union nor in European Union primary law are there any provisions which state that legal persons which are emanations of States are not entitled to the protection of fundamental rights.[362]

Therefore, the CJEU considered that it is necessary to accept that non-EU states may have standing to bring actions against EU acts – subject to the admissibility requirements of Article 263 TFEU – precisely because 'the very existence of effective judicial review designed to ensure compliance with provisions of EU law is inherent in the existence of the rule of law'.[363] According to the CJEU's Grand Chamber formation in *Venezuela v Council*,

> an interpretation of the fourth paragraph of Article 263 TFEU in the light of the principles of effective judicial review and the rule of law militates in favour of finding that a third State should have standing to bring proceedings, as a 'legal person', within the meaning of the fourth paragraph of Article 263 TFEU, where the other conditions laid down in that provision are satisfied. Such a legal person governed by public international law is equally likely as any another [*sic*] person or entity to have its rights or

[360] *Democratic Republic of the Congo v Belgium* App no 16554/19 ECLI:CE:ECHR:2020:1006DEC001655419 (ECtHR, 6 October 2020).

[361] *Slovenia v Croatia* App no 54155/16 ECLI:CE:ECHR:2020:1118DEC005415516 (ECtHR, 18 November 2020), para 66. See, on this judgment, E Stoppioni and O Baillet, 'Op-Ed: "Expanding on the Privatisation of the Inter-State Application: The ECtHR's Decision in the Slovenia v Croatia Case"' (*EU Law Live*, 22 December 2022), available at www.eulawlive.com, https://eulawlive.com/op-ed-expanding-on-the-privatisation-of-the-inter-state-application-the-ecthrs-decision-in-the-slovenia-v-croatia-case-by-edoardo-stoppioni-and-olivier-baillet.

[362] Case T-10/13 *Bank of Industry and Mine v Council of the European Union* ECLI:EU:T:2015:235 [2015], para 53.

[363] Case C-872/19 P *République bolivarienne du Venezuela v Council of the European Union* ECLI:EU:C:2021:507 [2021], para 48.

> interests adversely affected by an act of the European Union and must therefore be able, in compliance with those conditions, to seek the annulment of that act.[364]

These three examples illustrate how the protection of fundamental rights within the EU legal order – as developed by the CJEU – has evolved to operate independently from the framework provided by the ECHR, and as elaborated by the ECtHR. More generally, an examination of the CJEU's case law highlights a significant specialisation in the area of fundamental rights, evidenced by the establishment of a comprehensive and coherent body of jurisprudence at the EU level. Based on a series of interviews conducted by Jasper Krommendijk with members and employees of the CJEU, there appears to be a preference for resolving cases, wherever possible, on the basis of the CJEU's own jurisprudence and secondary EU legislation.[365]

However, as discussed, this 'autonomisation' does not always lead to enhanced protection. In some cases, the CJEU's interpretation has been regressive, raising serious concerns.[366] It is hoped that the EU's accession to the ECHR, as mandated by Article 6(2) TEU, will help put an end to such problematic dynamics. That said, there are also instances where this autonomy yields a positive impact on the protection of rights. In such cases, it is crucial that beneficiaries are able to fully leverage these improvements to ensure that their fundamental rights are upheld. This balance between independence and consistency highlights the importance of continuing to refine the relationship between the EU legal order and the broader European and international human rights framework.

VI.3. A Constitutional Balance under Tension

The EU is not an international human rights organisation. Its capacity to act as a protector of fundamental rights exists – I have just demonstrated its 'norm-setter capacity' – but it is limited. Its action complements that of the Member States and forms part of the broader European human rights landscape, in which the ECHR remains a cornerstone.

On paper, this appears straightforward. In practice, however, matters are considerably more complex when it comes to delineating the limits of this protection and understanding how the different layers of rights protection co-exist, particularly at the national and EU levels. The introduction of a new actor into an already regulated domain inevitably gives rise to questions concerning the interaction and co-ordination of the various layers of protection. Two general questions must be raised in relation to the ambit of EU Fundamental Rights Law: first,

[364] ibid, para 50.

[365] J Krommendijk, 'The Use of ECtHR Case Law by the Court of Justice after Lisbon: The View of Luxembourg Insiders' (2015) 22 *Maastricht Journal of European and Comparative Law* 829.

[366] On these two facets, see B De Witte, 'The Relative Autonomy of the European Union's Fundamental Rights' (2019) 88(1) *Nordic Journal of International Law* 65–85.

whether a given situation falls within the scope of EU law (scope of application); and second, if so, to what extent the leeway afforded to the Member States allows them, on the basis of their national law, to go beyond the standards of EU law within that scope (level of protection).

In this regard, a clear distinction must be drawn between two scenarios: on the one hand, situations in which EU Fundamental Rights Law may apply – through the prism of the EU Charter – even in the absence of EU legislation harmonising the matter at issue (VI.3.a); and, on the other hand, those in which such harmonising legislation does exist (VI.3.b). In each case, it is first necessary to address the difficulties arising from the determination of the EU Charter's scope of application. Thereafter, attention will be given to the extent of the discretion that remains in the hands of the Member States to apply higher national standards of protection when the situation at stake falls within the scope of EU fundamental rights law.

VI.3.a. The Ambit of EU Fundamental Rights Law in the Absence of EU Harmonisation

VI.3.a (i) The Scope of Application

Article 51 of the EU Charter provides that Member States are bound to respect its provisions 'when they are implementing Union law'. The most straightforward example of such implementation occurs when Member States give effect to a measure of EU law, such as a Directive or a Regulation adopted by the EU legislature. However, for a situation to fall within the scope of the EU Charter, it is not always necessary that it be expressly harmonised or regulated by secondary EU legislation. There are, indeed, cases in which, even in the absence of such harmonisation, the circumstances at issue nonetheless display a sufficiently close connection with EU law to trigger the applicability of the EU Charter.

Yet, a genuine difficulty persists in determining the precise boundaries of this scope, as defined in Article 51. While certain situations clearly fall within the EU Charter's remit, many others occupy an indeterminate 'grey zone' where the assessment of whether EU Fundamental Rights are engaged becomes complex, and at times, arguably, arbitrary.

Without entering into the full depth of a debate that has already generated extensive academic commentary and judicial disputes, it is nonetheless worth recalling some examples of these 'grey zone' cases. As just emphasised, the EU Charter applies to Member States when they 'implement' EU law. Yet, in its landmark *Åkerberg Fransson* judgment, the CJEU held that this notion must be read in light of its earlier jurisprudence on the general principles of EU law, and in particular the concept of situations 'falling within the scope of EU law'.[367] The

[367] Case C-617/10, *Åkerberg Fransson* ECLI:EU:C:2013:105, para 21.

first source of uncertainty thus lies in this lexical duality, which blurs the dividing line between the application of national law and that of EU Fundamental Rights Law.

The CJEU nevertheless attempted to address this by developing a set of criteria that should, supposedly, clarify what is encompassed by this scope of application. In its *Hernandez* judgment, it notably emphasised that,

> in order to determine whether a national measure involves the implementation of EU law for the purposes of Article 51(1) of the Charter, it is necessary to determine, inter alia, whether that national legislation is intended to implement a provision of EU law; the nature of the legislation at issue and whether it pursues objectives other than those covered by EU law, even if it is capable of indirectly affecting EU law; and also whether there are specific rules of EU law on the matter or rules which are capable of affecting it.[368]

These criteria, although very useful, nevertheless do not lift the veil on all uncertainties.

A recent case, *PT*, is particularly interesting for grasping the complexity of the scope of application of EU law. This case concerned a plea-bargaining mechanism providing for the possibility to impose a more lenient penalty on an accused who pleads guilty, in the context of the prosecution of offences for which minimum penalties are determined by EU law. The CJEU considered that, although such minimum penalties are indeed imposed by EU law on Member States, which must transpose them into substantive criminal law, the fact that Bulgarian procedural law provided for such a mechanism of sentence reduction did not constitute an implementation of EU law. Accordingly, the CJEU held that

> the relationship between the provisions of substantive criminal law of the European Union … and the provisions of Bulgarian criminal procedural law governing the agreement for settlement of the case at issue in the main proceedings does not go above and beyond the fact of the former provisions being closely related to, or having an indirect impact on, the latter provisions. In those circumstances, a degree of connection … cannot be established between them.[369]

The CJEU, therefore, considered that the EU Charter did not apply to the implementation of this mechanism, even though it was invoked in the prosecution of offences for which the minimum penalty is defined by EU law.

Interestingly, and in a way that arguably further blurs the lines, the CJEU nevertheless considered that this case fell within the scope of Article 19(1) TEU, which requires that 'Member States are to provide remedies sufficient to ensure effective legal protection for individual parties in the fields covered by EU law'.[370] As a reminder, this provision implies that Member States must, in particular, respect the requirement of judicial independence. As the CJEU explained,

[368] Case C-198/13 *Julian Hernandez e.a.* ECLI:EU:C:2014:2055 [2014], para 37.
[369] C-432/22 *PT (and the perpetrator of an offence)* ECLI:EU:C:2024:987 [2024], para 42.
[370] ibid, para 44.

> the principle of effective judicial protection referred to in the second subparagraph of Article 19(1) TEU is a general principle of EU law which has been enshrined, inter alia, in the second paragraph of Article 47 of the Charter. The latter provision must, therefore, be duly taken into consideration for the purpose of interpreting the second subparagraph of Article 19(1).[371]

The CJEU further added that

> [f]urthermore, in accordance with the first sentence of Article 52(3) of the Charter, the rights contained therein have the same meaning and scope as the corresponding rights guaranteed by the ECHR. In accordance with the second sentence of that provision, this does not preclude EU law from providing more extensive protection. According to the Explanations relating to the Charter, the second paragraph of Article 47 of the Charter corresponds to Article 6(1) ECHR. The Court must, accordingly, ensure that its interpretation in the present case ensures a level of protection which does not disregard that guaranteed by Article 6(1) ECHR, as interpreted by the European Court of Human Rights.[372]

In other words, Article 47 of the EU Charter, excluded by a restrictive reading of Article 51 on the scope of application, comes back in through the window thanks to Article 19(1) TEU, which mirrors this provision. A connection is also made with the ECHR, which serves as a minimum floor of protection. This multi-layered framework, stemming in particular from the EU's limited competences in the field of human rights, can hardly fail to generate confusion.[373]

VI.3.a (ii) The Level of Protection

As previously indicated, once the (difficult) question of the EU Charter's scope of application has been settled, a second and equally significant inquiry arises: the extent of the margin of discretion left to the Member States within that scope. In other words, once a situation is deemed to fall under the EU Charter, the minimum standard of protection prescribed therein – as authoritatively interpreted by the CJEU – must be respected. The normative issue that follows is whether Member States remain free to provide a higher level of protection under their own constitutional traditions. In this respect, a distinction must be drawn between two scenarios: first, where the provision of a higher national standard of protection does not conflict with a requirement of EU law; and second, where such a conflict may arise.

From the perspective of international human rights law, this may appear counter-intuitive. Under Article 53 ECHR, parties are, in all circumstances, permitted to provide a higher level of protection than that guaranteed by the ECHR.[374]

[371] ibid, para 51.

[372] ibid, para 52.

[373] E Spaventa, 'Should we "harmonize" fundamental rights in the EU? Some reflections about minimum standards and fundamental rights protection in the EU composite constitutional system' (2018) *Common Market Law Review* 997, 1001.

[374] The conclusion, however, must be reconsidered in the presence of conflicts of fundamental rights.

In contrast, within the EU framework, the logic is fundamentally different: the EU is not an international human rights organisation and must also pursue other legitimate objectives, which can legitimately justify the establishment of a ceiling on the protection of human rights.

There is, indeed, an Article 53 in the EU Charter of Fundamental Rights, commonly referred to as the 'level of protection' clause, which, not coincidentally, may be seen as a counterpart to Article 53 ECHR. It stipulates that

> [n]othing in this Charter shall be interpreted as restricting or adversely affecting human rights and fundamental freedoms as recognised, in their respective fields of application, by Union law and international law and by international agreements to which the Union or all the Member States are party, including the European Convention for the Protection of Human Rights and Fundamental Freedoms, and by the Member States' constitutions.

Its scope, however, has been significantly curtailed by the CJEU, in order to safeguard the effectiveness of EU law. In *Melloni*, the CJEU held that, within the scope of EU law, national authorities and courts may indeed apply their own standards of fundamental rights protection, but only insofar as such standards do not compromise the level of protection guaranteed by the EU Charter, nor undermine the primacy, unity, and effectiveness of EU law.[375] The principle of primacy thus retains its decisive force, underscoring the pivotal role of the EU legislature in determining the extent of leeway accorded to national authorities.

In situations falling within the scope of the EU Charter without being governed by a harmonising measure of EU law, the CJEU has occasionally resorted to the notion of a national margin of appreciation in order to afford Member States a degree of leeway. In addressing this issue, the CJEU assumes a central role in calibrating the delicate balance between the uniform protection of fundamental rights at EU level and the preservation of national autonomy. To that end, it employs contextual criteria reminiscent of the ECtHR's doctrine of the 'margin of appreciation'. In *BPC Lux 2 and Others*, for instance, the CJEU emphasised that Member States enjoy a broad discretion in the field of economic policy, on the understanding that national authorities are institutionally better placed to determine the measures necessary to attain the objectives pursued.[376] Within this framework, a wide margin is thus left to Member States in defining the level of protection applicable, provided that the minimum threshold established by the EU Charter is duly respected.

Matters become considerably more intricate, however, where the exercise of such discretion by a Member State risks generating a conflict with a competing objective of the EU. In a situation falling within the scope of the EU Charter, but in the absence of specific harmonising legislation, the application of a higher national standard of fundamental rights protection may come into direct tension

[375] C-399/11 *Melloni* ECLI:EU:C:2013:107 [2013], para 60.
[376] Case C-83/20 *BPC Lux 2 and Others* ECLI:EU:C:2022:346 [2022], para 56.

with an EU objective. It is precisely in such circumstances that the constitutional tension inherent in the elusive 'balance' between the EU and its Member States becomes most apparent. The '*Taricco* saga' provides a vivid illustration of this dynamic.

In *Taricco I*, the CJEU held that Italian rules on limitation periods for serious VAT fraud offences undermined the effectiveness of EU law under Article 325 TFEU, and thus had to be disapplied by national courts.[377] The conflict thus arose from a national rule on limitation periods in criminal matters – a field not harmonised by EU law, yet clearly falling within its scope insofar as it concerned the collection of VAT, which forms part of the EU's own resources. This national rule, designed to regulate the temporal limits of criminal liability, came into tension with the EU's interest in ensuring the effective protection of its financial interests, which requires the efficient and dissuasive prosecution of VAT-related fraud. As it afforded a higher level of protection than that guaranteed by the EU Charter – specifically under Article 49 – the CJEU required that this higher national standard be set aside.

The Italian Constitutional Court reacted forcefully, asserting that these limitation rules were not mere procedural mechanisms but, rather, substantive guarantees safeguarding the fundamental right to the legality of criminal penalties *(nullum crimen, nulla poena sine lege)*, a core principle of the Italian constitutional order. It therefore referred the matter back to the CJEU, notably raising the risks of incompatibility with the principle of legality as protected by the Italian constitutional order. In *M.A.S. and M.B. (Taricco II)*, the CJEU adopted a more conciliatory approach, recognising that EU law does not oblige national courts to disapply domestic provisions where doing so would violate the fundamental principles of legality and foreseeability in criminal matters.[378] This evolution has been widely analysed in the literature as a paradigm of constitutional pluralism, illustrating how tolerance and judicial dialogue can reconcile the primacy of EU law with the safeguarding of national constitutional traditions.[379]

The reasoning developed in *Lin*[380] builds upon and refines the *Taricco* line of cases. In *Lin*, concerning Romanian rules on the interruption of limitation periods in serious VAT frauds, the CJEU reaffirmed the binding nature of Article 325 TFEU, yet nuanced its approach to national constitutional limits. The CJEU accepted that Member States may apply higher domestic standards of fundamental rights protection, particularly in criminal matters, provided that such standards do not jeopardise the effectiveness, unity, and primacy of EU law. However, it simultaneously insisted that national courts cannot invoke constitutional principles so

[377] Case 105/14 *Taricco e.a.* ECLI:EU:C:2015:555 [2015].

[378] Case 42/17 *M.A.S. and M.B.* ECLI:EU:C:2017:936 [2017].

[379] See, among others, C Rauchegger, 'National constitutional rights and the primacy of EU law: *M.A.S*' (2018) 55 *Common Market Law Review* 1521–48; and M Bonelli, 'The Taricco saga and the consolidation of judicial dialogue in the European Union' (2018) 25(3) *Maastricht Journal of European and Comparative Law* 357–73.

[380] C-107/23 PPU *Lin* ECLI:EU:C:2023:606 [2023].

as to create systemic impunity for offences affecting the EU's financial interests. Although the case concerned a higher national standard in an area not harmonised by EU law, the CJEU nonetheless found that it could not prevail over EU requirements. This outcome underscores the enduring uncertainty surrounding the precise conditions under which national standards may be maintained within the EU constitutional framework. The CJEU's formula – that such standards must not undermine the primacy, unity, or effectiveness of EU law – is by now well established, but its concrete implementation remains uneven and, at times, unpredictable.[381]

In conclusion, when a situation falls within the scope of EU law in the absence of full harmonisation, Member States may apply a higher standard of fundamental rights protection than that guaranteed by the EU Charter. However, where the application of such a standard risks undermining the pursuit of other objectives of EU law, a balancing exercise must be undertaken to ensure that the effectiveness of EU law is not jeopardised. Yet, as the recent jurisprudence reveals, determining the precise contours of this balance remains far from straightforward and continues to pose significant interpretative challenges.

VI.3.b. The Ambit of EU Fundamental Rights Law where there is EU Harmonisation

Where there is EU legislation harmonising fundamental rights, similarly complex questions arise regarding the constitutional balance between the EU and its Member States regarding the scope of application (i) and the margin of discretion left to Member States to apply, where possible, higher national standards of protection (ii).

VI.3.b (i) The Scope of Application

As regards the scope of application, it is clear that, when a Member State implements EU legislation, it is thereby implementing EU law and, consequently, its action falls within the scope of the EU Charter. In such cases, the Member State is required to comply with the EU Charter's provisions. However, the limits of this assertion can prove difficult to define, depending on the ambit of the applied EU legislation. For example, should a national measure that transposes an EU Directive providing only for minimum harmonisation be regarded as falling within the scope of EU law and the EU Charter when it goes beyond those minimum requirements?

In such a scenario, while an obligation arising from EU law undoubtedly exists, it remains limited in scope, and the Member State, in implementing that Directive,

[381] M Bonelli, 'Growing pains: Direct effect, primacy and fundamental rights after *Lin*' (2024) 61(4) *Common Market Law Review* 1045–76.

voluntarily decides to extend protection further than what is strictly required by EU law. The answer to this question was not self-evident, but it was clarified in the *TSN* judgment, where the CJEU held that protection offered under national law that exceeds the minimum required by an EU Directive 'falls within the exercise of the powers retained by the Member States, without being governed by that directive or falling within its scope'.[382] Consequently, in such cases, Member States are not bound by the EU Charter when acting beyond the limits of EU harmonisation.

VI.3.b (ii) The Level of Protection

The second question, as previously indicated, concerns the margin of manoeuvre afforded to Member States when acting within the scope of the EU Charter in the context of EU harmonisation. It is crucial to distinguish between different scenarios depending on the degree of discretion granted to the Member States by the EU legislature, which may vary according to the density or comprehensiveness of the relevant legislative act. Unlike situations in which no harmonising measure exists, in this context the EU legislature itself plays a decisive role in defining the extent of the discretion left to national authorities.

Where the EU legislature has pursued full and precise harmonisation, setting out detailed and binding requirements, the margin of discretion available to Member States is narrowly circumscribed. This follows directly from the principles of primacy and effectiveness, which require uniform compliance with the common rule. In such circumstances, Member States may be precluded from relying on their own higher standards of protection to go beyond the minimum threshold imposed by EU law.

Nevertheless, there remain instances in which the legislature deliberately preserves a margin of discretion for *national authorities*, thereby allowing for a degree of national autonomy within the broader framework of EU law. This margin of discretion can, at times, enhance the level of protection of fundamental rights, but it may also justify more extensive limitations on those rights.

The CJEU has, for instance, construed the EU Regulation mandating the stunning of animals prior to slaughter[383] in this light. While this Regulation pursues the legitimate objective of protecting animal welfare,[384] it may nonetheless come into direct tension with the practice of ritual slaughter, which some individuals invoke as an exercise of their freedom of religion.[385]

Accordingly, the Regulation provides an exception to the stunning requirement, stipulating that, in 'the case of animals subject to particular methods of

[382] Case C-609/17 *TSN* ECLI:EU:C:2019:981 [2019], para 52. On this judgment, see V Davio, 'Aux frontières de la Charte des droits fondamentaux: l'arrêt TSN et AKT et l'harmonisation minimale en droit européen' in Picod and Blumann, *Annuaire de droit de l'Union européenne* (n 343) 245–58.

[383] Council Regulation (EC) No 1099/2009 of 24 September 2009 on the protection of animals at the time of killing (OJ 2009 L 303, p 1).

[384] TFEU, art 13.

[385] Charter of Fundamental Rights of the European Union, art 10.

slaughter prescribed by religious rites, the requirements of paragraph 1 shall not apply provided that the slaughter takes place in a slaughterhouse'.[386]

However, given the absence of consensus among Member States as to the appropriate balance between freedom of religion and animal welfare, Article 26 stipulates that the Regulation 'shall not prevent Member States from maintaining any national rules aimed at ensuring more extensive protection of animals at the time of killing in force at the time of entry into force of this Regulation'.

In the case of *Centraal Israëlitisch Consistorie van België*, the issue concerned the compatibility of the Flemish decree in Belgium which prohibits all slaughter, including ritual slaughter, without prior (reversible) stunning, with Article 10 of the EU Charter, which protects freedom of religion. In other words, the question was whether a Member State could rely on the possibility of providing a higher level of protection for animal welfare to exclude the exemption from the prior stunning requirement granted by the Regulation for ritual slaughter. Relying on the absence of European consensus and the jurisprudence of the ECtHR, the CJEU considered that, in this context, Member States should be afforded a wide margin of discretion. According to the CJEU, 'it is precisely the lack of consensus among Member States as to how they perceive ritual slaughter which led to the adoption of Articles 4 and 26 of that Regulation'.[387] Therefore, the state should, in this context, be afforded, 'within the scope of Article 9 of the ECHR, a wide margin of appreciation in deciding whether, and to what extent, a limitation of the right to manifest religion or beliefs is necessary'.[388] This approach exemplifies the CJEU's careful balancing of competing fundamental rights in the context of divergent national practices.

Another example of the margin of discretion granted by the EU legislature in the field of fundamental rights protection is elaborated by Martijn van den Brink in his study of legislative authority and interpretation.[389] Under German and Austrian constitutional law, religious employers, such as churches, hospitals, or kindergartens, benefit from far-reaching exemptions from the prohibition of discrimination, granting them significant leeway to treat non-believers differently in employment matters.[390] By contrast, as underlined by van den Brink, such an approach would be inconceivable in Sweden or the Netherlands, where the carve-outs from the ban on discrimination for religious institutions are framed much more narrowly. These constitutional divergences created serious challenges for the

[386] Regulation (EC) No 1099/2009, art 4(4).

[387] Case C-336/19 *Centraal Israëlitisch Consistorie van België* ECLI:EU:C:2020:1031 [2020], para 68.

[388] ibid, para 67.

[389] M van den Brink, *Legislative Authority and Interpretation in the European Union* (Oxford University Press, 2024) 105.

[390] Martijn van den Brink (ibid) relies upon the reports of the European Equality Law Network, 'Germany – Country Report on Non-discrimination 2020' (2020) 56–62, https://www.equalitylaw.eu/downloads/5226-germany-country-report-non-discrimination-2020-1-96-mb; and 'Austria – Country Report on Non-discrimination 2020' (2020) 43–44, https://www.equalitylaw.eu/downloads/5264-austria-country-report-non-discrimination-2020-1-37-mb.

EU legislature, which, when seeking to adopt anti-discrimination legislation, was confronted with the near-impossible task of reconciling such conflicting conceptions of equality.[391] As a compromise, the Directive includes a provision that grants Member States some room for manoeuvre, though its clarity remains lacking.[392] Article 4(2) of the Directive states the following:

> Member States may maintain national legislation in force at the date of adoption of this Directive or provide for future legislation incorporating national practices existing at the date of adoption of this Directive pursuant to which, in the case of occupational activities within churches and other public or private organisations the ethos of which is based on religion or belief, a difference of treatment based on a person's religion or belief shall not constitute discrimination where, by reason of the nature of these activities or of the context in which they are carried out, a person's religion or belief constitute a genuine, legitimate and justified occupational requirement, having regard to the organisation's ethos. This difference of treatment shall be implemented taking account of Member States' constitutional provisions and principles, as well as the general principles of Community law, and should not justify discrimination on another ground.
>
> Provided that its provisions are otherwise complied with, this Directive shall thus not prejudice the right of churches and other public or private organisations, the ethos of which is based on religion or belief, acting in conformity with national constitutions and laws, to require individuals working for them to act in good faith and with loyalty to the organisation's ethos.

Another feature of Directive 2000/78 that exemplifies the legislature's difficulty in achieving consensus among the Member States lies in its explicit reliance on a minimum harmonisation approach. Article 8, indeed, specifies that 'Member States may introduce or maintain provisions which are more favourable to the protection of the principle of equal treatment than those laid down in this Directive.'[393]

In its judgment in *Associazione Avvocatura per i diritti LGBTI*, the CJEU, relying on this provision, held for instance that the Directive does not preclude Italian law from being less stringent in recognising the right of a legal person to bring proceedings in respect of a violation of the Directive than what the Directive itself requires.[394] Indeed, Article 8 expressly allows Member States to adopt or maintain provisions that are more favourable to the protection of the principle of equal treatment than those laid down in the Directive. Accordingly, the Directive in no way prevents a Member State from granting, under its national legislation, the right for associations with a legitimate interest in ensuring compliance with the Directive to bring judicial or administrative proceedings aimed at securing its enforcement. Where a Member State opts for such a choice, it is for that state to determine under what conditions an association such as the

[391] van den Brink, *Legislative Authority and Interpretation in the European Union* (n 389) 105.

[392] E Ellis and P Watson, *EU Anti-Discrimination Law*, 2nd edn (Oxford University Press, 2012) 394.

[393] On the confusion generated by the minimum harmonisation approach in this field, see Spaventa, 'Should we "harmonize" fundamental rights in the EU?' (n 372) 997–1024. Emphasis added.

[394] Case C-507/18 *Associazione Avvocatura per i diritti LGBTI* ECLI:EU:C:2020:289 [2020].

one at issue in the main proceedings may bring an action before a court, seeking a finding that discrimination prohibited by Directive 2000/78 has occurred, and that appropriate sanctions be applied.

It is evident that, in such contexts, the legislature has intentionally conferred a margin of discretion upon the Member States. This discretion, however, is not unlimited. A central difficulty, recurrent in the comparison of divergent standards of fundamental rights protection, concerns the identification of which standard may properly be regarded as the 'most favourable'.[395] Such a determination is rarely straightforward.

Moreover, the exercise is often compounded by an additional complication: the enhancement of protection for one fundamental right may, in practice, entail a corresponding restriction of another.

In this respect, the CJEU considered that, even where a Directive grants a margin of discretion, a Member State cannot invoke it to adopt measures that would infringe the EU Charter. In the case *Alemo-Herron*, for instance, the CJEU held that a Member State could not adopt rules deemed 'more favourable' to employees in the context of a transfer of undertaking, if such rules would violate Article 16 of the EU Charter, which safeguards the freedom to conduct a business.[396] Accordingly, although Article 8 of Directive 2001/23[397] allows Member States to strengthen the protection of employees, this must always be done in conformity with the EU Charter. This reasoning, while coherent with the EU Charter, appears nonetheless to sit uneasily with the CJEU's findings in *TSN*[398] that were analysed above. As a reminder, in that judgment, the CJEU considered that, where Member States go beyond the minimum harmonisation established by the legislature, the enhanced level of protection falls outside the scope of the EU Charter.

In the context of Directive 2000/78, a central issue concerned the extent to which a Member State might impose requirements more stringent than those established by the CJEU, under which private undertakings could justify prohibitions on the wearing of religious symbols in the workplace. Enhancing the level of protection of freedom of religion in this way could, however, potentially restrict the scope of the freedom to conduct a business, as enshrined in Article 16 of the EU Charter. While the CJEU initially appeared somewhat restrictive in *Achbita*,[399] similarly to *Alemo-Herron*,[400] it unequivocally confirmed in *WABE*

[395] See, for instance, Case-345/89 *Stoeckel* ECLI:EU:C:1991:324 [1991], about the prohibition of women's night work. R Xenidis, 'Minimum Requirements' in E Dubout, *Directive 2000/78 du 27 novembre 2000 portant création d'un cadre général en faveur de l'égalité de traitement en matière d'emploi et de travail: Commentaire article par article* (Larcier, 2020) 209, 233.

[396] Case C-426/11 *Alemo-Herron* ECLI:EU:C:2013:521 [2013], para 31.

[397] Council Directive 2001/23/EC of 12 March 2001 on the approximation of the laws of the Member States relating to the safeguarding of employees' rights in the event of transfers of undertakings, businesses or parts of undertakings or businesses, [2001] OJ L 82/16.

[398] Case C-609/17 *TSN* ECLI:EU:C:2019:981 [2019], para 52.

[399] Case C-157/15 *Samira Achbita and Centrum voor gelijkheid van kansen en voor racismebestrijding v G4S Secure Solutions NV* ECLI:EU:C:2017:203 [2017], para 38.

[400] Case C-426/11 *Alemo-Herron* [2013] ECLI:EU:C:2013:521, para 31.

that such a possibility falls within the discretion of the Member States. According to the CJEU,

> national provisions protecting freedom of thought, belief and religion, as a value to which modern democratic societies have attached great importance for many years, may be taken into account as provisions more favourable to the protection of the principle of equal treatment, within the meaning of Article 8(1) of Directive 2000/78, when examining what constitutes a difference of treatment based on religion or belief.[401]

The consequences of minimal harmonisation also raise questions regarding the scope of protection afforded under secondary EU law. If one considers, again, Directive 2000/78,[402] which prohibits discrimination in employment on various grounds, including disability, the issue arises as to how far the Directive's protections extend when national law provides a broader or more generous conception of the protected categories.[403] What should happen where the national definition of 'disability' is broader than that adopted by the CJEU? In such cases, it is unclear whether the protection afforded by the Directive extends to the wider category recognised under national law. Questions of this nature are by no means isolated; they underscore both the intricate nature of the EU law framework and the critical importance of preserving the possible diversity of national standards of protection. This is especially salient in the domain of fundamental rights, where national variations may reflect historical, social, or constitutional considerations that the EU must respect while maintaining the coherence and primacy of EU law.

These examples, without claiming to be exhaustive, underscore the intricate nature of EU Fundamental Rights Law, which must navigate the delicate balance between fostering unity – essential for the coherence of the EU legal order – and accommodating diversity, which lies at the heart of human rights protection. While fostering pluralism within EU Fundamental Rights Law is unquestionably desirable, it inevitably introduces a level of complexity that can hinder its overall intelligibility. This tension between coherence and flexibility illustrates one of the enduring challenges in the development and application of EU Fundamental Rights Law.

Finally, it is worth emphasising that the EU's harmonisation powers do not erase the deficiencies within its system for protecting fundamental rights. On the contrary, significant gaps and imperfections persist, even within these harmonisation measures. For example, the absence of legal pathways for asylum seekers to access the EU,[404] or the diminished protection of fundamental rights for individuals subjected to inter-state co-operation in criminal matters,[405] exemplify areas where

[401] Joined Cases C-804/18 and C-341/19 *IX v WABE eV and MH Müller Handels GmbH v MJ* ECLI:EU:C:2021:594 [2021], para 89.

[402] Council Directive 2000/78/EC of 27 November 2000 establishing a general framework for equal treatment in employment and occupation [2000] OJ L 303/16.

[403] Spaventa, 'Should we "harmonize" fundamental rights in the EU?' (n 373) 1016.

[404] Costello, *The Human Rights of Migrants and Refugees in European Law* (n 281) 1.

[405] See the contributions of V Mitsilegas, 'Mutual Recognition and Fundamental Rights in EU Criminal Law' and A Frąckowiak-Adamska, 'Procedural Rights (and Obligations) of Parties to Civil Proceedings', both published in González Pascual and Iglesias Sánchez, *Fundamental Rights in the EU Area of Freedom, Security and Justice* (n 220).

EU legislation fails to meet adequate standards. Although the EU has emerged as a prominent standard-setter in the field of fundamental rights, EU standards are not flawless. While EU legislation sometimes strengthens the protection of such rights, this is not always the case. The multiplication of protective layers does not inherently translate into substantive enhancement. Indeed, secondary legislation may, in certain instances, constrain the rights enshrined in the EU Charter, or the complex, multi-level framework may render these rights less comprehensible and less accessible. Furthermore, the process of harmonisation necessarily involves the establishment of uniform standards, which can occasionally undermine higher national protections or stifle their progressive development. Thus, while the EU has made significant advances in institutionalising the protection of fundamental rights, its system is still characterised by notable limitations and inherent tensions that warrant critical examination.

Figure 1.1 below outlines the various types of situations that may arise within a national legal order, along with the corresponding scope of application of EU fundamental rights law.

Figure 1.1 Overview of the scope of EU fundamental rights law

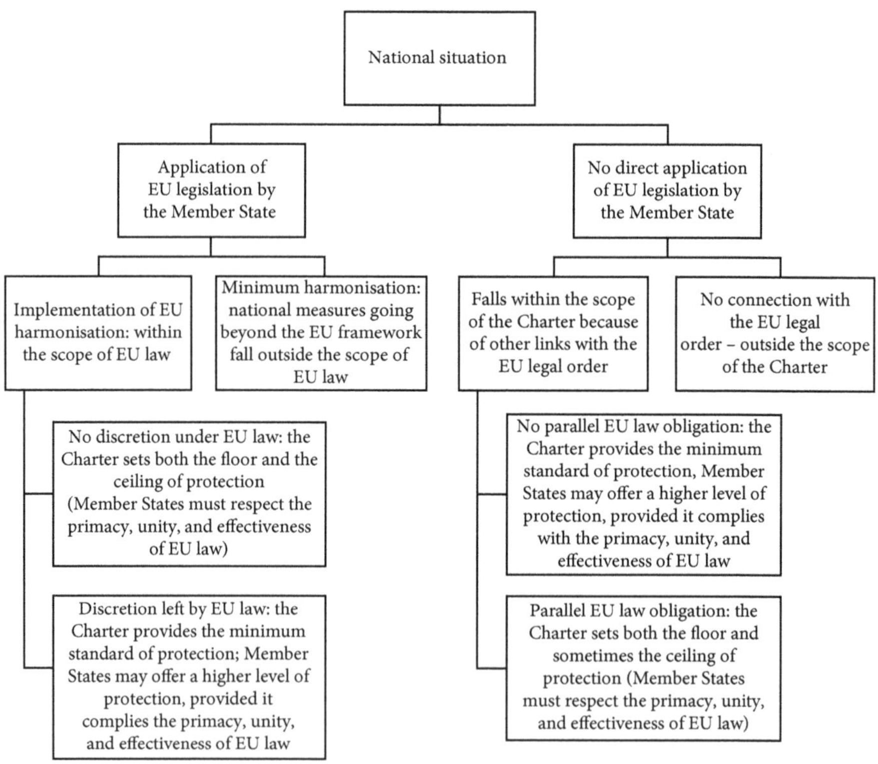

Conclusion

The evolution of the EU's role in the protection of fundamental rights reflects a remarkable and complex transformation. From an organisation initially lacking a general competence in this field, the EU has become a robust – albeit selective – protector of fundamental rights within Europe.

Although the EU does not fit neatly into the mould of an 'international human rights organisation', it has undeniably grown into a unique and influential 'international organisation protecting fundamental rights to a certain extent'. Despite the limitations and shortcomings that constrain its scope of action in this domain, the EU has emerged as an active and engaged actor, working within these boundaries and gradually exercising the competences entrusted to it. Its actions in the field of fundamental rights are by no means flawless, but they are nonetheless meaningful and increasingly impactful. This evolving role highlights the EU's potential to further enhance its contribution to the protection of fundamental rights, provided that it continues to address its weaknesses and refine its approach.

Initially, the EU positioned itself as a 'norm-*taker*', drawing on the common constitutional traditions of its Member States, and international human rights standards. Over time, however, it has evolved into a 'norm-*maker*' in certain areas, marking a significant departure from pre-existing standards. Despite the absence of a general human rights mandate, the Union has succeeded in constructing a sprawling and sophisticated web of protection, combining primary law, legislative developments, and judicial innovation. Through the creativity of the Court of Justice, general principles of EU law were transformed and consolidated into a genuine body of fundamental rights jurisprudence, paving the way for the enactment of the EU Charter. At the same time, the extensive reach of EU legislation in certain policy areas, such as non-discrimination, data protection, and the AFSJ, has given tangible effect to these rights across Member States.

This transformation is evident not only in the EU's growing assertiveness but also in its broader influence, which now extends to shaping the practices of other standard-setting bodies, including the ECtHR. The Strasbourg Court increasingly draws on EU law as a reference point for interpreting the ECHR, revealing the far-reaching impact of the EU's evolution into a proactive defender of individual rights.

The emergence of this new player does not come without difficulties, particularly in light of the constitutional balance with the Member States. The growing role of the EU in fundamental rights law naturally goes hand in hand with a stronger intrusion into national legal orders. The boundary between EU competences and those of the Member States, as well as the scope of EU Fundamental Rights Law, is, moreover, sometimes difficult to trace.

The EU's growing capacity to act in the field of fundamental rights is deeply rooted in the unique features of its legal architecture. The next chapter will explore how this EU Fundamental Rights framework sits within the structure of the distinctive characteristics of EU law, as well as the jurisdictional arsenal underpinning this framework.

2

The Power of EU Fundamental Rights Law

Community law ... not only imposes obligations on individuals but is also intended to confer upon them rights which become part of their legal heritage.[1]

Introduction

When the European Court of Justice handed down its landmark ruling in *Van Gend en Loos* back in 1964, it emphasised the distinctiveness of the Community, stating that it 'constitutes a new legal order of international law', and that it not 'only imposes obligations on individuals but is also intended to confer upon them rights which become part of their legal heritage'.[2] And the uniqueness of EU law has only been confirmed again and again over time. Without delving too deeply into the controversy on the nature of the EU,[3] it has become evident that, even though this legal order is based on international treaties concluded by the Member States, it has distinct attributes that distinguish it from traditional international law.

These distinctive features characterise *EU Fundamental Rights Law* too, giving it a singular authority and significance. Individuals who have fundamental rights protection under EU law may greatly benefit from these particularities. In the same way that it has developed separately from traditional international law generally, the EU legal framework has been developed separately from *traditional International Human Rights Law.*

The latter does not usually directly dictate how exactly it is supposed to be implemented in national legal systems.[4] On the contrary, for EU Fundamental Rights Law, explicit obligations are directly placed upon national authorities

[1] Case 26/62, *NV Algemene Transport- en Expeditie Onderneming van Gend & Loos v Netherlands Inland Revenue Administration* ECLI:EU:C:1963:1 [1963] ECR 1.

[2] ibid.

[3] See also the Introduction of this book.

[4] Little evolution can, nevertheless, be noticed in this context. The ECtHR, for instance, occasionally exhibits a greater degree of intrusion into the autonomy of contracting parties. Nonetheless, forthcoming evidence will show that this influence does not extend to the extent of the impact exerted by EU law on national legal systems.

within the EU legal framework, through legislative measures or the interpretative jurisprudence of the Court of Justice of the European Union (CJEU). This has a profound influence on the authority and robustness of EU law that provides fundamental rights protection. And the EU's specific characteristics are underpinned by the EU legal architecture's exceptionally well developed and highly organised system of judicial remedies. This remedy framework enables direct dialogue between national judges in the Member States and the CJEU, while also facilitating the European Commission's role as the Guardian of the Treaties. This, unsurprisingly, also further enhances the impact of EU Fundamental Rights Law.

Understanding the contribution of EU law to the protection of fundamental rights requires a much more in-depth appreciation of its distinct attributes, which is thus the objective of this chapter. Having examined the sources of fundamental rights protection within the EU's legal framework in the preceding chapter, the focus of the book now shifts to how authoritative those rights are. It will be observed that the distinctive features of EU law strengthen its overall efficacy and, by extension, the rules that govern fundamental rights (section I), and that the robustness of EU Fundamental Rights Law is also bolstered by the well-developed system of judicial remedies that ensures its effective enforcement (section II). The synergy of these two distinctive features enhances the EU's power to protect fundamental rights.

Nonetheless, as will be reiterated throughout this book, these characteristics are not confined solely to sources protecting fundamental rights: they also extend to other EU measures, which may pursue competing objectives. Consequently, they serve both as a shield for fundamental rights and, at times, as a sword against them. This dual role must not be overlooked where one wishes to grasp the full picture of the EU as a unique regional organisation that provides for the protection of human rights.

Section I – The Special Characteristics of EU Fundamental Rights Law

There has been well-established recognition, over time, of the special and specific characteristics inherent to EU law. EU law still has an international character, but the interpretations of it as provided by the CJEU have endowed it with unique strength. By emphasising the *'nature spécifique'*[5] of the EU's legal order, the fact that it emerges from a *'source autonome'*,[6] and the imperative to preserve its *'effet utile'*,[7] a set of casuistically established principles has indeed

[5] Case 6/64 *Flaminio Costa v ENEL* ECLI:EU:C:1964:66 [1964] ECR 585.

[6] ibid. The French term *'autonome'* was translated as 'independent' in English.

[7] Case 30/59 *De Gezamenlijke Steenkolenmijnen in Limburg v High Authority of the European Coal and Steel Community* ECLI:EU:C:1961:2 [1961] ECR Special Edition 1; and Case 106/77 *Amministrazione delle Finanze dello Stato v Simmenthal SpA* ECLI:EU:C:1978:49 [1978] ECR 629, para 20.

emerged, exhibiting a level of sophistication unparalleled in comparative public international law.[8] The CJEU stated very early on that, 'independently of the legislation of Member States', Community law 'not only imposes obligations on individuals but is also intended to confer upon them rights which become part of their legal heritage'.[9] As underlined by Elise Muir, 'the EU Treaties, and the law deriving therefrom, is integrated with the law of the Member States in a uniquely powerful way'.[10]

This section delves into the profound implications that the specific characteristics that attach to EU law have had, and which naturally extend to EU Fundamental Rights Law. It seeks to analyse what distinctive effects they have on individual rights protected by EU law, while also considering how that may deviate from traditional international human rights protection.

The objective of this chapter is, however, not to offer an exhaustive analysis of these specific characteristics in their entirety. Such an undertaking lies beyond the scope of this book and would be impractical given the constraints of space. Instead, the aim is to explore how these features contribute to the protection of fundamental rights within the framework of the EU. In light of this objective, I will first highlight the characteristics that distinguish the EU as a 'unique' international organisation (section I.1). I will then examine how the EU Fundamental Rights framework is grounded in the principle of primacy (section I.2) and the conferral of rights on individuals (section I.3). Finally, I will analyse the overarching commitment to effectiveness in EU fundamental rights law (section I.4).

I.1. The Special Characteristics of EU Law: A 'Unique' International Organisation

The legal order of the EU has long been recognised as possessing distinctive characteristics. The story is well known: the European Court of Justice ruled in its seminal *Van Gend en Loos* judgment far back in 1963 that a new legal order granting rights to individuals had emerged:

> [T]he Community constitutes a new legal order of international law for the benefit of which the states have limited their sovereign rights, albeit within limited fields, and the subjects of which comprise not only Member States but also their nationals. Independently of the legislation of Member States, Community law therefore not only imposes obligations on individuals but is also intended to confer upon them rights which become part of their legal heritage. These rights arise not only where they are expressly granted by the Treaty, but also by reason of obligations which the Treaty

[8] ME Mendez-Pinedo, 'The Principle of Effectiveness of EU Law: A Difficult Concept in Legal Scholarship' (2021) *Juridical Tribune* 5, 6.

[9] Case 26/62, *NV Algemene Transport- en Expeditie Onderneming van Gend & Loos v Netherlands Inland Revenue Administration* ECLI:EU:C:1963:1 [1963] ECR 1.

[10] E Muir, *An Introduction to the EU Legal Order* (Cambridge University Press, 2023) 50.

> imposes in a clearly defined way upon individuals as well as upon the Member States and upon the institutions of the Community.[11]

This judgment marked an acknowledgment of the subsequently developed doctrine of the direct effect of EU law, empowering individuals to invoke EU provisions directly before national courts.[12] This doctrine is now deeply entrenched in EU law, but represented a true legal revolution at the time, which had a crucial influence on the consequences of EU law in national legal orders.

One year later, in the *Costa v ENEL* case, the European Court of Justice enshrined the principle of primacy by stating that national law conflicting with Community law and the Treaties could not have precedence over Community law:

> The integration into the laws of each Member State of provisions which derive from the Community and more generally the terms and the spirit of the Treaty, make it impossible for the States, as a corollary, to accord precedence to a unilateral and subsequent measure over a legal system accepted by them on a basis of reciprocity. Such a measure cannot therefore be inconsistent with that legal system … The law stemming from the Treaty, an independent source of law, could not, because of its special and original nature, be overridden by domestic legal provisions, however framed, without being deprived of its character as Community law and without the legal basis of the Community itself being called into question.[13]

The primacy of EU law has now been firmly established, and it ensures that national authorities, particularly judicial authorities, must prioritise EU legal norms over their own conflicting domestic laws. In the renowned 1970 case *Internationale Handelsgesellschaft*, the European Court of Justice further expanded this precedent to the effect that conflicting national constitutional norms can also be overridden.[14]

The principles of primacy and direct effect are complemented by another cardinal principle of EU law: that of effectiveness, already mentioned above with regard to the EU's competing objectives.[15] The principle of effectiveness is rooted in the famous doctrine of '*effet utile*', which originates from public international law.[16] It was cited in Community law for the first time in 1963, in the *De gezamenlijke Steenkolenmijnen in Limburg* case. The European Court of Justice stated in that judgment that the jurisdiction of the Community could impinge on national sovereignty if it 'is necessary to prevent the *effectiveness*

[11] Case 26/62, *NV Algemene Transport- en Expeditie Onderneming van Gend & Loos v Netherlands Inland Revenue Administration* ECLI:EU:C:1963:1 [1963] ECR 1.

[12] On the place of the individual in the EU legal order, see J Rondu, *L'individu, sujet du droit de l'Union européenne* (Bruylant, 2020).

[13] Case 6/64 *Flaminio Costa v ENEL* ECLI:EU:C:1964:66 [1964] ECR 585.

[14] Case 11/70 *Internationale Handelsgesellschaft mbH v Einfuhr- und Vorratsstelle für Getreide und Futtermittel* ECLI:EU:C:1970:114 [1970].

[15] See ch 1, s V.2 of this book, 'The EU's Competing Objectives and the Specific Characteristics of EU Law'.

[16] Mendez-Pinedo, 'The Principle of Effectiveness of EU Law' (n 8) 7.

of the treaty from being considerably weakened and its purpose from being seriously compromised'.[17] The Court later developed the interpretation of this principle, often in combination with the above-mentioned principles of primacy and the doctrine of direct effect.[18]

These features – the principle of primacy, the doctrine of direct effect, and the principle of effectiveness (of Community and, later, EU law) – are now presented as specific characteristics of the EU legal order. But at the time – and also currently – none of them are or were entirely innovative doctrines under international law.[19] Indeed, any source of international law would naturally assert its primacy over national rules, and its *effet utile*, in order to ensure its viability. The same holds true with regard to direct effect: back in 1928, the International Court of Justice explicitly recognised that states could conclude treaties establishing 'rules creating individual rights and obligations' that were enforceable by domestic courts.[20]

What is particularly remarkable in the realm of EU law is not the existence of these characteristics per se, but the specific and far-reaching consequences that flow from them. These consequences are exceptionally robust, extending well beyond what is traditionally recognised in international law. Moreover, the distinctive nature of these characteristics arises from the synergy between the three of them, and also from the intricately elaborate system of judicial remedies available within the EU legal order, in particular the preliminary reference procedure.[21] This procedure, indeed, enables the Court of Justice of the European Union (CJEU) to offer a profound and nuanced interpretation of the consequences of these legal characteristics in national legal orders. The paragraphs that follow will elaborate on these particularities and show how they differentiate the EU system from traditional international human rights law.

I.1.a. The Principle of Primacy

With regard to the principle of primacy, in traditional public international law, states are typically given a discretion to determine the methods by which they will fulfil their international commitments. The focus is primarily on whether these obligations have been met or breached rather than on scrutinising how the

[17] Case 30/59 *De gezamenlijke Steenkolenmijnen in Limburg/Haute Autorité de la Communauté européenne du charbon et de l'acier* ECLI:EU:C:1961:2 [1961] (emphasis added).

[18] Mendez-Pinedo, 'The Principle of Effectiveness of EU Law' (n 8) 6.

[19] JHH Weiler, 'Van Gend En Loos: The Individual as Subject and Object and the Dilemma of European Legitimacy' in H Ruiz-Fabri, GF Sinclair, and A Rosen (eds), *Revisiting Van Gend en Loos* (Société de législation comparée, 2014) 16.

[20] ICJ, Advisory Opinion of 3 March 1928, *Jurisdiction of the Courts of Danzig* [1928] 17–18. See B de Witte, 'Direct Effect, Primacy, and the Nature of the Legal Order' in P Craig and G De Búrca, *The Evolution of EU Law*, 3rd edn (Oxford University Press, 2021) 226.

[21] Weiler, 'Van Gend En Loos' (n 19) 16.

consequences of international law are incorporated or recognised within domestic legal systems. As underlined by Anne Peters and Ulrich K. Preuss,

> from the standpoint of international law states are generally free as to the manner in which domestically, they put themselves in position to meet their international obligations; the choice between the direct reception and application of international law, or its transformation into national law by way of state, is a matter of indifference … These are matters for each state to determine for itself according to its own constitutional practice.[22]

By contrast, EU law has ventured further, with the CJEU progressively delineating, through its rulings interpreting Community and EU law, the tangible ramifications stemming from the principle of primacy. No matter what the national legal tradition is – whether EU law is given effect through a monist or dualist system – the effects of primacy must be immediately recognised by national authorities, 'without [it] being possible to make EU obligations conditional upon the adoption of measures authorising the emergence of, or reproducing, EU obligations in domestic legal orders'.[23] The principle of primacy is, moreover, 'unreserved and absolute', from the point of view of the CJEU at least,[24] as it applies, without any limitation, to all types of national rules, even if subsequently adopted.[25] From a practical standpoint, the CJEU has construed the principle of primacy in EU law as requiring all national judges to set aside any national provision that conflicts with a provision of EU law that has direct effect in the case pending before them.[26] Even more significantly, the CJEU has extended this power to all bodies of the Member States. This means that not only judicial authorities, but even national administrations, are required to disregard conflicting national laws in order to respect and enforce provisions of EU law with direct effect.[27]

This situation contributes to the unique character of EU law. Given that it is the CJEU itself that determines how EU law penetrates national legal systems (within the remit of the Treaties), Member States have no room for discretion in this matter, unless they intentionally contravene EU law. As acknowledged by Janneke Gerards and Joseph Fleuren, 'from a constitutional perspective, the implementation of EU law is of a very different nature than the implementation of ('ordinary') international law'.[28]

[22] A Peters and UK Preuss, 'International Relations and International Law' in MV Tushnet, T Fleiner, and C Saunders (eds), *Routledge Handbook of Constitutional Law* (Routledge, 2015) 36.

[23] Muir, *An Introduction to the EU Legal Order* (n 10) 51.

[24] On the reception of the principle of primacy in national legal orders, see, among others, A Bobić, *The Jurisprudence of Constitutional Conflict in the European Union* (Oxford University Press, 2022).

[25] M Bobek, 'The Effects of EU Law in the National Legal Systems' in C Barnard and S Peers (eds), *European Union Law*, 3rd edn (Oxford University Press, 2020) 177.

[26] See Case 106/77 *Amministrazione delle Finanze dello Stato v Simmenthal SpA* [1978], para 21; and C-573/17 *Popławski* ECLI:EU:C:1978:49 [2019] ECR 629, para 61.

[27] Case 103/88 *Fratelli Costanzo SpA v Comune di Milano* ECLI:EU:C:1989:256 [1989] ECR 1839, para 31; Bobek, 'The Effects of EU Law in the National Legal Systems' (n 25) 177.

[28] J Gerards and J Fleuren, 'Chapter 9: Comparative Analysis' in J Gerards and J Fleuren (eds), *Implementation of the European Convention on Human Rights and of the Judgments of the ECtHR in National Case Law: A Comparative Analysis* (Intersentia, 2014) 338.

I.1.b. Direct Effect

The doctrine of direct effect in EU law has also had a far greater influence at the national level, compared with traditional international law. In practice, direct effect enables individuals to invoke provisions of EU law before national courts, and, more broadly, before domestic authorities.[29] This holds true even if the EU law provision concerned does not enshrine, as such, a subjective right for the individual (although it does have to meet certain criteria before it can have direct effect). Provisions of EU law can serve both as a 'sword', empowering individuals to claim newly established rights, and as a 'shield', protecting them from the enforcement of national rules that conflict with them.[30] Direct effect is, thus, 'an obligation to apply' the relevant provision of EU law, 'either as a norm which governs the case or as a standard for legal review'.[31] As already emphasised, the concept of direct effect is not foreign to public international law. Nevertheless, it is undeniable that its influence is much more pronounced in EU law.

Firstly, numerous provisions have had such an effect attributed to them, both in vertical relations between the public bodies of Member States and individuals, and in horizontal relations between individuals and private parties.

Secondly, the growth and power of the doctrine of direct effect of EU law can also be attributed to the existence of the preliminary ruling procedure.[32] Indeed, as stated by Joseph HH Weiler, EU law that has direct effect as developed through the CJEU has the power of being uniform, authoritative, and binding:

> What makes direct effect so effective and seductive to national courts in the European system is the fact that the preliminary reference system eliminates both those impediments: the member state court does not have to grapple with hermeneutic uncertainty as to the correct interpretation of the treaty norm; it receives an authoritative interpretation from the European Court of Justice. And, what is more, that interpretation is de facto valid, erga omnes, i.e., binding equally on all. The member states' courts 'are not alone' when confronted with the higher norm of the international treaty.[33]

Moreover, even where it is found that an EU provision does not have direct effect, the obligation of 'consistent interpretation' still applies to it in EU law. This legal requirement applies to all national authorities, which must construe their national law in accordance with an EU law provision – even if it does not have direct effect – *to the fullest extent possible*.[34] Again, while this requirement is not a novel concept in the realm of traditional international law, it has also

[29] Case 103/88 *Fratelli Costanzo SpA v Comune di Milano* ECLI:EU:C:1989:256 [1989] ECR 1839, para 31.

[30] de Witte, 'Direct Effect, Primacy, and the Nature of the Legal Order' (n 20) 294.

[31] S Prechal, 'Direct Effect, Indirect Effect, Supremacy and the Evolving Constitution of the European Union' in C Barnard (ed), *The Fundamentals of EU Law Revisited* (Oxford University Press, 2007) 38.

[32] On this procedure, see s II.1 of this chapter, 'Individual Vigilance and National Judges as EU Fundamental Rights Guarantors'.

[33] Weiler, 'Van Gend En Loos' (n 19) 19.

[34] Case 14/83 *Sabine von Colson and Elisabeth Kamann v Land Nordrhein-Westfalen* ECLI:EU:C:1984:153 [1984] ECR 1891, para 26. Emphasis added.

gained both quantitative and qualitative significance in the context of EU law.[35] Indeed,

> the principle that national law must be interpreted in conformity with EU law requires national courts to do *whatever* lies within their jurisdiction, taking the whole body of domestic law into consideration and applying the interpretative methods recognised by it, with a view to ensuring that the framework decision in question is fully effective and to achieving an outcome consistent with the objective pursued by it.[36]

Although EU law cannot serve as the basis for a *contra legem* interpretation of national law,[37] the CJEU considers that jurisprudence should be adjusted accordingly:

> the obligation to interpret domestic law in conformity with EU law requires national courts to change established case-law, where necessary, if it is based on an interpretation of domestic law that is incompatible with the objectives of a framework decision.[38]

For example, a national court would, in principle, be bound by its supreme court's jurisprudence or ruling in a given case: but if the supreme court contradicts EU law requirements, that national court should bypass the usual domestic judicial hierarchy and ensure that EU law is given full effect. If necessary to do so, it must 'disapply, on its own authority, the interpretation adopted by the national Supreme Court, since that interpretation is not compatible with EU law'.[39] This duty thus has a very wide scope of application, as it concerns *all* national laws, *all* EU laws, and *all* national authorities.[40]

I.1.c. The Principle of Effectiveness

The principle of effectiveness has also been construed robustly in EU law, and it now plays a pivotal role in the functioning of the EU legal order. The functioning of this legal order indeed depends on indirect administration, and it quickly became evident that the implementation, enforcement, and compliance of/with EU law rely heavily on measures undertaken by the Member States.[41] Moreover, the law is the primary instrument for EU integration, and the success of this project was heavily dependent on the Member States all applying Community law

[35] Bobek, 'The Effects of EU Law in the National Legal Systems' (n 25) 169.
[36] C-579/15, *Popławski* ECLI:EU:C:2017:503 [2017], para 34 (emphasis added).
[37] ibid, para 33.
[38] ibid, para 35.
[39] C-554/14 *Ognyanov* ECLI:EU:C:2016:835 [2016], paras 69 and 70. See also C-792/22, *Energotehnica*, ECLI:EU:C:2024:788, para 66.
[40] Bobek, 'The Effects of EU Law in the National Legal Systems' (n 25) 169. For a comparison with the effect of the ECHR in national legal orders, see G Martinico, 'Is the European Convention Going to Be "Supreme"? A Comparative-Constitutional Overview of ECHR and EU Law before National Courts' (2012) 23 *European Journal of International Law* 401.
[41] M Accetto and S Zleptnig, 'The Principle of Effectiveness: Rethinking Its Role in Community Law' (2005) 11 *European Public Law* 375, 382.

equally.[42] Consequently, the CJEU elaborated upon the principle of effectiveness, to bolster the framework of the EU legal order. In the same way as for the EU's special characteristics (discussed above in sections I.1(a) and I.1(b)), the principle of effectiveness, even if its roots are in international law, has achieved a level of potential, advancement, and sophistication within EU law that is unprecedented in comparative constitutional law or public international law.[43]

While there is no unanimous definition of the principle of effectiveness, nor a comprehensive systematisation of it in the literature,[44] several judgments exemplify its consequences. The famous judgment *Factortame I* is one of them. By that ruling, the European Court of Justice established that the principle of effectiveness required national courts to grant interim relief in order to ensure the full effectiveness of EU law. If necessary, they had to suspend the application of the relevant national legislation, even if they were not granted the power to do so in their national legal order.[45]

On the basis of the principle of effectiveness, the European Court of Justice also developed the famous '*Rewe* test',[46] so that it could scrutinise the compatibility of national procedural rules with EU law. The CJEU has established two procedural principles for this. The first is the principle of equivalence, which stipulates that national procedural regulations governing actions to safeguard rights under Community law must not be less favourable than those governing analogous claims under national law. The second is the principle of effectiveness, which mandates that these regulations must not render the exercise of rights conferred by EU law practically impossible or excessively challenging. As stressed by Giulia Gentile, these principles do not have an equivalent in traditional international law, and the *Rewe* test 'creates a unique judicial tool which permits the [Court] to mould national procedural rules'.[47] A very strong dynamic has emerged enhancing the effectiveness of EU law, which has not occurred in other international legal orders.

The quest for effectiveness has also justified the adoption of *harmonised* procedural rules, aiming at supporting the effective application of substantive provisions. This has also been the case in the field of fundamental rights protection, as I will illustrate later on.

While I have presented the three principles individually for the sake of clarity, it is essential to realise that they work in combination, their synergy lending considerable strength to EU law. This triumvirate, in fact, acts as a potent ally in ensuring the efficacy of EU law within national legal frameworks.

[42] G Gentile, 'One, No One, One Hundred Thousand: The Multi-Faceted Effectiveness of EU Law' (2022) 34(3) *European Review of Public Law* 614, 617.

[43] Mendez-Pinedo, 'The Principle of Effectiveness of EU Law' (n 8) 6.

[44] Gentile, 'One, No One, One Hundred Thousand' (n 42) 624.

[45] Case C-213/89 *The Queen v Secretary of State for Transport, ex parte: Factortame Ltd and others* ECLI:EU:C:1990:257 [1990] ECR I-02433.

[46] Case 33/76 *Rewe-Zentralfinanz eG et Rewe-Zentral AG v Landwirtschaftskammer für das Saarland* ECLI:EU:C:1976:188 [1976] ECR 1989.

[47] Gentile, 'One, No One, One Hundred Thousand' (n 42) 634.

I.1.d. The Uniqueness of EU Law and its Specific Characteristics

As I have already underlined, the obligations deriving from these principles contrast with those generally recognised in international law, including international human rights law.

States are generally free to determine how they choose to implement the ECHR within their domestic legal systems.[48] According to the European Court of Human Rights (ECtHR), 'neither Article 13 nor the Convention in general lays down for the contracting States any given manner for ensuring within their internal law the effective implementation of any of the provisions on the Convention'.[49] Although the Council of Ministers recommended that the ECHR should become an 'integral part' of domestic legal systems, it also unequivocally emphasised that 'it is for member states to decide which system is most suited to ensuring the necessary protection of Convention rights, taking into consideration their constitutional traditions and particular circumstances'.[50] The contracting parties are required to 'secure' the rights and freedoms in the ECHR to individuals within their jurisdiction, but they are not required to directly incorporate the ECHR into their national law.[51]

As a consequence, the principle of direct effect does not apply to provisions of the ECHR.[52] States are granted discretion 'to fashion the remedy, subject to subsequent approval of the Committee of Ministers'.[53] And while the ECtHR also leverages the 'effectiveness' or '*effet utile*' of the ECHR,[54] enabling it to extend the ECHR's territorial reach,[55] acknowledge states' indirect liability,[56] or impose financial duties,[57] it has not gone to the extent of mandating national judges to

[48] M Beijer, *The Limits of Fundamental Rights Protection by the EU: The Scope for the Development of Positive Obligations* (Intersentia, 2017) 31.

[49] See *Swedish Engine Drivers' Union v Sweden* App no. 5614/72 ECLI:CE:ECHR:1976:0206JUD000561472 (ECHR, 6 February 1976), para 50.

[50] Recommendation Rec(2004)6 of the Committee of Ministers to Member States on the improvement of domestic remedies, adopted by the Committee of Ministers on 12 May 2004 (114th Session).

[51] D Harris, M O'Boyle, and C Warbrick, *Law of the European Convention on Human Rights*, 1st edn (Butterworths, 1995) 24.

[52] G Ulfstein, 'Transnational Constitutional Aspects of the European Court of Human Rights' (2021) 10 *Global Constitutionalism* 151, 157. My study does not aim to compare the effects reserved for the ECHR and EU law across all Member States. Such a comparison would go well beyond the scope of my study. Instead, I will focus on presenting the positions of the CJEU and the ECtHR.

[53] A Huneeus, 'Courts Resisting Courts: Lessons from the Inter-American Court's Struggle to Enforce Human Rights' (2011) 44 *Cornell International Law Journal* 494, 519. See *Kuric and others v Slovenia* App no 26828/06 ECLI:CE:ECHR:2012:0626JUD002682806 (ECHR, 26 June 2012), para 406; and *Scozzari and Giunta v Italy* App nos. 39221/98 and 41963/98, ECLI:CE:ECHR:2000:0713JUD003922198 (ECHR, 13 July 2000), para 249.

[54] J Gerards, *General Principles of the European Convention on Human Rights*, 2nd edn (Cambridge University Press, 2023) 5.

[55] *Soering v UK* App no 14038/88 ECLI:CE:ECHR:1989:0707JUD001403888 (ECHR, 7 July 1989).

[56] ibid.

[57] *Airey v Ireland* App no 6289/73 ECLI:CE:ECHR:1979:1009JUD00062897 (ECHR, 6 February 1981).

acknowledge the direct effect of the ECHR's provisions.[58] Instead, a state may satisfy its obligations by ensuring, in whatever manner it chooses, that its law and practice is such that an individual's ECHR rights are guaranteed.[59] The ECtHR has even stated that, although national judges have the option to set aside national laws conflicting with the ECHR, if they were instead to refer the matter to a state's constitutional court, that would not, in itself, violate Article 6.[60] The ECtHR points out that,

> this is all the more the case since neither the Convention in general nor Article 13 in particular prescribe to Contracting States a specific manner of ensuring, in their domestic law, the effective application of the provisions of this instrument.[61]

In exceptional cases, the ECtHR goes further, by offering guidance on the general or individual measures that states must adopt to implement specific judgments.[62] A notable example of this approach is the practice developed through pilot judgments, which first appeared in the jurisprudence of the ECtHR in 2004, in the case of *Broniowski v Poland*.[63] This practice has since been formalised in Article 61 of the ECtHR's Rules of Procedure, which states that the ECtHR can issue such judgments 'where the facts of an application reveal in the Contracting Party concerned the existence of a structural or systemic problem or other similar dysfunction which has given rise or may give rise to similar applications'.[64] The ECtHR thus chooses one case to discuss a wider problem present in the respondent state, to respond to repetitive cases. It is explicitly provided, in this context, that the ECtHR may specify in its judgment 'the type of remedial measures which the Contracting

[58] A single counter-example, to the author's knowledge, can be found in the case law, in *Giuseppe Mostacciuolo v Italy (No 2)* App no 65102/01 ECLI:CE:ECHR:2006:0329JUD006510201 (ECHR 29 March 2006), where it is stressed that 'the Court feels it important to stress that although the existence of a remedy is necessary, it is not in itself sufficient. The domestic courts must be able, *under domestic law, to apply European case-law directly*, and their knowledge of this case-law has to be facilitated by the State in question' (emphasis added), para 125. However, it immediately continued its reasoning by reiterating that, 'subject to monitoring by the Committee of Ministers, the respondent State remains free to choose the means by which it will discharge its legal obligation under Article 46 of the Convention, provided that such means are compatible with the conclusions set out in the Court's judgment' (para 126).

[59] ibid.

[60] *Dumitru Popescu v Romania (No 2)* App no 71525/01 ECLI:CE:ECHR:2007:0426JUD007152501 (ECHR, 26 April 2007), para 104 (own translation).

[61] ibid.

[62] Beijer, *The Limits of Fundamental Rights Protection by the EU* (n 48) 33. The ECtHR, for example, underlined in its judgment *Hovhannisyan and Shiroyan v Armenia* App no 5065/06 ECLI:CE:ECHR:2011:1115JUD000506506 (ECHR, 15 November 2011), para 10, that the 'Contracting States that are parties to a case are *in principle* free to choose the means whereby they will comply with a judgment in which the Court has found a breach. This discretion as to the manner of execution of a judgment reflects the freedom of choice attaching to the primary obligation of the Contracting States under the Convention to secure the rights and freedoms guaranteed' (emphasis added).

[63] *Broniowski v Poland* App no 31443/96 ECLI:CE:ECHR:2004:0622JUD003144396 (ECHR, 22 June 2004).

[64] On this proceeding, see K Dzehtsiarou, 'Pilot-Judgment Procedure at the European Court of Human Rights' in E Muir, S Garben and I Goveare (eds), *Activating Human and Fundamental Rights Before the European Courts* (Hart Publishing, 2026).

Party concerned is required to take at the domestic level by virtue of the operative provisions of the judgment'.

However, as underlined by Eline Kindt, 'the practice shows that the Court sometimes opts to not include general measures in the operative part of the judgment or does not even offer advice on general measures at all'.[65] Moreover, the fundamental principle in the ECHR's legal system still upholds the freedom of States Parties in determining the methods by which they fulfil their obligations, under the supervision of the Committee of Ministers.[66] Judgments specifying remedial measures are still only a small fraction of the ECtHR's case law.[67] Constitutional comparative law studies show, in that regard, that contracting states have opted to enact safeguards through varied methods, in accordance with their respective constitutional practices.[68] According to Giuseppe Martinico, while in certain states the disapplication of national norms that are contrary to the ECHR by national judges is allowed,[69] this is not a universal rule.[70] In fact, in some states, such practices are explicitly prohibited.

A detour into the realm of the American Convention on Human Rights (ACHR) is also instructive. The Inter-American Court of Human Rights (IACtHR) has developed a doctrine known as the 'conventionality control', which places stronger obligations on national American judges than the ones the ECHR places on national European judges. This doctrine, indeed, mandates national judges to control *ex officio* the compatibility of the national norms they apply with the ACHR.[71] In its judgment of 2006 in the case *Almonacid Arellano*, the IACtHR established that

> domestic judges and courts are bound to respect the rule of law, and therefore, they are bound to apply the provisions in force within the legal system. But when a State has ratified an international treaty such as the American Convention, its judges, as part of the State, are also bound by such Convention. *This forces them to see that all the effects of*

[65] E Kindt, 'Giving up on Individual Justice? The Effect of State Non-Execution of a Pilot Judgment on Victims' (2018) 36 *Netherlands Quarterly of Human Rights* 173, 176.

[66] M Fyrnys, 'Expanding Competences by Judicial Lawmaking: The Pilot Judgment Procedure of the European Court of Human Rights' (2011) 12 *German Law Journal* 1231, 1237.

[67] A Donald and A-K Speck, 'The European Court of Human Rights' Remedial Practice and Its Impact on the Execution of Judgments' (2019) 19 *Human Rights Law Review* 83, 87. On the different types of measures recommended by the ECtHR, see L-A Sicilianos, 'The Involvement of the European Court of Human Rights in the Implementation of Its Judgments: Recent Developments under Article 46 ECHR' (2014) 32 *Netherlands Quarterly of Human Rights* 235.

[68] B Rainey and others, *Jacobs, White and Ovey: The European Convention on Human Rights*, 7th edn (Oxford University Press, 2017) 84.

[69] See, among others, Belgian Court of Cassation *Le Ski* [1971] Pasicrisie 886.

[70] Martinico, 'Is the European Convention Going to Be "Supreme"?' (n 40) 417.

[71] For an in-depth analysis, see, among others, L Burgorgue-Larsen, 'Conventionality Control: Inter-American Court of Human Rights (IACtHR)' (2018) *Max Planck Encyclopedias of International Law*; J Contesse, 'The International Authority of the Inter-American Court of Human Rights: A Critique of the Conventionality Control Doctrine' (2018) 22 *The International Journal of Human Rights* 1168; S Garcia Ramirez, 'The Relationship between Inter-American Jurisdiction and States (National Systems): Some Pertinent Questions' (2015) 5(1) *Notre Dame Journal of International & Comparative Law* 116.

> *the provisions embodied in the Convention are not adversely affected by the enforcement of laws which are contrary to its purpose and that have not had any legal effects since their inception*. In other words, the Judiciary *must exercise a sort of 'conventionality control' between the domestic legal provisions which are applied to specific cases and the American Convention on Human Rights. To perform this task, the Judiciary has to take into account not only the treaty, but also the interpretation thereof made by the Inter-American Court, which is the ultimate interpreter of the American Convention*.[72]

This clearly goes a long way in terms of the responsibilities assigned to the national judiciary and reminds us of the jurisprudence of the CJEU regarding the effects that EU law must have in the legal systems of Member States. The IACtHR extended this duty to all public authorities in its *Gelman* judgment.[73]

However, a significant limitation was established no less than two months after the *Almonacid Arellano* judgment, in the *Dismissed Congressional Employees* case. In this case, the IACtHR explicitly established that the obligation of conventionality control only applies within the scope of the competencies recognised to the national judges and the higher rules that govern their jurisdiction. The judgment found that organs of the judiciary should indeed exercise this control, 'evidently in the context of their respective spheres of competence and the corresponding procedural regulations'.[74]

As underlined by Laurence Burgorgue-Larsen, this reference is 'essential' and should be understood as implying that, when exercising this control, each national authority should 'take into account the national legal system and circumstances (eg the international treaties' position in the hierarchy of norms, the existence of a constitutionality control that is more or less concentrated, etc)'.[75]

This kind of limitation does not come into play when analysing the effects that *EU* law should have in national legal systems. Article 4(2) of the TEU states that the EU must respect 'national identities, inherent in their fundamental structures, political and constitutional', from which principles of institutional and procedural autonomy are derived – but it has not prevented the CJEU from imposing the obligation on all national judges to set aside any norm conflicting with an EU law provision endowed with direct effect, even in states where ordinary judges originally lacked the authority to conduct legislative validity reviews.

Moreover, as stressed by Judge Sergio García Ramírez at the IACtHR, the Inter-American Convention system also differs from EU law due to the 'vague'[76] nature of the substantive obligations it imposes. Conversely, EU law is made up of more specific rules, particularly those that are designed to have a harmonising

[72] Inter-American Court on Human Rights, 26 September 2006, *Almonacid Arellano*, para 124 (emphasis added).

[73] Inter-American Court on Human Rights, 24 February 2011, *Gelman*, para 239.

[74] Inter-American Court on Human Rights, 24 November 2006, *Case of the Dismissed Congressional Employees (Aguado-Alfaro et al) v Peru*, para 128.

[75] Burgorgue-Larsen, 'Conventionality Control: Inter-American Court of Human Rights (IACtHR)' (n 71).

[76] Contesse, 'The International Authority of the Inter-American Court of Human Rights' (n 71) 1176.

effect. And, furthermore, EU provisions – including those of the EU Charter of Fundamental Rights – can be the subject of preliminary rulings to clarify their content. The judgments issued by the IACtHR do not have the same authority as those rendered by the CJEU, because of the lack of a strong system of surveillance and remedies in the American system.[77] These different elements explain the disparity in the impact and strength of the two international legal orders on or in national law, despite the enshrinement of conventionality control in the Inter-American system.

The features flowing from the EU triptych – primacy, direct effect, and effectiveness – thus constitute unusual attributes in the realm of international human rights law. They are, however, not incompatible with the international law nature of treaties.[78] Indeed, as underlined by Bruno de Witte, even if these doctrines could be seen as having a 'distinct federal flavour', they apply quite differently from the principle of supremacy in federal countries such as Germany, Switzerland, the US, or Canada.[79] For example, in those countries, there is no direct right of appeal to the CJEU against judgments of national courts that fail to recognise the primacy of EU law.[80] Moreover, the principle of primacy does not go so far as to nullify national provisions that may be in conflict with EU law; in fact, this principle does not impact on the validity of national law, which should subsequently be revised or replaced in accordance with national procedural rules.[81] Furthermore, 'the fact that, as a rule, international law leaves to States a choice among various methods of domestic enforcement of international obligations does not prevent specific Treaties or international decisions from imposing specific requirements in this respect'.[82] When testing the effectiveness of EU law, it is in fact the 'success of the EU as an international organisation' that is being measured.[83] As put by Wyatt and Dashwood, the EU can, therefore, be described 'as a developed form of international organisation which displays characteristics of an embryonic federation'.[84]

The enshrinement of these principles, unsurprisingly, had a significant impact on the position of the individual within the European construct. As Bruno de Witte emphasises, 'it is safe to say that those judgments (in *Van Gend en Loos* and *Costa*) and their progeny have helped to put the individual person, and her rights and interests, at the heart of European law'.[85] The following paragraphs provide an

[77] On their authority, see, among others, L Burgorgue-Larsen, *The 3 Regional Human Rights Courts in Context. Justice That Cannot Be Taken for Granted* (Oxford University Press, 2024), 432–40.

[78] de Witte, 'Direct Effect, Primacy, and the Nature of the Legal Order' (n 20) 226.

[79] B de Witte, 'EU Law: Is It International Law?' in C Barnard and S Peers (eds), *European Union Law* (n 25) 203.

[80] ibid.

[81] Bobek, 'The Effects of EU Law in the National Legal Systems' (n 25) 176.

[82] de Witte, 'EU Law: Is It International Law?' (n 79) 204.

[83] Gentile, 'One, No One, One Hundred Thousand' (n 42) 614.

[84] A Dashwood et al, *Wyatt and Dashwood's European Union Law*, 5th edn (Sweet & Maxwell, 2006) 132, quoted by de Witte, 'EU Law: Is It International Law?' (n 79) 210.

[85] de Witte, 'Direct Effect, Primacy, and the Nature of the Legal Order' (n 20) 223.

in-depth analysis of their consequences on the protection of fundamental rights provided by the EU.

I.2. The Supreme EU Fundamental Rights Law System

As already underlined, the principle of primacy, as construed by the European Court of Justice, has a profound influence on national legal systems. Its obliges all national authorities to set aside any domestic law provisions that are in conflict with EU law provisions that have direct effect. The strength of this obligation is equally manifest in the realm of fundamental rights protection as enshrined within the EU legal order.

The CJEU has recently clarified that the obligation to set aside a national norm can only arise in the event of a conflict with a provision of EU law *that can have direct effect*. In the past, this limit was not clearly established, and a strand of the literature distinguished the issue of direct effect from the obligation to set aside national norms contrary to EU law.[86] This is why several older judgments seem to impose this obligation even when there is an EU law norm that cannot have direct effect, such as a provision of an EU Directive. This is, for instance, the case in the *Kreil* judgment. The CJEU established that the principle of equal treatment between women and men concerning access to employment, as set out in Directive 76/207, precluded the application of national provisions that would contravene this principle, such as a general exclusion of women from military posts involving the use of arms, and which allowed them access only to the medical and military-music services.[87] The CJEU was asked to provide an interpretative judgment through the preliminary reference procedure. It went beyond merely recognising that there was an incompatibility between the national and EU laws – it went on to direct the national authorities to set aside the disputed national provision. This can probably also be explained because the conflicting practice was that of the State, and not of an individual.

It is now clear that the obligation to set aside a conflicting national rule can only be imposed with regard to an EU provision which had been recognised as having direct effect.[88] This has not prevented the CJEU from acknowledging numerous situations where there is such direct effect, notably by relying on the EU Charter to circumvent the lack of direct effect of EU Directives.

The *Bauer* case is illustrative in this regard, and we will delve into it extensively in the subsequent section, focused on direct effect. The CJEU enshrined the *Simmenthal* obligation in relation to the fundamental right to an annual period of

[86] See, among others, K Lenaerts and T Corthaut, 'Towards an Internally Consistent Doctrine on Invoking Norms of EU Law' in S Prechal and B Roermund (eds), *The Coherence of EU Law* (Oxford University Press, 2018).

[87] Case C-285/98 *Tanja Kreil v Bundesrepublik Deutschland* ECLI:EU:C:2000:2 [2000] ECR I-69, para 32.

[88] Case C-573/17 *Criminal proceedings against Daniel Adam Popławski* ECLI:EU:C:2019:530 [2019].

paid leave, as implemented by the Working Time Directive,[89] by relying directly on Article 31(2) of the EU Charter. This provision of the EU Charter was considered capable of having direct effect – despite the fact that it was implemented by a Directive, which is an instrument that, in principle, cannot have direct effect.[90] The CJEU confirmed that, where it is impossible to interpret a national rule in a manner consistent with this Article,

> the national court, before which a dispute between the legal heir of a deceased worker and the former employer of that worker has been brought, must disapply that national legislation and ensure that the legal heir receives payment from the employer of an allowance in lieu of paid annual leave.[91]

In this particular case, the national court had to disapply the national legislation, retroactively stripping inheritors of the right to paid annual leave earned before the death of an employee. This consequently denied their legal heirs a compensation allowance in lieu of such leave, through the financial settlement of those rights.[92]

Such an obligation may also arise to directly ensure compliance with a provision of the EU Charter that is capable of direct effect, even in this absence of secondary legislation. In the *Garlsson* case, the CJEU established that Article 50 of the EU Charter, which enshrines the *ne bis in idem* principle, has direct effect. Therefore,

> in the course of the assessment of the compatibility of provisions of domestic law with the rights guaranteed by the Charter, the national court which is called upon, within the exercise of its jurisdiction, to apply provisions of EU law is under a duty to give full effect to those provisions, if necessary refusing of its own motion to apply any conflicting provision of national legislation, even if adopted subsequently, and it is not necessary for the court to request or await the prior setting aside of such provision by legislative or other constitutional means.[93]

The CJEU also recalled the obligation for national judges to refrain from applying a national decision breaching EU law, in a judgment concerning the protection of the rule of law and of the principle of effective judicial protection. This case concerned a resolution adopted by the disciplinary chamber of the Supreme Court on the suspension of a judge from their role. The CJEU confirmed that such resolution should be set aside by national judges if it appears that it has been adopted in breach of the principle of judicial independence as protected by Article 19 TEU and Article 47 of the EU Charter. Moreover, the threat of disciplinary sanctions for

[89] Directive 2003/88/EC of the European Parliament and of the Council of 4 November 2003 concerning certain aspects of the organisation of working time [2003] OJ L 299/9 (Directive 2003/88/EC).

[90] Joined Cases C-569/16 and C-570/16 *Stadt Wuppertal v Maria Elisabeth Bauer and Volker Willmeroth v Martina Broßonn* ECLI:EU:C:2018:871 [2018], para 85.

[91] ibid, para 92.

[92] ibid, para 86.

[93] Case C-537/16 *Garlsson Real Estate SA and Others v Commissione Nazionale per le Società e la Borsa (Consob)* ECLI:EU:C:2018:193 [2018], para 67.

national judges setting aside national decisions could not hinder this obligation, arising from EU law.[94]

Even when the EU law provision protecting a fundamental right does not have direct effect, the individual injured as a result of conflicting domestic law is not left without any redress. To begin with, as previously underscored, the duty of consistent interpretation remains applicable to all national authorities, even with regard to EU law norms deprived of direct effect.[95] Moreover, the CJEU also considers that the individual in question can consistently invoke the principle of state liability as established in the *Francovich* judgment,[96] which establishes a right to obtain compensation for a loss suffered because of a Member State's failure to comply with EU law if certain conditions are met.[97] The principle of Member States' liability for failure to comply with EU law – including non-directly applicable provisions – indeed constitutes an additional tool for ensuring the precedence of the protection conferred by EU law upon individuals. In the *Smith* case, the CJEU explicitly confirmed that, when consistent interpretation with EU law was not feasible, and an individual was adversely affected by a Member State's failure to correctly implement or transpose a directive, he or she 'could nevertheless invoke the principles established in the judgment … Francovich and Others … to seek compensation from the Member State, if justified, for any resulting losses'.[98]

These consequences arising from the principle of primacy are, undeniably, a singularity of the fundamental rights protection offered by the EU.

Indeed, other international systems for safeguarding fundamental rights do not typically delineate the concrete implications of the rights they protect within national legal orders. As underlined by Laurence Burgogue-Larsen, about the ECHR, 'at no point has the Strasbourg Court, in fact, developed a similarly structured theory that explicitly and unapologetically governs the competencies of national courts'.[99] Although certain states have acknowledged comparable obligations to set aside national provisions conflicting with the ECHR, this duty does not stem from the international legal order but, rather, from their *domestic* legal frameworks.

The above encapsulates the specific authority of EU Fundamental Rights Law: its primacy is regarded as inherent to the system itself. In the following section, I will explore how the conjunction of this principle with other characteristics of

[94] Joined Cases C-615/20 and C-671/20 *YP e.a. (Levée d'immunité et suspension d'un juge)* ECLI:EU:C:2023:562 [2023].

[95] Case C-122/17 *David Smith v Patrick Meade and Others* ECLI:EU:C:2018:631 [2018], para 39.

[96] Joined Cases C-6/90 and C-9/90 *Andrea Francovich and Danila Bonifaci and others v Italian Republic* ECLI:EU:C:1991:428 [1991].

[97] Case C-282/10 *Maribel Dominguez v Centre informatique du Centre Ouest Atlantique and Préfet de la région Centre* ECLI:EU:C:2012:33 [2012], para 43.

[98] Case C-122/17 *David Smith v Patrick Meade and Others* ECLI:EU:C:2018:631 [2018], para 57.

[99] L Burgorgue-Larsen, 'Chronique d'une théorie en vogue en Amérique latine Décryptage du discours doctrinal sur le contrôle de conventionalité' (2014) 100 *Revue française de droit constitutionnel* 831.

EU law, along with the system of remedies, renders the EU Fundamental Rights system unique, compared with traditional international human rights law.

I.3. The Individual-rights-based EU Fundamental Rights Law

As highlighted earlier, recognition of direct effect is not unique to EU law; it has been acknowledged for the provisions of other international instruments too. Nevertheless, a stronger force can be attributed to the principle of direct effect in EU law. This is thanks to the preliminary ruling procedure, as it allows the CJEU to authoritatively interpret the consequences that derive from EU law within national legal orders. Indeed, a substantial dynamic emerges between, on the one hand, national judges who are entrusted with the direct application of EU law and, on the other, the CJEU, which provides guidance in that regard. The CJEU has issued numerous judgments concerning the recognition of effects pertaining to the fundamental rights that are set out in the EU's legal framework.

While direct effect is a foundational principle of EU law, not all EU rules benefit from it. Certain conditions must be met for a national judge to directly apply EU law norms in a case they are called to rule upon. These norms must possess specific qualities necessary for such application to occur. The traditional conditions required to recognise the direct effect of an EU provision include: (i) the clarity of the provision; (ii) the fact that it is unconditional, and thus does not allow for any margin of discretion on the part of the Member States; and (iii) that the provision is not dependent on further implementation measures so that it can be adopted by the EU or Member States.[100] The interpretation of such provisions by the case law is, however, not always consistent, and, as pointed out by former Advocate General Michal Bobek, the main question the test poses is, 'does the EU law provision in question contain an understandable and justiciable rule of behaviour, which can be applied by national authorities'?[101]

Without claiming to be exhaustive, I shall attempt, in the following, to provide a condensed overview illustrating the strength of recognised direct effect in the realm of EU Fundamental Rights Law. In light of this, I shall differentiate between the scenario where vertical direct effect is acknowledged, pertaining to the relationship between the individual and the state (I.3.a), and the situation concerning horizontal relations between individuals (1.3.b).

I.3.a. The Vertical Direct Effect of EU Fundamental Rights Law

Fundamental rights have traditionally been conceived as shields for individuals against public authorities. They were initially developed to govern the relationship between private and public entities – a vertical dimension – and they continue

[100] Bobek, 'The Effects of EU Law in the National Legal Systems' (n 25) 159.
[101] ibid.

to do so, including within the EU system of protection. In this regard, the EU Charter of Fundamental Rights explicitly states in Article 51 – as previously examined – that it is addressed 'to the institutions and bodies of the Union' and 'to the Member States only when they are implementing Union law'. Similarly, numerous legislative acts aim to protect the fundamental rights of individuals against EU institutions and Member States.

For these rights to be adjudicated before a *national* court, an ascending vertical direct effect must be recognised in order to enable individuals to invoke this protection against national governmental authorities in judicial proceedings. The recognition that EU law can have such an effect dates back to the 1963 *Van Gend en Loos* judgment.[102] Since then, case law has further refined the conditions under which this effect can be recognised, varying according to the different sources of EU law.

With regard to primary law, including the EU Charter, the CJEU has acknowledged the possibility of vertical upward direct effect for provisions that meet the required standards of precision, clarity, and unconditionality. This is, for instance, the case, according to the CJEU, of Article 50 of the EU Charter, which enshrines the *ne bis in idem* principle. As recalled earlier, the CJEU considered in the *Garlsson* case that 'the *ne bis in idem* principle guaranteed by Article 50 of the Charter of Fundamental Rights of the European Union confers on individuals a right which is directly applicable in the context of a dispute such as that at issue in the main proceedings'.[103]

The dispute concerned legal proceedings that were commenced on whether an administrative fine for an offence was a second penalty, given that a criminal penalty had already been imposed for the same offence. Article 47 of the EU Charter, which safeguards the right to an effective remedy, is also considered by the CJEU to be a provision that is clear and precise enough to be granted vertical direct effect. The CJEU indeed considers that this provision 'is sufficient in itself and does not need to be made more specific by provisions of EU or national law to confer on individuals a right which they may rely on as such'.[104] Therefore, national judges may be required to set aside any national legislation conflicting with the requirements flowing from Article 47 of the EU Charter. For example, in *B v Centre public d'action sociale belge*, the CJEU held that,

> in a situation where the national court concludes that the Belgian legislation does not offer a third-country national … a remedy against the return decision governed by clear, precise and foreseeable rules and leading to the automatic suspension of that decision, it is for that court to hold that the appeal brought by the third-country national has suspensive effect for the purpose of the annulment or suspension of the return

[102] Case C-26/62, *NV Algemene Transport- en Expeditie Onderneming van Gend & Loos v Netherlands Inland Revenue Administration* ECLI:EU:C:1963:1 [1963] English Special Edition 1.

[103] Case C-537/16 *Garlsson Real Estate SA and Others v Commissione Nazionale per le Società e la Borsa (Consob)* ECLI:EU:C:2018:193 [2018], para 68.

[104] Case C-414/16 *Vera Egenberger v Evangelisches Werk für Diakonie und Entwicklung e.V.* ECLI:EU:C:2018:257 [2018], para 78.

> decision taken in respect of that third-country national, if necessary refusing to apply the national legislation precluding that appeal from having such an effect.[105]

However, in order to be able to rely upon the EU Charter, the dispute must, of course, fall within its scope of application in a way that is in line with its Article 51.

Regarding secondary legislation, it is necessary to make a clear distinction between EU Regulations and EU Directives.

The provisions of Regulations are generally considered to be capable of having direct effect. This means that specific provisions of Regulations protecting fundamental rights can be relied upon by individuals in legal proceedings against public authorities – directly before national judges.

However, many rules harmonising fundamental rights are found within Directives.

It is not the case, though, for the well-known General Data Protection Regulation (GDPR),[106] which I have already discussed in the chapter one of this book. While the GDPR is primarily addressed to private entities, it also applies to public authorities who carry out data processing activities, except in certain exclusive cases that are listed.[107] Beyond that list, individuals can invoke the GDPR's provisions against public authorities that violate the rules it imposes. The CJEU recently confirmed, for example, that a committee of inquiry set up by the parliament of a Member State should respect the GDPR within the scope of its activities, unless the activities can fall within one of the exceptions enshrined in the GDPR, such as for national security.[108] The exceptions must, however, be construed narrowly: the main principle is the broad applicability of the GDPR, including where public authorities are concerned.[109]

Directives, by nature, have binding force 'as to the result to be achieved' in every Member State, giving national authorities the discretion to determine the form and methods to achieve this result.[110] Thus, when fundamental rights standards are contained in a Directive, Member States are required to transpose them into their national legal order. Individuals can then rely upon the national implementation measures in the context of their disputes. Nevertheless, it has long been established that if a Directive has not been implemented within the requisite deadline, it may acquire vertical direct effect, allowing individuals to rely on any

[105] Case C-233/19 *B v Centre public d'action sociale de Liège (CPAS)* ECLI:EU:C:2020:757 [2020], para 57.

[106] Regulation (EU) 2016/679 of the European Parliament and of the Council of 27 April 2016 on the protection of natural persons with regard to the processing of personal data and on the free movement of such data, and repealing Directive 95/46/EC (General Data Protection Regulation) [2016] OJ L 119/1 ('GDPR').

[107] Except when these public authorities act outside the scope of application of the Regulation, according to art 2(2)(a) to (d) GDPR.

[108] Case C-33/22 *Österreichische Datenschutzbehörde* ECLI:EU:C:2024:46 [2024], para 43.

[109] ibid, para 45.

[110] TFEU, art 288.

sufficiently precise provisions it has against the defaulting state.[111] This prevents a state from gaining an advantage from its own transgressions, such as failing to safeguard fundamental rights by not implementing EU Directives that enshrine those rights. For instance, concerning the Directive on the right to interpretation and translation[112] and the Directive on the right to information[113] in criminal proceedings, the CJEU recalled that,

> whenever the provisions of a directive appear, so far as their subject matter is concerned, to be unconditional and sufficiently precise, they may be relied upon before the national courts by individuals against the Member State concerned, where the latter has failed to implement the directive in domestic law by the end of the period prescribed or where it has failed to implement the directive correctly.[114]

And that,

> since … Article 2(1) and Article 3(1) of Directive 2010/64 and Article 3(1)(d) of Directive 2012/13 state, in a precise and unconditional manner, the content and scope of the rights of every suspected or accused person to receive interpretation services and the translation of essential documents, and to be informed of those rights, those provisions must be regarded as having direct effect, with the result that any person benefiting from those rights may rely on them against a Member State, before the national courts.[115]

A similar line of reasoning was adopted regarding the so-called 'Return Directive'.[116] That legislative text has harmonising provisions that establish minimum safeguards to govern the expulsion of third-country nationals staying irregularly on a Member State's territory. Article 5 of this Directive states that, 'when implementing this directive, Member States shall take due account of the best interests of the child; family life; the state of health of the third-country national concerned, and respect the principle of non-refoulement', which the CJEU held was sufficiently clear to have direct effect. It found that,

> even though a directive leaves the Member States a degree of latitude when they adopt rules in order to implement it, a provision of that directive may be regarded as unconditional and precise where it imposes on Member States in unequivocal terms a precise obligation as to the result to be achieved, which is not coupled with any condition regarding application of the rule laid down by it.[117]

[111] Case 41/74 *Yvonne van Duyn v Home Office* ECLI:EU:C:1974:133 [1974] ECR 1337.
[112] Directive (EU) 2010/64 of the European Parliament and of the Council of 20 October 2010 on the Right to Interpretation and Translation in Criminal Proceedings [2010] OJ L 280/1.
[113] Directive (EU) 2012/13 of the European Parliament and of the Council of 22 May 2012 on the Right to Information in Criminal Proceedings [2010] OJ L 142/1.
[114] Case C-242/22 PPU *TL (No interpreter or translation)* ECLI:EU:C:2022:611 [2022], para 49.
[115] ibid, para 52.
[116] Directive 2008/115/EC of the European Parliament and of the Council of 16 December 2008 on Common Standards and Procedures in Member States for Returning Illegally Staying Third-Country Nationals [2008] OJ L 348/ 98 (Directive 2008/115).
[117] Case C-528/21 *M.D. (Interdiction d'entrée en Hongrie)* ECLI:EU:C:2023:341 [2023], para 95.

Therefore, according to the CJEU,

> where Article 5 of Directive 2008/115 is invoked by an individual before a national court against a Member State which has transposed it incorrectly, it is for that court to ensure the full effectiveness of that directly effective EU law provision and, if it is unable to interpret the national legislation in conformity with that Article 5, to disapply, of its own motion, the national provisions which appear to be incompatible with it.[118]

The fact that an EU judge has in this way compelled national judges to directly apply EU law standards protecting fundamental rights undoubtedly contributes to the effectiveness of these rights. Indeed, it is common for national judges to be called upon to directly ensure the implementation of EU Fundamental Rights protection in disputes brought before them.[119]

I.3.b. The Horizontal Effects of EU Fundamental Rights Law

The notion of horizontal effects of fundamental rights refers to the obligation to protect, and the right to benefit from, such rights, in relationships between individuals/private parties, specifically whether that type of subject can rely on a norm of EU law before a national judge in a dispute against another private individual. Although, traditionally, fundamental rights have been conceived and thought of primarily as obligations imposed on the *State*, for several decades now, the horizontal applicability of certain rights between individuals has been increasingly recognised in human rights law globally, including in the EU context.[120]

Horizontal effects can manifest in various ways. The horizontal effect of fundamental rights can arise either as a result of the framing of EU legislation (i) or through the interpretative case law of the CJEU (ii).

I.3.b (i) Horizontal Effects Through Legislation

Within the scope of EU Fundamental Rights Law, there is a lot of legislation that imposes obligations on individuals or private parties in horizontal relationships, namely with other individuals or private parties. National measures transposing EU Directives can, therefore, directly impose obligations upon individuals or private parties, which are enforceable before a national court.

[118] ibid, para 110.

[119] However, as previously mentioned, it must be kept in mind that these specific characteristics of EU law not only favour rules *protecting* fundamental rights but also those within EU law that may *limit* them. Nonetheless, the impact of EU law rules that enshrine fundamental rights in national legal systems certainly benefits from these specific characteristics.

[120] E Frantziou, *The Horizontal Effect of Fundamental Rights in the European Union: A Constitutional Analysis* (Oxford University Press, 2019) 1. See also A Briegleb and N Vander Putten, 'Horizontalisation des droits fondamentaux. Enjeux et prégnance de l'influence des droits humains sur les litiges entre acteurs privés' in T Léonard and J van Meerbeeck (dir), *Droit privé et environnement: une alliance contre nature? (Re)découverte de la force mobilisatrice du droit privé à l'aune de l'intérêt général* (Presses universitaires Saint-Louis 2025, forthcoming).

A recent and highly illustrative example in this regard is the 'equal pay' Directive[121] that has already been mentioned. That Directive imposes numerous obligations on employers who are covered by its scope, especially transparency obligations concerning potential pay gaps between female and male workers.[122] This EU legislative text, which must be transposed by Member States into their national legal orders, translates the principle of non-discrimination between women and men into specific and explicit obligations for (private) employers, concerning their employees.

The EU's recent legislative package on digital services is also notable. It imposes a set of obligations on online platforms, to further its aim to enhance the fundamental rights protection of users in the digital space.[123] The Digital Markets Act (DMA) imposes several obligations on large online platforms to protect users' personal data, in line with the right to protection of personal data, which is an EU Fundamental Right.[124] The Digital Services Act (DSA) also imposes obligations on large online platforms to protect users' fundamental rights, including the right to respect for private and family life, the right to personal data protection, and the right to non-discrimination.[125] The platforms that are subject to these obligations are required to establish user-friendly mechanisms allowing individuals or entities to report the presence on their services of specific information that those individuals or entities consider to be illegal content.[126] They are also obliged to conduct risk assessments, examining aspects such as the dissemination of illegal content through their services; potential adverse effects on the exercise of fundamental rights, including human dignity, the right to privacy and family life, personal data protection, freedom of expression and information, and non-discrimination, and various other aspects.[127] Following these risk assessments, providers of very large online platforms and search engines must implement reasonable, proportionate, and effective mitigation measures tailored to the identified systemic risks.[128] It ought to be highlighted that the EU is a pioneer in this regard; rather than simply complementing existing national protection, it takes the lead. I will return to this question in chapter four, where I will examine the political project that the protection of fundamental rights in the digital sphere may represent for the EU.

[121] Directive (EU) 2023/970 of the European Parliament and of the Council of 10 May 2023 to Strengthen the Application of the Principle of Equal Pay for Equal Work or Work of Equal Value between Men and Women through Pay Transparency and Enforcement Mechanisms [2023] OJ L 132/21 (Directive 2023/970).

[122] ibid, arts 6–9.

[123] In addition, among others, to protect fair competition on the digital markets.

[124] Regulation (EU) 2022/1925 of the European Parliament and of the Council of 14 September 2022 on Contestable and Fair Markets in the Digital Sector and amending Directives (EU) 2019/1937 and (EU) 2020/1828 (Digital Markets Act) [2022] OJ L 265/1, art 5.

[125] Regulation (EU) 2022/2065 of the European Parliament and of the Council of 19 October 2022 on a Single Market For Digital Services and amending Directive 2000/31/EC (Digital Services Act) [2022] OJ L 277/1 (Regulation 2022/2065), recital 52.

[126] ibid, art 16.

[127] ibid, art 34.

[128] ibid, art 35.

I.3.b (ii) Horizontal Effects Through the CJEU's Case Law

Horizontal effects can also be attached to EU rules through judicial means: national judges may directly invoke EU Fundamental Rights provisions in disputes between private parties.

The first recognition of this kind of horizontal effect in EU law dates back to 1976, in the famous *Defrenne* case, where the European Court of Justice acknowledged the horizontal applicability of the principle of equal pay for men and women, then contained in Article 119 of the EEC Treaty.[129] Article 119 stipulated that 'each Member State shall ensure that the principle of equal pay for male and female workers for equal work or work of equal value is applied'. Gabrielle Defrenne, employed by the Belgian national airline Sabena, complained before a national judge of gender-based discrimination against her because she had fewer pension rights in comparison to her male counterpart. The Belgian judge sought interpretation of that provision through a reference for a preliminary ruling from the European Court of Justice, which determined that the principle of equal pay had direct horizontal effect. According to the Court, despite the fact that this provision was directed at the Member States,

> since Article 119 is mandatory in nature, the prohibition on discrimination between men and women applies not only to the action of public authorities but also extends to all agreements intended to regulate paid labour collectively, as well as to contracts between individuals.[130]

As a result, Ms Defrenne could demand that the principle be applied in the legal dispute she had with her employer, a private party.

Since then, the CJEU has developed rather extensive jurisprudence on this matter, which has, in turn, been the subject of abundant literature.[131] Despite the absence of a common doctrine on the horizontal applicability of fundamental rights in the Member States' legal systems, the concept of horizontal effect still played a prominent role in the CJEU's case law.[132] The individual was, indeed, seen 'not only as a bearer of rights, but, also, as an actor of whom specific types of conduct are legally required', very early on in the EU legal order.[133]

[129] Case 43/75 *Gabrielle Defrenne v Société anonyme belge de navigation aérienne Sabena* ECLI:EU:C:1976:56 [1976].

[130] ibid, para 39.

[131] See, among others, Frantziou, *The Horizontal Effect of Fundamental Rights in the European Union* (n 120); E Muir, 'The Horizontal Effects of Charter Rights Given Expression to in EU Legislation, from Mangold to Bauer' [2019] *Review of European Administrative Law* 185; S Prechal, 'Horizontal Direct Effect of the Charter of Fundamental Rights of the EU' (2020) 66 *Revista de Derecho Comunitario Europeo* 407.

[132] Frantziou, *The Horizontal Effect of Fundamental Rights in the European Union* (n 120) 51.

[133] ibid; see Case 26/62 *NV Algemene Transport- en Expeditie Onderneming van Gend & Loos v Netherlands Inland Revenue Administration* ECLI:EU:C:1963:1 [1963] English Special Edition 1, which states that 'Community law therefore not only imposes obligations on individuals but is also intended to confer upon them rights which become part of their legal heritage.'

Since the EU Charter became legally binding, in 2009, several judgments acknowledging the direct horizontal applicability of certain provisions have been handed down by the CJEU. To date, several provisions of the EU Charter have explicitly been granted horizontal direct effect: Article 21, which enshrines the principle of non-discrimination;[134] Article 31, which guarantees the right to fair working conditions, including paid annual leave;[135] and Article 47, which safeguards the right to effective judicial protection.[136] In contrast, Article 26, concerning the rights of disabled persons to integration;[137] Article 27, which establishes workers' right to information and consultation within the undertaking;[138] and Article 38, on consumer protection, have not been interpreted as having such legal effect.[139] And the limitation of the scope of the EU Charter, as set out in Article 51, remains relevant, including in the context of disputes between private individuals.

While there are still uncertainties that I will not fully address here, the case law seems to confirm that all provisions of the EU Charter that establish a mandatory right and are unconditional are capable of having horizontal direct effect.[140] Indeed, according to the CJEU, the right concerned must be 'both mandatory and unconditional in nature, the unconditional nature not needing to be given concrete expression by the provisions of EU or national law'.[141] As stressed by Lucia Serena Rossi, this test is similar but articulated with varying terminology, compared with the initial direct effect test established concerning EU Treaty provisions.[142] On the basis of this two-step test, a distinction is thus made between 'right-conferring

[134] Case C-414/16 *Vera Egenberger v Evangelisches Werk für Diakonie und Entwicklung e.V.* ECLI:EU:C:2018:257 [2018]; Case C-193/17 *Cresco Investigation GmbH v Markus Achatzi* ECLI:EU:C:2019:43 [2019]; Case C-68/17 *IR v JQ* ECLI:EU:C:2018:696 [2018].

[135] Joined Cases C-569/16 and C-570/16 *Stadt Wuppertal v Maria Elisabeth Bauer and Volker Willmeroth v Martina Broßonn* ECLI:EU:C:2018:871 [2018]; Case C-684/16 *Max-Planck-Gesellschaft zur Förderung der Wissenschaften eV v Tetsuji Shimizu* ECLI:EU:C:2018:874 [2018]; Case C-193/85 *Cooperativa Co-Frutta Srl contre Amministrazione delle finanze dello Stato* ECLI:EU:C:1987:210 [1987] ECR 2085.

[136] Case C-414/16 *Vera Egenberger v Evangelisches Werk für Diakonie und Entwicklung e.V.* ECLI:EU:C:2018:257 [2018].

[137] Case C-356/12 *Wolfgang Glatzel v Freistaat Bayern* ECLI:EU:C:2014:350 [2014], para 78. As Eleni Frantziou pointed out, the parties were in a vertical relationship (individual v state) in the *Glatzel* judgment, but it is evident from the wording of the judgment that this conclusion also applies to horizontal relations (between private parties) (E Frantziou, 'The Horizontal Effect of the Charter: Towards an Understanding of Horizontality as a Structural Constitutional Principle' (2020) 22 *Cambridge Yearbook of European Legal Studies* 208, 210).

[138] Case C-176/12 *Association de médiation sociale v Union locale des syndicats CGT and Others* ECLI:EU:C:2014:2 [2014], paras 45–49.

[139] Case C-122/17 *David Smith v Patrick Meade and Others* ECLI:EU:C:2018:631 [2018], para 49.

[140] Frantziou, 'The Horizontal Effect of the Charter' (n 137) 218. See, for an analogous conclusion, T Plat, 'The Effectiveness of Social Directives in the Light of the Charter of Fundamental Rights of the European Union – A Mirage on the Social Horizon?' [2023] *Revue des affaires européennes* 771–78.

[141] Joined Cases C-569/16 and C-570/16 *Stadt Wuppertal v Maria Elisabeth Bauer and Volker Willmeroth v Martina Broßonn* ECLI:EU:C:2018:871 [2018], para 85.

[142] LS Rossi, 'The Relationship between the EU Charter of Fundamental Rights and Directives in Horizontal Situations' (*EU Law Live Analysis*, 2019), available at http://eulawanalysis.blogspot.com/2019/02/the-relationship-between-eu-charter-of.html.

provisions' and 'non-right-conferring provisions'.[143] With regard to the 'mandatory nature' condition, EU Charter provisions requiring further implementation by national law and practice, therefore, seem not to be able to have such direct effect, even when there is an EU legislative text giving expression to the fundamental right concerned.[144] The condition of unconditionality seems, on the other hand, to refer to the traditional criteria of clarity and precision.[145]

It is, however, not easy to define the scope of protection provided by these provisions of the EU Charter in individual disputes. This difficulty is compounded by the CJEU's use of the 'enigmatic'[146] concept of the 'essence', 'very substance' or 'essential content' of rights, in several judgments on the issue.[147] A thorough analysis of the case law suggests that, when the CJEU refers to this notion, it implies that only the 'essential content' of the right in question can benefit from direct horizontal effect.[148] Conversely, in the absence of explicit reference to this notion of essence, it suggests that even more peripheral aspects of the law may be recognised with such an effect.[149] As underlined by the current President of the Court of Justice, Koen Lenaerts,

> There are Charter provisions that contain rights which may produce horizontal direct effect beyond the scope of their essence. This is because non-essential elements of those rights are sufficient in themselves and do not need to be made more specific by other provisions of EU or national law in order to confer on individuals a right on which they may rely as such. Therefore, those elements are mandatory and unconditional in nature and are fully effective at primary EU level. Accordingly, those rights may be relied upon in a dispute between private parties with a view to setting aside a national measure that, whilst not compromising the essence of those rights, constitutes a disproportionate limitation on their exercise. This appears to be the case of the rights enshrined in Articles 21 and 47 of the Charter.[150]

On the other hand, other 'non-essential' elements of certain EU Charter rights require action from the national or EU legislature to be fully effective. In this

[143] Frantziou, *The Horizontal Effect of Fundamental Rights in the European Union* (n 120) 100.

[144] Case C-176/12 *Association de médiation sociale v Union locale des syndicats CGT and Others* ECLI:EU:C:2014:2 [2014], paras 45–49 and Case C-684/16 *Max-Planck-Gesellschaft zur Förderung der Wissenschaften eV v Tetsuji Shimizu* ECLI:EU:C:2018:874 [2018], para 73.

[145] Rossi, 'The Relationship between the EU Charter of Fundamental Rights and Directives in Horizontal Situations' (n 142), relying upon Case C-537/16 *Garlsson Real Estate SA and Others v Commissione Nazionale per le Società e la Borsa (Consob)* ECLI:EU:C:2018:193 [2018], paras 65–66.

[146] Plat, 'The Effectiveness of Social Directives in the Light of the Charter' (n 140) 778.

[147] On this concept, see, among others, K Lenaerts, 'Limits on Limitations: The Essence of Fundamental Rights in the EU' (2019) 20 *German Law Journal* 779–93; and S Van Drooghenbroeck and C Rizcallah, 'The ECHR and the Essence of Fundamental Rights: Searching for Sugar in Hot Milk?' (2019) 20 *German Law Journal* 904–23.

[148] See, for instance, Joined Cases C-569/16 and C-570/16 *Stadt Wuppertal v Maria Elisabeth Bauer and Volker Willmeroth v Martina Broßonn* ECLI:EU:C:2018:871 [2018], para 49; and Case C-684/16 *Max-Planck-Gesellschaft zur Förderung der Wissenschaften eV v Tetsuji Shimizu* ECLI:EU:C:2018:874 [2018], para 61, about art 31(2) of the EU Charter.

[149] See, for instance, Case C-414/16 *Vera Egenberger v Evangelisches Werk für Diakonie und Entwicklung e.V.* ECLI:EU:C:2018:257 [2018], about arts 21 and 47 of the EU Charter.

[150] Lenaerts, 'Limits on Limitations' (n 147) 789.

context, 'only measures compromising the essence of those rights may be set aside'.[151]

As stressed below, the recognition of horizontal effect of EU Charter provisions has often occurred when there is EU legislation – especially when it is in the form of an EU Directive – providing 'specific expression' to the EU Charter right in question. In this regard, it appears that, when that kind of EU legislation exists, it is often its terms that define the content of the protection offered by the EU Charter provision it embodies.

As already underlined, harmonisation in the field of fundamental rights protection has often occurred through EU Directives, which, in principle, cannot have direct effect.[152] An upward vertical effect can be attributed to them in certain circumstances. On the other hand, horizontal direct effect is, in principle, excluded because EU Directives are addressed to the Member States concerning the result they have to achieve. This limitation has been balanced by several methods of interpretation by the CJEU – which have already been extensively analysed in the literature – including the broad interpretation of 'State emanation',[153] and the obligation of consistent interpretation. In the field of fundamental rights protection, the CJEU has, moreover, developed a creative line of case law which enables this obstacle to be circumvented based on the existence of 'general principles of EU law' or, later, the legally binding provisions of the EU Charter. This jurisprudence, indeed, recognises that there can be horizontal direct effect for general principles of EU law or provisions of the EU Charter which are given 'concrete expression' by a harmonisation measure.

It was in the famous *Mangold* case of 2000 that the CJEU laid the initial foundations for this jurisprudence.[154] This case concerned German legislation allowing employers to hire older workers on fixed-term contracts without temporal restrictions, whereas the general rule limited such contracts to a two-year period. This disparity reduced protection for older workers facing dismissal, in contrast to their younger counterparts. The legislation aimed to facilitate the employment of older workers. Mr Mangold, who was subject to one of these contracts, argued that there was a violation of EU law due to the age-based discrimination it entailed, in a dispute against his private-sector employer. At that time, Directive 2000/78, establishing a general framework for equal treatment in employment and occupation, had not yet been transposed into German law, as Germany had requested an extension for transposition until 2 December 2006. Nonetheless, the judgment, delivered on 22 November 2005, made reference to the Directive and considered

[151] ibid, 791.

[152] Case 152/84 *M.H. Marshall v Southampton and South-West Hampshire Area Health Authority (Teaching)* ECLI:EU:C:1986:84 [1986] ECR 723; Case 91/92 Paola Faccini Dori v Recreb *Srli* ECLI:EU:C:1994:292 [1994] ECR I-3325.

[153] See, among others, Case C-614/11 *Niederösterreichische Landes-Landwirtschaftskammer v Anneliese Kuso* ECLI:EU:C:2013:544 [2013], para 32; Case C-361/12 *Carmela Carratù v Poste Italiane SpA* ECLI:EU:C:2013:830 [2013], para 29.

[154] Case C-144/04 *Werner Mangold v Rüdiger Helm* ECLI:EU:C:2005:709 [2005] ECR I-9981.

that the fact the contract had been concluded before the transposition deadline did not prevent considering it, given the fact that, 'during the period prescribed for transposition of a directive, the Member States must refrain from taking any measures liable seriously to compromise the attainment of the result prescribed by that directive'.[155] Furthermore – and here comes the most innovative aspect of the ruling – the CJEU held that this Directive was not the primary source of the prohibition of age discrimination in EU law. According to the CJEU, it is the pre-existing principle of non-discrimination that constitutes a general principle of EU law which should serve as the primary source opposing such practices.[156] Therefore, 'observance of the general principle of equal treatment, particularly concerning age, cannot be conditional upon the expiration of the period allowed to Member States for transposing a directive intended to establish a general framework for combating age-based discrimination'.[157] Consequently,

> it is the responsibility of the national court, hearing a dispute involving the principle of non-discrimination in respect of age, to provide, in a case within its jurisdiction, the legal protection that individuals derive from EU law and to ensure that those rules are fully effective, setting aside any provision of national law that may conflict with that law.[158]

Implicitly, the CJEU thus circumvented the lack of horizontal direct effect of the Directive by requiring the national judge to consider the applicability of the general principle of law in this dispute between private parties. This ruling was confirmed by the *Kücükdeveci* judgment, where the CJEU explicitly stated that Directive 2000/78 was merely a 'specific expression' of 'the principle of non-discrimination on grounds of age, which must be considered a general principle of EU law'.[159] This jurisprudence, in practice, conferred effects on EU Directives that they typically lack, and understandably stirred considerable controversy among legal scholars,[160] and within national courts.[161] In its ruling in *Dansk Industri*, the CJEU then clarified the intricate relationship between these two sources of protection, emphasising that the scope of the general principle of non-discrimination on the ground of age in the field of employment depends on the content of the Directive.[162] It indeed considered that

[155] ibid, para 67.
[156] ibid, para 74.
[157] ibid, para 73.
[158] ibid, para 77.
[159] Case C-555/07 *Seda Kücükdeveci v Swedex GmbH & Co. KG* ECLI:EU:C:2010:21 [2010] ECR I-365, para 21.
[160] See, among others, A Dashwood, 'From Van Duyn to Mangold via Marshall: Reducing Direct Effect to Absurdity?' (2007) 9 *Cambridge Yearbook of European Legal Studies* 81; and 'Editorial Comments: Horizontal Direct Effect – A Law of Diminishing Coherence?' (2006) 43 *Common Market Law Review* 1.
[161] BVerfGE 126, 286, 6 July 2010 (*Honeywell*).
[162] Muir, 'The Horizontal Effects of Charter Rights Given Expression to in EU Legislation, from Mangold to Bauer' (n 131) 190.

> the EU legislature intended, by the adoption of the directive, to establish a more precise framework to facilitate the practical implementation of the principle of equal treatment and, in particular, to specify various possible exceptions to that principle, circumscribing those exceptions by using a clearer definition of their scope.[163]

Moreover, the general principle could only be applicable to situations falling within the scope of the Directive.[164]

Similar reasoning was applied with regard to the right to paid annual leave. The CJEU, indeed, recognised the horizontal direct effect of the 'very substance' of Article 31(2) of the EU Charter,[165] notably by relying upon the Working Time Directive.[166] The late Advocate General Bot underlined, in this regard, that, given 'the symbiotic interrelationship'[167] between the right enshrined in the EU Charter and the Directive,

> in the absence of a defined period in Article 31(2) of the Charter, a paid annual leave consistent with that provided for in Article 7(1) of Directive 2003/88 is sufficient to meet the requirements of the Charter. A right to paid leave beyond the minimum duration fixed by the EU legislature cannot be inferred from Article 31(2) of the Charter.[168]

While this jurisprudence has yet to provide definitive clarity on the overall effect to be attributed to EU Charter provisions and legislation that embodies concrete expressions of fundamental rights, it has already had an impact on national legal orders. The *Bauer* case law resulted, for instance, in a reversal of the case law of the French Court of Cassation, which accepted the extensive conception of the right to paid annual leave and its applicability in private disputes.[169]

A French scholar described the 'case' as being the one of a national judge that

> après avoir averti maintes foi le législateur de la non-conformité du droit français avec le droit de l'UE, perd patience, s'empare de la jurisprudence européenne et braque sa position dans le sens contraire à celui retenu dix ans plus tôt.[170]

The French Court of Cassation, applying the principle of primacy, set aside the French labour law provision that conflicted with Article 31(2) of the EU Charter.

[163] Case C-441/14 *Dansk Industri (DI), acting on behalf of Ajos A/S v Estate of Karsten Eigil Rasmussen* ECLI:EU:C:2016:278 [2016], para 23.

[164] ibid, para 24.

[165] Joined Cases C-569/16 and C-570/18 *Stadt Wuppertal v Maria Elisabeth Bauer and Volker Willmeroth v Martina Broßonn* ECLI:EU:C:2018:871 [2018], para 49.

[166] Directive 2003/88/EC.

[167] Joined Cases C-609/17 and C-610/17 *Terveys- ja sosiaalialan neuvottelujärjestö (TSN) ry v Hyvinvointialan liittory and Auto-ja Kuljetusalan Työntekijäliitto AKT ry v Satamaoperaattoritry* ECLI:EU:C:2019:459 [2019], Opinion of Advocate General Bot, para 109.

[168] ibid, para 108.

[169] L Xenou, 'Right to paid annual leave: The Cour de cassation recognized the direct horizontal effect of Article 31(2) of the EU Charter and strengthened the protection of employees' rights' (2025) 32(1) *Maastricht Journal of European and Comparative Law* 78–88.

[170] A Martinon, 'Affaire des congés payés: le justiciable au pays des sources' [2024] *Droit social* 580, 581 ('After having repeatedly warned the legislator about the non-compliance of French law with EU law, the national judge loses patience, seizes European case law, and shifts its position in the opposite direction to that taken ten years earlier.').

Thanks to the unique characteristics of EU law, the French judge was able to remedy the legislature's failure by directly relying on the EU Charter. This judgment – which has retroactive effect – eventually led to legislative reform in order to ensure compliance with EU Fundamental Rights Law requirements.

It seems clear, however, that the fact that there is a Directive does not necessarily mean that direct effect must be recognised for the provision of the EU Charter that it embodies. Indeed, as Théodore Plat highlights, 'a Directive cannot confer on a Charter provision the qualities required to be applicable in a horizontal dispute if it does not itself possess them'.[171] In the *Association de médiation sociale* judgment,[172] the CJEU, for instance, ruled that Article 27 of the EU Charter, which protects the fundamental right to information and consultation of workers, did not possess these qualities, despite the existence of Directive 2002/14 establishing a general framework for informing and consulting workers in the European Community.[173] When revisiting the two criteria of the direct effect of the EU Charter stated above, it indeed appears that Article 27 of the EU Charter does not meet the condition of being 'mandatory in nature', as it states that 'workers or their representatives must, at the appropriate levels, be guaranteed information and consultation in good time *in the cases and under the conditions provided for by Union law and national laws and practices*'.[174] Hence, it is the provision of the EU Charter itself, regardless of whether its content is complemented by the existence of a Directive, that the CJEU recognises as having horizontal direct effect.

The opposite is also true: certain provisions of the EU Charter may be granted direct effect even when they have not been given specific expression through a Directive. This appears to be the case in *X (Absence de motif de résiliation)*, which I will examine below in relation to the principles of effectiveness and effective judicial protection. In this instance, it was Article 47 of the EU Charter that enabled the CJEU to bypass the lack of direct effect of a Directive, even though the Directive in question – concerning the protection of workers on fixed-term contracts – did not itself serve to implement Article 47.[175]

The recognition that the EU Charter provision, in combination with an EU Directive, had direct effect (whether or not it gave specific expression to the stand-alone Charter provision) gives rise to significant questions regarding the constitutional equilibrium between the EU and its Member States. As emphasised, the CJEU, leveraging the Charter, navigates around the absence of direct effect of Directives – a principle that, in essence, is supposed to serve as a constraint on the authority of the EU. This dynamic also exemplifies the profound influence of EU harmonisation in the realm of fundamental rights protection on the enjoyment

[171] Plat, 'The Effectiveness of Social Directives in the Light of the Charter' (n 140) 774.

[172] Case C-176/12 *Association de médiation sociale* ECLI:EU:C:2014:2 [2014].

[173] Directive (EC) 2012/14 of the European Parliament and of the Council of 11 March 2002 establishing a general framework for informing and consulting workers in the European Community [2002] OJ L 80/29.

[174] Emphasis added.

[175] Case C-715/20 *X (absence de motif de résiliation)* ECLI:EU:C:2024:139 [2024].

of these rights, as discussed in chapter one. By legislating, the EU brings more situations within the scope of the EU Charter of Fundamental Rights, and the EU Charter can then come into play to address the lack of horizontal direct effect of the legislation. The latter will then play a role in determining the content of the protection offered by the EU Charter. As emphasised by the CJEU, the national court, when called upon to interpret and determine the obligations deriving from the EU Charter, while possibly balancing the various interests involved, 'will have to take into consideration the balance struck between those interests by the EU legislature'.[176] A genuine 'osmotic effect'[177] thus emerges between EU legislative acts and the EU Charter, widening the scope of application and the impact of fundamental rights protection offered by the EU in national legal systems.

The impact of EU Fundamental Rights protection on disputes between individuals is not limited to cases where horizontal direct effect has officially been recognised, or when it has been implemented by national measures. Indeed, through what Eleni Frantziou terms the 'radiating effect', the EU Charter also has a significant impact on how EU secondary legislation is construed, including in disputes between private parties.[178]

To illustrate, the CJEU interpreted Directive 95/46,[179] in conjunction with Articles 7 (the right to respect for private and family life) and 8 (the right to protection of personal data) of the EU Charter, in the *Google Spain* case as imposing an obligation on Google (a private entity) to respect an individual's right to be forgotten. In this context, the private entity was called upon to carry out a fair balancing act between, on the one hand, 'the legitimate interest of internet users potentially interested in having access to [the relevant] information', and, on the other hand, 'the data subject's fundamental rights under Articles 7 and 8 of the Charter'.[180]

As underlined by Frantziou, 'the effect of the ruling is that horizontal obligations flowing from the Charter are attributed to private entities in the case law, even though the horizontality question is not openly examined'.[181]

The *Test-Achats* case is also illustrative on this point. That judgment concerned Article 5(2) of Directive 2004/113,[182] which allowed Member States to continue

[176] Case C-414/16 *Vera Egenberger v Evangelisches Werk für Diakonie und Entwicklung e.V.* ECLI:EU:C:2018:257 [2018], para 81.

[177] Denys Simon uses the French expression *'effet direct osmotique'*: D Simon, 'Directive' *Répertoire de droit européen* (Dalloz, 2018), para 110.

[178] Frantziou, 'The Horizontal Effect of the Charter' (n 137) 220.

[179] Directive 95/46/EC of the European Parliament and of the Council of 24 October 1995 on the Protection of Individuals with regard to the Processing of Personal Data and on the Free Movement of such Data [1995] OJ L 281/31.

[180] Case C-131/12 *Google Spain SL and Google Inc. v Agencia Española de Protección de Datos (AEPD) and Mario Costeja González* ECLI:EU:C:2014:317 [2014], para 81.

[181] Frantziou, *The Horizontal Effect of Fundamental Rights in the European Union* (n 120) 111.

[182] Council Directive 2004/113/EC of 13 December 2004 implementing the principle of equal treatment between men and women in the access to and supply of goods and services [2004] OJ L373/37 (Directive 2004/113/EC).

permitting the use of gender as a factor in the calculation of premiums and benefits for the purposes of insurance and related financial services for a few more years. The CJEU found that this was incompatible with the principle of equal treatment between women and men, as protected by Articles 21 and 23 of the EU Charter.[183] Consequently, Article 5(2) of that Directive was declared invalid. This affected both public and private insurance companies, which were no longer authorised to use gender-related statistics in the calculation of their premiums.[184]

These phenomena illustrate how the EU protection system has evolved into a genuine individual-rights-based framework. National authorities may indeed be mandated, either by the EU legislature or by the CJEU, to directly implement a range of rights, even in disputes between private individuals. This situation also sets the EU legal system apart from conventional international protection frameworks. In traditional international law, there is no obligation to recognise direct horizontal effect, as it does not dictate to national authorities the exact manner in which they must incorporate its obligations into their domestic legal systems. For instance, the ECHR system does not mandate states to adopt such a stance. As a result, fundamental rights are safeguarded in interpersonal relationships only through the positive obligations placed on the contracting states.[185] These obligations require states to ensure the effective protection of ECHR rights in relations between private parties,[186] and this also extends to national courts.[187] Nevertheless, the scope of these positive obligations is 'inherently limited',[188] and the horizontal effect is, by its very nature, only indirect. In this regard, courts are not obliged to give the ECHR and the judgments of the ECtHR direct effect in the national law of their state, which is free to implement them in accordance with the rules of its national legal system. In EU law, as explored, the CJEU diverges from the traditional international law perspective by independently determining how EU law should operate within the legal systems of its Member States. The underlying logic of the EU system of protection distinguishes itself, once again, from traditional international human rights law. This singularity can prove highly advantageous for the beneficiaries of fundamental rights, as

[183] Case C-236/09 *Association Belge des Consommateurs Test-Achats ASBL and Others v Conseil des ministres* ECLI:EU:C:2011:100 [2011] 2011 ECR I-00773, para 32.

[184] Frantziou, 'The Horizontal Effect of the Charter' (n 137) 110.

[185] D Spielmann, 'The European Court of Human Rights' in D Oliver and J Fedtke (eds), *Human Rights and the Private Sphere: A Comparative Study* (Routledge, 2007) 427; Frantziou, *The Horizontal Effect of Fundamental Rights in the European Union* (n 120) 52.

[186] Gerards, *General Principles of the European Convention on Human Rights* (n 54) 222. On this concept, see, among others, V Stoyanova, *Positive Obligations under the European Convention on Human Rights Within and Beyond Boundaries* (Oxford University Press, 2023); and L Lavrysen, *Human Rights in a Positive State: Rethinking the Relationship between Positive and Negative Obligations under the European Convention on Human Rights*, 1st edn (Intersentia, 2016).

[187] Gerards, *General Principles of the European Convention on Human Rights* (n 54) 235.

[188] Beijer, *The Limits of Fundamental Rights Protection by the EU* (n 48) 64, quoting *Zehnalova and Zehnal v the Czech Republic* App no. 38621/97 ECLI:CE:ECHR:2002:0514DEC003862197 (ECHR, 14 May 2002).

exemplified, among many other cases, in the French case on paid annual leave (see above).

I.4. An Effective EU Fundamental Rights Law System

In addition to the principles of primacy and direct effect, a third principle is regularly invoked by the CJEU to enhance the protection of fundamental rights provided by EU law: the principle of effectiveness.

As mentioned earlier, this principle was enshrined early on by the CJEU, and was drawn from the traditional international law principle of *'effet utile'*. The CJEU has given it an extensive interpretation, allowing it to solidify the effects of EU law in national legal systems. This principle has also been embraced and incorporated by the EU legislature, which translated it into more specific requirements in certain pieces of legislation (I.4.a). In the absence of harmonisation rules, the principle of effectiveness is notably encapsulated in the '*Rewe* formula', according to which Member States can themselves define the procedural conditions governing actions intended to ensure the implementation of EU law, provided that they respect the principles of equivalence and effectiveness.[189] The CJEU has further substantiated the principle of effectiveness in the context of fundamental rights (I.4.b).

I.4.a. Effectiveness Through Legislation

The principle of effectiveness is frequently embodied in EU secondary legislation, in order to support the implementation of EU substantive law. This is equally relevant in the context of fundamental rights protection, where EU legislation led the way by imposing extensive obligations on Member States – or even private parties – to ensure the effectiveness of the rights it aims to protect. In this context, the EU progressively encroaches upon the procedural autonomy of Member States to strengthen the effective enforcement of human rights. This growing influence reflects a distinctive feature of the EU's Fundamental Rights framework, setting it apart from traditional national systems. While this intervention reshapes the balance between national and EU competences, it also offers significant advantages to rights-holders by enhancing legal protections and procedural guarantees. Recognising this specificity is crucial for leveraging it effectively whenever appropriate.

This dynamic is at work in most EU legislation harmonising fundamental rights, including in EU anti-discrimination law, EU data protection law, EU digital law, EU asylum law, and EU criminal law.

[189] S Prechal and R Widdershoven, 'Redefining the Relationship between "Rewe-Effectiveness" and Effective Judicial Protection' (2011) 4 *Review of European Administrative Law* 31, 32.

To ensure the effective implementation of the principle of equal treatment within national legal systems, EU legislation introduces a set of highly sophisticated and innovative procedural rules, particularly when compared with national equality law frameworks and the jurisprudence of the ECtHR.[190] Despite being dispersed across various sections of different EU equality Directives and lacking full uniformity, these procedural provisions share significant similarities. As a result, they contribute to the development of what Elise Muir describes as a 'common procedural law of EU equality policy'.[191]

This common procedural framework comprises five key elements present in most legislation designed to combat discrimination based on sex, ethnic origin/race, religion/belief, age, sexual orientation, and disability.[192] The first concerns access to judicial or administrative procedures, requiring Member States to enable legal entities to initiate or support actions on behalf of victims of discrimination, in judicial or administrative proceedings.[193] The second concerns a partial shift of the burden of proof, which dictates that, in the presence of prima facie evidence of discrimination, its existence should be presumed, and it is therefore the responsibility of the potential perpetrator to provide evidence to the contrary.[194] The obligation for Member States to adopt measures aimed at protecting victims from retaliatory actions following a complaint filed for discrimination constitutes a third element of this common framework.[195] The fourth key element is that Member States are required to establish 'bodies for the promotion of equal treatment', notably to assist victims to pursue complaints.[196] And the fifth is that the EU legislation imposes on the Member States the obligation to establish effective sanctions and to establish a system of compensation for the victims.[197] The exact wording of this obligation differs depending on the EU legislation in question.

[190] E Muir, 'Procedural Rules in the Service of the "Transformative Function" of EU Equality Law: Bringing the Prohibition of Nationality Discrimination Along' (2015) 8 *Review of European Administrative Law* 153.

[191] E Muir, *EU Equality Law: The First Fundamental Rights Policy of the EU* (Oxford University Press, 2018) 150.

[192] ibid. See, among others, Council Directive 2000/78/EC of 27 November 2000 establishing a General Framework for Equal Treatment in Employment and Occupation [2000] OJ L303/16 (Directive 2000/78/EC); Council Directive 2000/43/EC of 29 June 2000 Implementing the Principle of Equal Treatment between Persons Irrespective of Racial or Ethnic Origin [2000] OJ L 180/22 (Directive 2000/43/EC); Directive 2004/113/EC; Directive 2006/54/EC of the European Parliament and of the Council of 5 July 2006 on the Implementation of the Principle of Equal Opportunities and Equal Treatment of Men and Women in Matters of Employment and Occupation (recast) [2006] OJ L 204/23 (Directive 2006/54/EC); Directive (EU) 2019/1158 of the European Parliament and of the Council of 20 June 2019 on Work-life Balance for Parents and Carers and repealing Council Directive 2010/18/EU.

[193] Directive 2000/43/EC, art 7.

[194] ibid, art 8.

[195] ibid, art 9.

[196] See, among others, Directive 2004/113/EC, art 12; Directive 2006/54/EC, art 20; Directive 2010/41/EU, art 11.

[197] Directive 2000/43/EC, art 15.

The most innovative ones require Member States to 'ensure real and effective compensation or reparation … for loss or damage sustained by a person as a result of discrimination … such compensation or reparation being dissuasive and proportionate to the loss or damage suffered'.[198] For example, in the Directive on sex equality in self-employment, compensation or reparation 'shall not be limited by the fixing of a prior upper limit'.[199]

More recently, the EU has even taken a further step in the 'proceduralisation'[200] of the principle of effectiveness to combat gender discrimination with regard to wages. Directive 2023/970 aims at reinforcing the application of the equal pay for equal work or work of equal value principle through pay transparency and enforcement mechanisms.[201] It is, indeed, highly innovative in this regard. It goes as far as imposing a set of obligations directly on companies, particularly in terms of transparency. Moreover, like other equality Directives, it requires Member States to ensure that court proceedings for enforcing the rights and obligations it establishes are easily accessible to workers and individuals acting on their behalf, even after the termination of the employment relationship in which the discrimination is alleged to have occurred.[202] It also calls for the establishment of penalties that 'guarantee a real deterrent effect'.[203] In this context, associations, organisations, equality bodies, workers' representatives, or other legal entities with a legitimate interest in promoting gender equality, according to criteria set out in national law, should be able to engage in any administrative procedure or court proceedings concerning an alleged violation of rights or obligations related to the equal pay principle.[204] Furthermore, victims must be able to claim real and effective compensation and redress, without being limited by a prior upper limit, in any administrative procedure or court proceedings involving an alleged violation of rights or obligations linked to the equal pay principle.[205] They must also be protected against any potential retaliation.[206] A partial shift of the burden of proof is also provided for,[207] and the Directive even defines the standard of evidence required to establish the existence of equal work or work of equal value.[208] More innovatively, it further compels Member States to 'ensure that competent authorities or national courts have the power to order the disclosure of evidence containing confidential information where they

[198] Directive 2006/54/EC, art 18; Directive 2004/113/EC, art 8(2).
[199] Directive 2010/41/EU, art 10.
[200] Proceduralisation refers to the process of harmonising procedural guarantee requirements in order to ensure the effective protection of a substantive fundamental right.
[201] Directive 2023/970 (n 121).
[202] ibid, art 14.
[203] ibid, art 23.
[204] ibid, art 15.
[205] ibid, art 16.
[206] ibid, art 25.
[207] ibid, art 18.
[208] ibid.

consider it relevant to the equal pay claim'.[209] Another innovative aspect is that the Directive sets time limits for commencing the claim:

> [L]imitation periods shall not begin to run before the claimant is aware, or can reasonably be expected to be aware, of an infringement. Member States may decide that limitation periods do not begin to run while the infringement is ongoing or before the end of the employment contract or employment relationship.[210]

Such limitation periods shall, in addition, be no shorter than three years.[211] The Directive further specifies that the

> limitation period is suspended or, depending on national law, interrupted, as soon as a claimant undertakes action by bringing a complaint to the attention of the employer or by instituting proceedings before a court, directly or through the workers' representatives, the labour inspectorate, or the equality body.

Consequently, the Directive interferes quite extensively with the procedural autonomy of Member States.

These elements unquestionably contribute significantly to the effectiveness of the anti-discrimination efforts pursued by these Directives. As stressed by Elise Muir, the procedural dimension of fundamental rights legislation is 'extremely important in order to actually enhance the protection of the said fundamental right in domestic legal orders'.[212]

The GDPR also outlines various procedural requirements to ensure the effectiveness of the fundamental right to personal data protection. Notably, it stipulates that every 'data subject' has the right to lodge a complaint to a supervisory authority, especially in the Member State of their habitual residence, place of work, or the location of the alleged infringement, if they believe that the processing of their personal data breaches the GDPR.[213] Furthermore, natural or legal persons are entitled to an effective judicial remedy if a supervisory authority has made an adverse legally binding decision against them.[214] Additionally, the GDPR explicitly specifies that data subjects have the right to an effective judicial remedy when they believe that their rights under it have been breached due to non-compliance with it in the processing of their personal data.[215] In such disputes, the data subject has the right to be represented by an association, aiming at protecting the public interest, which is active in the field of data protection.[216] The GDPR also governs the right to compensation, indicating that any individual who has suffered material or non-material damage due to a violation of the GDPR has the right to receive compensation from

[209] ibid, art 20.
[210] ibid, art 21.
[211] ibid, art 21.
[212] E Muir, 'The Fundamental Rights Implications of EU Legislation: Some Constitutional Challenges' (2014) 51 *Common Market Law Review* 219, 225.
[213] GDPR, art 77.
[214] ibid, art 78.
[215] ibid, art 79.
[216] ibid, art 80.

the controller or processor for the harm endured.[217] Fines imposed by supervisory authorities for breaches of the GDPR must, in each individual case, be effective, proportionate, and dissuasive.[218] The GDPR also outlines criteria for determining the amount of the fine, including the nature, gravity, and duration of the violation, whether it was intentional or not, the categories of personal data affected by the infringement, and more. It even specifies the range of the fine, based on the GDPR Article that has been violated, which can go up to 10,000 or even 20,000 euros.[219]

Recent developments in EU digital law, among others aiming to 'contribute to the proper functioning of the internal market for intermediary services … in which fundamental rights enshrined in the Charter, including the principle of consumer protection, are effectively protected',[220] also contain procedural obligations implementing the principle of effectiveness. As underlined above, the DSA, for example, has numerous rules to guarantee respect for a person's fundamental rights in the digital sphere. In order to contribute to the effectiveness of these rights, it enshrines specific rules regarding the liability of service providers,[221] the obligation to designate a single point of contact to ease communication with national and European authorities,[222] and disclosure of information for recipients of their service.[223] It also requires providers of hosting services to 'put mechanisms in place to allow any individual or entity to notify them of the presence on their service of specific items of information that the individual or entity considers to be illegal content'.[224] It specifies that 'those mechanisms shall be easy to access and user-friendly, and shall allow for the submission of notices exclusively by electronic means'.[225] Such notices should be considered to 'give rise to actual knowledge or awareness' of the service provider, for the purposes of defining its liability.[226] The DSA even requires providers of very large online platforms, and of very large online search engines, to be subject, at their own expense and at least once a year, to independent audits to assess compliance with the many obligations it has imposed on them.[227] In addition, similarly to the EU's anti-discrimination Directives, the DSA requires Member States to lay down effective, proportionate, and dissuasive penalties.[228] It even goes as far as specifying that

> the maximum amount of fines that may be imposed for a failure to comply with an obligation laid down in this Regulation shall be 6% of the annual worldwide turnover of the provider of intermediary services concerned in the preceding financial year.[229]

[217] ibid, art 82.
[218] ibid, art 83.
[219] ibid.
[220] Regulation 2022/2065, art 1.
[221] Regulation 2022/2065, arts 4–10. See, above, s I.3.b(i) of this chapter on the DSA (I.3.b, 'The Horizontal Effects of EU Fundamental Rights Law').
[222] Regulation 2022/2065, art 11.
[223] ibid, art 14.
[224] ibid, art 16(1).
[225] ibid, art 16(2).
[226] ibid, art 16(3).
[227] ibid, art 37.
[228] ibid, art 52(3).
[229] ibid.

Rules regarding the right to lodge a complaint,[230] and compensation, are also enshrined in the DSA.[231] Given the often globalised nature of the online offences it concerns, and again to strengthen the effectiveness of combating them, it also lays down mutual assistance obligations,[232] rules on competences,[233] and mechanisms of joint investigations.[234]

This kind of 'proceduralisation' through harmonisation has also been at play for a long time now in the Area of Freedom, Security, and Justice (AFSJ). With regard to asylum seekers' fundamental rights, for instance, an EU Directive was specifically adopted 'in order to ensure a comprehensive and efficient assessment of the international protection needs of applicants'.[235] In this case, however, the objective is not solely the protection of fundamental rights. This objective is pursued in conjunction with the goal of ensuring the efficient processing of asylum applications. According to this Directive,

> every applicant should have an effective access to procedures, the opportunity to cooperate and properly communicate with the competent authorities so as to present the relevant facts of his or her case and sufficient procedural guarantees to pursue his or her case throughout all stages of the procedure.[236]

The preamble of the Directive continues by stating that

> [t]he procedure in which an application for international protection is examined should normally provide an applicant at least with: the right to stay pending a decision by the determining authority; access to the services of an interpreter for submitting his or her case if interviewed by the authorities; the opportunity to communicate with a representative of the United Nations High Commissioner for Refugees (UNHCR) and with organisations providing advice or counselling to applicants for international protection; the right to appropriate notification of a decision and of the reasons for that decision in fact and in law; the opportunity to consult a legal adviser or other counsellor; the right to be informed of his or her legal position at decisive moments in the course of the procedure, in a language which he or she understands or is reasonably supposed to understand; and, in the case of a negative decision, the right to an effective remedy before a court or a tribunal.[237]

This Directive has now been replaced by a Regulation, which should go even further in ensuring effectiveness, as it is directly applicable.[238]

[230] ibid, art 53.
[231] ibid, art 52(3).
[232] ibid, art 57.
[233] ibid, art 56.
[234] ibid, art 54.
[235] Directive 2013/32/EU of the European Parliament and of the Council of 26 June 2013 on common procedures for granting and withdrawing international protection (recast) [2013] OJ L 180/60 (Directive 2013/32/EU), recital 11. Regulation 2022/2065, art 52(3).
[236] Directive 2013/32/EU, recital 25.
[237] ibid.
[238] Regulation 2024/1348/EU of the European Parliament and of the Council of 14 May 2024 establishing a Common Procedure for International Protection in the Union and repealing Directive 2013/32/EU, OJ L, 2024/1348 (Regulation 2024/1348/EU).

The procedural rights of asylum seekers are, thus, defined within this context. As stressed by the CJEU with regard to the Common European Asylum System (CEAS), 'the EU legislature has not confined itself to establishing common substantive standards, but has also established common procedural standards'.[239] For instance, it outlines the guarantees that must be provided in terms of access to the legal process,[240] including specific assurances for minors or dependents.[241] It also specifies the information that should be conveyed to non-EU ('third-country') nationals in a language they understand,[242] as well as the right to an effective judicial remedy,[243] with the option of free legal assistance and representation when necessary.[244] These guarantees were subsequently strengthened by the CJEU, which, guided by the principle of effectiveness, interpreted them generously, notably in conjunction with the EU Charter. As we will delve into later in this discussion, the CJEU notably relied on the fact that a common procedural standard exists to justify an extensive interpretation of the procedural guarantees provided for by the EU Charter, illustrating once again the mutual reinforcement of this instrument with EU legislation.[245]

In the field of criminal law – as previously discussed in chapter one of this book – a series of EU Directives have also been adopted to harmonise procedural guarantees that protect the fundamental rights of suspects and accused individuals in criminal proceedings, as well as those of victims. In this context, the rationale diverges, as these Directives are not intended to establish procedural norms to safeguard the efficiency of another fundamental right, such as data protection, asylum rights, or the prohibition of discrimination. Instead, they represent a form of harmonisation designed to elucidate and, consequently, enhance the effectiveness of defence rights they give specific expression to. Within this context, these Directives also aim to bolster the effectiveness of procedural fundamental rights safeguarded by the EU Charter. This encompasses provisions such as the right to an effective remedy and a fair trial (Article 47), the presumption of innocence and the right of defence (Article 48), and the principles of legality and proportionality concerning criminal offences and penalties (Article 49), all of which are articulated in somewhat broad terms. As a reminder, six Directives pertaining to procedural rights for suspects and accused individuals have been enacted to specify, in detail, the guarantees flowing from these fundamental rights. These include the right to receive information,[246] the

[239] Joined Cases C-704 and C-39/21 *Staatssecretaris van Justitie en Veiligheid (Examen d'office de la rétention)* ECLI:EU:C:2022:858 [2022], para 86.

[240] Directive 2013/32/EU, art 6; Regulation 2024/1348/EU, arts 26–33.

[241] Directive 2013/32/EU, art 7; Regulation 2024/1348/EU, arts 20–23.

[242] Directive 2013/32/EU, arts 8 and 12; Regulation 2024/1348/EU, art 8.

[243] Directive 2013/32/EU, art 46; Regulation 2024/1348/EU, art 67.

[244] Directive 2013/32/EU, arts 20 and 22; Regulation 2024/1348/EU, arts 15–19.

[245] Joined Cases C-704 and C-39/21 *Staatssecretaris van Justitie en Veiligheid (Examen d'office de la rétention)* ECLI:EU:C:2022:858 [2022], para 86.

[246] Directive 2012/13/EU of the European Parliament and of the Council of 22 May 2012 on the Right to Information in Criminal Proceedings [2012] OJ L 142/1.

right to interpretation and translation,[247] the right to a lawyer,[248] the right to be presumed innocent and to be present at trial,[249] special safeguards for children who are suspects or accused in criminal proceedings,[250] and the right to legal aid.[251] The main objective of these Directives is to specify the obligations arising from these fundamental rights, and in doing so, make them more effective.

Initially, these measures were adopted with an instrumental focus, to ensure the efficient operation of a mutual recognition system to enable criminal law co-operation between Member States. Enforcing the mutual recognition of judgments requires the establishment of a shared minimum framework for safeguarding fundamental rights within criminal procedures. Over time, however, this rationale has evolved, giving rise to an independent objective aimed directly at protecting fundamental rights. Moreover, despite the fact that the measures were initially adopted to facilitate mutual recognition, their scope of application has now been extended to domestic situations, and not only those to do with co-operation between Member States.[252] This shift in scope was justified by the CJEU by the need to ensure that all judgments rendered in criminal matters by the Member States adhere to this common minimum foundation, to ensure the proper functioning of the AFSJ.[253]

Legislation of this kind that has been adopted in various fields of EU Fundamental Rights Law shows how the EU legislature has sought to strengthen the practical effectiveness of fundamental rights within national legal orders. This is a feature unique to the EU system, thanks to the possibility to harmonise rules for all Member States.

I.4.b. Effectiveness Through the CJEU's Case Law

Alongside these harmonisation measures, the principle of effectiveness also plays a pivotal role in the judicial interpretation of the obligations placed on Member States when they implement EU law. As emphasised earlier, the principle

[247] Directive 2010/64/EU of the European Parliament and of the Council of 20 October 2010 on the Right to Interpretation and Translation in Criminal Proceedings [2010] OJ L 280/1 (Directive 2010/64/EU).

[248] Directive 2013/48/EU of the European Parliament and of the Council of 22 October 2013 on the right of access to a lawyer in criminal proceedings and in European arrest warrant proceedings, and on the right to have a third party informed upon deprivation of liberty and to communicate with third persons and with consular authorities while deprived of liberty [2013] L 294/1.

[249] Directive (EU) 2016/343 of the European Parliament and of the Council of 9 March 2016 on the strengthening of certain aspects of the presumption of innocence and of the right to be present at the trial in criminal proceedings [2016] OJ L 65/1.

[250] Directive (EU) 2016/800 of the European Parliament and of the Council of 11 May 2016 on procedural safeguards for children who are suspects or accused persons in criminal proceedings [2016] OJ L 132/1.

[251] Directive (EU) 2016/1919 of the European Parliament and of the Council of 26 October 2016 on Legal Aid for Suspects and Accused Persons in Criminal proceedings and for Requested Persons in European Arrest Warrant Proceedings [2016] OJ L 297/1.

[252] Case C-646/17 *Criminal proceedings against Gianluca Moro* ECLI:EU:C:2019:489 [2019], para 36.

[253] ibid, para 35.

of effectiveness has long been enshrined in EU law and finds its roots in the international legal principle known as the '*effet utile*'. It has been construed in an expansive manner by the CJEU, which has had many ramifications, including in the field of fundamental rights.

To recall the *Rewe* formula, 'in the absence of Community rules' Member States enjoy discretion,[254] provided they respect the principles of effectiveness and equivalence. Put differently, where there are no EU harmonisation measures, Member States retain the freedom to regulate their own procedures facilitating the implementation of EU law, as long as they adhere to overarching EU law principles, including that of effectiveness. While the adoption of EU legislation is circumscribed by the principle of conferral, obligations pertaining to the enforcement of EU law, as construed by the CJEU, should be complied with by Member States in all circumstances.[255] As the principle of effectiveness is employed in a wide range of contexts, the purpose of this section is not to provide a comprehensive analysis, but to examine how it contributes to the effectiveness of the EU system for safeguarding fundamental rights.

The principle of effectiveness is traditionally described as having two facets, one negative and the other positive. Its negative aspect dictates that national provisions that do not meet the criteria of effectiveness must be set aside, or, in other words, 'eliminated'. Conversely, the positive side of the principle requires the establishment of new national procedures or remedies to ensure the successful enforcement of EU law.[256]

In the context of safeguarding fundamental rights, there has also been an extension of the principle of effectiveness found in the 'more stringent'[257] principle of effective judicial protection.[258] The latter is set out in the text of Article 47 of the EU Charter. According to the CJEU, the requirement of effectiveness indeed 'embod[ies] the general obligation on the Member States to ensure judicial protection of an individual's rights under Community law'.[259] While the exact nature of the relationship between these two principles is not entirely clear,[260] it is evident

[254] Case 33/76 *Rewe-Zentralfinanz eG and Rewe-Zentral AG v Landwirtschaftskammer für das Saarland* ECLI:EU:C:1976:188 [1976] ECR 1989, para 5.

[255] M Bonelli, 'Article 47 of the Charter, Effective Judicial Protection and the (Procedural) Autonomy of the Member States' in M Bonelli, M Eliantonio and G Gentile (eds), *Article 47 of the EU Charter and Effective Judicial Protection. Volume 1: The Court of Justice's Perspective* (Hart, 2022) 85, relying upon M Bobek, 'Why There Is No Principle of "Procedural Autonomy" of the Member States' in H-W Micklitz and B de Witte (eds), *The European Court of Justice and the Autonomy of the Member States* (Intersentia, 2011).

[256] Prechal and Widdershoven, 'Redefining the Relationship between "Rewe-Effectiveness" and Effective Judicial Protection' (n 189) 41.

[257] ibid, 39.

[258] First enshrined as a general principle in Case 222/84 *Marguerite Johnston v Chief Constable of the Royal Ulster Constabulary* ECLI:EU:C:1986:206 [1986] ECR 1651.

[259] Case C-268/06 *Impact v Minister for Agriculture and Food and Others* ECLI:EU:C:2008:223 [2008] ECR I-2483, para 47.

[260] On this issue, see among others, R Widdershoven, 'National Procedural Autonomy and General EU Law Limits' [2019] *Review of European Administrative Law* 5–34; Prechal and Widdershoven,

that both of them are invoked to fortify the effectiveness of EU law in safeguarding fundamental rights in national legal orders.[261] In the context of safeguarding individual rights, effective judicial protection as laid down in Article 47 of the EU Charter will certainly be the principle of reference,[262] even if the one of effectiveness is sometimes also referred to by the CJEU. As underlined by Matteo Bonelli, reliance on Article 47 of the EU Charter presents an advantage – the CJEU can justify its intervention where there is concern for protecting the position of individuals and their rights under EU law, rather than focusing on an instrumental interest of effectiveness.[263] Moreover, Article 47 of the EU Charter constitutes a 'more visible and highly legitimate legal basis upon which the Court can develop its standards of fundamental rights protection in relation to the right to an effective remedy'.[264] In this context, this provision is used to construe EU legislation, but also as a standard of validity of national practices. As underlined above, the CJEU has, in addition, recognised its capacity to provide a self-standing right that does not require further implementation, either at EU or national level, to apply directly in front of national judges, including in horizontal disputes.[265] According to Tobias Lock, the evolution of the case law implies that the most compelling aspect of the EU Charter now lies in its impact on remedies in national law, particularly in light of Article 47.[266] It indeed applies in all domestic proceedings dealing with EU law. This dimension is, therefore, crucial and should not be overlooked when exploring the potential of the EU Fundamental Rights system.

'Redefining the Relationship between "Rewe-Effectiveness" and Effective Judicial Protection' (n 189); and J Krommendijk, 'Is There Light on the Horizon? The Distinction between *Rewe* Effectiveness and the Principle of Effective Judicial Protection in Article 47 of the Charter after *Orizzonte*' (2016) 53 *Common Market Law Review* 1395. In a recent judgment, the Court of Justice has explicitly linked both principles, by declaring that the principle of effectiveness was enshrined in art 47 of the Charter (See Case C-289/21 *IG v Varhoven administrativen sad* ECLI:EU:C:2022:920 [2022], para 56). According to Nabil Khabirpour, in this judgment, 'the concept of effective judicial protection is an autonomous principle that undergirds the creation of a remedial framework. Although the particulars of this framework are within the autonomy of each Member States, it must be consistent with the principles of equivalence and effectiveness.': N Khabirpour, 'The Principles of Effectiveness, Effective Judicial Protection and the Rule of Law' (2023) 5 *European Human Rights Law Review* 477, 480.

[261] A caveat, however, is that the principle of effectiveness of EU law can, at times, be used to limit these fundamental rights, as discussed in s I.4.b of this chapter, 'Effectiveness through the CJEU's Case Law'.

[262] See, for instance, Case C-73/16 *Peter Puškár v Finančné riaditeľstvo Slovenskej republiky and Kriminálny úrad finančnej správy* ECLI:EU:C:2017:725 [2017], and a commentary on it by HK Ellingsen, 'Effective Judicial Protection of Individual Data Protection Rights: *Puškár*' (2018) 55 *Common Market Law Review* 1879.

[263] M Bonelli, 'Effective Judicial Protection in EU Law: An Evolving Principle of a Constitutional Nature' (2019) 12 *Review of European Administrative Law* 35, 53.

[264] S Drake, 'More Effective Private Enforcement of EU Law Post-Lisbon: Aligning Regulatory Goals and Constitutional Values' in S Drake and M Smith (eds), *New Directions in the Effective Enforcement of EU Law and Policy* (Edward Elgar Publishing, 2016) 35.

[265] Case C-414/16 *Vera Egenberger v Evangelisches Werk für Diakonie und Entwicklung e.V.* ECLI:EU:C:2018:257 [2018].

[266] T Lock, 'Why the EU Charter Matters, The Right to an Effective Remedy under Article 47' (*Verfassungsblog*, 31 October 2024), available at https://verfassungsblog.de/why-the-eu-charter-matters/.

Both the principles of 'effectiveness' and 'effective judicial protection' have been invoked in various fields of EU Fundamental Rights Law. The CJEU, indeed, frequently relies on these principles to ensure the strength of European standards within national legal systems. Following a brief and non-comprehensive overview of this case law, broader considerations will be made regarding these principles and their implications for the protection of EU Fundamental Rights.

The principles of effectiveness and effective judicial protection, for instance, play a crucial role in the case law of the CJEU in the field of asylum.[267] The CJEU has, indeed, often been required to construe EU legislation in this field in the light of the right to an effective remedy, or even review the compatibility of national legal procedures with this right. A commonly cited illustration in this framework is the *Samba Diouf* judgment, where the CJEU interpreted Directive 2005/85, the first 'Procedural Directive' in the field of asylum, which has now been replaced by an EU Regulation,[268] in light of Article 47 of the EU Charter, to enhance the remedies provided by this minimal harmonisation Directive. Although the text of the Directive did not explicitly mandate that there should be a remedy against a decision to use accelerated proceedings for international protection applications, the CJEU held that, under the principle of effective judicial protection enshrined in the EU Charter, the justification for applying such a procedure must be subject to judicial review. Similarly, the CJEU addressed a gap in the Dublin III Regulation, which did not provide for an appeal against a refusal to transfer an asylum seeker, but only against transfer decisions that had been made.[269] The CJEU indeed held that, in order to ensure the

> benefit from the effective protection of his or her rights which that regulation seeks … to establish, an unaccompanied minor applicant must be able to exercise a judicial remedy … not only where the requesting Member State adopts a transfer decision, but also where the requested Member State refuses to take charge of the person concerned.[270]

In this regard, the CJEU explicitly underscored that this interpretation is 'compelling', given that 'Article 8(2) of the Dublin III Regulation is intended to ensure full respect for the fundamental rights of unaccompanied minors, guaranteed in Articles 7 and 24 of the Charter.'[271]

[267] M Reneman, 'No Turning Back? The Empowerment of National Asylum and Migration Courts under Article 47 of the Charter' in Bonelli, Eliantonio, and Gentile, *Article 47 of the EU Charter and Effective Judicial Protection, Vol 1* (n 255) 141.

[268] Directive 2008/115/EC of the European Parliament and of the Council of 16 December 2008 on common standards and procedures in Member States for returning illegally staying third-country nationals [2005] OJ L 326/13, now replaced by Regulation 2024/1348/EU.

[269] Regulation (EU) No 604/2013 of the European Parliament and of the Council of 26 June 2013 establishing the criteria and mechanisms for determining the Member State responsible for examining an application for international protection lodged in one of the Member States by a third-country national or a stateless person (recast) [2013] OJ L180/31, art 27.

[270] Case C-19/21 *I and S v. Staatssecretaris van Justitie en Veiligheid* ECLI:EU:C:2022:605 [2022], para 45.

[271] ibid, para 46.

In the *PG* case, building upon the precedents set by the *Alheto*[272] and *Torubarov*[273] rulings, the CJEU held that – even if judges are not required to be able to directly modify administrative decisions related to international protection in order to directly grant a specific form of protection[274] – while courts are not required to directly alter administrative decisions on international protection in order to grant protection, an administrative authority is nevertheless bound by the court's assessment where a refusal decision is annulled and the applicant is found to meet the applicable criteria.[275] In such a situation, the principle of effective judicial protection requires that the administrative authority provide international protection unless new circumstances, making a fresh evaluation necessary, objectively arise. Moreover, if the national court's decision is not implemented and if national law does not empower the court to enforce its judgment, the national court should be able to amend the administrative decision and substitute it with its own. In this context, the national judge should bypass national regulations that obstruct this action, directly invoking Article 47 of the EU Charter.[276]

In the *FMS* case that was discussed earlier,[277] the CJEU took an even more decisive step. It established that, even in the absence of a specific national legal provision providing for such oversight, the principles of the primacy of EU law and the right to effective judicial protection (as guaranteed by Article 47 of the EU Charter) require that national judges assert their competence to assess the legality of the detention of an asylum seeker. To ensure the effective protection granted by EU law to non-EU nationals who are placed in detention, the CJEU thus requires national judges to *create*, *ex nihilo* – if not already present in national law – a direct avenue for judicial recourse based directly on Article 47 of the EU.[278] Always in the context of the detention of asylum seekers, the CJEU has also established that the relevant provisions of secondary law,

> read in conjunction with Articles 6 and 47 of the Charter, must be interpreted as meaning that a judicial authority's review of compliance with the conditions governing the lawfulness of the detention of a third-country national which derive from EU law must lead that authority *to raise of its own motion*, on the basis of the material in the file brought to its attention, as supplemented or clarified during the adversarial proceedings before it, any failure to comply with a condition governing lawfulness which has not been invoked by the person concerned.[279]

[272] Case C-585/16 *Serin Alheto v Zamestnik-predsedatel na Darzhavna agentsia za bezhantsite* ECLI:EU:C:2018:584 [2018].

[273] Case C-556/17 *Alekszij Torubarov v Bevándorlási és Menekültügyi Hivatal* ECLI:EU:C:2019:626 [2019], paras 68, 72, and 77.

[274] Case C-406/18 *PG v Bevándorlási és Menekültügyi Hivatal* ECLI:EU:C:2020:216 [2020].

[275] ibid, para 20.

[276] ibid, para 22.

[277] Joined Cases C-924/19 PPU and C-925/19 PPU *FMS and Others v Országos Idegenrendészeti Főigazgatóság Dél-alföldi Regionális Igazgatóság and Országos Idegenrendészeti Főigazgatóság* ECLI:EU:C:2020:367 [2020].

[278] ibid, para 290.

[279] Joined Cases C-704/20 and C-39/21 *Staatssecretaris van Justitie en Veiligheid (Examen d'office de la rétention)* ECLI:EU:C:2022:858 [2022], para 94. Emphasis added.

With regard to criminal judicial co-operation, the principles of effectiveness and effective judicial protection are also frequently used as a guiding compass. They have, notably, been regularly used by the CJEU in the framework of the implementation of the European Arrest Warrant, in order to guarantee that this mechanism is operated under judicial oversight.[280] These principles have also served to support a generous interpretation of EU Directives on procedural rights for suspects and accused persons. Numerous judgments highlight how the CJEU's teleological interpretation, driven by the quest for the '*effet utile*' of these Directives, enhances the protection of criminal procedural rights within the European area. The CJEU has, notably, enshrined the obligation for Member States to adopt 'specific measures' to implement the procedural rights Directives. With regard to the right to interpretation and translation, the CJEU moreover ruled, in the case *Criminal proceedings against IS*, that Member States must take specific measures to ensure the *quality* of the interpretation and translations provided, 'so as to guarantee, first, that the persons concerned have knowledge of the case against them and are able to exercise their right of defence and, secondly, the sound administration of justice'.[281] The CJEU thus, unsurprisingly, requires the effective and qualitative implementation, by the Member States, of the Directive.[282] It recalled in this framework that

> the information which must be communicated to any person suspected or accused of having committed a criminal act, in accordance with Article 6 of Directive 2012/13, must be provided in a language understood by that person, where necessary by means of linguistic assistance from an interpreter or by means of a written translation.[283]

According to the CJEU, this obligation should be recognised as having vertical direct effect, as it is expressed 'in a sufficiently precise and unconditional manner in order to be relied upon by an individual and applied by the national court'.[284] In order to guarantee the effectiveness of these rights, the CJEU went on to specify that, given the decisive character of the right to be informed, the fact that such linguistic assistance is not provided to a person who does not speak or understand the language of those proceedings is 'sufficient to deprive the proceedings of their fairness and to undermine the effective exercise of the rights of the defence'.[285] To ensure the effective enforcement of the Directive, the CJEU set out the specific consequences that should be acknowledged in the event of non-compliance. The CJEU further clarified that, even if the Directives protecting the right to

[280] Some authors nevertheless regret that art 47 of the Charter has not been relied upon to constrain the role of public prosecutors in surrender procedures. See, among others, Joined Cases C-508/18 and C-82/19 PPU *OG and PI* ECLI:EU:C:2019:456 [2019]; A Martufi, 'Article 47 of the Charter and the European Arrest Warrant: Chronicle of a Death Foretold?' in Bonelli, Eliantonio, and Gentile (eds), *Article 47 of the EU Charter and Effective Judicial Protection, Vol 1* (n 255) 167.

[281] Case C-564/19 *Criminal proceedings against IS* ECLI:EU:C:2021:949 [2021], paras 110–12.

[282] Directive 2010/64/EU.

[283] Case C-564/19 *Criminal proceedings against IS* ECLI:EU:C:2021:949 [2021], para 129.

[284] ibid, para 110.

[285] ibid, para 130.

information and the right to interpretation and translation in criminal proceedings do not set out detailed rules for the implementation of the rights which they lay down, the principle of effectiveness requires national implementation measures not to 'undermine the objective pursued by those directives, namely safeguarding the fairness of criminal proceedings and ensuring respect for the rights of the defence of suspects and accused persons during those proceedings'.[286] Therefore, according to the CJEU, requiring the person concerned

> to plead that he or she has not been informed of his or her rights to interpretation and translation … within a prescribed period, failing which that challenge will be time-barred, would have the effect of rendering meaningless the right to be informed … and would consequently undermine that person's rights to a fair trial, enshrined in Article 47 of the Charter, and to respect for the rights of the defence, enshrined in Article 48(2) of the Charter.[287]

Therefore, the relevant provisions of the Directives, read in the light of Articles 47 and 48(2) of the EU Charter, and the principle of effectiveness, preclude national legislation that requires the beneficiaries of the rights outlined in these Directives to raise any claims within a specific time frame,

> where that period begins to run before the person concerned has been informed, in a language which he or she speaks or understands, first, of the existence and scope of his or her right to interpretation and translation and, secondly, of the existence and content of the essential document in question and the effects thereof.[288]

It is worth noting, however, that unlike the principle established regarding the unlawful detention of asylum seekers, the CJEU has not gone so far as to establish an obligation for the criminal judge to raise, of their own motion, the breach of the duty placed on competent authorities to promptly inform suspects or individuals facing charges of their right to remain silent.[289]

The principle of effective judicial remedy has also been used to increase the protection of workers' social rights. The *X (absence de motif de résiliation) case*[290] illustrates how Article 47 of the EU Charter could support the right to fair dismissal, by deriving, from the principle of effective judicial protection, the requirement to inform the worker, in writing, of the reason(s) for his or her dismissal.[291] The case concerned a Polish law which allowed employers to terminate a fixed-term contract prematurely without providing any justification – unlike the requirements

[286] Case C-242/22 PPU *TL (Absence d'interprète et de traduction)* ECLI:EU:C:2022:611 [2022], para 77.
[287] ibid, para 79.
[288] ibid, para 89.
[289] Case C-660/21 *KB and FS (Relevé d'office dans le domaine pénal)* ECLI:EU:C:2023:498 [2023], para 49.
[290] Case C-715/20, *X (absence de motif de résiliation)* ECLI:EU:C:2024:139 [2024].
[291] On this judgment, see S Robin-Olivier, 'The Power of the Right to an Effective Remedy to Horizontalize Directives. Comment on Case C-715/20, X (Absence de motif de résiliation), 20 February 2024' (2025) 32(1) *Maastricht Journal of European and Comparative Law* 65–77.

for permanent contracts. The CJEU ruled that this practice was incompatible with Directive 1999/70, which implements the framework agreement on fixed-term work and seeks to reduce disparities between such contracts and permanent employment.[292] As the CJEU itself acknowledged, however, this Directive could not be directly invoked in a dispute between private parties, due to the absence of horizontal direct effect (see above). Nonetheless, the CJEU found a powerful ally in Article 47 of the EU Charter, which, as previously mentioned, does have such an effect. It held that the absence of a justification requirement for terminating fixed-term contracts undermines the worker's right to legal recourse – a right firmly enshrined in Article 47. Consequently, the CJEU required the national judge to set aside the national provision allowing for the dismissal without stating reasons, for fixed-term contracts, on the basis of Article 47 of the EU Charter read in conjunction with the relevant provision of the framework agreement.[293] Here, the principle of effective judicial protection, enshrined in the EU Charter, acts as a safeguard, allowing courts to overcome the fact that Directives do not have horizontal direct effect, so that they can give specific expression to fundamental EU social rights.

These illustrations demonstrate how the principle of effectiveness, and its extension – the principle of effective judicial protection – can bolster how the EU safeguards fundamental rights. As already emphasised, these two principles are closely interconnected and, in certain cases, even overlap. Yet, a crucial differentiation between these two principles lies in the fact that, while the principle of effective judicial protection is consistently invoked to bolster an individual's standing vis-à-vis public authorities, the principle of effectiveness may at times bolster rights, but can also occasionally function more as a double-edged sword. As I have already highlighted, the principle of effectiveness, much like other specific characteristics of EU law, can both support and constrain the fundamental rights of individuals. I will revisit this paradox in chapter four.[294] Nevertheless, at this stage, it is essential to underline that the 'protective' dimension of the principle of effectiveness in EU law should not be overlooked. As Armin von Bogdandy has pointed out, 'the effectiveness principle can only be grasped fully if one considers that this principle strengthens the legal subjects of the Member States and transforms them into subjects and actors of the supranational legal order'.[295]

Unsurprisingly, Article 47 of the EU Charter is increasingly referred to in the case law of the CJEU.[296] This provision has also been used to bolster

[292] Framework Agreement on Fixed-term Work concluded on 18 March 1999 annexed to Council Directive 1999/70/EC of 28 June 1999 concerning the Framework Agreement on Fixed-term work concluded by ETUC, UNICE and CEEP, [1999] OJ L 175, p 43.

[293] Case C-715/20, *X (absence de motif de résiliation)* ECLI:EU:C:2024:139 [2024], para 81.

[294] See ch 4, s II, 'A Field of Tensions and Contradictions'.

[295] A von Bogdandy, 'Founding Principles' in J Bast and A von Bogdandy (eds), *Principles of European Constitutional Law*, 2nd edn (Hart, 2011) 30.

[296] G Gentile and S Menzione, 'Searching for the Pieces of the EU Justice Puzzle: Articles 47, 48, 49 and 50 of the EU Charter of Fundamental Rights' in Bonelli, Eliantonio and Gentile, *Article 47 of the EU Charter and Effective Judicial Protection, Vol 1* (n 255) 28.

the preliminary ruling mechanism[297] – a tool that, as I will explore in detail below, greatly facilitates the infusion of EU Fundamental Rights protection into national legal frameworks.[298] Coupled with Article 19 TEU, which mandates Member States to 'provide remedies sufficient to ensure effective legal protection in the fields covered by Union law', it moreover exerts constraints on the Member States' structural decisions concerning the configuration of their national judicial systems. There is no doubt that the principle of effective judicial protection has a strong impact on national legal systems and the way the protection of fundamental rights offered by the EU penetrates them. These judgments take on particular significance in the context of the decline of the rule of law and judicial independence in several Member States of the EU, by offering, once again, a way out that is directly grounded in EU law, for judges whose work might be compromised by politically driven institutional changes that undermine their role.[299]

The principles of effectiveness and effective judicial protection undeniably strengthen the protection of fundamental rights in EU law. As previously noted, in the realm of traditional international law, states generally retain considerable discretion in the manner in which they fulfil their international obligations.[300] International law is not inherently designed to govern the consequences that should be attributed to its provisions within national legal systems or how they should come into effect. With regard to the ECHR, 'a party may satisfy Article 1 instead by ensuring, in whatever manner it chooses, that its law and practice is such that an individual's Convention rights are guaranteed'.[301] It is, nevertheless, true that principles of effectiveness and of effective remedy are also found within the realm of the ECHR. As noted by Janneke Gerards, the notion of effectiveness 'provides the Court with important guidance in interpreting the Convention and in assessing the reasonableness and acceptability of interferences with the Convention rights'.[302] The requirement of effectiveness in that context dates back to the early case *Marckx v Belgium*, by which the ECtHR established that the ECHR should be construed in an effective way so that 'it does not merely compel the State to abstain from such interference: in addition

[297] A Wallerman Ghavanini and C Rauchegger, 'Effective Judicial Protection before National Courts: Article 47 of the Charter, National Constitutional Remedies and the Preliminary Reference Procedure' in Bonelli, Eliantonio, and Gentile (eds), *Article 47 of the EU Charter and Effective Judicial Protection, Vol 1* (n 255).

[298] See s II.1 of this chapter, 'Individual Vigilance and National Judges as EU Fundamental Rights Guarantors'.

[299] On this issue, see, among others, L Pech and K Lane Scheppele, 'Illiberalism Within: Rule of Law Backsliding in the EU' (2017) 19 *Cambridge Yearbook of European Legal Studies* 3.

[300] R Jennings and A Watts (eds), *Oppenheim's International Law. Vol I: Peace*, 9th edn (Longman, 1992) 82–83.

[301] Harris, O'Boyle, and Warbrick, *Law of the European Convention on Human Rights* (n 51) 24.

[302] Gerards, *General Principles of the European Convention on Human Rights* (n 54) 5.

to this primarily negative undertaking, there may be positive obligations'.[303] In this context, the principle of effectiveness is, nevertheless, importantly balanced by another structural principle of the ECHR: the principle of subsidiarity. The latter implies that there is leeway for the contracting parties 'to regulate and restrict the exercise of Convention rights in the way they think is best suited to national views and national (legal and constitutional) traditions'.[304]

In this regard, it is evident that Article 47 of the EU Charter offers far stronger protection than its counterpart in the ECHR. Both Article 13 and Article 6 of the ECHR have a significantly narrower scope. On the one hand, Article 13 guarantees the right to an effective remedy for rights enshrined in the ECHR but does not require that remedy to be judicial in nature, unlike Article 47 of the EU Charter. On the other hand, Article 6, which ensures the right to a fair trial and judicial remedy, applies only to disputes of a civil or criminal nature. This substantive limitation does not constrain the scope of Article 47 of the EU Charter, although it does remain restricted to disputes falling within the ambit of EU law, as defined in Article 51 of the EU Charter. As previously mentioned, however, the latter limitation must be significantly qualified due to the interpretation the CJEU has given to the second paragraph of Article 19(1) TEU. As a reminder, it indeed considered that this provision requires Member States to uphold the principle of effective judicial protection 'in the areas covered by Union law'.[305] This scope is much broader than that of Article 51 of the EU Charter, resulting in the consequence that the principle of effective judicial protection, safeguarded by EU law, has the potential to benefit litigants in practically any matter. The exact scope of the second paragraph of Article 19(1) TEU, and its relationship with Article 47 of the EU Charter, still have to be further clarified by case law.

To conclude, it is apparent that the structural principles of primacy, direct effect, and effectiveness serve to fortify the fundamental rights bestowed by the EU legal order. While these principles are not foreign to international law, what distinguishes this context is the precise guidance offered by the CJEU and the EU legislature concerning the tangible implementation of EU law within national legal frameworks. In this regard, the CJEU has been remarkably creative in shaping the concrete consequences attached to these otherwise traditional principles of international law. This reinforces the broader point emphasised throughout this book: EU law, though limited in scope, can be profoundly rich in its contribution to the protection of human rights. This influential dynamic is further accentuated by the system of remedies that underpins EU Fundamental Rights Law, which I will explore further in the ensuing paragraphs.

[303] *Marckx v. Belgium* App no 6833/74 ECLI:CE:ECHR:1979:0613JUD000683374 (ECHR, 13 June 1979), para 30.

[304] Gerards, *General Principles of the European Convention on Human Rights* (n 54) 5.

[305] See ch 1, ss II–IV, and VI.

Section II – A Strong System of Judicial Remedies to Enforce EU Fundamental Rights Law

Beyond the distinctive features that underpin the potency of EU Fundamental Rights Law, its effectiveness within the common area of protection of fundamental rights is further strengthened by a comprehensive and cohesive system of judicial remedies. As highlighted by Koen Lenaerts, Kathleen Gutman, and Janek Tomasz Nowak, this aspect also sets the EU apart from other international organisations, in the framework of which 'enforceability is often far less certain'.[306] In the context of the EU, the CJEU plays a major role, which has earned it the description of 'most effective supranational judicial body in the history of the world'.[307] Along with the deepening of EU integration, the CJEU's jurisdiction has been extended to cover an increasing number of issues related to fundamental rights protection.[308]

The judicial framework of the EU operates on a dual level. While the CJEU serves as the authoritative interpreter of EU law,[309] an equally crucial role is played by national judges, who can be regarded as the natural adjudicators of EU law. In their daily responsibilities, these judges are tasked with implementing EU law, using, when necessary, the mechanism to request a preliminary ruling from the CJEU to address interpretative questions and ensure the consistent application of EU law (section II.1). Beyond this dual-level implementation system of EU law, its effective enforcement is also guaranteed by an institutional framework that enables the European Commission and the other Member States to commence legal proceedings against other Member States breaching EU law, with infringement proceedings. As 'Guardian of the Treaties', the European Commission does this regularly, including in cases on fundamental rights protection (section II.2). In urgent cases, procedures can be accelerated, and the CJEU may be able to issue interim measures.

The aim of this section is not to provide an exhaustive reproduction of all the details regarding these procedures, as that would greatly exceed the scope of this book.[310] There is, moreover, already a wealth of literature on the subject. Instead, the focus is, as in the previous section, on briefly illustrating how these tools can enhance the effectiveness of the protection of fundamental rights offered by the EU.

[306] K Lenaerts, K Gutman, and JT Nowak, *EU Procedural Law*, 2nd edn (Oxford University Press, 2023) 1.

[307] A Stone Sweet, *The Judicial Construction of Europe* (Oxford University Press, 2004) 1.

[308] V Passalacqua, 'Who Mobilizes the Court? Migrant Rights Defenders Before the Court of Justice of the EU' (2022) 15 *Law and Development Review* 381, 382.

[309] TEU, art 19.

[310] On this topic, see Muir, Garben and Govaere, *Activating Human and Fundamental Rights Before the European Courts* (n 64).

II.1. Individual Vigilance and National Judges as EU Fundamental Rights Guarantors

Individuals play a crucial role in enforcing EU law, including in the field of fundamental rights protection. In the *Van Gend en Loos* judgment, delivered in 1963, the European Court of Justice had already stated that 'the vigilance of individuals concerned to protect their rights amounts to an effective supervision' of EU law.[311] While they do not primarily exercise this supervisory role before the CJEU, they do so before national judges – the 'natural' judges of EU law – who are tasked with applying it in their daily rulings. National judges are regularly called upon to directly enforce EU law. As stressed by Sacha Prechal and Aniel Pahladsingh, 'in this setting, it is primarily the domestic courts which are responsible for protecting fundamental rights that litigants derive from EU law'.[312] Within this framework, national judges can (or sometimes must, depending on the case) seek assistance from the CJEU through the preliminary ruling procedure. This procedure also allows the CJEU to support the implementation of EU law at the national level, including to protect fundamental rights; it constitutes a cornerstone of the EU legal order and greatly contributes to the strength of EU law.

The primary raison d'être of the preliminary ruling procedure is to ensure the uniform application of EU law throughout the Member States,[313] but it also appears to constitute a genuine tool for legal challenges concerning fundamental rights violations. Indeed, as observed by Virginia Passalacqua, combined with the doctrines of primacy and direct effect, such proceedings started being used as an 'individual's infringement procedure', allowing individuals to question the compatibility of national law, notably with EU Fundamental Rights Law.[314] In this context, national judges have the ability to seek guidance from the CJEU regarding the interpretation of EU law, in order to assess the compatibility of their national provisions. Although the CJEU lacks the authority to annul national laws, it is not uncommon for national courts to set aside domestic legislation following a preliminary ruling because it prevents or undermines individuals from exercising their rights under EU law as construed by the CJEU.[315] For this procedure to be used, a case must be brought before national courts, and the answer to

[311] Case C-26/62, *NV Algemene Transport- en Expeditie Onderneming van Gend & Loos v Netherlands Inland Revenue Administration* ECLI:EU:C:1963:1 [1963] English Special Edition 1.

[312] S Prechal and A Pahladsingh, 'Urgency and Human Rights in EU Law: Procedures Before the Court of Justice of the EU' in E Rieter and K Zwaan (eds), *Urgency and human rights: the protective potential and legitimacy of interim measures* (Asser Press, 2021) 38.

[313] M Broberg, 'Preliminary References as a Means for Enforcing EU Law' in A Jakab and D Kochenov (eds), *The Enforcement of EU Law and Values: Ensuring Member States' Compliance, Vol 1* (Oxford University Press, 2017) 105.

[314] V Passalacqua, 'Legal Mobilization via Preliminary Reference: Insights from the Case of Migrant Rights' (2021) 58 *Common Market Law Review* 751, 752.

[315] C Lacchi, *Preliminary References to the Court of Justice of the European Union and Effective Judicial Protection* (Larcier Luxembourg, 2020) 60.

the question must be necessary to resolve the dispute. This mechanism cannot be invoked to seek answers to hypothetical or abstract questions.[316] Should the interpretation provided by the CJEU clash with national law, it becomes the responsibility of national authorities to implement all necessary general or specific measures to uphold compliance with EU law. As highlighted earlier, the principles of primacy and loyal co-operation specifically require judges and administrative bodies to refrain from applying any national norm conflicting with an EU law norm possessing direct effect. Furthermore, competent authorities are obliged to repeal such measures through procedures outlined in national law. In addition to being binding on the referring judge, the preliminary ruling delivered by the CJEU is endowed with an *erga omnes* effect,[317] and it is precisely because of that characteristic that this procedure becomes so powerful when it comes to the enforcement of EU law.[318] Under Article 267 of the TFEU, any national judge can make use of this mechanism. Moreover, where any such question is raised in a case pending before a court or tribunal of a Member State against whose decisions there is no judicial remedy under national law, that court or tribunal is required to bring the matter before the CJEU.

Many judgments have been delivered by the CJEU as a result of preliminary ruling requests, specifying the substance of the protection of fundamental rights provided by EU law. According to a recent study conducted by Eleni Frantziou, about 30 per cent of preliminary rulings between 2018 and 2023 had a fundamental rights dimension.[319] As a result, national rules or practices have often had to cease being implemented, to ensure compliance. A major difference that precisely distinguishes the protection offered by EU law from other international sources of protection is the existence of this procedure: indeed, a national judge can suspend proceedings to ask the CJEU about the content of the protection provided by EU law even during the initial steps of the judicial process.

The ECHR process diverges significantly, requiring individuals to exhaust domestic remedies before accessing the courtrooms of the ECtHR in Strasbourg with an individual complaint. Since the entry into force of Protocol 16, in 2018, the ECtHR can also now provide Advisory Opinions, but these opinions are not binding on states. Additionally, such requests are restricted to the highest courts and tribunals, excluding lower instances.[320] For the time being, the use of this

[316] Broberg, 'Preliminary References as a Means for Enforcing EU Law' (n 313) 101.

[317] On this issue, see G Martinico, 'Retracing Old (Scholarly) Paths: The Erga Omnes Effects of the Interpretative Preliminary Rulings' (2023) 15 (Special Issue) *European Journal of Legal Studies* 37.

[318] Broberg, 'Preliminary References as a Means for Enforcing EU Law' (n 313) 107.

[319] E Frantziou, 'Human Rights as an Example of Cooperative Federalism? A Chronology of the Use of the Preliminary Reference Procedure in Human Rights Cases between 1957 and 2023' (2023) 15 (Special Issue) *European Journal of Legal Studies* 191.

[320] On this proceeding, see J Krommendijk, 'Purposeless or promising? Advisory opinions from the European Court of Human Rights' in Muir, Garben, and Govaere, *Activating Human and Fundamental Rights Before the European Courts* (n 64); and, for a comparison with the preliminary ruling procedure, in the same edited collection, see F Ronkes Agerbeek 'Knowing whom to ask: judicial dialogue under Protocol n°16 and Article 167 TFEU considered in light of EU accession to the ECHR'.

mechanism is relatively modest: fewer than 10 opinions have been delivered at present. As the Protocol has only recently come into effect, time will reveal whether the success of this mechanism will grow.

The preliminary ruling proceeding remains a genuinely unique characteristic of the EU fundamental rights protection system. As underlined by Thomas Horsley,

> [w]hilst entirely conventional in many respects, the EU Treaty framework has nonetheless always contained some more distinctive and innovative features. … The preliminary reference procedure is …, without doubt, the EU Treaty framework's most innovative feature and an instrument of international law. In international law, states are generally held to account for infringements of their international obligations ex post. … The preliminary reference procedure in Article 267 TFEU complements this framework by providing an additional mechanism to address potential compliance issues within domestic legal orders ex ante in collaboration with the Court of Justice.[321]

This observation even leads Takis Tridimas to say that Article 267 TFEU is perhaps 'the most important provision of the Treaty' and 'a true facilitator of political change'. For him, 'it is difficult to think of another procedural provision in an international treaty that has had such an empowering effect'.[322]

When the CJEU is called upon to clarify the interpretation of EU law within this framework, it often appears that it treats the conflict submitted to it abstractly, and enters into the heart of the legal question it poses. In this context, it ultimately exercises a power of review, akin to that wielded by the constitutional courts of certain Member States.[323] According to Koen Lenaerts, it sometimes goes as far as it can 'to reach the same practical outcome as the one that would be obtained through direct invalidation of Member State law'.[324]

Over time, the procedure has been further refined. An accelerated procedure – the 'PPU' – was put in place to urgently deal with preliminary rulings where important risks for fundamental rights are at stake in the AFSJ. As EU law can effectively address such situations, particularly in fields such as judicial co-operation in criminal or family matters, and asylum and immigration, the possibility for the CJEU to intervene with minimum delay was seen as necessary to preserve fundamental rights to the greatest extent possible.[325] The PPU can only be used for questions relevant to the AFSJ. This procedure used to be activated in two main scenarios: first, where the persons in question were deprived of their liberty and the answer to the question referred would be decisive to the assessment of the legality of this

[321] T Horsley, *The Court of Justice of the European Union as an Institutional Actor: Judicial Lawmaking and its Limits* (Cambridge University Press, 2018) 114.
[322] T Tridimas, 'The preliminary ruling procedure and fundamental rights: a tale of jurisdictional supremacy' in Muir, Garben, and Govaere, *Activating Human and Fundamental Rights Before the European Courts* (n 64).
[323] ibid, 125.
[324] K Lenaerts, 'Constitutionalism and the Many Faces of Federalism' (1990) 38 *The American Journal of Comparative Law* 205, 256.
[325] TFEU, art 267.

deprivation;[326] and second, where there was a risk of serious and potentially irreparable harm to a parent/child relationship or some other psychological damage.[327] For a few years now, the scope of this procedure seems to have been broadened to AFSJ cases implying real and irreparable risks for absolute fundamental rights, such as the prohibition of inhuman and degrading treatment.[328] There are two main differences between the PPU and the ordinary preliminary procedure: only the parties, the Member State concerned, the European Commission, and the EU institutions whose acts are relevant may participate in the written procedure, and these references are dealt with by a chamber of five judges deciding on the case, before it is discussed at the weekly General Meeting (Réunion Générale) of the Court of Justice.[329]

An Expedited Procedure (PPA) has also been enshrined in Article 105 of the Rules of Procedure, according to which the President of the Court may decide to transfer the matter from the normal to the expedited procedure for the sake of urgency, including in fields outside the AFSJ. This tool may be used when the question referred is a matter of 'exceptional urgency'.[330] In contrast to the PPU, the PPA essentially consists of shortening the different steps of the normal preliminary ruling procedure without dispensing with any of them, and can be used for cases beyond that of the field of the AFSJ.[331]

The 'priority treatment' provided for in Article 53(3) of the Rules of Procedure of the Court of Justice enables the President to decide that a case should 'jump the queue' of pending cases and be given temporal priority, while its procedural handling nonetheless follows the ordinary rules.[332]

At national level, structural principles, such as of loyal co-operation, effectiveness, and effective judicial protection, may require the establishment of interim measures in urgent cases that may lead to irreparable harm.[333] For instance, the principle of effective judicial protection requires, according to the CJEU,

> that it be possible in the legal order of a Member State for interim relief to be granted until the competent court has given a ruling on whether national provisions are compatible with Union law, where the grant of such interim relief is necessary to ensure the full

[326] See, among others, Case C-168/13 PPU *Jeremy F v Premier ministre* ECLI:EU:C:2013:358 [2013].

[327] See, among others, Case C-491/10 PPU *Joseba Andoni Aguirre Zarraga v Simone Pelz* ECLI:EU:C:2010:828 [2010] ECR I-14247.

[328] See, among others, Case C–638/16 PPU *X and X v État belge* ECLI:EU:C:2017:173 [2017], para 33.

[329] Lenaerts, Gutman, and Nowak, EU Procedural Law (n 306) 750.

[330] Case C-158/21 *Puig Gordi e.a.* ECLI:EU:C:2023:57 [2023], para 27. See, on this proceeding, ibid 746–55.

[331] ibid, 749.

[332] S Iglesias Sanchez, 'Reasonable Time before EU Courts: What is at Stake? Expedited and Urgent Preliminary Rulings as a Vehicle for Fundamental Rights Protection' in Muir, Garben, and Govaere, *Activating Human and Fundamental Rights Before the European Courts* (n 64).

[333] On this topic, see K Gutman and A Kornezov, 'Interim Measures and Fundamental Rights in EU Law: Some Reflections and Possible Reforms' in Muir, Garben, and Govaere, *Activating Human and Fundamental Rights Before the European Courts* (n 64).

effectiveness of the judgment to be given on the existence of such EU law rights in the main proceedings.[334]

The form, as such, of interim relief is a matter for the Member States, provided that they respect the principles of equivalence and effectiveness.[335] Additionally, a lot of EU laws expressly provide for temporary protective measures, for example with regard to individuals seeking international protection,[336] or those subject to a return decision,[337] in order to remain on a Member State's territory during the time of contestation of the measure.

Notwithstanding the great impact of the preliminary ruling procedure on the protection of fundamental rights provided by the EU, it is worth noting that there are still numerous obstacles to the effectiveness of the vigilance that individuals can exercise. The mobilisation of EU law, whether by litigants, lawyers, or national judges, still encounters challenges such as a lack of knowledge of EU law by these stakeholders.[338] Although the preliminary ruling procedure is certainly an important tool that strengthens the enforcement of the protection of fundamental rights provided by EU law, progress can still be made to make this procedure more accessible.

II.2. Institutional Enforcement to Protect EU Fundamental Rights Protection

In addition to the individual oversight permitted through the preliminary proceeding, EU fundamental rights are also monitored from an institutional perspective.[339] The European Commission, as the Guardian of the Treaties, has a central role in this regard. Indeed, it may invoke the well-established mechanism of infringement proceedings, a supervisory mechanism in EU law that empowers the European Commission to deal with non-compliant states.[340] This power, which has existed since the very beginnings of the EU, allowed the CJEU to establish very early on that the general rule of international law that permits states to retaliate when other parties fail to comply with the same treaty

[334] Case C-432/05 *Unibet (London) Ltd and Unibet (International) Ltd v Justitiekanslern* ECLI:EU:C:2007:163 [2007] ECR I-2271, para 77.

[335] Prechal and Pahladsingh, 'Urgency and Human Rights in EU Law' (n 312) 46.

[336] Directive 2013/32/EU, art 46; Regulation (EU) No 604/2013 of the European Parliament and of the Council of 26 June 2013 establishing the criteria and mechanisms for determining the Member State responsible for examining an application for international protection lodged in one of the Member States by a third-country national or a stateless person (recast) [2013] OJ L 180/31, art 27.

[337] Directive 2008/115, art 13.

[338] One of the objectives of this book is precisely to help address this issue.

[339] On the distinction between individual and institutional enforcement, see A Tomkins, 'Of Institutions and Individuals: The Enforcement of EC Law' in P Craig and R Rawlings (eds), *Law and Administration in Europe: Essays in Honour of Carole Harlow* (Oxford University Press, 2003).

[340] TFEU, art 258.

(inadimplenti non est adimplendum) does not apply within the context of EU law.[341]

The EU Treaties also grant Member States the authority to exert this institutional oversight and to commence legal proceedings before the CJEU concerning any violations of EU law committed by their counterparts.[342] However, this mechanism has limited success, primarily due to clear diplomatic considerations.[343]

Institutional oversight complements the avenues available to individuals before their national courts. As emphasised by Albertina Albors-Llorens, 'viewed together, all these avenues have the common aim of securing the protection of EU rights against possible infringements by Member States and national authorities'.[344] This consideration is particularly relevant to safeguarding fundamental rights. This aspect represents a distinctive feature of the protection system at the EU level: institutional oversight is established, reinforcing the authority of fundamental rights protected by this legal framework.

Without delving into the intricate details of this,[345] as that is beyond the purview of this book, it is worth noting that the infringement procedure unfolds in two distinct phases. The initial administrative phase involves a discussion based on a reasoned opinion between the European Commission and the Member State concerned. During this phase, the state may seek to justify its actions, while the European Commission, in turn, endeavours to persuade the state to cease its unlawful behaviour. Should this preliminary phase prove to be unsuccessful, the European Commission has the subsequent option to initiate legal proceedings before the CJEU. The CJEU then issues a declarative decision, deliberating on whether the Member State has breached EU law or not.

As a matter of fact, the uniqueness of this tool lies not so much in the procedure itself, through which the European Commission (or another Member State) secures a declaratory judgment regarding a potential breach of EU law, as this type of decision is not uncommon in the sphere of international public law.[346] Instead, it resides in the manner of its application, coupled with the procedural intricacies associated with it. Due to this element, this proceeding is generally regarded as being very effective.[347]

[341] de Witte, 'EU Law: Is It International Law?' (n 79) 201.

[342] TFEU, art 259.

[343] A Albors-Llorens, 'Judicial Protection before the Court of Justice of the European Union' in Barnard and Peers, *European Union Law* (n 25) 289.

[344] ibid.

[345] B Smulders and L Prete, 'The Age of Maturity of Infringement Proceedings' (2021) 58 *Common Market Law Review* 285; LW Gormley, 'Infringement Proceedings' in Jakab and Kochenov (eds), *The Enforcement of EU Law and Values* (n 313); and S Andersen, *The Enforcement of EU Law: The Role of the European Commission* (Oxford University Press, 2012).

[346] Horsley, *The Court of Justice of the EU as an Institutional Actor* (n 321) 113.

[347] L Prete, 'Infringement Procedures and Sanctions under Article 260 TFEU: Evolution, Limits and Future Prospects' in S Montaldo, F Costamagna, and A Miglio (eds), *EU Law Enforcement: The Evolution of Sanctioning Powers* (Routledge, 2021) 86.

Concerning its application, it appears that the European Commission uses the leeway it has in a manner aimed at increasingly and effectively supporting the protection of fundamental rights provided by EU law. Indeed, there has been a discernible shift in its use of Article 258 TFEU in recent years, with a growing inclination to obtain judgments finding that there have been violations of fundamental rights.[348] These endeavours have been favourably received by the CJEU, granting the European Commission the authority to fulfil its role as the Guardian of the Treaties in this area.

As Matteo Bonelli aptly points out, historically the European Commission's approach within the framework of infringement actions was 'piecemeal', as it 'decided to concentrate on fairly technical questions'.[349] In the context of the decline of the rule of law witnessed in certain Member States, the European Commission indeed engaged with precise technical rules to counter certain reforms that systematically undermined the independence of the judiciary. For instance, it leveraged Directive 2000/78, which establishes a general framework for equal treatment in employment and occupation,[350] to condemn Hungary's reform lowering the retirement age for judges, a move that effectively aimed at a purge of the judiciary. The CJEU sided with the European Commission, condemning Hungary due to the discriminatory nature of this measure.[351] While this action demonstrates the potential of infringement proceedings to ensure compliance with rules harmonising the protection of fundamental rights, such as Directive 2000/78, it was nonetheless criticised for its narrow focus in the broader problematic context of the decline of the rule of law.[352]

Gradually, the European Commission embraced a more comprehensive approach to issues concerning the EU's founding values. In its 2017 Communication entitled 'EU Law: Better Results through Better Application', the European Commission had already declared its intention to adopt a more strategic stance, emphasising the need to 'focus and prioritize enforcement efforts on the most significant breaches of EU law that impact the interests of its citizens and businesses'.[353]

Over time, the CJEU has progressively and directly leaned on provisions of the EU Charter to launch infringement proceedings. The landmark *Usufruct* case marked the initial instance of this evolution, revolving around the annulment of

[348] For a general overview, see L Prete, 'Infringement actions for the protection of fundamental rights' in Muir, Garben, and Govaere, *Activating Human and Fundamental Rights Before the European Courts* (n 64).

[349] M Bonelli, 'Infringement Actions 2.0: How to Protect EU Values before the Court of Justice' (2022) 18 *European Constitutional Law Review* 30, 32.

[350] Directive 2000/78/EC (n 192).

[351] Case C-286/12 *European Commission v Hungary* ECLI:EU:C:2012:687 [2012]. See, among others, Case C-288/12 *European Commission v Hungary* ECLI:EU:C:2014:237 [2014], about the premature ending of the term of the supervisory authority for the protection of personal data.

[352] Pech and Lane Scheppele, 'Illiberalism Within: Rule of Law Backsliding in the EU' (n 299).

[353] Communication (2017/C 18/02) from the European Commission of 19 January 2017, 'EU law: Better results through better application' [2017].

usufruct rights on agricultural land in Hungary held either directly or indirectly by nationals of other Member States. In response, the European Commission filed infringement proceedings, citing violations of Article 63 TFEU, safeguarding the free movement of capital, but also Article 17 of the EU Charter, protecting the fundamental right to property.

In his Opinion, Advocate General Saugmandsgaard Øe considered that invoking an EU Charter violation should only be admissible in the context of the implementation of EU rules, rather than when merely derogating from them, as was the case here (a derogation from the free movement of capital).[354] Recalling that, '[u]nlike national constitutional courts and the ECtHR, the Court does not have a *specific mandate to penalise possible infringements of fundamental rights committed by the Member States*',[355] he considered that, in the area of fundamental rights, the CJEU's intervention should focus on the areas for which it is genuinely responsible; thus, first and foremost, 'the actions of the Union itself and of the Member States when they are implementing EU policies'.[356]

The CJEU abstained from delving into the intricacies of this question, but asserted that the measures in question contravened Article 63 TFEU (free movement of capital) in conjunction with Article 17 of the EU Charter.[357]

The *Transparency of Associations* case provided an unequivocal avenue for clarification that a violation of a provision of the EU Charter can independently form the basis for an infringement action.[358] This case revolved around a 2017 law in Hungary concerning the 'transparency of civil society organisations'. The law imposed various restrictions on the funding of associations by persons established outside Hungary. Penalties had been imposed there on registration, declaration, and disclosure obligations on certain categories of civil society organisations receiving direct or indirect foreign assistance exceeding a certain threshold, and sanctions could be imposed on organisations not complying with these obligations. The CJEU observed that, in doing that, Hungary had imposed discriminatory and unjustified restrictions on both the organisations in question and the individuals providing such assistance. These obligations violated the freedom of movement of capital as outlined in Article 63 TFEU, on the one hand, and, on the other hand, infringed Articles 7 (right to respect for private life), 8 (right to the protection of personal data), and 12 (freedom of association) of the EU Charter. The fundamental rights issue was analysed entirely independently by the CJEU, recalling that:

> [W]here a Member State argues that a measure of which it is the author and which restricts a fundamental freedom guaranteed by the FEU Treaty is justified on the basis

[354] Case C-235/17 *European Commission v Hungary* ECLI:EU:C:2018:971 [2019] Opinion of Advocate General Saugmandsgaard Øe, paras 64–112.

[355] ibid, para 111.

[356] ibid, para 110.

[357] Case C-235/17 *European Commission v Hungary* ECLI:EU:C:2018:971 [2019]. See, among others, Smulders and Prete, 'The Age of Maturity of Infringement Proceedings' (n 345) 289.

[358] Case C-78/18 *Commission v Hungary (Transparency of associations)* ECLI:EU:C:2020:476 [2020].

> of that Treaty or by an overriding reason in the public interest recognised by EU law, such a measure must be regarded as implementing Union law within the meaning of Article 51(1) of the Charter, such that it must comply with the fundamental rights enshrined in the Charter.[359]

The *CEU* case illustrates a similar dynamic, where the law imposing restrictions on foreign higher education institutions in Hungary was challenged by the European Commission. In this ruling, the CJEU established that, in addition to the violation of the free movement of services, the measures also infringed upon the right to academic freedom (Article 13 of the EU Charter), the right to education (Article 14), and the freedom to conduct a business (Article 16).[360] As underlined by Advocate General Kokott in her Opinion,

> [t]he finding of a separate breach of a fundamental right has no particular repercussions in this case, as the action for failure to fulfil obligations is already well founded on account of the infringements of the Services Directive and Article 49 TFEU. The separate examination of fundamental rights nevertheless reflects the particular significance and nature of the infringement more clearly. This holds especially if, as in this case, the alleged breach of fundamental rights goes beyond the detrimental economic effects which are already covered by a finding of infringements of the internal market rules.[361]

While these judgments demonstrate that the authority for protecting fundamental rights provided by the EU is strengthened by the existence of infringement proceedings and the European Commission's exercise of a watchdog role, they do not conclusively resolve the question of the scope of application of this protection. As has been highlighted, the typical constraints of Article 51 of the EU Charter indeed 'continue to apply in the context of an Article 258 TFEU procedure'.[362]

In the context of the ongoing decline in the rule of law within the EU for several years now, an approach has, nevertheless, been developed to circumvent this limitation, particularly concerning the fundamental right to effective judicial protection. This jurisprudence is now well known and has been extensively commented upon:[363] the European Commission and the CJEU have found

[359] ibid, para 101.

[360] Case C-66/18 *Commission v Hungary (Enseignement supérieur)* ECLI:EU:C:2020:792 [2020], para 242.

[361] Case C-66/18 *Commission v. Hungary (Enseignement supérieur)* ECLI:EU:C:2020:172 [2020] Opinion of Advocate General Kokott, para 180.

[362] Bonelli, 'Infringement Actions 2.0' (n 349) 43.

[363] See, among others, L Pech and D Kochenov, 'Respect for the Rule of Law in the Case Law of the European Court of Justice: A Casebook Overview of Key Judgments since the Portuguese Judges Case' (*SIEPS*, March 2021) 1; M Leloup, 'The Untapped Potential of the Systemic Criterion in the ECJ's Case Law on Judicial Independence' (2023) 24 *German Law Journal* 995; C Rizcallah and V Davio, 'L'article 19 Du Traité Sur l'Union Européenne: Sésame de l'Union de Droit: Analyse de La Jurisprudence Récente de La Cour de Justice de l'Union Européenne Relative à l'indépendance Des Juges Nationaux' (2020) N° 122 *Revue Trimestrielle des Droits de l'Homme* 155; C Rizcallah and V Davio, 'The Requirement That Tribunals Be Established by Law: A Valuable Principle Safeguarding the Rule of Law and the Separation of Powers in a Context of Trust' (2021) 17 *European Constitutional Law Review* 581.

a 'skeleton key' in Article 19 TEU to enable the condemnation of violations of the principle of judicial independence, outside the scope of the Charter. Indeed, according to the CJEU, the protection provided by Article 19 TEU of the principle of judicial protection applies to '"the fields covered by Union law", irrespective of whether the Member States are implementing EU law within the meaning of Article 51(1) of the EU Charter'.[364] Thanks to this innovative interpretation, the European Commission has initiated numerous infringement proceedings to safeguard the principle of independence in Member States, with a particular focus on Poland.[365]

More recently, the European Commission has also decided to initiate infringement proceedings against Hungary for alleged violations of LGBTIQ+ rights, invoking Article 2 TEU as a free-standing provision.[366] As a reminder, Article 2 TEU states that the 'Union is founded on the values of respect for human dignity, freedom, democracy, equality, the rule of law and respect for human rights, including the rights of persons belonging to minorities'. The question quickly arose as to whether the European Commission could use this provision to push the boundaries of the scope of the EU Charter, to which Article 2 TEU does not apply. Calls have been made for the European Commission to initiate infringement proceedings on this basis against certain states that have experienced, or are experiencing, an illiberal shift.[367] Doubts may nevertheless arise regarding the possible direct effect of Article 2 TEU as a stand-alone provision, due to its vagueness.[368] Despite these doubts, the European Commission finally decided to try this option. The ruling of the CJEU is eagerly anticipated.

In my view, it seems that Article 2 TEU could, in any case, only be invoked for safeguarding fundamental rights in the presence of 'systemic' issues.[369] Otherwise, it risks indirectly undermining the scope of Article 51 of the EU Charter and the principle of conferral. On the other hand, the applicability of Article 2 TEU to systemic issues could be justified by the premise that the functioning of the EU

[364] Case C-791/19 *European Commission v Republic of Poland* ECLI:EU:C:2021:596 [2021], para 53.

[365] See, among others, Case C-619/18 *European Commission v Poland (Independence of the Supreme Court)* ECLI:EU:C:2019:531 [2019]; Case C-791/19 *European Commission v Poland (Disciplinary Regime Applicable to Judges)* ECLI:EU:C:2021:596 [2021]; and Case C-204/21 *Commission v Poland (Independence and Privacy of Judges)* ECLI:EU:C:2023:442 [2023].

[366] See the details of the action that has been brought against Hungary, in the Official Journal: Case C-769/22, *Commission v Hungary*, OJ 2023/C 54/19. The case is pending at the time of writing, and the Opinion of Advocate General Ćapeta was delivered on 5 June 2025, ECLI:EU:C:2025:408.

[367] K Lane Scheppele, 'Enforcing the Basic Principles of EU Law through Systemic Infringement Procedures' in C Closa and D Kochenov (eds), *Reinforcing Rule of Law Oversight in the European Union* (Cambridge University Press, 2016).

[368] See, among others, LD Spieker, 'Beyond the Rule of Law: How the Court of Justice can Protect Conditions for Democratic Change in the Member States' in A Södersten and E Hercock, *The Rule of Law in the EU: Crisis and Solutions* (SIEPS, 2023) 83–84; and Gormley (n 345) 78.

[369] On the notion of 'systemic and particular' in EU law, see the Special Issue edited by R Gadbled and C Rizcallah in (2023) 24(6) *German Law Journal*, 'The Systemic and the Particular in European Law', available at https://www.cambridge.org/core/journals/german-law-journal/issue/8C83A91220A6192D8A3A611BA768B9FF.

hinges on the shared values among its Member States. If systemic failures were to arise in this regard, it could jeopardise the entire structure of the EU, including the principle of mutual trust among its Member States. The European Commission also seems to embrace this understanding. It stressed, in its latest annual report on the application of the EU Charter of Fundamental Rights, that it 'has continued to uphold fundamental rights through infringement proceedings', referring, for example, to the Hungarian case. According to the European Commission, the Hungarian law which discriminates against people based on their sexual orientation and gender identity 'violates in a *systematic manner* several fundamental rights'.[370] Moreover, in the words of the European Commission, due to 'the gravity of these violations, the contested provisions also violate the common values laid down in Article 2 TEU'.[371]

On the other hand, actions based on Article 2 TEU combined with other specific provisions of the Treaty or legislation protecting fundamental rights can be easily contemplated. As stressed above, the CJEU has already used this technique to come to the rescue of the independence of national judiciaries on the basis of subparagraph 2 of Article 19(1) in combination with the value of the rule of law enshrined in Article 2 TEU.[372] The literature suggests that this operationalisation could also be implemented concerning the values of democracy and the essence of fundamental rights.[373] In this regard, the European Commission also recently initiated proceedings against Poland based on the principles of democracy as enshrined in Articles 2 and 10 TEU, along with several provisions of the EU Charter. This is due to the new law in Poland regarding the State Committee for the Examination of Russian influence on the internal security of Poland between 2007 and 2022.[374]

Forthcoming judgments of the CJEU will thus offer further clarification regarding the possible invocation of Article 2 TEU, whether or not combined with other provisions to protect EU values, including fundamental rights.

While these endeavours have yielded positive effects, it is essential to acknowledge that infringement actions alone may not be exhaustive in addressing the profound constitutional crises unfolding in certain Member States.[375] Infringement proceedings can be used to address systemic deficiencies in EU

[370] Report from the Commission to the European Parliament, the Council, the European Economic and Social Committee and the Committee of the Regions, Effective Legal Protection and Access to Justice – 2023 Annual Report on the Application of the EU Charter of Fundamental Rights, Brussels, 4.12.2023, COM(2023) 786 final, 2. Emphasis added.

[371] ibid.

[372] Case C-64/16 *Associação Sindical dos Juízes Portugueses v Tribunal de Contas* ECLI:EU:C:2018:117 [2018].

[373] LD Spieker, *EU Values before the Court of Justice: Foundations, Potential, Risks*, 1st edn (Oxford University Press, 2023) 197.

[374] See Press Release (8 June 2023), 'Rule of Law: Commission launches infringement procedure against Poland for violating EU law with the new law establishing a special committee', available at https://ec.europa.eu/commission/presscorner/detail/en/ip_23_3134.

[375] Bonelli, 'Infringement Actions 2.0' (n 349) 45.

law.[376] However, it is undeniable that those related to the rule of law have a fundamentally political dimension that can hardly be resolved (only) through such actions.

On the other hand, in the fight against specific violations of fundamental rights, infringement proceedings can prove to be a powerful tool, owing in part to the procedural intricacies associated with them.[377] Firstly, the Treaty stipulates that the CJEU may impose financial sanctions in the event of non-compliance with a judgment that has been handed down. According to Article 260(1) TFEU,

> if the Court of Justice of the European Union finds that a Member State has failed to fulfil an obligation under the Treaties, the State shall be required to take the necessary measures to comply with the judgment of the Court.

If the failure nevertheless persists, Article 260(2) TFEU allows the European Commission to request that the CJEU impose penalties against a Member State that has not taken the necessary measures to comply with the judgment of the CJEU. The Lisbon Treaty has facilitated the use of such a measure by removing the requirement for a reasoned opinion preceding the European Commission's action in this matter. A state that fails to comply with a judgment of the CJEU – including in the field of fundamental rights – can, therefore, easily be condemned to financial sanctions. When the breach concerns the failure to notify the transposition of an EU Directive, Article 260(3) TFEU provides that the European Commission can directly, from its first infringement proceedings based on Article 258 TFEU, ask the CJEU to directly condemn the state to the payment of a financial sanction. The sanctions can include a lump sum to sanction the breach of EU law, and/or a penalty payment to be paid until the cessation of the violation.[378] These should be proportionate to the gravity of the infringement and the ability of the Member State to pay.[379] Secondly, the Treaty also provides for measures that can be taken in emergency situations, for instance when a breach of EU law could result in irreparable violations of fundamental rights. Article 279 TFEU enshrines that 'the Court of Justice of the European Union may in any cases before it prescribe any necessary interim measures'. The purpose of this procedure is to support the effectiveness of EU law and, in particular, of the final decision of the CJEU, avoiding a lacuna in the legal protection afforded by it.[380] The CJEU will provide for interim measures if: (i) the granting of the measure is prima facie justified in fact and in law;

[376] L Prete, 'The Systemic Criterion in the Use of Infringement Proceedings' (2023) 24 *German Law Journal* 1011.

[377] For a more in-depth analysis, see, among others, Prete, 'Infringement Procedures and Sanctions under Article 260 TFEU' (n 347).

[378] P Pohjankoski, 'Rule of Law with Leverage: Policing Structural Obligations in EU Law with the Infringement Procedure, Fines, and Set-Off' (2021) 58 *Common Market Law Review* 1341, 1354.

[379] Case C-304/02 *Commission of the European Communities v French Republic* ECLI:EU:C:2005:444 [2005] ECR I-06263, para 103.

[380] Order of the Court of the Grand Chamber of 20 November 2017 in Case C-441/17 R *Commission v Republic of Poland* ECLI:EU:C:2017:877 [2017], para 94.

(ii) there is an urgency and a threat of serious and irreparable harm; (iii) effects of the order are needed before a decision is reached in the main action.[381] Within the context of the assessment, the CJEU balances the interests involved.[382]

There are several examples of this procedure having been used in the field of safeguarding the rule of law in the Member States. For instance, through an order dated 19 October 2018, the Vice-President of the Court of Justice instructed Poland to suspend the effects of a national measure aiming to lower the retirement age of judges of the Supreme Court.[383] According to the European Commission, this measure violated the principle of judicial protection, and its implementation was capable of resulting in irreparable harm. The Vice-President found in favour of the European Commission, relying on Article 160(7) of the Rules of Procedure, which empowers the Court of Justice to grant provisional measures even before hearing the defendant party. Shortly thereafter, the President of the Court of Justice decided to apply the expedited procedure (PPA) to the case in question.[384] According to the order, the use of this procedure was justified, as

> a response from the Court within a short time is such as … to remove the uncertainties relating to fundamental questions of EU law and concerning in particular the existence of possible interference with certain fundamental rights safeguarded by EU law.[385]

The Grand Chamber simultaneously confirmed the grant of interim measures by the Vice-President.[386] It thus required Poland to suspend the application of the contested measures, take all necessary measures to ensure that the judges of the Supreme Court affected by those provisions may continue to perform their duties, refrain from adopting any measure concerning the appointment of judges to replace the judges affected by those provisions, and regularly inform the European Commission of all the measures it has adopted or plans to adopt in order to fully comply with that order.

Following a generous interpretation of Article 279 TFEU, the CJEU moreover considers that it could, based on this provision, also impose financial sanctions in the event of non-compliance with interim measures. This interpretation was first developed in the *Białowieża* case, which involved an infringement action against Poland for violating the Habitats Directive and the Birds Directive in the context

[381] Prechal and Pahladsingh, 'Urgency and Human Rights in EU Law' (n 312) 40. See also Order of the Court of 20 November 2017 in Case C-441/17 R *Commission v Republic of Poland* ECLI:EU:C:2017:877 [2018], paras 29–30.

[382] See n 381 above.

[383] Order of the Vice-President of the Court of 19 October 2018 in Case C-619/18 R *European Commission v Republic of Poland* [2019].

[384] Order of the President of the Court of 15 November 2018 in Case C-619/18 R *European Commission v Republic of Poland* ECLI:EU:C:2018:910 [2019].

[385] ibid, para 25.

[386] Order of the Court of 17 December 2018 in Case C-619/18 R *European Commission v Republic of Poland* ECLI:EU:C:2018:1021 [2019].

of environmental protection. According to the CJEU, if it hears an application for interim measures and considers

> that the circumstances of the case require additional measures to be taken in order to ensure the effectiveness of the measures requested, it has power under Article 279 TFEU, inter alia, to provide for a periodic penalty payment to be imposed on a Member State in the event that that Member State fails to comply with the interim measures ordered.[387]

The CJEU exercised this possibility in another case related to the protection of the independence of the judiciary in Poland. The European Commission initiated another action against Poland concerning additional measures undermining the independence of its judicial system, including a 'muzzle law' that explicitly prohibited any national court from reviewing compliance with EU requirements regarding an independent and impartial tribunal previously established by law. In the context of these infringement proceedings, it obtained an order imposing interim measures on Poland, including the suspension of the application of the contested measures.[388] Noting Poland's non-compliance with this order, the European Commission filed another action based on Article 279 TFEU, asking the CJEU to impose a penalty on Poland to compel compliance with the interim order.

The CJEU, sitting in Grand Chamber formation, found that Poland could not convincingly demonstrate that it had implemented the required interim measures, with the contested measures continuing to be implemented. According to the CJEU,

> in those circumstances, it appears necessary to strengthen the effectiveness of the interim measures set out in that order by providing for the imposition of a periodic penalty payment on the Republic of Poland in order to deter that Member State from delaying bringing its conduct into line with that order.[389]

In light of this, the CJEU decided to impose a periodic penalty of 1 million euros per day, until Poland complied with its obligations arising from the first order.[390] This use of Article 279 TFEU represents a noteworthy evolution, addressing certain past criticisms regarding the slowness of the procedure, which was deemed insufficient in responding to fast-moving developments.[391]

A remaining question is how to address a situation where a state adopts a confrontational stance against the EU, refusing to adhere to the CJEU's rulings and

[387] Order of the Court of the Grand Chamber of 20 November 2017 in Case C-441/17 R *European Commission v Republic of Poland* ECLI:EU:C:2017:877 [2018] para 104.

[388] Order of the Vice-President of the Court of 14 July 2021 in Case C-204/21 R *Commission v Poland (Indépendance et vie privée des juges)* ECLI:EU:C:2021:593 [2021].

[389] Order of the Vice-President of the Court of 27 October 2021 in Case C-204/21 R *Commission v Poland (Indépendance et vie privée des juges)* ECLI:EU:C:2021:878 [2021], para 57.

[390] ibid, para 64.

[391] M Dawson and E Muir, 'Individual, Institutional and Collective Vigilance in Protecting Fundamental Rights in the EU: Lessons from the Roma' (2011) 48 *Common Market Law Review* 751, 761.

to meet imposed financial sanctions. As emphasised by Piotr Bogdanowicz and Matthias Schmidt, the existing Treaties offer no recourse in such circumstances:[392] the Member State can unilaterally invoke Article 50 TEU to exit the EU.[393] Nevertheless, should the state opt to remain in the EU, the latter retains budgetary leverage to exert influence by revisiting outstanding fines.[394] This possibility also underscores a unique facet of the EU enforcement system, as demonstrated by Pekka Pohjankoski.[395] Should a Member State resist meeting financial sanctions, the European Commission possesses the authority to orchestrate recovery through a set-off against EU funds. The set-off mechanism can effectively apply between the fine amount and the payments anticipated to be disbursed to the Member State from the EU budget.

It is evident that infringement proceedings constitute a valuable instrument for upholding EU law, including fundamental rights. If the European Commission seizes this opportunity, further refinement is possible. As recently stressed by Olivier de Schutter, 'infringement proceedings should seamlessly integrate into the fundamental rights policy of the EU'.[396] The European Commission emphasised in a 2020 Communication that:

> [T]he Commission as guardian of the Treaties ensures that national legislation complies with EU law so that people can assert their rights, including their fundamental rights, and fully benefit from EU legislation. The Commission reaffirms its commitment to monitor the application of the Charter and related EU laws, strengthen its dialogue with Member States and launch infringements as appropriate where there is a breach of EU law. It will continue to closely monitor cases where a Member State is showing a systemic failure in applying the Charter when implementing EU law.[397]

Nevertheless, one might question, as Elise Muir and Mark Dawson already did in 2011, whether institutional enforcement mechanisms for safeguarding fundamental rights in the EU should be less reliant on the discretion of the European Commission, given its potential lack of political will to advance such actions.[398] Jorrit Rijpma and Apostolis Fotiadis, for instance, regretted lack of use of the infringement procedure in the field of fundamental rights violations by Member States in the context of external border management.[399] A factor of

[392] M Schmidt and P Bogdanowicz, 'The Infringement Procedure in the Rule of Law Crisis: How to Make Effective Use of Article 258 TFEU' (2018) 55 *Common Market Law Review* 1061, 1074.

[393] Pohjankoski, 'Rule of Law with Leverage' (n 378) 1356.

[394] ibid.

[395] ibid, 1358.

[396] O De Schutter, 'Infringement Proceedings as a Tool for the Enforcement of Fundamental Rights in the European Union' [2017] *Report for the Open Society Foundation* 1, 4.

[397] Communication from the Commission to the European Parliament, the Council, the European Economic and Social Committee and the Committee of the Regions, Strategy to Strengthen the Application of the Charter of Fundamental Rights in the EU, 2.12.2020, COM(2020) 711 final, 6.

[398] Dawson and Muir, 'Individual, Institutional and Collective Vigilance' (n 391) 765.

[399] J Rijpma and A Fotiadis, 'Addressing the Violation of Fundamental Rights at the External Borders of the European Union. Infringement Proceedings and Conditionality in EU Funding Instruments' (2022) 9 <https://www.greens-efa.eu/files/assets/docs/budgetconditionality_study_web_28_pages.pdf>.

explanation of this passivism is the increasing politicisation of the procedure, accompanied by the growing role of the President of the European Commission and the Secretariat General.[400] Broader political factors come into play when determining whether to initiate infringement proceedings, which may not necessarily be directly related to the actual infringement. Daniel Kelemen and Tommaso Pavone highlight the limits of this role by identifying a supranational politics of forbearance – a pattern of deliberate underenforcement of EU law resulting from the politicisation of international institutions and the competing pressures faced by executives who function both as prosecutors and as policy-makers.[401] Muir and Dawson already emphasised in this regard that it might be useful to give less weight to the Directorates General in prioritising infringement proceedings, and to leave more decision-making authority to the Legal Service of the European Commission.[402] Furthermore, an increased role could be given to the European Parliament, enabling it to request, or at least exercise political pressure on, the European Commission to initiate infringement actions in fundamental rights cases.[403] Finally, enhanced transparency during the pre-litigation phase of infringement proceedings could assist the European Commission in acquiring the required evidence regarding the presence of a breach in complex situations, such as those at the external borders of the EU.[404]

Conclusion

'Effectiveness is the very soul of legal rules' stated Pierre Pescatore in 1983.[405] Yet, this is where the weakness often lies in international law, including where it governs the protection of fundamental rights. This is precisely where the EU Fundamental Rights framework can distinguish itself from international human rights law: supported by specific features and a range of judicial procedures, its effectiveness can prove stronger than that of other legal instruments for protecting fundamental rights. That was the subject of analysis of this chapter: how these specific characteristics and the system of judicial remedies contribute added value to the EU fundamental rights system.

In this regard, this new layer of human rights protection seeks to be supreme, grounded in individual rights, and effective. Within this framework, it benefits

[400] D Kelemen and T Pavone, *Where Have the Guardians Gone? Law Enforcement and the Politics of Supranational Forbearance in the European Union* (Johns Hopkins University Press, 2023) 779–825.

[401] ibid.

[402] Dawson and Muir, 'Individual, Institutional and Collective Vigilance' (n 391) 766.

[403] ibid.

[404] Rijpma and Fotiadis, 'Addressing the Violation of Fundamental Rights at the External Borders of the EU' (n 399) 19.

[405] P Pescatore, 'The Doctrine of "Direct Effect": An Infant Disease of Community Law' [1983] *European Law Review* 155, 177.

from the CJEU's generous and unparalleled interpretation of the principles of primacy, direct effect, and effectiveness in international law.

Furthermore, its system of judicial remedies provides highly innovative tools to ensure the effectiveness of EU Fundamental Rights. With the mechanism to request preliminary rulings, national judges can request the intervention of the CJEU at the earliest stages of the case. In this procedure, the CJEU has often proved to act as a genuine guardian of EU Fundamental Rights. Moreover, the enforcement of these rights also benefits from an institutional oversight system, through the procedure of infringement proceedings. In this regard, the European Commission has explicitly expressed its intention to strengthen its monitoring of respect for fundamental rights by Member States. These words have been followed up by actual actions, with an increasing number of cases brought in connection with human rights, some of which are still pending, and which are crucial.

While these rather optimistic considerations should not be dismissed, they must not obscure the persistent and multifaceted limitations that continue to constrain the effectiveness of EU Fundamental Rights Law. The mere fact that these rights are embedded in the structural principles of direct effect, effectiveness, and primacy cannot, by itself, guarantee their consistent respect or full realisation across all Member States and policy domains. The authority of these principles, though doctrinally powerful, remains contingent upon the political, institutional, and procedural conditions in which they are applied. In practice, the constitutional promise of supremacy and self-executing rights frequently encounters the complex realities of political discretion, administrative inertia, and uneven judicial engagement within the EU's legal order.

Nonetheless, one may contend that EU law offers a comparatively enhanced degree of effectiveness when set against international human rights law, insofar as its institutional design provides judicial mechanisms capable of ensuring at least partial compliance. Yet, this relative advantage should not be overstated.

Moreover, these characteristics were never intended to expand the material or territorial scope of EU Fundamental Rights protection, which remains narrowly circumscribed within the field of application of EU law, as previously discussed in chapter one. Furthermore, the CJEU, in exercising its judicial functions, pursues a careful equilibrium between the protection of fundamental rights and the advancement of other, sometimes competing, objectives pursued by the EU, such as market integration, economic stability, and security. This structural balancing, which lies at the heart of the CJEU's constitutional adjudication, inevitably tempers the transformative potential of EU Fundamental Rights. Similarly, the institutional supervision exercised by the European Commission through infringement proceedings is itself constrained by political considerations and the variable intensity of Member State compliance. A lack of political will may thus undermine the consistent enforcement of EU Fundamental Rights Law in certain situations.

Accordingly, while the distinctive features of the EU legal order – its doctrines of primacy, direct effect, and effectiveness, as well as its system of judicial remedies – undeniably strengthen the protection of fundamental rights within the EU, they cannot, in and of themselves, transcend the structural, political, and doctrinal limits that continue to shape and delimit the scope of EU Fundamental Rights Law.

3

A Sophisticated Oversight Over Fundamental Rights

> In recent months we have seen threats to the legal and democratic fabric in some of our European states. The European Parliament and the Commission were the first to raise the alarm and played the decisive role in seeing these worrying developments brought into check.
>
> But these situations also revealed limits of our institutional arrangements. We need a better developed set of instruments – not just the alternative between the 'soft power' of political persuasion and the 'nuclear option' of article 7 of the Treaty.[1]

The EU is not an international human rights organisation. The protection of human rights is not its sole or primary mission. It has, nevertheless, become a pivotal player in this field in Europe. As explored in chapter one of this book, the EU has progressively reinforced its role in this domain, integrating fundamental rights into its very foundations. This evolution is reflected in several key developments: the recognition of fundamental rights as a core value of the EU; the elevation of the EU Charter of Fundamental Rights (EU Charter) to the same legally binding status as primary law; and the EU's active exercise of its specific competences in this field, in particular through legislative initiatives.

The unique characteristics of EU law and the jurisprudence of the Court of Justice of the European Union (CJEU) confer a particular strength on the protection and enforcement of EU Fundamental Rights within the national legal systems of the EU's Member States. Several factors contribute to their deep integration into domestic legal orders, notably the dynamic interplay between the doctrine of direct effect, the principle of primacy over national law and that of effectiveness, and the comprehensive system of judicial remedies established within the EU's legal order. This framework means that EU Fundamental Rights have a distinctive effect, allowing them to shape and influence national legal systems in ways that go beyond those of traditional human rights catalogues.

The EU also has a distinctive monitoring system and unique administrative tools to enforce fundamental rights, compared with traditional international human rights organisations.

[1] European Commission, State of the Union Address (Barroso), Speech/12/596 [2012].

I will examine that monitoring system and those tools further in this chapter. First, there is a long-established system of political oversight which has emerged alongside the elevation of the EU's founding values (section I). This political oversight reinforces the EU's judicial system of remedies. Second, and more recently, financial mechanisms have been introduced to ensure Member States' adherence to fundamental rights (section II). Finally, an independent monitoring and supervision system has also been implemented at the EU level (section III).

These systems, of course, have their flaws, and it must be clearly acknowledged that they are not sufficient on their own to ensure that Member States fully comply with their obligations flowing from EU Fundamental Rights Law. Nevertheless, it would be wrong to overlook the fact that they do offer, even if only marginally, meaningful added value to this protective framework.

Section I – Political Oversight

Although the EU does not have a direct and general competence to ensure respect for fundamental rights, the need to do so at the national level so that they function properly quickly became evident. For a long time now, the EU has been developing a system of political oversight to ensure that Member States adhere to fundamental rights. Numerous writers have already addressed and evaluated various political review mechanisms, but this matter cannot be overlooked in a discussion on the unique aspects of the EU's Fundamental Rights protection system. I will, however, keep this analysis concise and refer the reader to more comprehensive studies on the subject.

There are three distinct methods of political oversight discussed further below: *ex ante* scrutiny during a third country's accession process to the EU (section I.1); permanent monitoring mechanisms (section I.2); and political sanctions that are applied when there are serious and persistent breaches of fundamental rights by a Member State (section I.3).

I.1. Using the Accession Procedure as a Political Means to Impose EU Fundamental Rights

Membership of the EU comes with conditions that candidate countries have to meet, which are set out in Article 49 TEU and include respect for, and promotion of, the values set out in Article 2 TEU, including fundamental rights. Although the text of Article 49 TEU is compact and imprecise, a large number of legal and political documents since the 1990s have developed the conditions for accession to the EU.

In primary law, the Treaty of Amsterdam of 1999 formally established respect for fundamental rights as a prerequisite for EU membership. However, even prior to that, during the preparatory phase of the eastern enlargement, that criterion was already considered essential.

General conditions for membership were first articulated and codified six years earlier, in the conclusions of the Copenhagen European Council held on 21–22 June 1993. The aim was to provide a clear set of legal rules and criteria to frame the enlargement process. These accession conditions, initially defined in the Copenhagen setting, were later reaffirmed by the Madrid European Council in 1995.[2] Some of these 'political' conditions required that 'the candidate country has achieved stability of institutions guaranteeing democracy, the rule of law, human rights and respect for and protection of minorities'.[3] This is anchored in various requirements, including participation in the Council of Europe and, therefore, accession to the European Convention on Human Rights.[4]

In addition to developing the substantive conditions for membership, a 'pre-accession strategy' was also developed. That strategy involves a phase of monitoring and guidance during the period in which the candidate countries prepare for accession.[5] In practice, the European Commission, acting on behalf of the Council of the EU and the European Council, is responsible for vetting the candidate countries, to see whether they respect the accession conditions. It is not supposed to limit itself only to conducting a formal examination of the candidate country's legislation: it must undertake a thorough and concrete assessment of compliance with these conditions.[6] As underlined by Dimitry Kochenov, there has been an evolution in this regard: 'neighbours and future family members are no longer trusted but thoroughly checked before entering the house'.[7] In this context, 'the fulfilment of the EU accession conditions, and particularly the respect for fundamental and minority rights, thus became subject to *systematic* EU monitoring'.[8]

The accession process amounts to a probation period for the new Member States, possibly involving far-reaching reforms of their legal systems.[9] Once the negotiations have come to an end, an accession treaty encapsulating them still requires the consent of a majority of the Members of the European Parliament and

[2] Presidency Conclusions of the Madrid European Council of 15 and 16 December 1995, pt A, s III, available at https://www.europarl.europa.eu/summits/mad1_en.htm.

[3] Presidency Conclusions of the Copenhagen European Council of 21 and 22 June 1993, SN 180/1/93, available at https://www.europarl.europa.eu/summits/copenhagen/default_en.htm. For a study of these conditions, see M Cremona, 'Accession to the European Union: Membership Conditionality and Accession Criteria' (2002) 25 *Polish Yearbook of the European Union* 219–40.

[4] D Kochenov, *EU Enlargement and the Failure of Conditionality: Pre-Accession Conditionality in the Fields of Democracy and the Rule of Law* (Kluwer Law International, 2008) 38.

[5] C Hillion, 'Enlarging the European Union and Deepening Its Fundamental Rights Protection' (2013) 11 *Swedish Institute for Policy Studies* 1, 3.

[6] J-C Barbato, 'Les garanties du respect des valeurs par les Etats membres' in L Potvin-Solis (ed), *Les valeurs communes dans l'Union européenne: Onzièmes journées Jean Monnet* (Bruylant, 2014) 88.

[7] Kochenov, *EU Enlargement and the Failure of Conditionality* (n 4) 53.

[8] Hillion, 'Enlarging the European Union and Deepening Its Fundamental Rights Protection' (n 5) 3. Emphasis added.

[9] Barbato, 'Les garanties du respect des valeurs par les Etats membres' (n 6) 90.

the unanimous approval of the Council of the EU, before the EU Member States and candidate country go on to sign it.

Considering the above steps, the so-called 'Copenhagen criteria' therefore aimed to ensure in advance that new Member States share the common values on which the EU is based – in particular, fundamental rights.[10]

The fundamental rights aspect of the pre-accession process was significantly developed, however, during the 2004 'big bang' enlargement, during which there was a drive to improve the rule of law.[11] Chapter 23 on 'Judiciary and Fundamental Rights' was added to the list of negotiated chapters. As Hillion points out, this development stems from the fact that respect for fundamental rights is no longer merely a 'negative' condition for eligibility, but has become an integral part of the EU acquis that the candidate state must demonstrate it has positively integrated into its legal order.[12] Moreover, in 2011, the European Commission emphasised that it would develop a new strategy where issues related to the judiciary and fundamental rights should be tackled early in the accession process.[13] From 2012, Chapter 23 was, therefore, considered at the very beginning of the accession process, as well as at the end.[14] The EU may even choose to halt the entire accession negotiation process if issues occur with Chapter 23, because of its critical role in the comprehensive implementation of the acquis.[15] Fundamental rights requirements are also present in other chapters, notably the ones on 'Social Policy and Employment' (Chapter 19) and 'Justice, Freedom and Security' (Chapter 24). Since 2018, issues related to fundamental rights and, in particular, Chapters 23 and 24 have been included in Cluster no 1, 'the fundamentals of the accession process'. Negotiations on the fundamentals open first and close last, and the progress under this first cluster determines the overall pace of negotiations.

Financial assistance is, furthermore, provided to support states in their pre-accession process, through the Instruments for Pre-Accession Assistance (IPA). The programme, established for the 2021–27 period,[16] covers Albania, Bosnia and Herzegovina, Iceland, Kosovo, Montenegro, North Macedonia, Serbia, and Turkey, with the overarching goal of helping 'Instrument for Pre-accession Assistance III' beneficiaries to align with EU rules, standards, policies, and practices in

[10] B de Witte, 'The Relative Autonomy of the European Union's Fundamental Rights Regime' (2019) *Nordic Journal of International Law* 65, 82.

[11] Hillion, 'Enlarging the European Union and Deepening Its Fundamental Rights Protection' (n 5) 3.

[12] ibid.

[13] Communication from the European Commission to the European Parliament and the Council, Enlargement Strategy and Main Challenges 2011–2012, COM(2011) 666 final, 12.10.2011, p 5. On this approach, see Hillion, 'Enlarging the European Union and Deepening Its Fundamental Rights Protection' (n 5) 6.

[14] M Coli, 'The Values of the European Union as Legal Rules' (PhD defended at the University of Maastricht, 2024) 370.

[15] ibid, 7. See, for instance, Council of the European Union, 2012, General EU Position, Ministerial meeting opening the Intergovernmental Conference on the Accession of Montenegro to the European Union, 23/1. Brussels, 29 June 2012, para 25.

[16] Regulation (EU) 2021/1529 of the European Parliament and of the Council of 15 September 2021 establishing the Instrument for Pre-Accession assistance (IPA III), OJ L 330, 20.9.2021, pp 1–26.

preparation for their future accession. In this context, it sets specific objectives, including strengthening compliance with the values enshrined in Article 2 TEU, with a particular emphasis on human rights. The total budget allocated for this programme amounts to over 14.1 billion euros. The European Commission also announced that it would open up Rule of Law Reports to accession countries,[17] as an additional process of oversight.

Such preventive control, which requires prior alignment with fundamental rights standards,[18] has undoubtedly contributed to strengthening their protection across Europe. However, this mechanism alone cannot reliably ensure that Member States will continue to meet their fundamental rights obligations once they have joined the EU.

Firstly, the scope of the conditions is limited in time: they only apply during the pre-accession phase. There is, in fact, no equivalent system of oversight that continues after accession. Given the persistence – and, in some cases, resurgence – of human rights issues in an increasing number of Member States, there have been growing calls for the establishment of a 'Copenhagen Commission' to maintain ongoing monitoring.[19] As it stands, the safeguard offered by Article 49 of the TEU merely ensures compliance with the EU's founding values *at the time of accession*. It does not guarantee that the progress achieved in these areas will be sustained once a candidate country has become a Member State.[20]

Secondly, the effectiveness of the guarantee provided by pre-accession monitoring has itself been called into question. This criticism emerged notably in relation to the 2004[21] and 2007[22] enlargements. Kochenov, for instance, described the monitoring of compliance with democratic values and the rule of law during these accession procedures as a 'resounding failure'. He highlighted serious shortcomings in the European Commission's approach, particularly due to the complete lack of clarity regarding the applicable standards in this field.[23] The limitations of pre-accession monitoring were further illustrated by the establishment of a 'Cooperation and Verification Mechanism' for two new Member States – Bulgaria and Romania – owing to persistent issues, especially in the area of justice, at the time of their accession. The ongoing shortcomings in terms of respect for the rule of law, democracy, and human rights did not prevent them being accepted for accession. In 2023, the European Commission formally decided to close the

[17] European Commission, State of the Union Address (von der Leyen), SPEECH/23/4426 [2023].

[18] On the practice of assessing human rights, see M Möstl and others, 'EU practices on measuring human rights', in J Wouters and others *The European Union and Human Rights: Law and Policy* (Oxford University Press, 2020) 523–40.

[19] See, among others, J-W Müller, 'Should the EU Protect Democracy and the Rule of Law inside Member States?' (2015) 21 *European Law Journal* 141.

[20] On this issue, see 'Editorial Comments: Fundamental Rights and EU Membership: Do as I Say, Not as I Do!' (2012) 49 *Common Market Law Review* 481–488.

[21] 10 new Member States joined in 2004: Cyprus, Czechia, Estonia, Hungary, Latvia, Lithuania, Malta, Poland, Slovakia, and Slovenia.

[22] Romania and Bulgaria joined in 2007.

[23] Kochenov, *EU Enlargement and the Failure of Conditionality* (n 4) 300.

Cooperation and Verification Mechanism for Bulgaria and Romania, after 16 years of transitional monitoring.

Despite the weakness of the accession process, the CJEU reinforced the legal impact of Article 49 TEU by considering that it enshrines a 'standstill clause', implying the prohibition of regression in the respect of the accession conditions laid down in this provision.[24] According to the CJEU, the Member States are

> required to ensure that, in the light of [the value of the rule of law], any regression of their laws on the organisation of justice is prevented, by refraining from adopting rules which would undermine the independence of the judiciary.[25]

It considered that 'compliance by a Member State with the values enshrined in Article 2 TEU is a condition for the enjoyment of all of the rights deriving from the application of the Treaties to that Member State', and that

> a member State cannot therefore amend its legislation in such a way as to bring about a reduction in the protection of the value of the rule of law, a value which is given concrete expression by, inter alia, Article 19 TEU.[26]

The CJEU has not explicitly addressed the same issue in relation to the protection of fundamental rights, but it appears reasonable to infer that a similar conclusion would apply to all the values specified in Article 2 of the TEU.

I.2. Permanent Political Oversight of Respect for Fundamental Rights

As already underlined, the EU does not, per se, establish permanent monitoring of a Member State's post-accession respect for values, including fundamental rights. However, there are various political mechanisms through which the EU monitors the respect for fundamental rights by its Member States, with varying degrees of rigour and comprehensiveness. These mechanisms have been extensively studied, especially in light of the ongoing 'values crisis' faced by the EU.[27] I will, therefore, limit myself to a concise analysis of the role played by the EU's 'institutional triangle', comprising (a) the European Parliament; (b) the Council of the European Union; and (c) the European Commission. While most of these mechanisms fall under the umbrella of soft governance, they nonetheless play a crucial role in the enforcement of both political ('hard') sanctions and financial penalties, which will be explored later in this chapter. Additionally, they maintain a strong connection

[24] C-896/19 *Repubblika v Il-Prim Ministru*, ECLI:EU:C:2021:311 [2021].

[25] Kochenov, *EU Enlargement and the Failure of Conditionality* (n 4) 64.

[26] ibid, 63.

[27] See, among others, M Dawson, *The Governance of EU Fundamental Rights* (Cambridge University Press, 2017); C Closa and D Kochenov (eds), *Reinforcing Rule of Law Oversight in the European Union* (Cambridge University Press, 2016); and A Jakab and D Kochenov (eds), *The Enforcement of EU Law and Values* (Oxford University Press, 2017).

with judicial sanctions, as discussed in chapter two. Indeed, when the European Commission decides to initiate infringement proceedings, or when the CJEU finds a Member State in breach of EU law, this often follows numerous red flags raised by political soft-law instruments. Despite their seemingly low normative strength, these instruments prove highly effective in facilitating the implementation of hard-law sanctions, particularly judicial ones. Similarly, financial sanctions can only be considered after warning signals have been issued through these political dialogue mechanisms.

I.2.a. The European Parliament's Oversight

Described as the 'white knight' of human rights in Europe, the European Parliament has long served as a key defender of fundamental rights on the European stage.[28] This commitment is reflected in various ways, in particular through the actions of the Committee on Civil Liberties, Justice and Home Affairs and its working monitoring group on Democracy, Rule of Law and Fundamental Rights (DRFMG). Additionally, in its role as co-legislator, the European Parliament has expressed its commitment to comply with the requirements flowing from the EU Charter in its legislative processes.[29]

While the European Parliament does not have a direct mandate to politically oversee Member States' compliance with fundamental rights, it actively exercises political oversight through its powers and competences. This oversight includes adopting resolutions, recommendations, and reports, in addition to its legislative activities. Through these resolutions, the European Parliament seeks to promote the respect of fundamental rights within the EU[30] and to draw attention to potential violations occurring in certain Member States.[31] Although European Parliament resolutions are not legally binding, they play a certain role in raising political awareness, and can even be referenced in legal proceedings. Courts – both national and European – can consider these resolutions as supporting evidence in disputes.

[28] R Tinière and C Vial, *Droit de l'Union européenne des droits fondamentaux* (Bruylant, 2023) 187; and R Tinière, 'Le Parlement européen et la protection des droits fondamentaux ou le chevalier blanc des droits de l'homme à l'épreuve de la réalité' in T Marguery, S Platon, and H van Eijken, *Les élections européennes, 40 ans après: bilan, enjeux et perspectives* (Bruylant, 2020) 69–84.

[29] European Parliament Resolution of 15 March 2007 on compliance with the Charter of Fundamental Rights in the European Commission's legislative proposals: methodology for systematic and rigorous monitoring (2005/2169(INI)).

[30] See, for instance, European Parliament Resolution of 14 February 2019 on the right to peaceful protest and the proportionate use of force (2019/2569(RSP)), OJ C 449, 23.12.2020, pp 139–41.

[31] See, for instance, European Parliament Resolution of 26 November 2020 on the de facto ban on the right to abortion in Poland (2020/2876(RSP)), OJ C 425, 20.10.2021, pp 147–54; and European Parliament Resolution of 8 July 2021 on breaches of EU law and of the rights of LGBTIQ citizens in Hungary as a result of the legal changes adopted by the Hungarian Parliament (2021/2780(RSP)), OJ C 99, 1.3.2022, pp 218–25.

Additionally, these political instruments contribute to broader mechanisms such as Article 7 TEU, which allows for measures against Member States that threaten EU values, as well as the activation of financial sanctions at the EU level. In this context, in recent years the European Parliament has, notably, triggered the Article 7 TEU procedure against Hungary, calling on the Council of the EU to assess whether Hungary represents a serious risk of breaching the EU's founding principles[32] (on this, see more below). However, as noted by Ramona Coman, the question of the protection of values sparked deep divisions among EU parliamentary groups. Some argue that the protection of the values of the rule of law, human rights, and democracy should remain anchored at the national level, while others advocate for a stronger 'EU Polity' framework.[33]

Despite these divisions, the European Parliament has called for the establishment of a mechanism independent from political influence to monitor respect for fundamental rights, democracy, and the rule of law in Member States. In 2016, it adopted a resolution urging the European Commission to launch a legislative initiative to create an EU mechanism on democracy, the rule of law, and fundamental rights (DRF).[34] Regarding the legal basis for such a mechanism, several options have been suggested, such as the use of an interinstitutional agreement under Article 295 TFEU, or the use of Article 352 TFEU, which was the legal basis used to establish the Fundamental Rights Agency (FRA).[35] The European Commission has not formally followed up on the proposal with a legislative initiative.

In addition, the European Parliament has the power to receive and examine petitions from EU citizens, which may concern alleged violations of fundamental rights within Member States.[36] This participatory mechanism allows individuals to bring attention to systemic issues on the ground, offering the European Parliament a unique grass-roots perspective that can complement formal monitoring and enforcement procedures. While it does not have binding force, the petitions process can serve as a valuable early-warning tool.

The European Parliament can also join infringement proceedings initiated by the European Commission, a power it has exercised on multiple occasions in cases related to the protection of fundamental rights. For instance, the Committee on Legal Affairs (JURI) voted in favour of the European Parliament

[32] European Parliament Resolution of 12 September 2018 on a proposal calling on the Council of the European Union to determine, pursuant to Article 7(1) of the Treaty on European Union, the existence of a clear risk of a serious breach by Hungary of the values on which the EU is founded (2017/2131(INL)), OJ C 433, 23.12.2019, pp 66–85.

[33] R Coman, *The Politics of the Rule of Law in the EU Polity* (Palgrave Macmillan, 2023) 165.

[34] European Parliament Resolution of 25 October 2016 with recommendations to the European Commission on the establishment of an EU mechanism on democracy, the rule of law and fundamental rights (2015/2254(INL)).

[35] European Added Value Assessment accompanying the legislative initiative report: An EU mechanism on democracy, the rule of law and fundamental rights, 2016, PE 579.328.

[36] TFEU, art 227 and Charter of Fundamental Rights, art 44; see Rules of Procedure of the European Parliament, 2024–2029, 232–36.

joining the European Commission's infringement procedure against Hungary's so-called 'child protection law', citing, among other concerns, a violation of Article 2 TEU. Furthermore, the European Parliament decided to take legal action against the European Commission's decision to release funds to Hungary, challenging the suspension of financial sanctions linked to the rule-of-law conditionality mechanism. This move highlights the European Parliament's commitment to upholding fundamental rights and ensuring compliance with EU legal standards.

Although the European Parliament's primary role is not to oversee the enforcement of fundamental rights, it has undeniably positioned itself as a defender of these rights in recent years. However, this stance is inherently dependent on the composition of its elected members. As a result, there is no guarantee that the institution will continue to uphold this position in the future.

I.2.b. The European Commission's Oversight

As Guardian of the Treaties, the European Commission has developed several political tools to monitor and ensure Member States' adherence to EU fundamental rights, which it can use in addition to the infringement procedure.[37] Various tools are available, and the aim here is not to provide a detailed, exhaustive analysis, but rather to highlight the most significant ones. Key continuous monitoring mechanisms include: (i) the Annual Report on the application of the Charter of Fundamental Rights and the new strategy to strengthen the application of the Charter in the EU; (ii) the EU Justice Scoreboard; and (iii) the more recently established Rule of Law Report.

In addition to these tools, we should also recall that Member States are under a legal obligation to report to the European Commission on the implementation of EU Directives within their national legal systems. This reporting typically includes information on transposition measures, practical application, and compliance with the objectives of Directives. This obligation, which also applies in relation to harmonisation measures in the field of fundamental rights protection, enables the European Commission to assess whether Member States have correctly and fully implemented the Directives, and to take further steps – such as infringement procedures – if necessary.

I.2.b (i) The Annual Report on the Application of the Charter

Since 2010, the European Commission has been publishing an Annual Report on the application of the Charter of Fundamental Rights within the EU. In 2020, the European Commission additionally adopted a new strategy, with three pillars directly aiming to contribute to the effective application of the EU Charter within

[37] See ch 2, s II.2, 'Institutional Enforcement to Protect EU Fundamental Rights Protection'.

Member States.[38] The first pillar aims to strengthen respect for this instrument by the states, primarily through dialogue with national authorities. The second pillar aims to empower civil society and ensure that Member States have fully operational national human rights institutions. Finally, the third pillar focuses on raising awareness among European citizens about the EU Charter, to enhance its recognition and understanding within Member States. In view of this, the European Commission encourages Member States to also develop their own initiatives to promote awareness. Since the 2020 Strategy to enhance the application of the EU Charter, the Annual Report has, moreover, concentrated on various strategically significant areas governed by EU law. These reports offer an overview of both the progress made and the challenges encountered within each selected policy area. The 2021 Annual Report focused on fundamental rights in the digital age,[39] while the 2023 Annual Report was dedicated to effective legal protection and access to justice as prerequisites for enjoying fundamental rights.[40] The 2024 Annual Report focused on EU funding directed towards promoting, protecting, and enforcing fundamental rights across the EU.[41]

Although this process is classified as soft law, it holds the potential to enhance fundamental rights protection within Member States. By fostering dialogue between the Member States and the European Commission, it helps in preventing or addressing violations. Though its impact may be constrained if a Member State directly challenges the EU's core values, it remains a valuable reference for political and judicial actors alike.

I.2.b (ii) The EU Justice Scoreboard

Since 2012, the European Commission has also been publishing the Annual EU Justice Scoreboard. This soft-law instrument is sectoral, as it focuses exclusively on the fundamental right to effective judicial protection. It involves conducting a yearly comparative analysis of the quality, independence, and efficiency of judicial systems across Europe, using various indicators, as part of the European Semester. Originally designed to counteract 'the negative growth spiral' following the 2008

[38] Communication 2.12.2020 from the Commission to the European Parliament, the Council, the European Economic and Social Committee and the Committee of the Regions Strategy to strengthen the application of the Charter of Fundamental Rights in the EU, COM/2020/711 final.

[39] Report from the European Commission to the European Parliament, the Council of the EU, the European Economic and Social Committee and the Committee of the Regions Protecting Fundamental Rights in the Digital Age – 2021 Annual Report on the Application of the EU Charter of Fundamental Rights, COM/2021/819 final, 10.12.2021.

[40] Report from the European Commission to the European Parliament, the Council of the EU, the European Economic and Social Committee and the Committee of the Regions Effective legal protection and access to justice 2023 – Annual report on the application of the EU Charter of Fundamental Rights, COM/2023/786 final, 4.12.2023.

[41] Report from the European Commission to the European Parliament, the Council of the EU, the European Economic and Social Committee and the Committee of the Regions Funding to promote, protect and enforce fundamental rights – 2024 Annual Report on the application of the EU Charter of Fundamental Rights COM/2024/456 final.

economic and financial crisis,[42] it is now also used to monitor compliance with the right to a fair trial in the context of the rule of law's decline. In the same vein, it initially only analysed justice in civil matters, but has since expanded to include Member States' judicial systems in criminal matters.

Similarly to the report on the Charter, even though it is a non-binding instrument, the EU Justice Scoreboard has the potential to contribute to the protection of the right to a fair trial in the Member States. As underlined by Adriani Dori,

> since the Commission is dealing with policy areas that are closely linked to Member States' sovereignty instead of advancing a supranational harmonisation, it is using alternative and soft methods, such as the soft coordination of domestic policies, evaluation and benchmarking, exchange of good practices, mutual learning processes, peer pressure etc.[43]

Although this instrument can be useful, caution must be exercised in its use: the indicator-based approach is probably not the most suitable for monitoring the rule of law and human rights. As demonstrated by Kim Lane Scheppele, such an approach may fail to capture the most systemic breaches of the rule of law because it analyses criteria in isolation rather than taking a holistic view of the situation.[44]

1.2.b (iii) The Annual Rule of Law Report

Alongside the report on the EU Charter of Fundamental Rights and the EU Justice Scoreboard, the European Commission introduced the Annual Rule of Law Report in 2020. Against the backdrop of ongoing rule-of-law challenges in recent years, it sought to develop a more holistic tool aimed at preventing violations and promoting respect for the rule of law within Member States and – as of 2024 – also in candidate countries. It aims at inclusivity by fostering dialogue between the European Commission and a wide array of stakeholders, including governmental and non-governmental entities. The report focuses on four key pillars, two of which directly address the protection of fundamental rights: national judicial systems and media pluralism and freedom. These are complemented by anti-corruption frameworks and institutional issues related to the balance of powers.

The Rule of Law Report follows a specific methodology.[45] Each autumn, Member States participate in consultations via detailed questionnaires. Through a

[42] A Jakab and L Kirchmair, 'How to Develop the EU Justice Scoreboard into a Rule of Law Index: Using an Existing Tool in the EU Rule of Law Crisis in a More Efficient Way' (2021) 22(6) *German Law Journal* 936, 937.

[43] A Dori, 'The EU Justice Scoreboard – Judicial Evaluation as a New Governance Tool' (2015) Max Planck Institute Luxembourg, Working Paper Series, no 2, 23.

[44] K Lane Scheppele, 'The Rule of Law and the Frankenstate: Why Governance Checklists Do Not Work' (2013) 26(4) Governance 559–62.

[45] European Commission, '2023 Rule of law report – methodology', 5 July 2023, available at https://commission.europa.eu/document/72ff8a72-5d69-49ba-8cb6-4300859ee175_en.

'network of national contact points for the rule of law', a communication channel is maintained to develop the report and share best practices. In spring, Member States, along with public and private stakeholders, submit contributions to the European Commission. The European Commission facilitated over 530 meetings for the 2023 Rule of Law Report, both online and in person, to engage with these stakeholders. In Belgium, the participants included three supreme courts, the High Council of Justice, the Belgian League of Human Rights, the Federal Institute for the Protection and Promotion of Human Rights, the three Flemish bar associations, and others. By early summer, Member States receive draft chapters for review and updating.

Published in July, the Report is discussed within EU institutions and at the national level. It includes a communication outlining the overall EU situation and 27 chapters (one per Member State) detailing country-specific developments since the previous report. The Report evaluates progress on previous recommendations, with the 2023 edition noting progress in 65 per cent of cases.

The Report's standout feature is its thorough coverage of all Member States. Although it lacks a direct sanctioning mechanism, it has proved to be highly valuable. First, it offers a comprehensive overview of the progress and challenges faced by each Member State in the four key areas related to the rule of law. Second, it can serve as a crucial reference for other political or judicial sanction processes.

I.2.c. The Council of the EU's Oversight of Respect of Fundamental Rights by the Member States

As Mark Dawson already pointed out several years ago, the Council of the EU was the last of the three political institutions to fully integrate the protection of fundamental rights into its agenda.[46] It was within the development of the Area of Freedom, Security, and Justice (AFSJ) that the Council began to explicitly acknowledge its concern for this issue and its commitment to ensuring the protection of human rights, particularly in the context of its legislative action.[47]

Regarding the monitoring of fundamental rights compliance within Member States, the Council of the EU, unsurprisingly, favours peer-review mechanisms

[46] Dawson, The Governance of EU Fundamental Rights (n 27) 110.

[47] See Presidency Conclusions of the Helsinki European Council, 11 and 12 December 2009, inviting the EU institutions to ensure that legal initiatives respect the EU Charter, and the following establishment by the Council of the EU of a permanent Working Party on Fundamental Rights and Citizenship (FREMP) in charge of fundamental rights, citizenship of the Union, and free movement of persons, which was institutionalised and made permanent by the Council. On this topic, see O de Schutter, 'The Implementation of the Charter by the Institutions of the European Union', CRIDHO Working Paper 2013/1.

and internal monitoring over the adoption of hard-law sanctioning tools.[48] In this spirit, it introduced the Annual Rule of Law Dialogue in 2014, in response to the rule of law crisis.[49] This initiative established a peer-review and soft-law co-ordination process in which Member States engage in discussions on an equal footing, aiming to promote and safeguard the rule of law through dialogue among all Member States. Predictably, the effectiveness of this mechanism remains limited, particularly due to rule-of-law backsliding in certain Member States, which hinders genuine co-operation in good faith in this field. Against that background, the Rule of Law Dialogue was described as a 'façade action', in terms of outcomes.[50] This observation also highlights the shortcomings of intergovernmentalism in protecting fundamental values[51] – shortcomings that are well known, particularly given the ineffectiveness of the Article 7 TEU procedure, which I will discuss below.[52] A more optimistic perspective, however, may see this mechanism as an additional avenue through which Member States can, in certain cases, benefit from their peers' advice to strengthen legal safeguards – including fundamental rights – within their own systems.[53] Nevertheless, it would be difficult to consider it a truly effective tool for ensuring genuine oversight of human rights compliance across the EU. While such positive effects may occur in practice, they rely on the concerned Member State's systemic adherence to rule-of-law principles and fundamental rights.

I.3. Political Sanctions in Case of Serious and Persistent Breach of Fundamental Rights

As I have reiterated on several occasions, there is currently no permanent overarching political mechanism in EU law to monitor compliance with Article 2 TEU values, nor is there any provision allowing for the exclusion of a Member State from the EU in cases of systemic disrespect, even on a temporary basis.[54] However, there is a specific political sanction mechanism to enforce the EU's founding values, outlined in the well-known Article 7 TEU. The objective of this mechanism is to prevent or halt serious and persistent violations of the values enshrined in Article 2 of the TEU, including the protection of fundamental rights.

[48] Dawson, The Governance of EU Fundamental Rights (n 27) 108.

[49] Council of the European Union, 'Ensuring Respect for the Rule of Law in the EU', 15206/14, 14 November 2014, p 12.

[50] Coman, *The Politics of the Rule of Law in the EU Polity* (n 33) 184.

[51] B Lobina, 'Beating a Dead Horse: Is There Any Value in the Council's Annual Rule of Law Dialogue?' (*Verfassungsblog*, 7 December 2023), https://verfassungsblog.de/beating-a-dead-horse/.

[52] On these dynamics, see, among others, the insightful and meticulous analysis of Coman, *The Politics of the Rule of Law in the EU Polity* (n 33) 171– 195.

[53] Dawson, *The Governance of EU Fundamental Rights* (n 27) 110.

[54] Contrary to the provision of art 8 of the Statute of the Council of Europe, which allows for such an exclusion.

Its application is thus intended not for isolated breaches of values or fundamental rights, but for systemic violations by a Member State. Many texts have already been dedicated to this provision, most of which acknowledge the weaknesses of this mechanism.[55] I will briefly recall its main features here.

Article 7 TEU, which originated from Article F.1. of the Treaty of Amsterdam,[56] establishes two mechanisms to prevent or sanction the existence of a 'serious and persistent breach' of the EU founding values by a Member State. Article 7(1) TEU establishes a so-called 'preventive' procedure, which allows the Council of the EU, acting by a majority of four-fifths of its members, to determine, based on a reasoned proposal from one-third of the Member States, the European Parliament, or the European Commission, the existence of a clear risk of a serious breach by a Member State of the values referred to in Article 2 TEU. Article 7(2) TEU sets out a 'remedial' procedure, which allows the Council of the EU to establish, by unanimity,[57] the existence of a serious and persistent breach by a Member State of the values laid down in Article 2. Once this determination has been made, the Council may then impose sanctions, which could consist of suspending certain political rights of a Member State. Both the preventive and remedial procedures are political tools, as Article 7 TEU grants the Council of the EU a discretionary power to assess whether there is (a clear risk of) a serious and persistent breach of Article 2 values in the Member State concerned.

The use of this mechanism should, thus, not be envisaged as a reaction to an individual case of the founding values being breached, but rather when the problem acquires a systemic dimension. Such a systemic problem may, nonetheless, appear in any policy area. Unlike the EU Charter, Article 7 TEU does not contain a clause limiting its scope of application to the actions of Member States 'implementing' EU law.[58] The mechanism enshrined in Article 7 TEU can thus be exercised in the event of a breach of common values, either in areas governed by EU law or in areas of competences reserved to the Member States.[59]

While Article 7 TEU is, theoretically, the EU's ultimate sanction mechanism for breaches of its common values, its practical impact has proven largely illusory. The highly demanding procedural thresholds that govern both its preventive and remedial arms render any concrete outcome unlikely. This is

[55] See, among others, Coman, *The Politics of the Rule of Law* (n 33) 184–93; and D Kochenov, 'Article 7: A Commentary on a Much Talked-About "Dead" Provision' in A von Bogdandy, P Bogdanowicz, I Canor et al (eds), *Defending Checks and Balances in EU Member States* (Springer, 2021) 127–55.

[56] At the time of the Amsterdam Treaty, only the remedial aspect was enshrined. The preventive aspect was inserted by the Treaty of Nice.

[57] Logically, excluding the state subject to the procedure: see TFEU, art 354.

[58] Charter of Fundamental Rights of the European Union, art 51.

[59] Communication of 15 October 2003 from the Commission to the Council and the European Parliament on Article 7 of the Treaty on European Union – Respect for and promotion of the values on which the Union is based, COM(2003) 606 final, p 5.

especially the case when multiple Member States are involved, as it is politically unrealistic to expect them to sanction one another. Recent developments have clearly illustrated this weakness. Years ago, the European Commission triggered the preventive procedure against Poland,[60] and the European Parliament did the same against Hungary,[61] in response to evident risks of systemic violations of the rule of law and fundamental rights. Yet, despite the gravity of the concerns raised, these procedures have stalled, exposing the limits of Article 7 TEU as an effective enforcement tool.

Section II – Financial Tools Supporting EU Fundamental Rights Protection

The relationship between EU funds and human rights is rarely a focal point of discussion, as these are typically viewed as two distinct and unrelated areas of EU law and policy. The topic of EU funds has, moreover, garnered less scholarly attention. Recently, however, this issue has gained prominence, particularly due to the substantial increase in EU financial resources in response to the COVID-19 pandemic.[62] Additionally, the EU is increasingly adopting a new mode of governance through funding.[63]

Though these two domains may not appear closely connected at first glance, a deeper analysis reveals that the EU's 'power of the purse'[64] has increasingly been leveraged to foster compliance with EU values,[65] including fundamental rights. The use of financial support and monitoring in relation to fundamental rights protection is, however, not entirely new. European funds have long been allocated to initiatives that can contribute to the protection of fundamental rights.

[60] Proposal for a Council Decision on the determination of a clear risk of a serious breach by the Republic of Poland of the rule of law, COM(2017) 835 final, available at: https://eur-lex.europa.eu/legal-content/EN/TXT/HTML/?uri=CELEX:52017PC0835&from=EN.

[61] European Parliament Resolution of 12 September 2018 on a proposal calling on the Council to determine, in accordance with Article 7(1) of the Treaty on European Union, the existence of a clear risk of a serious breach by Hungary of the values on which the Union is founded (2017/2131(INL)), P8_TA-PROV(2018)0340, available at http://www.europarl.europa.eu/sides/getDoc.do?pubRef=-//EP//NONSGML+TA+P8-TA-2018-0340+0+DOC+PDF+V0//EN.

[62] See, on this evolution, C Kilpatrick, 'Explaining and Remedying the Near Absence of the Budget in EU Law Scholarship' (2024) 61(3) *Common Market Law Review* 623–654.

[63] R Weber (ed), *The Financial Constitution of European Integration: Follow the Money?*, 1st edn (Hart Publishing, 2023); and C Kilpatrick and J Scott (eds), *New Frontiers of EU Funding* (Oxford University Press, 2024).

[64] M Fisicaro, 'Beyond the Rule of Law Conditionality: Exploiting the EU Spending Power to Foster the Union's Values' (2022) 7 *European Papers – A Journal on Law and Integration* 697–719.

[65] On this phenomenon, see L Fromont and A van Waeyenberge, 'Trading Rule of Law for Recovery? The New EU Strategy in the post-Covid Era' (2021) 27 *European Law Journal* 132–147; and Fisicaro, 'Beyond the Rule of Law Conditionality' (n 65) 697–719 . See also, for a comparable analysis in relation to the protection of environment, N Vander Putten, 'Funding the green. Environmental Governance Through Spending and Its Effectiveness-Related Risks' (2026) *Common Market Law Review*, forthcoming.

Conditioning funding on human rights compliance, moreover, emerged long ago within the realm of EU external relations. Measures were implemented to ensure that EU financial assistance to third countries was used in full compliance with human rights and democratic principles.[66] However, the explicit connection between the protection of fundamental rights within the EU and funding has only been clearly established in recent years, in response to the decline in adherence among Member States. This section seeks to explore this new trend and examine how EU funding is used to support the protection of fundamental rights at the national level within the EU.

In this context, it is useful to distinguish between two types of governance method that the EU can deploy through its financial instruments. The first has a 'positive' dimension that entails funding initiatives supporting fundamental rights – a 'carrot' approach. The second has a 'negative' dimension, which involves financially sanctioning behaviour that violates fundamental rights – a 'stick' approach. Some instruments, moreover, combine this stick-and-carrot approach. For many years now, European funds have been directly or indirectly supporting initiatives that contribute to the protection of fundamental rights in Europe (carrot approach). A portion of European financial resources is allocated to actions aimed at financing public services such as hospitals, education, and other sectors that sustain the flourishing of fundamental rights. The EU, in this framework, positively encourages the adoption of human rights-friendly initiatives at the national level. The 'stick' approach is more recent.[67] With the 'rule-of-law crisis' that has emerged within the EU since the 2010s, voices have been raised calling for the use of financial sanctions against Member States that undermine the EU's founding values.[68] Although no explicit mechanisms existed for financially sanctioning breaches of these values, some believed that existing tools could be used for this purpose.[69] Additionally, there have been increasing calls for the creation of new financial instruments specifically designed for the protection of EU founding values. In 2013, four foreign affairs ministers proposed the establishment of such a financial sanction mechanism to protect the rule of law in the EU.[70] This initiative culminated in the adoption of the Conditionality

[66] For an overview of the former methods used in order to support fundamental rights in EU external relations, see, among others, Report from the Commission on the implementation of measures intended to promote observance of human rights and democratic principles in external relations for 1996–1999 [2000] COM(2000) 726.

[67] For a pioneering study on the topic, see V Viţă, 'The Rise of Spending Conditionality in the European Union: What Can EU Learn from the U.S. Conditional Spending Doctrine and Policies?' (2018) European University Institute, Department of Law Research Paper No. 2017/16.

[68] See, among others, G Halmai, 'The Possibility and Desirability of Rule of Law Conditionality' (2019) 11 *Hague Journal on the Rule of Law* 171–188.

[69] See, among others, ibid.

[70] Letter to José Manuel Barosso from Dr Guido Weterwelle (Germany), Frans Timmermans (Netherlands), Villy Sovndal (Denmark), and Erkki Tuomioja (Finland) (6 March 2013), available at https://www.eerstekamer.nl/eu/documenteu/_brief_nederland_duitsland/f=/vji8oh6slx9o.pdf.

Regulation[71] in 2020. In addition to this cross-cutting Regulation protecting the EU's financial interests, other financial instruments have also evolved to include a 'value dimension'.

Under the EU budget, several funds may have this kind of carrot-and-stick impact on the protection of fundamental rights in the Member States. Outside the EU budget *sensu stricto*, the EU has also recently expanded its financial resources thanks to the NextGenerationEU (NGEU) programme, implemented by the Resilience and Recovery Facility. This initiative also seeks, to some extent, to ensure that the new investments envisaged by this programme align with EU values, in particular the European Pillar of Social Rights. After analysing the role of fundamental rights in the EU's budget as such (section II.1), I will review their place in the NGEU initiative (section II.2). I will then briefly examine the conditionality regulation that applies across these financial instruments (section II.3), and end with a brief cross-cutting conclusion (section II.4).

While this section attempts to be as complete and accurate as possible, it is important to note that, when describing these instruments, we must consider the relatively short period of their implementation. This limited time frame means a cautious approach must be taken when evaluating their effectiveness, as comprehensive assessments require adequate data and longer-term observation to draw accurate conclusions.

II.1. The Protection of Fundamental Rights within the EU Budget

Each year, a general budget of the EU is drawn up,[72] mostly financed by the EU's own resources.[73] In addition, a Multiannual Financial Framework (MFF), established for a period of at least five years,[74] is adopted. The MFF must be in line with the annual budget, and determines the amounts of the annual ceilings on commitment appropriations by category of expenditure, and of the annual ceiling on payment appropriations.[75] The last MFF, covering the 2021–27 period, amounts to over 1.2 trillion euros (1.074 trillion euros in 2018 prices), and has been topped up by 806.9 billion euros (750 billion euros in 2018 prices) through

[71] Regulation (EU, Euratom) 2020/2092 of the European Parliament and of the Council of 16 December 2020 on a general regime of conditionality for the protection of the Union budget [2020] OJ L433I ('Conditionality Regulation').

[72] TFEU, art 314.

[73] K Lenaerts, P Van Nuffel and T Corthaut, *EU Constitutional Law* (Oxford University Press, 2021) 480.

[74] TFEU, art 312. In practice, this is done every seven years.

[75] TFEU, art 312.

NGEU, the temporary instrument to power the recovery, which I will analyse below.[76]

The funds made available by the EU budget are implemented either by direct management (by the European Commission), by shared management (by the European Commission and national authorities), or by indirect management (by partner organisations or other authorities inside or outside the EU). The latter type notably comprises the majority of the EU budget allocated to humanitarian aid and international development. As it mainly concerns the protection of rights outside the EU, it exceeds the scope of this book.

It would be impossible to conduct a comprehensive analysis of the vast number of different EU funds. Therefore, I have chosen to focus on two types of funds: the funds concerned by the current Common Provision Regulation (section II.1(a)), and the EU Justice, Rights and Values Fund (section II.1(b)). I selected the first group due to their significant coverage and their explicit fundamental rights conditionality. The second choice is appropriate because it specifically focuses on the protection of values. Furthermore, these two types of funds are managed differently: the funds under the Common Provision Regulation are subject to shared management, whereas the EU Justice, Rights and Values Fund is managed through both direct and indirect administration.

II.1.a. Shared-management Funds Impacting the Protection of Fundamental Rights

About 80 per cent of the EU budget is currently allocated through shared management by the European Commission and Member States.[77] The two main areas covered by these funds are, on the one hand, the Common Agricultural Policy (CAP) and, on the other, the Cohesion Policy established to strengthen the economic, social and territorial cohesion of the EU. On the basis of Article 177 TFEU, a 'Common Provision Regulation' (CPR) is adopted each programming period, in order to define the organisation of – including tasks, priorities, and objectives – the Cohesion and Structural Funds. During the current programming period, a few funds established under the Home Affairs policy were also included within the scope of the last CPR.[78]

[76] European Commission, Directorate-General for Budget, 'The EU's 2021–2027 long-term budget and NextGenerationEU – Facts and figures' (Publications Office of the European Union, 2021).

[77] Kilpatrick, 'Explaining and Remedying the Near Absence of the Budget in EU Law Scholarship' (n 63) 627.

[78] Regulation (EU) 2021/1060 of the European Parliament and of the Council of 24 June 2021 laying down common provisions on the European Regional Development Fund, the European Social Fund Plus, the Cohesion Fund, the Just Transition Fund and the European Maritime, Fisheries and Aquaculture Fund and financial rules for those and for the Asylum, Migration and Integration Fund, the Internal Security Fund and the Instrument for Financial Support for Border Management and Visa Policy [2021] OJ L231/159 ('CPR Regulation').

While there is a dimension of human rights protection in the funds distributed under the CAP – particularly in protecting the social rights of farmers – the link between these funds and the strict protection of fundamental rights is rather remote. The CAP instruments do not explicitly reference the protection of fundamental rights. In contrast, the Cohesion Funds and the Home Affairs Funds, which are subject to the current CPR,[79] are more closely connected to the protection of fundamental rights. It is notable that the current CPR explicitly includes conditionality based on fundamental rights protection. Therefore, I will focus my analysis on these funds.

As already underlined, the implementation of these funds is characterised by 'shared management' between the EU, on the one hand, and the Member States, on the other.[80] Member States are primarily responsible for implementing them, but the European Commission nevertheless plays an important role, as it negotiates investment priorities with the Member States and ultimately validates their investment choices. EU shared-management funds thus give EU institutions the opportunity to pursue specific policy goals through their administration.

The functioning of EU funds, their foundation, and even how they are labelled, have evolved over the course of the different programming periods. I will not delve into these changes in detail, as that goes beyond the scope of the book.[81] Let me simply note that reference has often been made to the 'Cohesion Fund' or the 'European Structural and Investment Funds' (ESIF). These funds are long-established financial instruments within the framework of EU regional policy, aimed at reducing economic and social disparities among Europe's regions by investing in job creation, transportation infrastructure, research, innovation, and more. In this section, I will use the term 'CPR Funds' to describe all funds covered by the current CPR, because, as already underlined, the latest programming period, 2021–27, also encompasses a series of funds established next to the structural and cohesion policy.[82] The CPR Funds cover, under the current programming period of 2021–27, five funds aligned with the 'Cohesion Policy' (the ERDF,[83] the ESF+,[84] the CF,[85] the JTF,[86] and the EMFAF),[87] alongside resources earmarked

[79] ibid.

[80] On this concept, see 'Shared Management' in P Craig (ed), *EU Administrative Law* (Oxford University Press, 2018) 80–110.

[81] For a historical evolution of EU budget and related conditionality regimes, see I Gambardella, 'The Promise and Perils of Fundamental Rights through Funding in the EU' (PhD thesis at Katholieke Universiteit Leuven and Université libre de Bruxelles, forthcoming).

[82] As noted by Ilaria Gambardella in 'EU Governance Through Funding: What consequences for the scope of application of EU fundamental rights?' (2024) 31 *Maastricht Journal of European and Comparative Law* 221. The ESI acronym is no longer used in the new version of the CPR, probably because 'the CPR includes spending programmes which go well beyond the strict understanding of "cohesion policy"'.

[83] European Regional Development Fund.

[84] European Social Fund Plus.

[85] Cohesion Fund.

[86] Just Transition Fund.

[87] European Maritime, Fisheries and Aquaculture Fund.

for the development of the AFSJ ('Home Funds', including the AMIF,[88] the ISF,[89] and the BMVI).[90] Together, they account for roughly 30 per cent of the European budget.

The narrative surrounding these funds is not primarily focused on the protection of fundamental rights. The Cohesion Policy, indeed, aims to ensure the reduction of social and economic disparities between countries and between different areas and regions within the same country.

However, the success of the Cohesion Policy involves raising the standard of living for European citizens, and thus contributes to the implementation of their fundamental rights.[91] Moreover, there has been a gradual inclusion of individual rights concerns within the framework of their management. The Home Funds covered by the CPR can also have a more or less direct impact on the protection of fundamental rights in the Member States. It is, therefore, essential to consider these funds when analysing the EU system for protecting fundamental rights.

Firstly, I will analyse (II.1(a)(i)) how these funds can be used to support initiatives aimed at upholding fundamental rights in Europe ('carrot'); and, secondly, (II.1(a)(ii)) how the fundamental rights imperative comes into play to frame their management ('stick').

II.1.a (i) CPR Funds Supporting Fundamental Rights Protection ('Carrot')

As previously mentioned, the main explicit goal of CPR Funds is not, as such, the protection of fundamental rights or EU values. The use of these funds, particularly the Home Funds, may even restrict certain fundamental rights: for instance, financing border management could potentially clash with the rights of non-EU nationals who seek asylum in Europe. Since they are not designed as funds for the protection of fundamental rights, they may serve other competing objectives, as outlined in chapter one of this book.[92]

However, these funds have, for some time, also been effectively used to finance various initiatives which, in fact, enhance the protection of fundamental rights in Europe. As underlined earlier, the explicit objective of Cohesion Funds is to promote economic, social, and territorial cohesion within the EU.[93] These objectives are relatively vague, and can therefore serve as a 'capacious umbrella for a host of more fine-grained policy aims'.[94] Cohesion Funds are even described

[88] EU Asylum, Migration and Integration Fund.

[89] Internal Security Fund.

[90] Border Management and Visa Instruments Fund.

[91] On the evolution of the Cohesion Policy, see L Diéz Sánchez, 'Why cohesion policy is not about cohesion' (2025) 62(1) *Common Market Law Review* 13–48.

[92] See ch 1, s V.2, 'The EU's Competing Objectives and the Specific Characteristics of EU Law'.

[93] TFEU, art 174.

[94] B de Witte, 'Integration Through Funding' in Weber (ed), *The Financial Constitution of European Integration: Follow the Money?* (n 63) 227.

as 'half-empty shells that can be filled with new policy goals every seven years, when the revised fund regulations are being adopted, and occasionally even within the seven-year period, in order to address new needs'.[95] In practice, these funds have long been used to support initiatives that enhance the protection of fundamental rights in Member States, particularly those that are economically disadvantaged.

The European Regional Development Fund (ERDF), part of the Cohesion Policy, and which receives the largest allocation of funds among the CPR Funds, is a good illustration of this trend. Its primary goal is to foster social and economic development in various EU regions and cities, ultimately striving to minimise disparities in development across Europe. While it does not appear, at first sight, to be immediately linked to fundamental rights concerns, closer examination reveals that this fund has strong fundamental rights implications.[96] One of the 2021–27 key goals of the ERDF is to enable investments to make Europe and its regions 'more social, by supporting employment, education, skills, social inclusion and equal access to healthcare'.[97] To promote social inclusion and combat poverty, particularly among marginalised communities, the ERDF supports investments 'to improve access, including through infrastructure, to social, educational, cultural and recreational services, including sports, taking into account the specific needs of persons with disabilities, children and the elderly',[98] and it is stated that particular attention should be paid to the inclusion of marginalised[99] communities such as Roma. The ERDF is also highly relevant regarding the prohibition of discrimination[100] and the integration of persons with disabilities. We can thus easily identify the fundamental rights patterns of ERDF-funded initiatives, which could support, among others, the right to social security and social assistance (Article 34 of the EU Charter), the right to health care (Article 35 of the EU Charter), the right to education (Article 14 of the EU Charter), and the rights of the elderly (Article 25 of the EU Charter). The principle of non-discrimination (Article 21 of the EU Charter) and the right of persons with disabilities to benefit from inclusion measures

[95] ibid.

[96] JP Aus, 'Fundamental Rights Monitoring of EU Funds in Germany' (2022) 12, available at https://fra.europa.eu/sites/default/files/fra_uploads/country-research-eu-funds-nhris-germany_en.pdf.

[97] European Commission web page, 'European Regional Development Fund', available at https://ec.europa.eu/regional_policy/funding/erdf_en.

[98] Regulation (EU) 2021/1058 of the European Parliament and of the Council of 24 June 2021 on the European Regional Development Fund and on the Cohesion Fund [2021] OJ L231/60, recital 20.

[99] ibid, recital 21. See also Communication from the Commission to the European Parliament, the Council, the European Economic and Social Committee and the Committee of the Regions – An EU Framework for National Roma Integration Strategies up to 2020 [2011] COM(2011)173 final, which explicitly underlies the need to use structural funds to support Roma targeted projects.

[100] Aus, 'Fundamental Rights Monitoring of EU Funds in Germany' (n 97) 12; and Regulation (EU) 2021/1058 of the European Parliament and of the Council of 24 June 2021 on the European Regional Development Fund and on the Cohesion Fund [2021] OJ L231/60, recital 5.

(Article 26 of the EU Charter) are also implemented by actions supported by the ERDF.

In addition to the ERDF, CPR Funds include the European Social Fund Plus (ESF+), the goal of which is to support Member States and regions

> to achieve high employment levels, fair social protection and a skilled and resilient workforce ready for the future world of work, as well as inclusive and cohesive societies aiming to eradicating poverty and delivering on the principles set out in the European Pillar of Social Rights.[101]

Here also, the relationship with fundamental rights, particularly social rights, can be readily inferred. One of the goals of the ESF+ is to support the principles announced in the European Pillar of Social Rights.[102] In this regard, the regulation notably enshrines that

> the ESF+ should support the efforts of Member States to contribute to the eradication of poverty with a view to breaking the cycle of disadvantage across generations and promote social inclusion by ensuring equal opportunities for all, reducing barriers, tackling discrimination and addressing health inequalities.[103]

In view of this, it should be used 'to enhance timely and equal access to affordable, sustainable and high-quality services that promote the access to housing and person-centred care such as healthcare and long-term care', and to 'contribute to the modernisation of social protection systems with a particular focus on children and disadvantaged groups and with a view, in particular, to promoting the accessibility of such systems, including for persons with disabilities'.[104] Moreover, the ESF+ should also be used in the view of eradicating poverty by supporting schemes aiming to alleviate food and material deprivation and promote social integration of the most deprived persons.[105] The European Commission even went as far as demanding a specific breakdown of the funds: a minimum of 25 per cent of national ESF+ funding should be allocated towards addressing poverty and social exclusion. Moreover, Member States with significant issues of child poverty are required to allocate at least 5 per cent of their funding to initiatives aimed at reducing child poverty. Every Member State must also allocate at least 3 per cent of its ESF+ budget to combat material deprivation.[106] In this context as well, numerous

[101] Regulation (EU) 2021/1057 of the European Parliament and of the Council of 24 June 2021 establishing the European Social Fund Plus (ESF+) [2021] OJ L231/21, art 3.

[102] Communication from the European Commission to the European Parliament, Council of the EU, the EESC and the Committee of the Regions – Establishing a European Pillar of Social Rights [2017] COM(2017)250.

[103] Regulation (EU) 2021/1057 of the European Parliament and of the Council of the EU of 24 June 2021 establishing the European Social Fund Plus (ESF+) [2021] OJ L231/21, recital 18.

[104] ibid, recital 18.

[105] ibid, recital 19.

[106] Communication from the Commission to the European Parliament, the Council, the European Economic and Social Committee and the Committee of the Regions – The European Pillar of Social Rights Action Plan [2021] COM(2021)102 final.

rights established by the EU Charter can thus receive financial support, such as the principle of human dignity (Article 1), the freedom to choose an occupation and right to engage in work (Article 15), the rights of the child (Article 24), the right of persons with disabilities to benefit from inclusion measures (Article 26), and so on.

As has been observed, the ERDF and the ESF+ represent 'a significant asset which hold the potential of developing inclusion policies which would otherwise not be feasible',[107] in particular in the poorest Member States, which benefit the most from them. The FRA noted the 'very significant fundamental rights' impact of these funds, for example in the framework of the process of deinstitutionalisation of people with disabilities.[108] While the dimension of fundamental rights is clearly present, further research would be needed to precisely identify the exact effects of these funds on the protection of rights on the ground.[109]

Home Funds can also, to a certain extent, support the strengthening of certain fundamental rights. The Asylum, Migration and Integration Fund, set up for the period 2021–27 with a total of about 10 billion euros, is among others used to support dignified facilities for asylum applicants.[110] Nevertheless, their influence on safeguarding fundamental rights appears somewhat restricted, given the primary focus on border protection and security priorities. Additionally, critical voices have emerged to denounce the use of these funds, particularly in establishing migrant detention camps that breach fundamental rights.[111] However, as I will explore below, the allocation of these funds – at least in principle – is constrained by the obligation to uphold the EU Charter of Fundamental Rights.

[107] T Magazzini, E Chiozza, and M Rossi, 'Conformism or Inadequacy of Roma Inclusion Policies? Missed Opportunities at the European and Local Levels' in T Magazzini and S Piemontese (eds), *Constructing Roma Migrants: European Narratives and Local Governance* (Springer International Publishing, 2019) 60.

[108] European Union Agency for Fundamental Rights, 'EU Funds – Ensuring Compliance with Fundamental Rights' (19 December 2023) 19, available at https://fra.europa.eu/en/publication/2023/eu-funds. Criticism has, nevertheless, been raised about the support by EU Funds of overcrowded institutions for disabled persons despite the risk it entails for their fundamental rights, *cf* European Network on Independent Living, 'Shadow report on the implementation of the UN Convention on the Rights of Persons with Disabilities in the European Union', Brussels, February 2022, 13.

[109] K Hermans et al, 'Delivering on the European Pillar of Social Rights: Towards a Needs-based Distribution of the European Social Funds?' (2023) 57 *Social Policy & Administration* 464, 477.

[110] European Union Agency for Fundamental Rights, 'EU Funds – Ensuring Compliance with Fundamental Rights' (n 109) 19.

[111] Evidence showing that EU Funds directly or indirectly supported actions breaching fundamental rights in the context of border management in Croatia, Bulgaria, and Hungary has, notably, been collected: see Lighthouse Reports, 'Europe's Black Sites: Refugees arbitrarily detained, tortured at secret facilities in EU' (8 December 2022), available at https://www.lighthousereports.com/investigation/europes-black-sites/. See also E Guild, 'What Monitoring for Fundamental Rights at EU Borders? Frontex and Rule of Law' (*Verfassungsblog*, 7 September 2022) 3, available at https://verfassungsblog.de/what-monitoring-for-fundamental-rights-at-eu-borders/.

II.1.a (ii) Sanctions to Ensure Respect of Fundamental Rights under the Common Provision Regulation ('Stick')

In addition to the financial aid that funds may offer to support initiatives enhancing fundamental rights protection, conditionality mechanisms have slowly emerged that require respect of these rights during their implementation. This process has undergone significant evolution, culminating in the latest programming period, spanning from 2021 to 2027. As noted by Nathalie Rubio and Romain Tinière, whereas the matters concerning the management of European funds and fundamental rights were previously marked by mutual indifference, their intersection has recently reached a peak.[112] I will summarise this evolution in the following paragraphs. As a new CPR has been adopted for each programming period since 1988,[113] the framework is expected to continue evolving. Therefore, having an overview of this evolution is useful for understanding the different types of conditionalities that can be implemented.

While the first CPR, of 1988,[114] did not explicitly include references to the protection of fundamental rights, the second one – adopted to regulate the programming period of 1994–99 – inserted the requirement that all measures receiving financial support should be in conformity with the EU Treaties, including the principle of equal opportunities for men and women.[115] The Cohesion Policy is, therefore, among the earliest EU policies to embrace gender equality mainstreaming.[116] According to Viorica Viţă, fundamental rights imperatives were, nevertheless, at that time 'limited to the gender perspective', and built 'very much on the functional, worker rationale' aimed at supporting free movement of workers.[117]

The introduction of the third CPR, in 2006, governing the cohesion plan for 2007–13, marked the initial step towards a more comprehensive obligation to fight discrimination within the framework of fund management.[118] A new provision, incorporated in Article 16, indeed imposed an obligation on the Member States and the European Commission to take measures to prevent discrimination in the implementation framework of the funds. According to this provision, 'the

[112] N Rubio and R Tinière, 'Quand les fonds européens rencontrent les droits fondamentaux' (2024) *Revue de l'Union européenne* 196.

[113] Council Regulation (EEC) No 2052/88 of 24 June 1988 on the tasks of the Structural Funds and their effectiveness and on coordination of their activities between themselves and with the operations of the European Investment Bank and the other existing financial instruments [1988] OJ L185, 9.

[114] ibid.

[115] ibid, 5; and art 7 of Council Resolution of 22 June 1994 on the promotion of equal opportunities for men and women through action by the European Structural Funds [1994] OJ C231/01.

[116] MA Pollack and E Hafner-Burton, 'Mainstreaming Gender in the European Union' (2000) 7 *Journal of European Public Policy* 432, 441.

[117] V Viţă, 'Ex Ante Fundamental Rights Conditionalities – a Novel Fundamental Rights Tool in the European Structural and Investment Funds Architecture: Locating it in the broader EU fundamental rights conditionality landscape' (LLM thesis, European University Institute 2014) 59.

[118] Council Regulation (EC) No 1083/2006 of 11 July 2006 laying down general provisions on the European Regional Development Fund, the European Social Fund and the Cohesion Fund and repealing Regulation (EC) No 1260/1999 [2006] OJ L210/25.

Member States and the Commission shall ensure that equality between men and women and the integration of the gender perspective is promoted during the various stages of implementation of the Funds'. Moreover, the Member States were required to 'take appropriate steps to prevent any discrimination based on sex, racial or ethnic origin, religion or belief, disability, age or sexual orientation during the various stages of implementation of the Funds and, in particular, in the access to them'.

This situation continued to evolve with the 2014–20 programming period. The related 2013 CPR established three *ex ante* fundamental rights conditionalities, concerning, respectively, non-discrimination, gender equality, and the rights of people with disabilities. Member States were required, *before* being able to conclude the partnership agreement enabling the release of funds, to demonstrate the existence of administrative capacity for the implementation and application during the use of the funds of: (i) 'Union gender equality law and policy'; (ii) 'Union anti-discrimination law and policy'; and (iii) 'the United Nations Convention on the rights of persons with disabilities (UNCRPD)'.[119] The three fundamental rights conditionalities were 'general', and thus applied to all 2014–20 European Structural and Investments Funds.[120]

The European Commission outlined very precisely the requirements of these conditions. According to its 'Guidance on Ex Ante Conditionalities', they required the presence of a robust regulatory framework and administrative capacity pertaining to non-discrimination, gender equality, and inclusion of people with disabilities.[121] In relation to non-discrimination, the European Commission insisted on the following requirements: (i) the setting-up of a national equality body under Article 13 of Directive 2000/43/EC; (ii) the elaboration of a plan to consult with and involve bodies in charge of anti-discrimination; and (iii) the indication of the steps taken to facilitate active involvement of the national equality body. Moreover, it required a plan for training on EU anti-discrimination law and policy covering all staff involved in the implementation of the ESI Funds (managing authorities, intermediate bodies, certifying authorities, and audit authorities).[122] Similar obligations were imposed under the gender equality conditionality clause.[123] With regard

[119] Regulation (EU) No 1303/2013 of the European Parliament and of the Council of 17 December 2013 laying down common provisions on the European Regional Development Fund, the European Social Fund, the Cohesion Fund, the European Agricultural Fund for Rural Development and the European Maritime and Fisheries Fund and laying down general provisions on the European Regional Development Fund, the European Social Fund, the Cohesion Fund and the European Maritime and Fisheries Fund and repealing Council Regulation (EC) No 1083/2006 [2013] OJ L347/320, Annex XI.

[120] Viţă, 'Ex Ante Fundamental Rights Conditionalities' (n 118) 78.

[121] European Commission, 'Guidance on Ex Ante Conditionalities for the European Structural and Investment Funds – Part II', available at https://ec.europa.eu/regional_policy/information-sources/legislation-and-guidance/guidance_en, 337–56.

[122] ibid, 340.

[123] ibid; 349.

to disability rights, in addition to similar requirements, the Guidance also specified that there should be arrangements ensuring the implementation of Article 9 of the UNCRPD:

> to ensure to persons with disabilities access, on an equal basis with others, to the physical environment, to transportation, to information and communications, including information and communications technologies and systems, and to other facilities and services open or provided to the public, both in urban and in rural areas.

In this regard, the European Commission required monitoring mechanisms to be in place, ensuring 'notification and resolution of problems as well as, redress and enforcement mechanisms in relation to accessibility for persons with disabilities in interventions co-funded by ESI Funds'.[124] Planned interventions, therefore, had to ensure the accessibility of 'the built environment, transport, information and communication, including new technologies, as well as services open or provided to the public'.[125] The Guidance also obliged the Member States to develop 'clear technical guidance documents which refer to applicable Union and national rules and standards, in order to ensure consistent and objective assessment of accessibility'.[126] Hence, the 2013 CPR, as implemented by the European Commission, imposed stringent and meticulously defined obligations on the Member States to uphold these fundamental rights when implementing the funds during the 2014–20 programming period.

The 2013 CPR nevertheless restricted the scope of application of fundamental rights conditionality by establishing that they should only apply in the case of 'a direct and genuine link to, and direct impact on, the effective and efficient achievement of a specific objective for an investment priority or a Union priority'.[127] The Regulation, moreover, specified that the

> assessment of applicability by the Commission shall … take account of the principle of proportionality having regard to the level of support allocated, where appropriate.[128]

As previously underlined by Viorica Viță, the introduction of fundamental rights conditionality in the 2013 system has thus been counterbalanced by this relevance test, making it very much conditional whether they are even applicable.[129] In its Guidance on Ex Ante Conditionalities, the European Commission,

[124] ibid, 354.
[125] ibid.
[126] ibid, 355.
[127] Regulation (EU) No 1303/2013 of the European Parliament and of the Council of 17 December 2013 laying down common provisions on the European Regional Development Fund, the European Social Fund, the Cohesion Fund, the European Agricultural Fund for Rural Development and the European Maritime and Fisheries Fund and laying down general provisions on the European Regional Development Fund, the European Social Fund, the Cohesion Fund and the European Maritime and Fisheries Fund and repealing Council Regulation (EC) No 1083/2006 [2013] OJ L347/320, arts 2.33 and 19.
[128] ibid, art 19.3.
[129] Viță, 'Ex Ante Fundamental Rights Conditionalities' (n 118) 83.

among other things, underlined that a key question to determine the applicability was whether the fulfilment of fundamental rights conditionality is required to achieve the specific objective of the investment.[130] In situations where the non-application of these conditions had little impact on the achievement of specific spending objectives, states were, conversely, exempted from fulfilling them. Moreover, as already underscored, even if conditionality was found to be applicable, a subsequent proportionality test had to be undertaken, with due consideration given to 'the level of allocated support' and the 'overall aim of reducing the administrative burden on the management and control bodies'.[131] The responsibility for evaluating the applicability of, and compliance with, these conditions lay with the Member States, followed by a subsequent review by the European Commission to confirm the self-assessment conducted. In the case of disagreement on the applicability of the condition or its fulfilment, it was for the European Commission to demonstrate both the applicability and the non-fulfilment.[132] Despite its limitations, this mechanism constituted a genuine innovation in the EU's efforts to safeguard fundamental rights within its Member States.

A major shift occurred with the last programming period plan. The latest CPR, which oversees eight EU funds for the 2021–27 period,[133] accounting for a third of the EU budget,[134] indeed expands and deepens fundamental rights conditionality. As a reminder, the eight funds covered by this Regulation are the European Regional Development Fund (ERDF), the European Social Fund Plus (ESF+), the Cohesion Fund, the Just Transition Fund (JTF), the European Maritime, Fisheries and Aquaculture Fund (EMFAF), the Asylum, Migration and Integration Fund (AMIF), the Internal Security Fund (ISF), and the Border Management and Visa Instrument (BMVI).[135] In this new framework, oversight of adherence to fundamental rights operates on two fronts: both prior to and following the implementation of investments financed by EU funds.

[130] European Commission, 'Guidance on Ex Ante Conditionalities for the European Structural and Investment Funds – Part I', 27 February 2014, 11–12, available at https://ec.europa.eu/regional_policy/en/information/publications/guidelines/2014/guidance-fiche-guidance-on-ex-ante-conditionalities-for-the-european-structural-and-investment-funds-part-i.

[131] Viţă, 'Ex Ante Fundamental Rights Conditionalities' (n 118) 89, relying upon CPR Regulation, arts 4.5 and 19.3.

[132] Regulation (EU) No 1303/2013 of the European Parliament and of the Council of 17 December 2013 laying down common provisions on the European Regional Development Fund, the European Social Fund, the Cohesion Fund, the European Agricultural Fund for Rural Development and the European Maritime and Fisheries Fund and laying down general provisions on the European Regional Development Fund, the European Social Fund, the Cohesion Fund and the European Maritime and Fisheries Fund and repealing Council Regulation (EC) No 1083/2006 [2013] OJ L347/320, art 19.4.

[133] CPR Regulation.

[134] European Commission web page, 'Common Provisions Regulation: The single rulebook of EU funds jointly delivered with member states and regions', available at https://commission.europa.eu/funding-tenders/find-funding/funding-management-mode/common-provisions-regulation_en.

[135] CPR Regulation, art 1.

First, a general obligation to ensure the respect of *all* fundamental rights (not only non-discrimination principles, as before) in the implementation of the funds is now explicitly enshrined in the new 2021 CPR. According to its Article 9(1), which establishes the 'Horizontal Principles' applicable to the implementation of these funds, 'Member States and the Commission shall ensure respect for fundamental rights and compliance with the Charter of Fundamental Rights of the European Union in the implementation of the Funds'.

These horizontal principles also include obligations to ensure 'that equality between men and women, gender mainstreaming and the integration of a gender perspective are taken into account and promoted throughout the preparation, implementation, monitoring, reporting and evaluation of programmes',[136] and to prevent 'any discrimination based on gender, racial or ethnic origin, religion or belief, disability, age or sexual orientation during the preparation, implementation, monitoring, reporting and evaluation of programmes'.[137] Within this framework, 'accessibility for persons with disabilities shall be taken into account throughout the preparation and implementation of programmes'.[138] The Regulation establishing the ISF, moreover, adds, with regard to the specific case of actions funded by the ISF, that Member States shall, in addition, 'pay special attention to assisting and protecting vulnerable persons, in particular children and unaccompanied minors'.[139]

Respect for these obligations is assessed by the European Commission at the moment of the approval of partnership agreements[140] and programmes[141] or their future amendments. Horizontal principles are applied before the approval by the European Commission, but do not, as such, guarantee compliance during the implementation phase.[142]

Second, the Regulation also establishes a new system of permanent conditionality regarding respect of the EU Charter. According to Annex III of the Regulation, the 'effective application and implementation of the Charter of Fundamental Rights' constitutes a 'horizontal enabling condition' under the meaning of Article 15 of the Regulation. According to this provision, enabling conditions must be fulfilled at the time of approval of the programme, but Member States shall also 'ensure that enabling conditions remain fulfilled and respected throughout the programming period'. They thus establish a *permanent* conditionality mechanism, compliance with which is assessed before the reimbursement of the costs.

[136] ibid, art 9(1).
[137] ibid, art 9(3).
[138] ibid.
[139] Regulation (EU) 2021/1149 of the European Parliament and of the Council of 7 July 2021 establishing the Internal Security Fund [2021] OJ L 251/94 ('ISF Regulation'), art 4.
[140] ibid, art 12(1).
[141] ibid, art 23(1).
[142] E Rubio et al, 'The Tools for Protecting the EU Budget from Breaches of the Rule of Law: The Conditionality Regulation in Context' (Requested by the BUDG Committee of the European Parliament 2023) 45.

The 'implementation and application of the United Nations Convention on the Rights of Persons with Disabilities (UNCRPD) in accordance with Council Decision 2010/48/EC' also constitutes an enabling condition, according to Annex III. With regard to gender equality – which constituted a self-standing *ex ante* condition in the previous system – the European Commission underlined that the general 'Charter enabling condition … includes gender equality as one of its key principles and applies to all the investments under this regulation'.[143] The Regulation goes to great lengths in the obligations required of Member States regarding the protection of fundamental rights. Annex III to the CPR, indeed, specifies that the EU Charter-enabling condition requires that:

> Effective mechanisms are in place to ensure compliance [with the EU Charter], which include:
>
> 1. Arrangements to ensure compliance of the programmes supported by the Funds and their implementation with the relevant provisions of the Charter.
> 2. Reporting arrangements to the monitoring committee regarding cases of non-compliance of operations supported by the Funds with the Charter and complaints regarding the Charter submitted in accordance with the arrangements made pursuant to Article 69(7).

Member States should, in this context, when preparing the programmes, communicate the arrangement put in place to the European Commission. Permanent monitoring committees, including representation by national fundamental rights bodies, should be established to help assess compliance with the EU Charter.[144] According to the European Commission, 'given their independent status and expertise in monitoring and advising authorities, national human rights institutions (NHRIs) could play a role in ensuring that EU funded programmes are designed and implemented in compliance with the Charter'.[145] The Regulation establishing the AMIF additionally renders the participation of 'relevant international organisations, non-governmental organisations, such as refugee organisations and migrant-led organisations, as well as national human rights institutions and equality bodies, and economic and social partners' mandatory.[146] With regard to the development of programmes under the AMIF and BMVI, EU legislation, moreover, requires early consultation of the FRA.[147]

[143] Communication from the Commission to the European Parliament, the Council, the European Economic and Social Committee and the Committee of the Regions – A Union of Equality: Gender Equality Strategy 2020–2025 [2020] COM(2020)152 final, 16.

[144] CPR Regulation, art 8(1)(b).

[145] Communication from the Commission to the European Parliament, the Council, the European Economic and Social Committee and the Committee of the Regions – Strategy to strengthen the application of the Charter of Fundamental Rights in the EU [2020] COM(2020)711, 8.

[146] Regulation (EU) 2021/1147 of the European Parliament and of the Council of 7 July 2021 establishing the Asylum, Migration and Integration Fund [2021] OJ L 251/1 ('AMIF Regulation'), art 4.

[147] AMIF Regulation; art 13.4 of Regulation (EU) 2021/1148 of the European Parliament and of the Council of 7 July 2021 establishing, as part of the Integrated Border Management Fund, the Instrument for Financial Support for Border Management and Visa Policy [2021] OJ L251/48 ('BMVI Regulation'), art 16(4).

With regard to the UNCRPD, the 2021 CPR additionally specifies that there should be a national framework ensuring its implementation, including: (i) objectives with measurable goals, data collection and monitoring mechanisms; (ii) arrangements to ensure that the accessibility policy, legislation and standards are properly reflected in the preparation and implementation of the programmes; and (iii) reporting arrangements to the monitoring committee regarding cases of non-compliance of operations supported by the funds with the UNCRPD and complaints regarding the UNCRPD submitted in accordance with the arrangements made pursuant to Article 69(7).

In practice, the Member States prepared partnerships agreements for the period 2021–27, determining the policy objectives and arrangements for the use of five funds (the ERDF, the ESF+, the Cohesion Fund, the JTF, and the EMFAF).[148]

These partnership agreements were examined by the European Commission, which could make observations. These observations could concern, among others, the obligation to respect the EU Charter, but also the country-specific recommendations (CSRs) addressed to the Member States in the framework of the European Semester and the European Pillar of Social Rights that the Member States have to take into account when drafting their partnership agreements.[149]

Member States then had to adapt their proposed partnership agreement in light of these observations. If satisfied, the European Commission adopted an implementing act on the approval of the agreement.[150] The partnership agreements are complemented by 'programmes', prepared by the Member States in co-operation with the relevant partners and stakeholders (such as local or regional authorities, civil society organisations, and NHRIs), for the eight funds covered by the CPR.[151] These programmes set out priorities, corresponding to police objectives, to be supported by the funds. Their compliance with the CPR and the Fund-specific Regulations was also examined by the European Commission, which has to validate them through the adoption of implementing decisions.[152]

When preparing these programmes, Member States were required to assess whether the enabling conditions were fulfilled. The European Commission reviewed this assessment and could suspend its approval for several months (four months for approval of partnership agreements, and five for programmes).

[148] L Detre, A Jakab, and T Lukácsi, 'Comparing Three Financial Conditionality Regimes and Their Application to Hungary: The Conditionality Regulation, the Recovery and Resilience Facility Regulation, and the Common Provisions Regulation', *Max Planck Institute for Comparative Public Law & International Law (MPIL) Research Paper* (No 2023–23) 24.

[149] CPR Regulation, arts 11(1)(a) and 12(1).

[150] ibid, arts 10–14.

[151] ibid, arts 21–22.

[152] ibid, art 23.

Although theoretically possible, the relevant literature considered it unlikely that the European Commission would refuse approval after this time period, unless a Member State was confrontational.[153] However, in some cases, the European Commission issued observations along with the approval, which could be used during the cost-reimbursement period when assessing compliance with the enabling conditions.

Following this, prior to a Member State's request for reimbursement of expenses linked to the operation in question, another assessment of compliance with the enabling conditions is conducted by the European Commission.

Unlike the previous system established in the 2013 CPR, the conditionality is thus now also *permanent*, meaning that expenditure costs may be included in payment applications but will be reimbursed later *only if* enabling conditions were adhered to when they were incurred.[154] This means that the condition must also be fulfilled during the whole programming period, and not just at the beginning of the programming stage.[155] The non-reimbursement of payment is automatic and does not require the adoption of a specific decision by the European Commission: if one of the enabling conditions is not met, the costs (except pre-financing that occurred at moment of the approval of the programme) will not be reimbursed until the enabling condition is fulfilled.[156] As stated by Marco Fisicaro, this situation 'mitigates the risk of cosmetic compliance, and gives the Commission a more meaningful instrument to address eventual steps back by the Member States occurring after the assessment carried out at the very start of the programming period'.[157]

After the approval of the partnership agreements and programmes, Member States are required to set up monitoring committees to monitor the implementation of each programme, including whether the enabling conditions are being respected (a committee may cover several programmes).[158] Their composition should be representative of the different stakeholders, and, as underlined above, they may or shall include NHRIs' representatives.[159]

Nevertheless, the system is not flawless. Indeed, once expenditure has been reimbursed, it cannot be reclaimed, even if the conditions are no longer met. Only future reimbursements may be halted. Furthermore, a non-compliant Member State might remain so for several years, only to become compliant at the end of the period, in order to request full reimbursement.[160]

[153] Rubio et al, 'The Tools for Protecting the EU Budget' (n 143) 45.
[154] CPR Regulation, arts 15(5) and 15(6).
[155] ibid, art 15(6).
[156] Rubio et al, 'The Tools for Protecting the EU Budget' (n 143) 41.
[157] Fisicaro, 'Beyond the Rule of Law Conditionality' (n 65) 703.
[158] CPR Regulation, arts 38 and 40.
[159] ibid, art 39.
[160] I thank Pauline Thinus for flagging this to me.

This process can be schematised as follows:

Figure 3.1 Control of the respect of EU Fundamental Rights law within the framework of the 2021 Common Provision Regulation

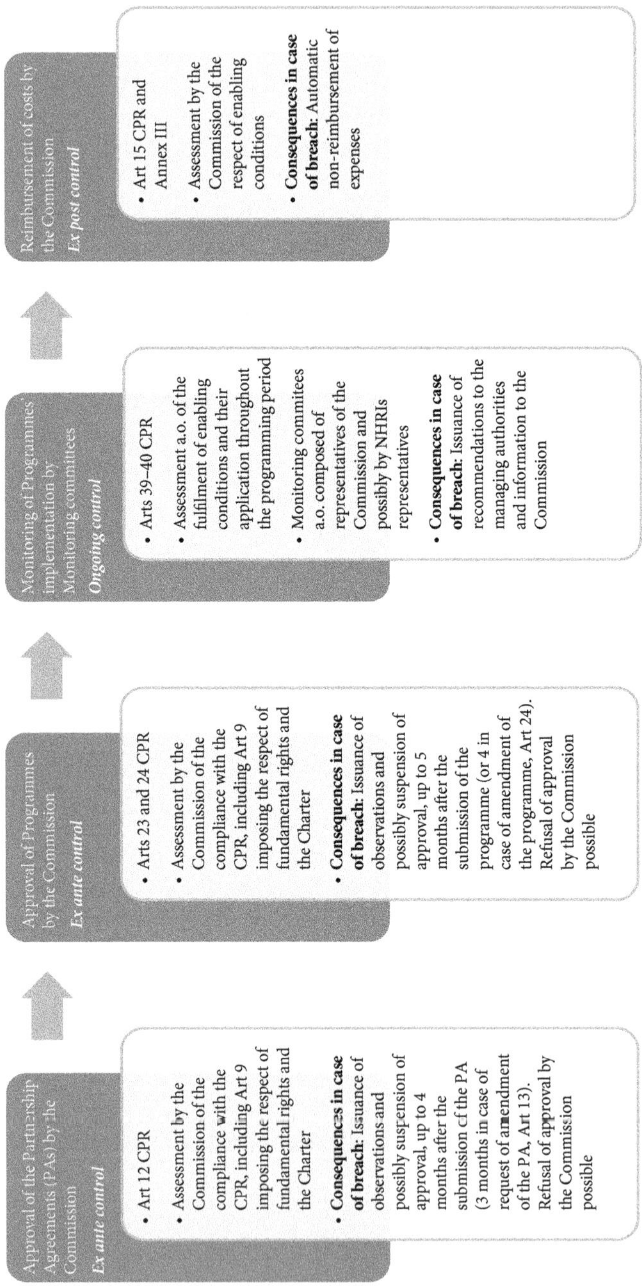

The pivotal question ahead revolves around whether the reforms enacted for the 2021–27 programming period can effectively mitigate the weaknesses of the preceding phase and thus enhance efficiency. As noted by Marco Fisicaro, various indicators hint at a trajectory towards improvement.[161] First, conditionality is no longer submitted to a high applicability threshold, such as in the previous system. As underlined above, for the *ex ante* condition to be applicable, there had to be

> a concrete and precisely pre-defined critical factor, which is a prerequisite for and has a direct and genuine link to, and direct impact on, the effective and efficient achievement of a specific objective for an investment priority or a Union priority.[162]

Now, conditionality extends across all specific objectives of the Cohesion Plan. Second, the assessment of compliance with the conditionality is now conducted not only during the programming stage but throughout the entirety of the financial period.[163] Discussions are, nevertheless, still under way regarding the outcomes attained through conditionality. Concerning the 2014–20 programming period, the European Commission lauded their efficiency, asserting that they had prompted structural reforms and enhanced adherence to EU legislation.[164] Conversely, the Court of Auditors offered a more nuanced perspective, deeming the *ex ante* conditionalities 'innovative but not yet effective instruments'.[165]

In any case, we can identify a 'shift towards using financing rather than rule-making to influence how European Member States work',[166] and it is clear that these new instruments could serve the protection of fundamental rights within the implementation of EU funds.[167]

However, as highlighted by Bruno de Witte, the impact of these instruments should not be overestimated, as the EU budget remains limited.[168] Furthermore, we can lament the lack of transparency in decisions related to the implementation of funds. Indeed, the implementation of this system remains very opaque to

[161] Fisicaro, 'Beyond the Rule of Law Conditionality' (n 65) 702.

[162] Recital 33, Regulation (EU) No 1303/2013 of the European Parliament and of the Council of 17 December 2013 laying down common provisions on the European Regional Development Fund, the European Social Fund, the Cohesion Fund, the European Agricultural Fund for Rural Development and the European Maritime and Fisheries Fund and laying down general provisions on the European Regional Development Fund, the European Social Fund, the Cohesion Fund and the European Maritime and Fisheries Fund and repealing Council Regulation (EC) No 1083/2006.

[163] CPR Regulation, art 15(6).

[164] European Commission, Directorate-General for Regional and Urban Policy, and L Dijkstra, 'My Region, My Europe, Our Future: Seventh Report on Economic, Social and Territorial Cohesion' (10 September 2017) 179, available at https://op.europa.eu/en/publication-detail/-/publication/014d75b6-aefa-11e7-837e-01aa75ed71a1.

[165] European Court of Auditors, 'Special report 15/2017, Ex-ante conditionalities and performance reserve in Cohesion: innovative but not yet effective instruments' (2017), available at https://www.eca.europa.eu/Lists/ECADocuments/SR17_15/SR_PARTNERSHIP_EN.pdf.

[166] M Dawson and F de Witte, *EU Law and Governance* (Cambridge University Press, 2022) 49.

[167] Gambardella, 'EU Governance Through Funding' (n 83) 224.

[168] de Witte, 'Integration Through Funding' (n 95) 222.

this day – legal documents in this field are very difficult to find,[169] making it difficult to assess its effectiveness.[170] Moreover, the significant challenge of accessing information regarding the content and results of the evaluations conducted by the European Commission and Member States diminishes accountability in the national-level process.[171] The staff responsible for implementing these conditions at both the national and EU levels may also lack adequate knowledge, information, and instructions to effectively apply them.

Despite the weaknesses of the system, the European Commission has used fundamental rights conditionality, notably concerning Hungary and Poland.

Regarding Poland, in the partnership agreement concluded on 20 June 2022,[172] and covering about 75 billion euros, the European Commission (only) highlighted issues related to gender equality and the rights of persons with disabilities, without mentioning judicial independence.[173] While the *ex ante* conditionality seems to have been implemented in a rather minimalist fashion, the European Commission ultimately opted to withdraw funds *ex post* as a consequence of Poland's failure to fulfil pledged judicial reforms.[174] Poland itself stated that the enabling condition related to the EU Charter was not fulfilled.[175] More recently, this suspension was lifted due to the progress that had been made by the new Polish government, which aims to restore the rule of law in Poland.[176]

In the partnership agreement concluded with Hungary on 22 December 2022, covering 22 billion euros,[177] of which only a summary is available in English,[178] the

[169] Kilpatrick, 'Explaining and Remedying the Near Absence of the Budget in EU Law Scholarship' (n 63) 647.

[170] On the lack of transparency and difficulty of accessing documents in this field, see Gambardella, 'The Promise and Perils of Fundamental Rights through Funding in the EU' (n 82).

[171] European Council on Refugees and Exiles and Platform for International Cooperation on Undocumented Migrants, 'Fundamental Rights Compliance of Funding Supporting Migrants, Asylum Applicants and Refugees inside the European Union – Policy Note' (March 2023), available at https://ecre.org/wp-content/uploads/2023/03/PIC-ECR-Rights-and-EU-funds-March-2023.pdf.

[172] 'EU Cohesion Policy: Commission Adopts €76.5 billion Partnership Agreement with Poland for 2021–2027' (30 June 2022), available at https://ec.europa.eu/commission/presscorner/detail/en/ip_22_4223.

[173] K Lane Scheppele and J Morijn, 'What Price Rule of Law?' in A Södersten and E Hercock (eds), *The Rule of Law in the EU: Crisis and Solutions* (Swedish Institute for European Policy Studies, Report no 1, April 2023) 44.

[174] A Krysztoszek, 'European Commission to release frozen €137bn for Poland' (18 October 2022), availableathttps://www.euractiv.com/section/all/short_news/european-commission-to-freeze-polands-cohesion-money/.

[175] CPR Regulation, art 15(2).

[176] R Coman and A Buzogány, 'The European Union's Response to the Rule of Law Crisis and the Making of the New Conditionality Regime' (2024) 62(2) *Journal of Common Market Studies* 1, 7.

[177] Commission Implementing Decision of 22 December 2022 approving the partnership Agreement with Hungary [2022] C(2022)10002 final.

[178] European Commission website, 'EU Cohesion Policy 2021–2027: Investing in a fair climate and digital transition while strengthening Hungary's administrative capacity, transparency and prevention of corruption', available at https://ec.europa.eu/regional_policy/whats-new/newsroom/22-12-2022-eu-cohesion-policy-2021-2027-investing-in-a-fair-climate-and-digital-

European Commission emphasised the obligation for Member States to respect the enabling conditions in the implementation of cohesion policy and Home Affairs programmes. The European Commission identified several areas where problems could be observed in this regard.

Firstly, it noted deficiencies in relation to judicial independence. According to the European Commission, the horizontal enabling condition on the EU Charter should be considered fulfilled for the reimbursement of expenses only when 'Hungary has taken the measures on the judiciary to which it has committed under the country's Recovery and Resilience Plan'. In other words, the European Commission established judicial independence as a cross-cutting enabling condition, potentially leading to the suspension of the entire 22 billion euros of funds.[179] Under this framework, it linked the release of funds to the fulfilment of the 27 milestones outlined in the RRF (see below).

Secondly, the European Commission highlighted serious risks to the EU Charter arising from the so-called child protection law that infringes LGBTQ+ equality rights, the current asylum policy, and measures threatening academic freedom. In this regard, the European Commission explicitly stated that it 'cannot reimburse the related expenditure submitted other than for technical assistance and for fulfilling the enabling conditions'. The European Commission also used the threat of suspending programme approvals to combat the discriminatory policies enacted by five Hungarian regions against LGBTQ+ individuals, labelling themselves as 'LGBTQ-free zones'. The European Commission notified those that were categorising territories as LGBTQ-free/unwelcome that this violates the EU Charter. As a result, the European Commission suspended recovery assistance for cohesion and the territories of Europe (REACT-EU) programme amendments associated with these regions. This threat prompted all five regions to retract their anti-LGBTQ+ resolutions.[180]

In December 2023, the European Commission considered that Hungary had met the judicial independence horizontal enabling condition, allowing over 10 billion euros to be released for payment.[181] Coincidentally or not, this decision came before the December European Council meeting on support for Ukraine, at which Viktor Orbán ultimately reversed his stance and agreed not to block the aid.[182]

transition-while-strengthening-hungary-s-administrative-capacity-transparency-and-prevention-of-corruption_en.

[179] E Maurice, 'The Rule of Law: The Uncertain Gamble on Conditionality' (*Schuman Papers* no 660, 13 March 2023).

[180] Rubio et al, 'The Tools for Protecting the EU Budget' (n 143) 45.

[181] Kilpatrick, 'Explaining and Remedying the Near Absence of the Budget in EU Law Scholarship' (n 63) 648. However, a part of the funds are still suspended because of violations of academic freedom, child protection, and asylum law.

[182] Coman and Buzogány, 'The European Union's Response to the Rule of Law Crisis' (n 177) 7.

According to information held by the European Council on Refugees and Exiles (ECRE), eight national programmes under the Home Funds were also suspended because they were in breach of the Charter of Fundamental Rights. These programmes were proposed by Hungary, Poland, and Cyprus and covered a total of around 1 billion euros of the EU budget. As underlined by the report, 'the implication is that, for as long as the enabling conditions are not fulfilled, while the Member States can start implementing the programmes, they will not be able to receive reimbursements of expenditure for the activities', except the financial support for technical assistance and activities themselves aimed at fulfilling the enabling conditions.[183]

To conclude on CPR funds, the importance of fundamental rights, including social rights, in the expenditure and management of these funds has thus significantly increased. As observed by Claire Kilpatrick, the evolution of EU funds shows 'an important social inclusion turn in EU spending in the last decade, including a notable shift towards direct financial support for the most deprived'.[184] Recently, European institutions have, moreover, employed the sanction mechanism provided by these instruments against two Member States. While this tool can indeed enhance the enforcement of fundamental rights within the EU, it is constrained by several factors, including the politicisation of the European Commission, which is the only entity operating in this area. A more in-depth and long-term analysis of the use of these instruments will be necessary to evaluate their effectiveness.

II.1.b. The Justice, Rights and Values Fund Supporting Fundamental Rights Initiatives

Alongside these shared-management funds, there are several funds managed directly by the European Commission or indirectly through other stakeholders. An EU Justice, Rights, and Values Fund was established in 2021[185] as part of the EU's Multiannual Financial Framework (MFF) for the period 2021–27, directly linking to the protection of fundamental rights. This fund is aimed at promoting, strengthening, and defending EU founding values, including fundamental rights and the rule of law, internally. It encompasses two programmes: the Citizens, Equality Rights and Values (CERV)[186] and Justice[187] Programmes. They are

[183] European Council on Refugees and Exiles and Platform for International Cooperation on Undocumented Migrants, 'Fundamental Rights Compliance' (n 172).

[184] Kilpatrick, 'Explaining and Remedying the Near Absence of the Budget in EU Law Scholarship' (n 63) 642.

[185] The previous programming period included a Rights, Equality and Citizenship Fund covering a budget of 439.5 million euros over the period 2014–20 and a Justice Programme covering 378 million euros for the same period.

[186] Regulation (EU) 2021/692 of the European Parliament and of the Council of 28 April 2021 establishing the Citizens, Equality, Rights and Values Programme and repealing Regulation (EU) No 1381/2013 of the European Parliament and of the Council and Council Regulation (EU) No 390/2014 [2021] OJ L156/1.

[187] Regulation (EU) 2021/693 of the European Parliament and of the Council of 28 April 2021 establishing the Justice Programme and repealing Regulation (EU) No 1382/2013 [2021] OJ L156/21.

managed centrally, directly or indirectly,[188] by the European Commission, and amount to 1,641 million euros under the current MFF.[189]

This funding, although limited, supports initiatives focusing (among others) on the protection of fundamental rights in the Member States, and thus deserves to be mentioned ('carrot'). More precisely, it aims at providing direct support to a diverse range of participants involved in rights and values efforts, such as NGOs, equality bodies, public-sector organisations, legal networks, and academic institutions. The singularity of this fund lies in the fact that oversight of its resources is entrusted to the European Commission rather than the Member States. This strategy has the potential to sidestep certain challenges, particularly amidst the weakening of fundamental rights and the rule of law observed in some Member States.

The CERV is structured in four strands: (i) Union values – aimed at protecting, promoting, and raising awareness on the values of Article 2 TEU; (ii) equality, rights and gender equality – aimed at promoting rights, non-discrimination, equality, including gender equality, and advancing gender and non-discrimination mainstreaming; (iii) citizens' engagement and participation – aimed at promoting citizens' engagement and participation in the democratic life; and (iv) Daphne – aimed at fighting violence, including gender-based violence.[190] A significant portion of this funding is allocated to support activities conducted by civil society organisations, especially those at the local and regional levels.[191] For the 2021–27 period, the budget of the CERV programme was significantly expanded, following a proposal by the European Parliament that more than doubled its funding to over 1.5 billion euros. This substantial increase elevated CERV to the status of the largest EU fund devoted to promoting the EU's founding values and fundamental rights, while also strengthening an EU grounded in equality, justice, rights, and shared values.[192]

[188] art 7(1) of Regulation (EU) 2021/692 of the European Parliament and of the Council of 28 April 2021 establishing the Citizens, Equality, Rights and Values Programme and repealing Regulation (EU) No 1381/2013 of the European Parliament and of the Council and Council Regulation (EU) No 390/2014 [2021] OJ L156/1, art 9(1); and Regulation (EU) 2021/693 of the European Parliament and of the Council of 28 April 2021 establishing the Justice Programme and repealing Regulation (EU) No 1382/2013 [2021] OJ L156/21.

[189] M Sapala, 'Cohesion, resilience and values: Heading 2 of the 2021–2027 MFF' (April 2021) 9, available at https://www.europarl.europa.eu/RegData/etudes/BRIE/2021/690542/EPRS_BRI(2021)690542_EN.pdf.

[190] Regulation (EU) 2021/692 of the European Parliament and of the Council of 28 April 2021 establishing the Citizens, Equality, Rights and Values Programme and repealing Regulation (EU) No 1381/2013 of the European Parliament and of the Council and Council Regulation (EU) No 390/2014 [2021] OJ L156/1, arts 2–6.

[191] ibid, art 7(5).

[192] Report from the Commission to the European Parliament, the Council, the European Economic and Social Committee and the Committee of the Regions, 'Funding to promote, protect and enforce fundamental rights 2024', annual report on the application of the EU Charter of Fundamental Rights, Brussels, 10/10/2024, COM(2024) 456 Final, p 5.

The Justice Programme aims to provide support in legal matters, both civil and criminal, and to uphold the rule of law, including the independence of the judiciary.[193] This involves aiding efforts to enhance the efficiency of national legal systems and the effective implementation of judicial decisions. A key focus of this fund is to ensure effective access to justice across Europe, which includes upholding the rights of victims of crime, and procedural rights in criminal cases. Within this scope, the fund aims to facilitate equitable and non-discriminatory justice for everyone, as well as effective remedies, by advancing efficient procedures in both civil and criminal matters. It also aims to protect and uphold the rights of all crime victims, along with the procedural rights of suspects and those accused in criminal trials. The Justice Programme, for instance, co-finances the Human Rights Education for Legal Professionals (HELP) programme, which is a free e-learning course on the EU Charter and the European Convention on Human Rights.

As Marco Fisicaro emphasises, the establishment of the Justice, Rights and Values Fund is of critical importance, as the reduction in funding experienced by civil society organisations in the EU jeopardises their proper functioning.[194] By centralising the distribution of this funding, it allows civil society organisations to access financial aid independently of national frameworks. The European Commission is thus equipped to bolster these associations, supporting their capacity to counterbalance democratic backlash.[195] The Special Rapporteur on the Situation of Human Rights Defenders highlighted, in this regard, in 2017, that the EU should:

> review its policy on funding civil society organisations exclusively through the State budget and explore alternative sources and means of funding for independent civil society, with a view to ensuring free and non-politicized access to funding, including small grants, for all civil society organisations.[196]

Establishing this fund represents a significant step towards bolstering human rights protection across Europe. However, it is crucial to acknowledge that the fund's allocated budget is relatively modest. Moreover, the procedural hurdles and bureaucratic layers associated with accessing the fund could diminish its potential benefits, especially for local groups unfamiliar or inexperienced with navigating EU funding mechanisms. Here again, a thorough long-term analysis will be essential to fully understand the fund's effectiveness and impact.

[193] Regulation (EU) 2021/693 of the European Parliament and of the Council of 28 April 2021 establishing the Justice Programme and repealing Regulation (EU) No 1382/2013 [2021] OJ L156/21, art 3.

[194] Fisicaro, 'Beyond the Rule of Law Conditionality' (n 65) 712.

[195] ibid.

[196] Report of the Special Rapporteur on the Situation of Human Rights Defenders on His Mission to Hungary (2017) A/HRC/34/52/Add.2 (19 January 2017) para 113, available at https://digitallibrary.un.org/record/861182?ln=fr&v=pdf.

II.2. The Role of Fundamental Rights in the Recovery and Resilience Facility

Alongside the Multiannual Financial Framework (MFF), as I have previously highlighted, the NGEU plan was decided in 2020. This plan aimed to increase the EU's financial capacity to address the consequences of the COVID-19 crisis. This plan adds 750 billion euros to European resources, with the majority being implemented through the Resilience and Recovery Facility (RRF), covering 360 billion euros of loans and over 312 billion euros of grants.[197] The RRF seeks to offer financial assistance to Member States for investments and reforms outlined in National Recovery and Resilience Plans (NRRP).[198] It is under the direct management of the European Commission, with the Member States as its beneficiaries. In practice, NRRPs are agreed upon by the European Commission, and validated by the Council of the EU through implementing decisions. RRF payments are conditioned upon the achievement of agreed objectives, designed as milestones and targets.[199] The RRF operates on a performance-based approach, implying that the European Commission disburses funds to each country only upon the achievement of the reforms and investments outlined in their plan. While this initiative represents a significant evolution in EU funding, particularly because of the extensive use of grants rather than loans, it is designed to be temporary. Member States' projects must be completed between February 2020 and 31 December 2026.

Similarly to what has been observed with the CPR Funds, various national initiatives supported by the RRF contribute to strengthening fundamental rights across Europe. A positive support ('carrot') for the development of fundamental rights in Member States is thus provided by NGEU (section II.2(a)). However, in contrast to the system in place under the current CPR, the RRF lacks a proper conditionality regime directly linked to the safeguarding of fundamental rights. Nevertheless, the European Commission plays a crucial role in validating the NRRPs and approving the planned reimbursements, which are performance-based ('stick'). Additionally, for some states, the European Commission has established 'super milestones' that need to be achieved before eligibility for RRF funding is granted. A few of these milestones indirectly address fundamental rights protection and the rule of law, in particular the principle of effective judicial protection ('stick') (section II.2(b)).

[197] L van Middelaar, 'Investment Politics. A New Capacity to Project Union Action into the Future?' in Weber (ed), *The Financial Constitution of European Integration: Follow the Money?* (n 63) 245.
[198] Regulation (EU) 2021/241 of the European Parliament and of the Council of 12 February 2021 establishing the Recovery and Resilience Facility [2021] OJ L57/17 ('RRF Regulation'), art 4(2).
[199] Rubio et al, 'The Tools for Protecting the EU Budget' (n 143) 50.

II.2.a. Fundamental Rights Milestones Supported by the RRF ('Carrot')

Similarly to the CPR Funds, the RRF can also support reforms aimed at strengthening fundamental rights. Although supporting fundamental rights is not the explicit focus of the RRF, it can, like the Cohesion Funds, contribute to their enhancement.

The RRF Regulation outlines six policy areas falling under its scope: the green transition; digital transformation; smart, sustainable, and inclusive growth; social and territorial cohesion; health, economic, social, and institutional resilience; and policies aimed at the next generation, children, and youth, encompassing education and skills development. It is not surprising that measures related to fundamental rights may fall under these objectives. Moreover, the RRF is characterised by its integration with the European Semester, which allows for the consideration – albeit limited – of the respect of certain fundamental rights by the Member States. Indeed, through the RRF, the country-specific recommendations (CSRs) made during the European Semester gain strength, as national reports (NRRPs) are required to take them into account. Article 18 of the RRF Regulation further stipulates that national plans must explain how the measures in the recovery and resilience plan are expected to contribute to gender equality and equal opportunities for all.[200]

With regard to the initiatives funded by the RRF, many of these may contribute to the protection of fundamental rights in Europe. Milestones contributing to the fundamental right to education (Article 14 of the EU Charter) have been established, for instance, to provide support to students from underprivileged socioeconomic and migrant backgrounds.[201] Others strengthen the fundamental right to health (Article 35 of the EU Charter) by backing the financing of national health care systems.[202] Funding has also been granted for improving both the accessibility and quality of social housing,[203] and for increasing the labour-market participation of women.[204] Reforms aimed at strengthening judicial independence have been required from the Czech Republic, Hungary, Malta, Poland, Romania, and Slovakia.[205] Many milestones and targets financed

[200] However, this objective has been criticised for being too narrow, particularly in view of the broader aim of tackling inequality and poverty. Furthermore, it has been lamented that, within this instrument, the fight against inequality has been directly linked to the objective of economic growth. See L Fromont, 'The place of inequality and poverty in the Recovery and Resilience Facility' in C Brière and A Crespy, *Inequality and the European Union* (Routledge, 2025) 113–25.

[201] Council Recommendation of 14 July 2023 on the 2023 National Reform Programme of Sweden and delivering a Council opinion on the 2023 Convergence Programme of Sweden [2023] OJ C312/252.

[202] Council Recommendation of 12 July 2022 on the 2022 National Reform Programme of Poland and delivering a Council opinion on the 2022 Convergence Programme of Poland [2022] OJ C334/171.

[203] Council Recommendation of 14 July 2023 on the 2023 National Reform Programme of Lithuania and delivering a Council opinion on the 2023 Stability Programme of Lithuania [2023] OJ C312/135.

[204] Council Recommendation of 14 July 2023 on the 2023 National Reform Programme of Austria and delivering a Council opinion on the 2023 Stability Programme of Austria [2023] OJ C 312/186.

[205] Rubio et al, 'The Tools for Protecting the EU Budget' (n 143) 53.

by the RRF are thus addressing challenges in the field of fundamental rights.[206] According to the analysis of the European Commission, 216 measures, accounting for 13.4 billion euros in grants and loans, are linked to social and inclusion measures.[207] The RRF, indeed, enables the EU to invest in national welfare state policies and reforms.[208] Even though not all social measures have a direct impact on the protection of fundamental rights, some of them cover areas such as education, health, long-term care, housing, and employment, and include specific actions aimed at the integration, equality, and wellbeing of socioeconomically disadvantaged people and specific vulnerable groups, such as people with disabilities, the elderly, Roma people, or migrants.

II.2.b. Sanctions to Respect Fundamental Rights under the RRF ('Stick')

While the RRF does not include a strict conditionality mechanism for the respect of fundamental rights like the CPR does, the European Commission can still exercise significant control over how these funds are spent, through the validation of the NRRPs. There are no general obligations related to the protection of fundamental rights in this framework, but these rights can still have an indirect influence.

As already underlined, the NRRPs are, moreover, expected to align with the country-specific challenges and priorities identified within the framework of the European Semester.[209] The majority of these recommendations are of an economic nature, but some of them are more or less directly related to fundamental rights. The CSRs focus on specific problems encountered within the Member States and are discussed by the Council of Ministers, which gives them a strong functional legitimacy. According to Louise Fromont and Arnaud van Waeyenberge, this implies that the conditionality enshrined in the European Semester 'will be more easily accepted by Member States'.[210] The fundamental rights aspect of the CSRs is constrained, yet it is present.[211] It encompasses mainly elements pertaining to effective judicial protection and the principles of the European Pillar of Social

[206] European Union Agency on Fundamental Rights, 'EU Funds – Ensuring Compliance with Fundamental Rights' (n 109) 20.

[207] European Commission, 'Recovery and Resilience Scoreboard – Thematic analysis: social protection' (April 2022) 3, available at https://ec.europa.eu/economy_finance/recovery-and-resilience-scoreboard/assets/thematic_analysis/scoreboard_thematic_analysis_social_protection.pdf.

[208] DJ Bokhorst, 'Steering National Social Reforms through the EU's Recovery Plan' in B Vanhercke and S Spasova (eds), *Social policy in the European Union: State of play 2022* (European Trade Union Institute, 2023) 36.

[209] RRF Regulation, art 17(3).

[210] Fromont and Van Waeyenberge, 'Trading Rule of Law for Recovery?' (n 66) 139.

[211] However, it should be noted that CSRs can, conversely, sometimes be seen as threatening fundamental rights, particularly when imposing certain austerity policies. As with most instruments analysed in this book, the protection of fundamental rights is balanced with competing objectives pursued by the EU.

Rights.[212] By incorporating the CSRs established within the European Semester into the process of the RRF, the European Commission is thus equipped with augmented monitoring capabilities. It assesses whether the plans – and, more significantly, any future deviations from these plans – align with the CSRs and adhere to the milestones and targets.[213] However, it should be emphasised that some CSRs can negatively impact the protection of fundamental rights. The primary aim of the European Semester was to impose budgetary constraints on several Member States. As Eleni De Becker observes,

> An analysis of the CSRs and the Annual Growth Surveys (period 2011–2015) shows that several EU Member States were asked to reduce the duration of unemployment benefits (e.g., Belgium and France). EU Member States have also been urged to increase labor market participation, especially among vulnerable groups of workers who have difficulties entering labor markets.[214]

Although the European Pillar of Social Rights is now considered within the European Semester framework, some recommendations from the CSRs still call for the reduction of certain social protections, potentially harming the protection of fundamental rights.

The scope of fundamental rights covered by the RRF combined with the CSRs is, additionally, much narrower than the cross-cutting clause of compliance of the CPR with the Charter. As underlined by Eulalia Rubio et al, one of the major drawbacks of the RRF is also that it is a 'one-shot' measure: unless the Member State requests to amend its plan, the milestones and targets identified in NRRPs cannot be changed.[215] A loophole can occur if the milestones, such as those related to protecting certain fundamental rights, are inadequate, or if a significant drawback is discovered after the plan's approval. The European Commission cannot add milestones to the NRRP retroactively. Moreover, unlike what is foreseen in the CPR, once the NRRPs are approved, the European Commission is unable to halt or suspend RRF payments because of a use of these funds non-compliant with the EU Charter. Unlike the horizontal principles outlined in the CPR, those established in the RRF Regulation[216] do not include the respect for fundamental rights and the EU Charter. The European Commission can only take such action if this irregularity poses a threat to the satisfactory achievement of RRF milestones and targets.[217] However, the 'key novelty' of the RRF is the performance-based financing.[218] Payments are, thus, conditioned on the achievement of reforms

[212] E De Becker, 'The principle of adequate social protection in the European Pillar of Social Rights: Assessing the instruments used to realise its potential' (2024) 26(2) *European Journal of Social Security* 284, 287.

[213] Bokhorst, 'Steering National Social Reforms' (n 209) 27.

[214] De Becker, 'The principle of adequate social protection in the European Pillar of Social Rights' (n 212) 286.

[215] Rubio et al, 'The Tools for Protecting the EU Budget' (n 143) 53.

[216] RRF Regulation, art 5.

[217] Rubio et al, 'The Tools for Protecting the EU Budget' (n 143) 50.

[218] Bokhorst, 'Steering National Social Reforms' (n 209) 27.

identified in the national plans. As already underlined, the European Commission is responsible for scrutinising compliance with these criteria. Should the evaluation yield a negative outcome, it reserves the right to partially or fully suspend payments.[219] Progress is evaluated through milestones (qualitative objectives) and targets (quantitative objectives).[220] In cases of backtracking on previously fulfilled milestones, the funds may also be recovered.[221] Failure by the Member State to implement necessary measures within six months will prompt the European Commission to proportionally decrease the financial contribution, and, if applicable, the loan amount.[222] The RRF Regulation, moreover, establishes that loan agreements shall be terminated if, within the 18 months of the adoption of the Council Implementing Decision, no progress has been made in respect of any relevant milestones and targets.[223]

Additionally, although there is no explicit conditional clause in the RRF, 'audits and controls' milestones have been added in many NRRPs as prerequisites for certain Member States to access the initial disbursements from the RRF. These conditions, also referred to as 'super milestones', are designed to rectify shortcomings within the RRF's management and oversight mechanisms, in order to protect the EU's financial interests.[224] Though not directly connected to safeguarding fundamental rights, a few of them hold the potential to influence the fundamental right to effective judicial protection. The proper functioning of the judicial system has, indeed, been identified as a critical condition for the effective utilisation of the RRF. Therefore, requirements related to the protection of the fundamental right to effective judicial protection are incorporated into some NRRPs, serving as a condition for the allocation of funds for projects under the RRF.[225]

The European Commission recommended reforms focusing on the independence of the judicial system as a precondition in the Hungarian and Polish NRRPs.[226] With regard to Hungary, it considered that,

> taking into account that effective judicial independence is a prerequisite for the functioning of an internal control system, milestones should be set out for reforms to strengthen the relative role and powers of the National Judicial Council in relation to the powers of the President of the National Office for the Judiciary, strengthen the judicial independence of the Supreme Court (Kúria), remove obstacles to references for preliminary rulings to the Court of Justice of the European Union and remove

[219] RRF Regulation, art 24(6).
[220] ibid, art 2(4).
[221] ibid, art 24(3).
[222] ibid, art 24(8).
[223] ibid, art 24(9).
[224] ibid, arts 5(e) and 22.
[225] For an in-depth analysis of these 'super milestones' and the stage of their fulfilment in January 2023, see, among others, A Schwarcz, 'Rule of law-related "super milestones" in the recovery and resilience plans of Hungary and Poland. Briefing requested by the CONT committee of the European Parliament' (January 2023), available at https://www.europarl.europa.eu/RegData/etudes/BRIE/2023/741581/IPOL_BRI(2023)741581_EN.pdf.
[226] Lane Scheppele and Morijn, 'What Price Rule of Law?' (n 173) 42.

the possibility for public authorities to challenge final judicial decisions before the Constitutional Court.[227]

Twenty-seven 'super milestones' were defined, four of which relate to judicial independence, covering the remedial measures agreed upon under the general conditionality mechanism (see below). With regard to Poland, the European Commission established super milestones requiring a reform strengthening the independence and impartiality of courts and a reform to remedy the situation of judges affected by the decisions of the Disciplinary Chamber of the Supreme Court. As set out in the European Commission's proposal, 'Poland should fulfil those milestones before the submission of the first payment request and no payment under the Facility may be made before their fulfilment'.[228] Hence, the RRF has been leveraged to strengthen the fundamental right to effective judicial protection, as enshrined in Article 47 of the EU Charter. Although the super milestones for Poland are fewer (only 4), compared with those in the Hungarian plan (up to 60), this can be explained by their much broader scope.

As these super milestones act as prerequisites for the first disbursements, they mainly entail formal obligations, such as the adoption of new rules. As underlined by Rubio and others, the fulfilment of these conditions does not ensure the effective operation of these new frameworks throughout the entire RRF implementation period.[229] However, any reversal would enable the European Commission to suspend, and possibly recover, RRF funding.[230] Furthermore, it should be noted that, as indicated in Article 8 of the RRF Regulation, the Conditionality Regulation, which will be analysed below, applies throughout the implementation of the RRF.

At the time of writing, it is still too early to judge the effectiveness of these super milestones. However, it is the European Commission that has been entrusted with the task to evaluate the achievement of the milestones, which will undoubtedly entail a political dimension.[231] The political factor is already present right from the establishment of the super milestones: these do not always align perfectly with the demands arising from the jurisprudence of the CJEU, which may create 'an alternative legal reality' where a Member State 'may be financially rewarded for enacting "reforms" that fall short of its true obligations under EU law, undermining the authority of the ECJ and its decisions'.[232] According to a joint assessment

[227] Proposal for a Council Implementing Decision on the approval of the assessment of the recovery and resilience plan for Hungary [2022] COM/2022/686 final, recital 60.

[228] Proposal for a Council Implementing Decision on the approval of the assessment of the recovery and resilience plan for Poland [2022] COM/2022/268 final, recital 44.

[229] Rubio et al, 'The Tools for Protecting the EU Budget' (n 143) 52.

[230] RRF Regulation, art 24(3).

[231] Maurice, 'The Rule of Law' (n 180).

[232] F Corti and others, 'Study Supporting the Mid-Term Evaluation of the Recovery and Resilience Facility' (December 2023) 165, available at https://commission.europa.eu/document/download/7fff9205-b77a-4a3f-ad85-8a4c88cb6503_en?filename=study-supporting-the-mid-term-evaluation-of-the-recovery-and-resilience-facility.pdf.

made in November 2023 by different NGOs, including Amnesty International, in relation to Hungarian reforms following the EU requirements, 'the implementation of the reforms falls short of expectations, also lacking both pace and genuine commitment, and the effectiveness and sustainability of the already adopted changes remain largely to be seen'.[233] Nevertheless, other studies indicate that, without the RRF, difficult reforms related to the rule of law, especially in Poland, Hungary, and Romania, would likely not have occurred.[234]

To conclude on the role of fundamental rights in the RRF, it is important to note that, while the RRF has significant potential to financially support initiatives protecting fundamental rights in Member States, its 'sanctioning' dimension is much less pronounced than in the CPR regime. There is no general requirement ensuring that the funds are used in compliance with the Charter. This difference raises questions, particularly because, although the two types of funds are not subject to the same fundamental rights rules, both are governed by the Conditionality Regulation, which we will now examine.

II.3. The Conditionality Regulation

One cannot delve into the discussion of the new financial mechanisms instituted to safeguard the founding values of the EU without highlighting the Conditionality Regulation,[235] which was adopted in 2021. Initially conceived as a mechanism to protect the rule of law, its scope underwent significant reduction during the legislative process, turning it into a safeguard for the EU's budget. While it is often labelled as 'the rule of law conditionality regulation', one must not overlook its restricted scope, which was confirmed by the CJEU.[236] This limitation notably arises from the legal basis used to adopt the Regulation,[237] and prevents competence creep in budget management. Although the ties to the protection of values have diminished, it remains possible that this instrument indirectly, and to a certain extent only, serves to protect fundamental rights. Given the limited connection to the protection of fundamental rights, I will confine my analysis to this instrument.[238]

[233] Joint assessment by Amnesty International Hungary, Eötvös Károly Institute, Hungarian Civil Liberties Union, Hungarian Helsinki Committee, K-Monitor, and Transparency International Hungary, 'Assessment of Hungary's compliance with conditions to access EU funds' (16 November 2023), available at https://www.amnesty.hu/assessment-of-hungarys-compliance-with-conditions-to-access-eu-funds/.

[234] Corti and others, 'Study Supporting the Mid-Term Evaluation of the Recovery and Resilience Facility' (n 233) 133.

[235] Conditionality Regulation (n 72).

[236] C-156/21 *Hungary v the European Parliament and Council of the European Union* ECLI:EU:C:2022:97 [2022]; and C-157/21 *Republic of Poland v the European Parliament and Council of the European Union* ECLI:EU:C:2022:98 [2022].

[237] TFEU, art 322(1)(a).

[238] For a more in-depth analysis, see, among others, A Baraggia and M Bonelli, 'Linking Money to Values: The New Rule of Law Conditionality Regulation and Its Constitutional Challenges' (2022) 23 *German Law Journal* 131; and A De Gregorio Merino, 'Follow the Money, Follow the Values' in Weber, *The Financial Constitution of European Integration: Follow the Money?* (n 63).

The Conditionality Regulation was introduced to serve as a measure balancing the substantial collective funding expected from the NGEU, ensuring that such financial allocations align with the principles of the rule of law ('stick'). This Regulation applies broadly, covering all funds provided to Member States by the EU. As already underscored, its scope was considerably diluted during the legislative journey, rendering it somewhat inappropriate to present it as a robust guardian of the rule of law and the EU's founding values. In essence, as it stands, especially following its endorsement by the CJEU,[239] the Conditionality Regulation primarily functions as a mechanism to shield the EU's financial interests. After much heated debate in EU institutions, it was finally decided to adopt a Regulation aimed at safeguarding the EU financial interests – albeit with a connection to the rule of law, but only when violations of the rule of law pose a financial threat.[240] Thus, not every violation of the rule of law can warrant the use of this sanction mechanism, only those capable of endangering EU monies. The benefit of this instrument in bolstering the protection of fundamental rights as such is thus very much constrained. In any event, it will be imperative to ascertain that any potential breach of fundamental rights could undermine the financial interests of the EU, to justify the use of this mechanism. This scenario appears to be relatively uncommon, except in cases involving the fundamental right to effective judicial protection. The Regulation explicitly underlines that 'breaches of the principles of the rule of law, in particular those that affect the proper functioning of public authorities and effective judicial review, can seriously harm the financial interests of the Union'.[241] Conversely, a policy that violates the EU Charter – such as, for example, one discriminating against LGBTQ+ individuals – could not justify the use of this instrument unless it can be shown to affect the EU's budget.

In terms of procedure, it falls upon the European Commission to identify the existence of breaches of the rule of law that may affect the sound financial management of the EU budget.[242] Following this, it engages in dialogue with the relevant Member State, potentially also involving the European Parliament.[243] Ultimately, the Council of the EU, by a qualified majority, decides on the implementation of appropriate sanction measures, which may include the suspension of fund allocation, including cohesion funds.[244]

The instrument was used in relation to Hungary, resulting in a decision to suspend funds amounting to 6.3 billion euros.[245] Seventeen 'remedial measures'

[239] C-156/21 *Hungary v the European Parliament and Council of the European Union* ECLI:EU:C:2022:97 [2022]; and C-157/21 *Republic of Poland v the European Parliament and Council of the European Union* ECLI:EU:C:2022:98 [2022].

[240] On the evolution that led to the final text, see, among others, Coman, *The Politics of the Rule of Law in the EU Polity* (n 33) 195–241.

[241] Conditionality Regulation, recital 15. See also art 4(2)(d).

[242] ibid, art 6(1).

[243] ibid, art 6(2)–6(7).

[244] ibid, art 6(10)–6(11).

[245] Council Implementing Decision (EU) 2022/2506 of 15 December 2022 on measures for the protection of the Union budget against breaches of the principles of the rule of law in Hungary [2022] OJ L325/94.

have been identified to halt the suspension of funds, primarily covering efforts to combat corruption.[246] None of them have a direct link to the protection of fundamental rights. With regard to Poland, the European Commission has refrained from activating the budgetary conditionality mechanism because it could not establish that the breaches of judicial independence directly jeopardise EU budget management and the financial interests.[247]

II.4. EU Spending Powers and Fundamental Rights: A Cross-cutting Analysis

A new monitoring approach to fundamental rights is emerging within EU financial and budgetary instruments, supplementing the previously mentioned political conditionalities and sanctions. For some time now, the EU's budget has increasingly financed national initiatives aimed at enhancing the protection of fundamental rights in Member States (the 'carrot approach'). More recently, the EU has begun developing financial mechanisms that allow for sanctions in cases of potential violations of EU founding values, including fundamental rights (the 'stick approach'). Some instruments, such as the RRF, combine both approaches.

This shift can be attributed to two key factors: the ongoing 'values crisis' that the EU has been experiencing for over a decade, and the increasing financial integration within the EU, marked by a rise in the EU budget and culminating in the establishment of the NGEU programme. These factors have necessitated the implementation of new financial monitoring mechanisms for EU values. With the risk of EU founding values being increasingly violated in certain Member States, how can the justification for greater financial integration be further promoted and justified? The systemic impact and effectiveness of these new mechanisms remain, nevertheless, to be seen.

While we can observe occasional developments within the Member States as a result of these mechanisms, it is doubtful whether they will be sufficient to address the crisis of values currently faced by the EU. While the share of European funds plays a more substantial role in government expenditure within states with lower GDPs,[248] EU funds remain considerably constrained in comparison with the budgets of its Member States.[249] Moreover, as underlined by Coman and Buzogany, the new conditionality mechanisms only enable the European

[246] Communication from the Commission to the Council on the remedial measures notified by Hungary under Regulation (EU, Euratom) 2020/2092 for the protection of the Union budget [2022] COM(2022)687 final.

[247] Maurice, 'The Rule of Law' (n 180).

[248] European Union Agency on Fundamental Rights, 'EU Funds – Ensuring Compliance with Fundamental Rights' (n 109) 16.

[249] de Witte, 'Integration Through Funding' (n 95) 235.

Commission to assess formal change rather than substantive transformation.[250] Additionally, there is uncertainty regarding the proficiency of the actors tasked with the implementation of these 'fundamental rights conditionalities'. It is not guaranteed that the Directorates-General of the European Commission, and national stakeholders, possess the requisite expertise to adeptly implement these intricate, opaque, and complex mechanisms.[251] Research conducted by the FRA underscores the imperative need for enhanced training in fundamental rights for officials engaged in managing authorities or other functions tied to the administration of EU funds, particularly at regional and local levels. Many individuals involved find instruments such as the EU Charter and CPR to be abstract and encounter challenges in applying them effectively to their daily responsibilities.[252] In view of this, there is a regrettable lack of coherence and clarity in these mechanisms, due to the varying regimes applicable to different funds. Expecting national stakeholders, who must implement or contribute to these mechanisms, to master all these different conditionality regimes is unrealistic. A unified regime would be more straightforward and likely more effective in practice. Another lingering question pertains to the co-ordination of these diverse sanction mechanisms. These instruments significantly overlap, resulting in insufficient clarity regarding their application and associated conditions.

The use of these new financial tools also raises questions regarding legitimacy. A central issue, strongly linked to fundamental rights, is the question of competence creep.[253] Through these tools, EU institutions gain influence in areas beyond the EU's attributed powers. As extensively discussed in chapter one of this book, while the EU has a certain capacity to protect fundamental rights, it still remains limited. Indeed, the EU lacks a general competence in the realm of fundamental rights. Therefore, how can we account for the broad scope of these financial instruments, which often extend beyond the EU's competences? This inquiry delves into the implications of the EU's evolving role in the field of fundamental rights protection for the distribution of powers between the EU and its Member States, a topic I will explore further in chapter four of this book.

To conclude, presented below is a comparative table illustrating the various instruments examined and the fundamental rights aspects addressed by each of them.

[250] Coman and Buzogány, 'The EU's Response to the Rule of Law Crisis' (n 177) 7.

[251] On this point, see, further, Gambardella, 'The Promise and Perils of Fundamental Rights through Funding in the EU' (n 82).

[252] Coman and Buzogány, 'The EU's Response to the Rule of Law Crisis' (n 177) 7.

[253] M Fisicaro, 'Conditionality and the making of the EU spending power: the question of competence', forthcoming in the *Common Market Law Review*; and I Gambardella, 'Finanziamenti dell'Unione europea come mezzi alternativi per orientare le politiche degli Stati membri: quale impatto sulla ripartizione delle competenze?' (2024) 3 *Quaderni AISDUE* 217–34.

Table 3.1 Table illustrating the various forms of financial support and conditionality in relation to EU Fundamental Rights Law

	The Common Provision Regulation	**The Recovery and Resilience Facility**	**Conditionality Regulation**
Funds concerned	Cohesion and Home Funds	RRF Funds	All EU Funds
Management	Shared management by the European Commission and the Council of the EU and the Member States	Direct management by the European Commission; Member States are beneficiaries	Sanction mechanism implemented directly by the European Commission and the Council of the EU
Fundamental Rights Components	• Funding of initiatives contributing to the protection of FR • General obligation to respect the Charter and the UNCRPD • Cross-cutting enabling conditions, including the respect of the EU Charter of Fundamental Rights and the implementation of the UNCRPD	• Funding of initiatives contributing to the protection of FR • NRRPs implement CSRs which integrate the European Pillar of Social Rights' principles and the rule of law imperative (including the principle of effective judicial protection)	• Limited to rule of law issues threatening EU budget • Possibly includes the protection of the fundamental right to an effective judicial protection, to the extent that it protects EU financial interests
Possible sanctions	• *Ex ante* – Refusal of approval of partnership agreements • *Ex post* – Non-reimbursement of expenses	• *Ex ante* – Refusal of approval of NRRPs and determination of the super milestones' *ex ante* conditionality • Performance-based: (super) milestones must be achieved to request (a first) reimbursement	• Cross-cutting suspension or reduction, interruption of payments or reimbursements

Section III – Independent Monitoring and Supervision of EU Fundamental Rights Protection

In addition to the political and financial mechanisms underpinning the effectiveness of EU Fundamental Rights Law, the EU has triggered the creation of a network of independent bodies tasked with supervising and monitoring respect for EU Fundamental Rights Law. The creation of such guardians – both at the EU and domestic levels – is a distinctive feature of this layer of protection, shaping a genuine governance structure for human rights within the EU. In 2007, the EU set up a general agency with a broad mandate covering all sectors: the Fundamental Rights Agency (section III.1). Alongside this, a number of sectoral bodies have also been established to carry out sector-specific monitoring functions (section III.2).

III.1. The Fundamental Rights Agency

The Fundamental Rights Agency (FRA) is the most important and cross-cutting independent monitoring agency in the EU for fundamental rights protection. This expert body, which is already well-documented in the literature,[254] operates independently, with the mission of providing EU institutions, bodies, offices, and agencies, and the Member States[255] (when implementing EU law), with expertise and support concerning the implementation and protection of EU Fundamental Rights, as laid out in its Founding Regulation (Article 2).[256] It was established following the model of independent human rights institutions, initially promoted by the United Nations through the 'Paris Principles', and now present in a large majority of EU Member States.

The origins of the FRA lie in academic debates, notably those initiated by Alston and Weiler in 1999.[257] Following a prolonged political struggle,[258] the FRA was formally established in 2007.[259] Its institutional predecessor, the European

[254] See P Alston and O de Schutter (eds), *Monitoring Fundamental Rights in the EU: The Contribution of the Fundamental Rights Agency* (Hart Publishing, 2005).

[255] One area remains excluded from the scope of the FRA: the Common Foreign and Security Policy (Founding Regulation, art 3(2)).

[256] Council Regulation (EC) 168/2007 of 15 February 2007 establishing a European Union Agency for Fundamental Rights, OJ L 53 of 22 February 2007 ('Founding Regulation'), pp 1–14.

[257] P Alston and JHH Weiler, 'An "Ever Closer Union" in need of a Human Rights Policy: The European Union and Human Rights' in P Alston (ed), *The EU and Human Rights* (Oxford University Press, 1999) 3–66.

[258] M Ovadek, 'The Curious Case of the Fundamental Rights Agency's Mandate: Legal Shrouding and Democratic Politics' (2019) 25(4) *European Public Law* 517–34.

[259] On this process, see L Violini, 'The Fundamental Rights Agency of the EU: A step on the way toward an integrated EU policy in the domain of fundamental rights' in L Violini and A Baraggia (eds), *The Fragmented Landscape of Fundamental Rights Protection in Europe* (Edward Elgar, 2018) 139–52.

Monitoring Centre on Racism and Xenophobia, was created in 1997, notably in response to the inclusion of a far-right party in the Austrian government.

Within the EU's institutional framework, and international human rights law, the FRA stands out for its distinct status and mandate.[260] As underlined by von Bogdandy and von Bernstorff, its creation 'was another step in the expansion of an EU policy on fundamental rights'.[261] Interestingly, it was once again the term 'fundamental rights' that was chosen over 'human rights', reflecting, as emphasised in the Introduction to this book, the EU's tendency to refer to something more 'domestic' than international. As already stressed, the adjective 'fundamental' is typically used in constitutional contexts, while 'human' is more commonly associated with the multilevel international human rights architecture.[262] According to its Founding Regulation, the FRA is made up of four key bodies: a management board, an executive board, a scientific committee, and a director. The management board is not composed of representatives from the Member States, but rather of independent individuals who, nonetheless, are appointed by the Member States.

The FRA's main function is advisory, which it fulfils through several means. First, it collects and analyses data (provisions of evidence), disseminating its findings through the publication of reports.[263] Second, it issues expert opinions (policy advice).[264] Third, it works to raise awareness of fundamental rights issues within civil society (communication of rights).[265] Importantly, it can only act within the limits of the powers conferred on the EU.[266] Moreover, it lacks regulatory or quasi-judicial authority and is not empowered to make binding decisions on third parties.

However, although it may seem limited, this advisory power can serve as the foundation for significant administrative action.[267] The FRA, notably, provide legal opinions on legislative proposals being discussed at the EU level. Crucially, for the purposes of our study, it also offers practical guidance to national stakeholders in the context of implementing EU Fundamental Rights at the domestic level.[268] In this capacity, the Agency engages actively with Member States to support and enhance the national implementation of EU fundamental rights.

[260] GN Toggenburg, 'The European Union Fundamental Rights Agency' in G Oberleitner (ed), *International Human Rights Institutions, Tribunals, and Courts* (Springer, 2018) 446.

[261] A von Bogdandy and J von Bernstorff, 'The EU Fundamental Rights Agency within the European and International Human Rights Architecture' (2009) 46(4) *Common Market Law Review* 1035–1068.

[262] ibid, 1036.

[263] On this mission, see B Sokhi-Bulley, 'The Fundamental Rights Agency of the European Union: A New Panopticism' (2011) 11(4) *Human Rights Law Review* 683–706.

[264] GN Toggenburg, 'The EU Fundamental Rights Agency and the Fundamental Rights Charter: How Fundamental is the Link Between Them?' in S Peers et al (eds), *The EU Charter of Fundamental Rights: A Commentary* (Hart Publishing, 2014) 1614.

[265] Toggenburg, 'The European Union Fundamental Rights Agency' (n 261) 452.

[266] Council Regulation 168/2007/EC of 15 February 2007 establishing a European Union Agency for Fundamental Rights, OJ L 53 of 22 February 2007, p 1, art 3.

[267] von Bogdandy and von Bernstoff, 'The EU Fundamental Rights Agency' (n 262) 1051.

[268] Toggenburg, 'The European Union Fundamental Rights Agency' (n 261) 450.

As Gabriel N. Toggenburg emphasises, beyond its formal structures, the Agency functions as a 'network of networks' that reaches into diverse national contexts.[269] To this end, the Founding Regulation mandates that each Member State appoint a National Liaison Officer (NLO). In practice, these are civil servants working in ministries of interior or foreign affairs, or within the office of the prime minister. They serve to ensure a continuous flow of information between the Agency and individual Member States. These NLOs convene annually at the Agency's headquarters in Vienna to review its work and exchange updates on national developments. In addition, this collaborative network is reinforced by national parliamentary focal points, who act as the Agency's main partners within the parliamentary administrations of the Member States.[270]

Before 2022, the scope of action for the FRA was significantly limited. At the time, it could only act on its own initiative within specific 'thematic areas' defined every five years by the Council of the EU in a multi-annual framework,[271] excluding the field of police and judicial co-operation in criminal matters. As Lorenza Violini has noted, this fragmented approach to defining its fields of intervention weakened the Agency's overall effectiveness.[272] While it could, upon request from the European Parliament, the Council of the EU, or the European Commission, issue opinions on matters outside these predefined areas, such matters still had to fall within the scope of EU law.[273] This meant that its ability to act was largely dependent on the political will of these institutions.[274]

However, things have since evolved. Following the 2022 amendment to the Founding Regulation, the FRA may now also undertake own-initiative work in broader fields, including on police and judicial co-operation in criminal matters.[275] The Common Foreign and Security Policy, nevertheless, remains excluded from its realm.[276] The former multi-annual framework used to define its work programme has been replaced by a more flexible and operational system of annual and multi-annual programming, which is no longer in the sole hands of the Council of the EU. This programming is prepared by the Agency's director and subsequently discussed with the Council of the EU, the European Commission, the Member States, and the scientific committee. Based on these consultations, the

[269] ibid, 447.

[270] ibid.

[271] Council Regulation 168/2007/EC of 15 February 2007 establishing a European Union Agency for Fundamental Rights, OJ L 53 of 22 February 2007, art 5(3).

[272] Violini, 'The Fundamental Rights Agency of the EU' (n 260) 144.

[273] Council Regulation 168/2007/EC of 15 February 2007 establishing a European Union Agency for Fundamental Rights, OJ L 53 of 22 February 2007, art 3.

[274] However, the Agency has had the opportunity to report on an area closely related to mutual trust – detention conditions – on the basis of a request from the European Commission: see the report, European Union Agency for Fundamental Rights, 'Criminal detention conditions in the European Union: rules and reality' (December 2019), available at https://fra.europa.eu/sites/default/files/fra_uploads/fra-2019-criminal-detention-conditions-in-the-eu_en.pdf.

[275] Council Regulation (EU) 2022/555 of 5 April 2022 amending Regulation (EC) No 168/2007 establishing a European Union Agency for Fundamental Rights, OJ L 108, 7.4.2022, pp 1–12.

[276] see Founding Regulation, art 3(2).

final programme is then adopted by the Agency's management board.[277] The FRA's scope of action is, therefore, not as strictly circumscribed as, for instance, the field of application of the EU Charter of Fundamental Rights, as set out in Article 51.[278] In this sense, its broad mandate comes against the backdrop of a delicate balance with the EU's limited competences in the field of human rights. The Agency's legal basis – the so-called flexibility clause, now enshrined in Article 352 TFEU – is one of the 'least specific' provisions in the Treaties.[279] As a result, the connection between its activities and the EU's areas of competence has not always been clearly delineated.

In light of these developments, the FRA adopted a strategic framework for the period 2023–28, structured around three core priorities. First, it aims to support the safeguarding of fundamental rights standards in the creation of new EU laws and policies. Second, it seeks to contribute to the respect, protection, and fulfilment of fundamental rights within the domains already governed by existing EU legislation. Finally, the strategy includes a set of cross-cutting actions designed to reinforce the broader realisation of the EU's Fundamental Rights goals and vision across all areas of governance. In connection with the strengthening of fundamental rights protection within Member States, the FRA has set out specific strategic objectives as part of the second strategic priority. These include supporting the implementation of EU laws and policies by providing advice, expert opinions, research, and real-time assistance to EU institutions, Member States, and other relevant stakeholders; promoting the integration of a fundamental rights perspective in the application of relevant laws and policies at both EU and national levels; and assisting the EU institutions and Member States in adopting practical measures to address emerging fundamental rights risks and challenges.[280] In terms of content, the Agency also outlined a number of megatrends that seem most relevant to fundamental rights, in its Strategic Plan 2023–28,[281] including: (i) challenges to justice and the rise of a security-based agenda; (ii) threats to democratic values; (iii) inequality and increased discrimination; (iv) changing patterns of migration; (v) economic and social trends; (vi) digital transformation and artificial intelligence; and (vii) climate change.

The FRA thus plays a crucial role in supporting the effective implementation of fundamental rights standards across EU Member States, particularly in

[277] Council Regulation (EU) 2022/555 of 5 April 2022 amending Regulation (EC) No 168/2007 establishing a European Union Agency for Fundamental Rights, OJ L 108, 7.4.2022, pp 1–12, art 5a.

[278] On the scope of application of EU Fundamental Rights, see ch I, s IV, 'Limitation: A Paradoxically Restricted Mandate'.

[279] E Muir, *EU Equality Law: The First Fundamental Rights Policy of the EU* (Oxford University Press, 2018) 179.

[280] European Union Agency for Fundamental Rights, 'Single Programming Document, 2025–2027', available at https://fra.europa.eu/sites/default/files/fra_uploads/fra_spd_2025-2027_en.pdf.

[281] FRA Strategic Plan 2023–2028, available at https://fra.europa.eu/sites/default/files/fra_uploads/fra-2023-fra-strategic-plan-2023-2028_en.pdf.

increasingly sensitive and politically charged areas. Its very existence reflects a noteworthy innovation when compared with the general framework of international human rights law, where such independent and specialised agencies remain rare. However, like many of the EU's Fundamental Rights mechanisms, the Agency operates primarily through non-binding instruments and advisory outputs. This 'soft' nature inherently limits its capacity to constrain or influence Member States that actively resist or undermine the liberal democratic values at the heart of the EU legal order. Nevertheless, the Agency contributes meaningfully to the broader governance of fundamental rights within the EU, serving as both a watchdog and a knowledge hub, and reinforcing the normative architecture that underpins the EU's commitment to fundamental rights protection.

III.2. Sector-specific Human Rights Monitoring Bodies

In addition to the FRA, the EU has gradually established a network of sector-specific monitoring bodies tasked with ensuring compliance with EU Fundamental Rights Law, both within its institutional structure and across Member States. This layered oversight system also reflects a distinctive feature of the EU's institutional architecture in the broader landscape of international human rights law. Without seeking to be exhaustive in either the examples selected or the depth of analysis, I will briefly highlight some of the key players that illustrate this evolving architecture.

In domains where it holds autonomous competences, the EU has mandated the creation of monitoring bodies that support the implementation of its policies. In the area of non-discrimination, and within the framework of the EU's anti-discrimination policy, EU law requires the establishment of independent equality bodies in each Member State, mandated to promote equal treatment and support victims of discrimination in accessing justice (section III.2(a)). In the field of data protection, Member States were required to establish independent national data protection authorities, thereby contributing to a coherent and multi-layered oversight system. At the EU level, the European Data Protection Supervisor (EDPS), established in 2004, is entrusted with ensuring the protection of personal data processed by EU institutions and bodies. In parallel, data protection officers have been appointed within several EU agencies, including Europol and Eurojust, to ensure internal compliance and reinforce institutional accountability (section III.2(b)).

Furthermore, in policy areas more indirectly connected to fundamental rights, the EU has likewise promoted the creation of dedicated monitoring mechanisms. As an example, in the field of migration and border management, the EU agency Frontex has both a Fundamental Rights Officer and a Consultative Forum on Fundamental Rights, designed to monitor the agency's compliance with fundamental rights obligations and to provide expert advice on relevant issues (section III.2(c)).

Together, these developments underscore the EU's distinctive approach to fundamental rights protection: a multi-level governance model that not only formulates high normative standards but also seeks to ensure their effective implementation through a network of institutionalised monitoring mechanisms.

III.2.a. Equality Bodies

In the field of non-discrimination law, the EU has firmly established itself as a normative leader, as highlighted in chapter one of this book. This leadership is not only reflected in the development of a sophisticated legal framework but also in the institutional infrastructure it has helped shape across Member States.[282] One of the most significant contributions in this regard is the emergence of a transnational network of equality,[283] entrusted with ensuring the effective implementation of EU anti-discrimination legislation at the national level.

While certain equality bodies already existed prior to EU anti-discrimination policy,[284] their generalised establishment can be directly traced back to the Race Equality Directive,[285] which imposed a binding obligation, for the first time, on all Member States and candidate countries to designate or create such bodies. Initially focused on combating discrimination on the grounds of racial or ethnic origin, this requirement was progressively extended through subsequent Directives, such as the Directive implementing the principle of equal treatment between men and women in the access to and supply of goods and services,[286] and the Directive on the implementation of the principle of equal opportunities and equal treatment of men and women in matters of employment and occupation,[287] in the field of gender discrimination. All the EU Directives subsequently adopted as part of the EU's anti-discrimination policy have continued this trend – with the notable exception of the Framework Employment Directive[288] – by requiring the establishment of bodies tasked with promoting the principles they enshrine.[289]

[282] Ch I, s VI.1, 'The EU's Harmonisation Power'; and M Bell, 'The implementation of European Anti-Discrimination Directives: Converging Towards a Common Model' (2008) 79(1) *The Political Quarterly* 36–44.

[283] On the governance model resulting from this innovation, see B de Witte, 'New Institutions for Promoting Equality in Europe: Legal Transfers, National Bricolage and European Governance' (2012) 60(1) *The American Journal of Comparative Law* 49–74

[284] For a history of equality bodies, see T Kadar, 'Equality bodies: a European phenomenon' (2018) 18 (2–3) *International Journal of Discrimination and the Law* 144–62.

[285] Directive (EC) 2000/43 of 29 June 2000 implementing the principle of equal treatment between persons irrespective of racial or ethnic origin OJ L 180, 19.7.2000, pp 22–26.

[286] Directive (EC) 2004/ 113 of 13 December 2004 implementing the principle of equal treatment between men and women in the access to and supply of goods and services OJ L 373, 21.12.2004, pp 37–43.

[287] Council Directive 2000/78/EC of 27 November 2000 establishing a general framework for equal treatment in employment and occupation. OJ L 303, 2.12.2000, pp. 16–22.

[288] Council Directive (EC) 2000/78 of 27 November 2000 establishing a general framework for equal treatment in employment and occupation OJ L 303, 2.12.2000, 16–22. This gap has, however, now been filled by Directive (EU) 2024/1499 of 7 May 2024 on standards for equality bodies in the field of equal treatment between persons irrespective of their racial or ethnic origin, equal treatment in matters of employment and occupation between persons irrespective of their religion or belief, disability, age or sexual orientation, equal treatment between women and men in matters of social security and in the access to and supply of goods and services, and amending Directives 2000/43/EC and 2004/113/EC OJ L, 2024/1499, 29.5.2024.

[289] Muir, *EU Equality Law* (n 280) 180.

Equality bodies are typically tasked with a multifaceted mandate: conducting independent analyses of discrimination, making recommendations to public authorities, raising awareness, and, crucially, providing support to victims. As such, equality bodies serve not only as enforcement actors but also as norm-shaping institutions, participating in the interpretation, dissemination, and internalisation of EU equality standards within domestic legal systems. While their institutional form and specific powers differ from one Member State to another, EU law imposes core requirements – most notably, that they operate with a high degree of independence and possess sufficient resources and competences to perform their duties effectively. Their dual function, as both guardians of individual rights and contributors to policy development, positions them as key components of the EU's multi-level fundamental rights architecture.

The broad discretion granted to Member States in establishing equality bodies has, however, resulted in inconsistencies in the level of protection against discrimination, along with significant disparities in the mandates, powers, and resources of the designated institutions.[290] A further point of concern was the relatively weak guarantees of independence required by the EU Directives for equality bodies – particularly when contrasted with the stronger safeguards granted to data protection authorities, to which I return below.[291]

In this context, a significant reform was introduced in 2024 with the adoption of two key EU Directives – Directive 2024/1499[292] and Directive 2024/1500[293] – with the purpose of establishing

> minimum standards for the functioning of Equality Bodies, to guarantee their independence and ensure their effectiveness in strengthening the application of the principle of equal treatment.[294]

The adoption of Directives (EU) 2024/1499 and 2024/1500 marked a significant milestone in the EU's anti-discrimination framework, addressing long-standing concerns about the uneven effectiveness and status of equality bodies across Member States. These texts introduce, for the first time, EU-wide minimum requirements regarding the mandates, independence, and resources of such bodies. Under Article 4 of both Directives, Member States are now required to

[290] Equinet, 'Key Principles for Equality Bodies' (October 2024) 5, available at https://equineteurope.org/wp-content/uploads/2024/10/Key-principles_for-web.pdf.

[291] Muir, *EU Equality Law* (n 280) 197.

[292] Council Directive (EU) 2024/1499 of 7 May 2024 on standards for equality bodies in the field of equal treatment between persons irrespective of their racial or ethnic origin, equal treatment in matters of employment and occupation between persons irrespective of their religion or belief, disability, age or sexual orientation, equal treatment between women and men in matters of social security and in the access to and supply of goods and services, and amending Directives 2000/43/EC and 2004/113/EC, OJ L, 2024/1499, 29.5.2024.

[293] Directive (EU) 2024/1500 of the European Parliament and of the Council of 14 May 2024 on standards for equality bodies in the field of equal treatment and equal opportunities between women and men in matters of employment and occupation, and amending Directives 2006/54/EC and 2010/41/EU, OJ L 2024/1500, 29.5.2024.

[294] art 1(1) of both Directives.

ensure that equality bodies have clearly defined competences covering discrimination on a wide range of grounds, including sex, racial, or ethnic origin, religion or belief, disability, age, and sexual orientation. Importantly, these competences must apply across all areas of life covered by EU anti-discrimination law – including, crucially, the fields of employment and occupation governed by Directive 2000/78/EC, which had not previously imposed such obligations.

One of the most notable innovations is the explicit and strong requirement that equality bodies operate independently and free from external influence (Articles 6 and 7), an obligation that draws inspiration from the model of data protection authorities under the GDPR (see below). The Directives also compel Member States to provide these bodies with adequate human, technical, and financial resources (Article 8), and to involve them in policymaking through formal consultation mechanisms (Article 10). Moreover, Articles 9 and 11 strengthen their investigatory and dispute resolution powers, allowing them to conduct independent inquiries and provide assistance to victims of discrimination.

Particularly significant is the obligation for the Member States to recognise equality bodies' powers to intervene in legal proceedings. Article 10 of both Directives requires that litigation powers be granted to these institutions, allowing them to take part in judicial and administrative proceedings – either in support of claimants or on their own initiative – depending on national procedural rules. It also affirms their role as legal experts, allowing them to contribute their specialised knowledge to the interpretation and application of equality law. This development marks a substantial step forward in enhancing the practical enforceability of anti-discrimination norms across the EU.

Together, these reforms represent a shift towards institutionalising equality bodies as core players in the governance of EU anti-discrimination law, moving away from fragmented national models and towards a more coherent and effective European standard.

The Member States are required to transpose and implement these changes into their national legal orders by June 2026, ensuring that the newly established minimum standards for equality bodies are fully operational by that date.

III.2.b. Data Protection Authorities and Officers

As previously noted, much like its approach to non-discrimination law, the EU has progressively crafted a sophisticated and comprehensive policy framework for the protection of personal data, now most notably codified in the landmark General Data Protection Regulation (GDPR). Within this legal architecture, a range of institutional mechanisms has been established to facilitate the effective enforcement of this fundamental right, which occupies a central position within the EU's legal order. In this regard, EU law has fostered the emergence of a transnational regulatory network that plays a pivotal role in safeguarding personal data – an inherently intangible asset capable of circulating freely across jurisdictions.[295] This framework represents a uniquely advanced and distinctive model within the broader context of international data protection governance.

At the EU level, the European Data Protection Supervisor (EDPS) serves as the independent supervisory authority responsible for overseeing the processing of personal data by the EU's institutions, bodies, offices, and agencies.[296] In addition to its supervisory role, the EDPS provides expert advice on new legislative initiatives concerning data protection, monitors the implications of technological developments for privacy, and co-operates closely with national supervisory authorities to ensure the consistent and coherent application of EU data protection standards.

Similarly, at the national level, Member States are required by EU law to establish independent national data protection authorities (DPAs),[297] responsible for monitoring the application of the GDPR and ensuring that data controllers and processors within their jurisdiction comply with their obligations. Each EU country has an independent data protection authority responsible for enforcing the GDPR and managing complaints. When data processing activities span multiple EU countries, the GDPR establishes a co-operation mechanism among the relevant authorities to ensure they work together and reach a common decision.[298] As Élise Degrave highlights, these authorities constitute a key component of the EU's data protection policy.[299] They occupy a particularly distinctive status: they are national public authorities, governed by domestic administrative law, yet entrusted with tasks imposed by EU law.[300] As is the case for equality bodies, their role is multifaceted:[301] (i) as co-regulators, they are occasionally called upon to supplement EU legislation in the field of data protection; (ii) as advisors, they engage in awareness-raising and guidance activities aimed at data controllers and processors; and (iii) as supervisory bodies, they are responsible for ensuring the effective enforcement of data protection rules. In this regard, they are endowed with real enforcement powers, ranging from warnings and reprimands to administrative fines, and even referrals to judicial authorities where necessary. Their status is, furthermore, protected under EU law, and has been safeguarded by the CJEU, which has issued several rulings reaffirming the strict requirement of

[295] E Degrave, 'Chapitre II – Protection des données à caractère personnel et régime transnational' in J-B Auby and J Dutheil de la Rochère (eds), *Traité de droit administratif européen*, 3rd edn (Bruylant, 2022) 937–60, 938.

[296] Regulation (EU) 2016/679 of the European Parliament and of the Council of 27 April 2016 on the protection of natural persons with regard to the processing of personal data and on the free movement of such data, and repealing Directive 95/46/EC (General Data Protection Regulation) [2016] OJ L 119/1 ('GDPR'), art 68.

[297] ibid, arts 51–59.

[298] ibid, art 60.

[299] Degrave, 'Chapitre II – Protection des données à caractère personnel et régime transnational' (n 296) 939.

[300] ibid.

[301] ibid.

independence that must be ensured by Member States in relation to these authorities.[302] The GDPR also establishes a framework to ensure effective co-operation between these authorities in cases involving cross-border data processing within the EU,[303] while guaranteeing a high level of proximity with citizens by enabling them to lodge complaints to the authority of the Member State of his or her habitual residence or place of work, or place of the alleged infringement.[304] The GDPR also establishes the European Data Protection Board (EDPB), which plays a co-ordination role among national authorities to ensure the consistent application of the Regulation.[305]

As a further point in relation to data protection, it is notable that the CJEU has recently affirmed that a national competition authority may, in the course of investigating an abuse of a dominant market position, identify a violation of the GDPR. In its judgment in the *Meta Platforms* case,[306] the CJEU indeed clarified that, while examining a potential abuse of dominance by a company, it may be necessary for the national competition authority to also assess the company's compliance with legal standards beyond competition law, such as those outlined in the GDPR. However, the CJEU made it clear that, when a competition authority identifies a GDPR violation, it does not replace the data protection authorities established under the Regulation. Instead, the competition authority must collaborate with these authorities, taking into account their decisions and ongoing investigations. Through this interpretation, the CJEU effectively expands the scope of oversight bodies, ensuring a more robust enforcement of GDPR compliance while maintaining a co-operative approach among the relevant authorities.

In parallel to these developments, the role of the data protection officer (DPO) has also emerged as a cornerstone of the EU's data protection governance. Pursuant to the GDPR, certain public and private entities are required to appoint a DPO to ensure adherence to data protection obligations.[307] The DPO's core responsibilities include overseeing the organisation's data processing activities, advising management on compliance with the GDPR, conducting data protection impact assessments, monitoring internal practices, and acting as the main point of contact for both data subjects and supervisory authorities. Through these functions, DPOs help embed a culture of data protection compliance within their organisations. Within national administrations, DPOs thus

[302] See, amongst others, C-518/07 *European Commission v Federal Republic of Germany* ECLI:EU:C:2010:125 [2010], para 25; C-288/12 *European Commission v Hungary* ECLI:EU:C:2014:237 [2014], paras 59–60; and C-362/14 *Maximillian Schrems v Data Protection Commissioner* ECLI:EU:C:2015:650 [2015], paras 41–42 and 57.

[303] GDPR, arts 4 and 16.

[304] ibid, art 77.

[305] ibid, art 68 et seq.

[306] C-252/21 Meta Platforms and Others (General terms of use of a social network) ECLI:EU:C:2023:537 [2023].

[307] GDPR, art 37.

play an essential role in advising public bodies and ensuring that public sector data processing activities conform to the rigorous standards set by EU law. At the level of EU agencies, bodies such as Europol and Eurojust have designated DPOs to ensure that their internal data processing activities are consistent with EU data protection standards. These officers play a crucial role in ensuring that the agencies' operational activities, which often involve cross-border co-operation with Member States, respect the fundamental rights to data protection and privacy. The establishment of DPAs and DPOs at both the EU and national levels plays an important role in enhancing personal data protection within the public and private sectors across the EU.

These developments reflect the extent to which the EU has positioned itself as a global leader in the field of data protection – not only by developing robust and comprehensive standards, but also by establishing a multi-level governance network composed of both EU and national bodies responsible for ensuring their effective implementation. This institutional architecture demonstrates a level of integration and co-ordination that remains relatively advanced compared with traditional international human rights law, once again illustrating the distinctive nature of the EU's Fundamental Rights system. As Élise Degrave has pointed out, the effectiveness of this set of common standards does not depend solely on the EU itself, but also on national bodies and the EDPB, which is called upon to play a key role in the construction of this shared legal regime.[308]

III.2.c. Frontex's Fundamental Rights Officer and Fundamental Rights Consultative Forum

The EU has not confined the establishment of institutional mechanisms for the protection of fundamental rights to areas where it holds explicit and autonomous competences – namely, equality law and data protection. Rather, it has also contributed to developments in sectors where fundamental rights considerations are more ancillary or indirect. While a comprehensive review lies beyond the scope of this discussion, one particularly illustrative example can be found in the field of external border management, where the integration of fundamental rights safeguards has become increasingly prominent – most notably within the institutional framework of Frontex.

Established in 2005, Frontex was initially tasked with co-ordinating co-operation among Member States in the management of the EU's external borders, without replacing national border control authorities. From its inception, however, it has been the subject of sustained criticism for failing to fully uphold fundamental rights standards.[309] Over time, its mandate and competences have

[308] Degrave, 'Chapitre II – Protection des données à caractère personnel et régime transnational' (n 296) 959.

[309] See, among others, M Fink, *Frontex and Human Rights: Responsibility in 'Multi-Actor Situations' under the ECHR and EU Public Liability Law* (Oxford University Press, 2018); and J De Coninck,

expanded significantly, transforming it into a central actor within the EU's border governance architecture. In this evolving context, addressing fundamental rights concerns has become an increasingly urgent necessity to ensure effective and credible human rights protection at the EU's external frontiers.[310]

In response to these concerns, the 2011 revision of Frontex's Founding Regulation[311] introduced several measures aimed at strengthening its fundamental rights framework. Notably, Frontex was required to adopt a Fundamental Rights Strategy,[312] and a Code of Conduct for all individuals participating in its operations,[313] and to establish both a Fundamental Rights Officer (FRO) and a Consultative Forum on Fundamental Rights. These bodies are mandated to monitor Frontex's compliance with EU and international human rights obligations, and to advise on fundamental-rights-related issues. The FRO and the Fundamental Rights Office – alongside the Consultative Forum – are intended to operate independently within Frontex to ensure the respect, protection, and promotion of fundamental rights. Their tasks include monitoring operations, conducting investigations and field visits, and providing advice, training, and capacity-building activities, particularly in relation to access to international protection.

While these institutional reforms represent a significant step forward, they have not resolved the deeper structural and normative tensions inherent in Frontex's role. Persistent concerns remain, particularly regarding the protection of migrants' rights at the EU's external borders.[314] Numerous studies and investigative reports continue to highlight serious deficiencies in Frontex's practices.[315] Scholars have argued that initiatives like the Consultative Forum often serve primarily symbolic or public relations functions, reflecting a rhetorical rather than substantive commitment to human rights.[316] As Perkowski aptly observed, rather than reflecting a clear and consistent commitment to rights-based governance, these changes

The EU's Human Rights Responsibility Gap: Deconstructing Human Rights Impunity of International Organisations (Hart Publishing, 2024).

[310] Dawson, *The Governance of EU Fundamental Rights* (n 27) 113.

[311] Regulation (EU) No 1168/2011 of the European Parliament and of the Council of 25 October 2011 amending Council Regulation (EC) No 2007/2004 establishing a European Agency for the Management of Operational Cooperation at the External Borders of the Member States of the European Union OJ L 304, 22.11.2011, pp 1–17.

[312] Frontex, 'Fundamental Rights Strategy' (31 March 2011), www.gdr-elsj.eu. In February 2021, an updated version was adopted: See 'Fundamental Rights Strategy' (14 February 2021), frontex.europa.eu.

[313] Frontex, Code of Conduct: For all Persons Participating in Frontex Operational Activities (21 March 2011).

[314] See, for an interesting analysis from a Member of the European Parliament, T Strik, 'Frontex's expanding mandate: Has democratic control caught up?' (2024) 30(1–2) *European Law Journal* 217–37.

[315] See, among others, E Guild (ed), *Monitoring Border Violence in the EU: Frontex in Focus* (Routledge, 2023); and G Raimondo, *The European Integrated Border Management: Frontex, Human Rights and International Responsibility* (Hart Publishing, 2024).

[316] N Perkowski, 'There Are Voices in Every Direction: Organizational Decoupling in Frontex' (2019) 57(5) *Journal of Common Market Studies* 1182.

have frequently been mobilised to 'conceal and legitimise dominant structures',[317] portraying Frontex simultaneously as a bulwark against perceived migratory threats, a saviour in humanitarian crises at sea, and a champion of fundamental rights. This duality shows the inherently ambivalent – and, at times, contradictory – nature of the agency's role, caught between security imperatives and human rights obligations.

That said, empirical research conducted by Chiara Loschi and Peter Slominski offers a more nuanced perspective.[318] Their findings suggest that, notwithstanding significant restrictions limiting their work, the creation of the Consultative Forum has created a space for fundamental rights stakeholders to engage in institutionalised dialogue with Frontex's internal and external stakeholders. While the Forum has not yet significantly strengthened Frontex's accountability, these dialogues have the potential to facilitate information-sharing, foster collective learning processes, and, over time, enhance Frontex's compliance with fundamental rights standards.

Conclusion

In this chapter, I have examined the distinctive institutional architecture that underpins EU Fundamental Rights Law. This intricate web of instruments, mechanisms, agencies, and bodies not only fortifies the EU's Fundamental Rights framework but also distinguishes it within the global landscape of human rights protection. The EU's institutional architecture for safeguarding fundamental rights is both comprehensive and multifaceted, encompassing political oversight, financial instruments, and independent monitoring bodies. While this structure underscores the robustness of the EU's additional layer of fundamental rights protection, it simultaneously brings to light the inherent limitations previously highlighted in the first part of this book.

As previously discussed, the EU's approach to political supervision of fundamental rights at the national level exemplifies the ambiguous position that it occupies in this field – caught between ambition and limitation. As repeatedly emphasised throughout this volume, the EU's proper functioning is intrinsically tied to the respect by its Member States for the values enshrined in Article 2 TEU, including fundamental rights. But the EU, unlike the Council of Europe, is not a human rights organisation. It lacks the institutional architecture and enforcement powers to act as a true guarantor of these rights when they are under threat within Member States. This structural ambiguity runs through the EU's entire engagement with fundamental rights. In contrast to the Council of Europe's

[317] N Perkowski, 'Frontex and the convergence of humanitarianism, human rights and security' (2018) 49(6) *Security Dialogue* 457, 461.

[318] C Loschi and P Slominski, 'Frontex's consultative forum and fundamental rights protection: enhancing accountability through dialogue?' (2022) 7(1) *European Papers* 195–214.

Committee of Ministers – which exercises political oversight over the execution of judgments by the European Court of Human Rights[319] – the EU has no permanent or centralised mechanism capable of monitoring and ensuring compliance in a similar fashion. Nor does it possess a continuous system for identifying and addressing systemic issues. This difference reinforces the central thesis of this book: the EU is not an international human rights organisation, but rather a supranational polity that can support and promote rights protection, yet only to a certain extent and within the boundaries of its legal and political mandate. In practice, this has resulted in a fragmented mosaic of tools through which the EU institutions may – albeit often cautiously – scrutinise Member States' adherence to fundamental rights. Most of these instruments fall within the realm of soft law: recommendations, evaluations, and dialogues that, while lacking binding force, still carry political and normative weight. Far from being ineffectual, these mechanisms can provide a solid basis for national reform and, in cases of persistent non-compliance, may help justify the initiation of legal action, such as infringement proceedings by the European Commission. Indeed, such judicial responses often rely on the data, assessments, and insights gathered through these softer mechanisms. Alongside this landscape stands Article 7 TEU, the EU's most prominent political tool for addressing serious and systemic breaches of its core values. However, its procedural complexity and political sensitivity have rendered it largely ineffective in practice. As seen in the stalled proceedings against Hungary and Poland, the high bar of procedural requirements, combined with political alliances between Member States, severely undermine the mechanism's deterrent capacity. Ultimately, the EU remains constrained by the absence of a coherent and effective political mechanism to ensure respect for fundamental rights within its own membership. This institutional gap continues to challenge the EU's credibility as a values-based community and highlights the need for renewed reflection on how best to reconcile its foundational commitments with its current capabilities.

It is likely due to the limitations of existing mechanisms that a new monitoring approach to fundamental rights is emerging within EU financial and budgetary instruments, supplementing the previously mentioned political conditionalities and sanctions. The EU has long supported national efforts to protect fundamental rights through financial incentives ('carrot'), and now increasingly employs sanctions to enforce its values ('stick'), especially via tools like the CPR. This shift stems from a decade-long 'values crisis' and deepening financial integration. Yet, the effectiveness of these mechanisms is uncertain: EU funds remain limited compared with national budgets, and conditionalities often assess form over substance. A lack of expertise among implementing European and national stakeholders further weakens impact, as does the complexity and inconsistency across different funding regimes. Calls for a unified system grow

[319] European Convention on Human Rights, art 46.

stronger. Co-ordination issues also persist, with overlapping instruments and unclear application rules. Legitimacy concerns arise, especially regarding the EU's expanding role beyond its formal competences. These developments raise important constitutional questions about power distribution between the EU and its Member States.

Finally, this chapter has revisited the third dimension of the EU's institutional oversight framework: the gradual establishment of independent monitoring and supervision mechanisms specifically designed to support the implementation of EU Fundamental Rights Law. What has emerged, incrementally and unevenly, is a network of independent bodies tasked with safeguarding fundamental rights – an institutional development that is largely unique within the broader landscape of international human rights law. At the EU level, a dedicated agency with a horizontal mandate – the Fundamental Rights Agency (FRA) – has been established. In addition, growing attention to fundamental rights can be observed across various EU agencies and bodies, as illustrated by the evolving institutional framework of Frontex. By contrast, obligations imposed by EU law on Member States in the field of fundamental rights have, to date, emerged only within specific policy areas – most notably, data protection and equality law, which remain the two main domains where the EU holds an autonomous competence in the field of fundamental rights protection. While this evolving institutional architecture represents a valuable contribution to the protection of fundamental rights within the EU, it is not without its limitations. Chief among these are its fragmented character and the absence of a comprehensive legal framework governing the mandate and operation of EU Fundamental Rights oversight mechanisms. Encouragingly, recent legislative initiatives, such as the adoption of the two new Directives on equality bodies,[320] mark a welcome move towards greater coherence and ambition in this domain. Ultimately, while the current state of affairs still reflects important structural and normative gaps, the creation of independent fundamental rights oversight mechanisms marks a cautious yet meaningful move towards institutionalising a more robust culture of rights within the EU.

In conclusion, the EU's institutional framework for fundamental rights protection embodies both its strengths and inherent limitations. While the development of political oversight, financial instruments, and independent monitoring bodies marks significant progress, the system remains fragmented and lacks a cohesive legal foundation. Addressing these structural and normative gaps is essential to enhance the EU's credibility as a values-based community and to ensure the effective safeguarding of fundamental rights across its Member States.

[320] Directives (EU) 2024/1499 and 2024/1500.

4

EU Fundamental Rights: A Political Project for the European Society

> In 2025, digital technologies are everywhere. Our phones have become an extension of ourselves. Algorithms are used to decide what we see on our social media feeds. They influence our everyday decisions, and more importantly, they affect how we experience and enjoy our fundamental rights. Whether it is our right to data protection, our right to non-discrimination, our freedom of expression – and even our right to free and fair elections.[1]

Introduction

The previous chapters examined how EU law is distinct in the realm of fundamental rights protection, particularly when compared with international human rights law. Those chapters were partly guided by a clear didactic ambition: to render EU law's singularities intelligible and engaging – even for those more familiar with international human rights law than EU law. This approach seeks to broaden access to the field of EU Fundamental Rights Law for those who can benefit from it on the ground, by illuminating its unique logic and its potential in the broader human rights landscape.

However, the ambition of this book is not confined to a one-directional inquiry. It aims instead to operate as a two-way bridge: on the one hand, moving from international human rights law towards the specific framework of EU Fundamental Rights, and, on the other, from the latter back to the EU's broader legal system and constitutional design.

In this context, it is worth asking whether examining the distinctive nature of the EU's Fundamental Rights Law framework might provide deeper insight into the EU itself – not only as a political and normative project, but also as a vision of the future it seeks to shape. The singularity of the EU's Fundamental Rights Law framework, I am convinced, not only distinguishes it from other systems, but also illuminates the EU's very nature and its underlying aspirations.

[1] European Union Agency for Fundamental Rights, Speech by Director Sirpa Rautio at the University of Florence, 'The Future of Democracy in the Digital Era', University of Florence Conference on 'The Future of Democracy in the Digital Era' (15 May 2025).

The study of the particular features of EU Fundamental Rights Law reveals that this legal order now constitutes a key layer within a global multi-level system of human rights protection (section I). It acts as a resonance chamber, reinforcing and enhancing the normative strength of human rights within the EU. But it goes further than that: it also provides fertile ground for the development and evolution of human rights. Moreover, it offers up a strategic and highly relevant arena in which they can be recognised and institutionally anchored. This contribution deserves to be more widely acknowledged among practitioners of international human rights law, so that they may draw upon this body of norms when it proves relevant and useful to do so for beneficiaries of human rights protection.

Nonetheless, EU Fundamental Rights Law continues to be characterised by substantial internal tensions. As highlighted throughout this volume, it is in many respects a domain defined by inherent contradictions (section II). It reflects the broader dilemmas inherent to the EU itself. The system of protection remains fragmented, in part due to the EU's limited competence in the area of fundamental rights. And, crucially, this field encapsulates both the richness and challenge of the European project, namely the ongoing task of (and tension between) preserving diversity and safeguarding unity.

More fundamentally, these very features – its sophistication, structural complexity, underlying dissonances, and capacity for transformation – invite us to appreciate the distinctive promise embodied in EU Fundamental Rights Law. To engage more deeply with this field is not merely a legal opportunity, but a societal one: the opportunity to draw the contours of European society, or, as one might say in French, 'faire société en Europe'. I believe that EU Fundamental Rights Law should be understood as a political project for the EU. This perspective represents an opportunity – one that I think European institutions, Member States, and political actors would do well to embrace if the EU is to not only maintain internal cohesion but also assert a meaningful presence on the international stage (section III).

Section I – A Key Voice in the Human Rights Polyphony

EU Fundamental Rights Law now occupies a pivotal role within the broader European human rights architecture. It operates as a chamber of resonance for international human rights law (section I.1), but its contribution does not end there: the EU's legal order also provides a fertile ground for the development and normative *evolution* of these rights (section I.2). In certain areas, it may even represent the most strategic and meaningful arena for the advancement and deepening of specific fundamental rights (section 1.3).

I.1. A Resonance Chamber

From its earliest stages, the legal order of the EU has drawn on external sources to shape its own fundamental rights framework: the national constitutional traditions of the Member States, and international human rights law, predominantly the European Convention on Human Rights (ECHR). As early as 1975, the Court of Justice of the European Union (CJEU) began referring to provisions of the ECHR in its case law.[2] By 1989, it had acknowledged the ECHR's particular importance for the development of fundamental rights within the EU.[3] This reliance is no longer incidental; it has been explicitly embraced. Article 6(3) TEU provides that

> fundamental rights, as guaranteed by the European Convention for the Protection of Human Rights and Fundamental Freedoms and as they result from the constitutional traditions common to the Member States, shall constitute general principles of the Union's law.[4]

What I seek to emphasise here is that this process is not merely about the passive reception of external norms. On the contrary, it transformatively dynamises the rights it duplicates. EU law not only imports and repeats international and national human rights standards – it *amplifies* and can enhance their impact. Through its unique structure and mechanisms, the EU legal order acts as a resonance chamber for international human rights law: it echoes, reinforces, and in some respects revitalises, reinvigorates, and even amplifies the norms it borrows.[5]

This effect is due in large part to the distinctive strength of EU law. As demonstrated in this book, EU law benefits from a set of specific features which give it a special power – most notably, the principles of primacy, direct effect, and effectiveness[6] – and support its penetration into the national legal orders. These characteristics allow fundamental rights under EU law to be invoked by individuals before national courts, and to be raised by individual national judges who have doubts, through the preliminary ruling procedure, giving them a degree of enforceability that many international norms lack. Moreover, the institutional framework of the EU – including its legislative arm (which includes the Council of the EU and the European Parliament), the supervisory role (of the European Commission), and judicial oversight (provided by the CJEU) – ensures not only the articulation but also the implementation and supervision of fundamental rights, to ensure that they are effectively enforced.

To illustrate this point briefly, reference may be made to the example already examined in chapter two: the fundamental right to paid annual leave, enshrined

[2] Case C-36/75 *Rutili* ECLI:EU:C:1975:137 [1975], para 32.

[3] Joined Cases 46/87 and 227/88 *Hoescht AG v Commission of the European Communities* ECLI:EU:C:1989:337 [1989], para 13.

[4] See ch 1 of this book, 'A Simultaneously Strong and Limited Human Rights Protector'.

[5] See ch 1, s VI of this book, 'Emancipation: A New Norm-maker'.

[6] See ch 2 of this book, 'The Power of EU Fundamental Rights Law'.

in Article 31(2) of the EU Charter of Fundamental Rights, constitutes a particularly instructive case. The CJEU has recognised that this provision has horizontal direct effect, enabling individuals to invoke it in disputes between private parties.[7] The CJEU interprets the obligations arising from this right in the light of Directive 2003/88/EC,[8] which does not itself have direct effect. This jurisprudence has had a significant impact, notably on the French legal order. For many years, the French Court of Cassation held that an employee who fell ill during paid leave could not claim the postponement of untaken days.[9] In a notable reversal, grounded in the EU Charter and the case law of the CJEU, the French Court of Cassation brought its interpretation into line with EU Fundamental Rights law. Interpreting Article L.3141-3 of the French Labour Code in the light of the Directive, it now recognises the right of an employee who becomes ill during paid leave to defer those days and take them subsequently.[10] This development illustrates the depth of EU Fundamental Rights Law's penetration into national legal systems – a phenomenon facilitated by the EU's distinctive structural and judicial features, and by the pivotal role played by the CJEU through the preliminary ruling procedure.

It remains uncertain whether traditional international law would have generated a comparable effect within the domestic legal order. The EU comprehensive system, therefore, provides a fertile ground in which international human rights norms, once integrated, can thrive. In this way, EU Fundamental Rights Law does more than mirror international standards; it empowers them. It gives them a renewed normative force, anchored in a legal system with far-reaching national impact and strong enforcement mechanisms. As such, one can meaningfully describe EU Fundamental Rights Law as a resonance chamber for international human rights law: not merely reflecting, but actively projecting and reinforcing, the standards it transposes.

I.2. A Ground for Growth

The EU is no longer content with simply reflecting international human rights standards; it has emerged as a space in which these rights can develop. As has been demonstrated throughout this book, the EU's role extends far beyond that of a 'norm-taker'. Indeed, the EU has gradually evolved into a 'norm-maker' in the field of human rights.

[7] See ch 2 of this book, 'The Power of EU Fundamental Rights Law'.

[8] Directive of the European Parliament and of the Council of 4 November 2003 concerning certain aspects of the organisation of working time OJ L 299/2003, pp 9–19; C-78/11 *Asociación Nacional de Grandes Empresas de Distribución (ANGED) v Federación de Asociaciones Sindicales (FASGA) and Others* ECLI:EU:C:2012:372 [2012].

[9] French Court of Cassation, 4 December 1996, Cass. soc., n° 93-44.907.

[10] French Court of Cassation, 10 September 2025, Cass. soc., n° 23-14.456, ECLI:FR:CCASS:2025:SO00790.

This extension is evident in several ways. Whether through its legislative powers or the autonomous interpretation of EU law by the CJEU, the EU has increasingly become a 'standard-setter' in the realm of fundamental rights protection. This capacity for innovation is explicitly foreseen within the EU's legal framework. Article 52(3) of the EU Charter states that

> Insofar as this Charter contains rights corresponding to rights guaranteed by the European Convention for the Protection of Human Rights and Fundamental Freedoms, their meaning and scope shall be the same as those laid down by the said Convention.

However, it further stipulates that 'This provision shall not prevent EU law from providing more extensive protection.'

In other words, the EU adheres to the minimum standards established by the ECHR, but is fully entitled to surpass these standards and provide a higher level of protection.

As Victor Davio aptly notes, 'the evolving role of the EU in the field of fundamental rights is not a binary or sudden shift between being a standard-taker and a standard-setter, but rather a gradual process marked by changes in intensity and diversity'.[11] The diversity of this process has lain in the fact that the EU's ability to set its own fundamental rights standards is not uniform across all areas. This process of autonomisation is most evident in areas where the EU has fully-fledged fundamental rights competences, such as in the fields of equality, non-discrimination, and data protection law. It is equally apparent in sectors where the EU has established comprehensive policies, such as EU procedural criminal law designed to facilitate mutual recognition, and the Common European Asylum System in migration law.[12] The intensity of the autonomisation also varies significantly between these areas. In some fields, such as data protection and gender equality law, the EU has been able to construct a strong and sophisticated legal framework that not only reflects but actively develops the standards of international human rights law. In other fields, the development of EU law is less advanced, and the EU's role as a norm-maker remains more circumscribed. Such instances are, however, increasingly rare. Even in areas where the EU has no fully-fledged competence, certain aspects nevertheless fall within the realm of EU Fundamental Rights Law. One may think, for example, of the protection of the fundamental rights of the child. Although the EU lacks explicit competence in this domain, a substantial body of case law has emerged in connection with civil judicial co-operation, particularly in matters involving child custody.

In any event, it is undeniable that, in certain domains, EU law has come to serve as the primary benchmark for human rights protection within the Member States of the EU. This is not merely because of the strength of EU law, but also due to the depth of its development in certain areas. In these specific domains, the

[11] V Davio, *EU Fundamental Rights: A Source of Special Significance for the European Court of Human Rights* (Larcier, 2026) 14.

[12] See ch 1 of this book, 'A Simultaneously Strong and Limited Human Rights Protector'.

EU does not merely incorporate international human rights standards and allow them to resonate within its legal framework; it actively reshapes and refines them, setting a new benchmark for the protection of fundamental rights. In this regard, the EU has evolved from passively adopting international human rights law to becoming a proactive architect and shaper of these standards.

It is also worth recalling that, on an external level, EU Fundamental Rights Law as elaborated through EU legislation has also shown that it has a profound influence. EU legislation is increasingly relied upon by the European Court of Human Rights (ECtHR)[13] to shape its jurisprudence, and, more broadly, has influenced the practices of global market actors. Anu Bradford has famously described this phenomenon as the 'Brussels Effect', and this dynamic of influence extends to some degree into the field of fundamental rights, highlighting the EU's remarkable global reach.[14]

I.3. A Strategic and Relevant Arena

It is an undeniable fact that EU law must be regarded as a reference framework for the protection of certain fundamental rights within the Member States, particularly in specific domains. The central question, however, is whether this configuration is both relevant and desirable. In certain areas, not only is it relevant, but it is also strategically significant for the EU to assume such a role. I contend that the effective protection of certain fundamental rights in particular contexts can only be ensured at the level of the EU. Indeed, certain challenges call for a co-ordinated and supranational response which, to be truly effective, must transcend the limits of national legislation and be articulated through the European legal framework. As a powerful international player, the EU has the ability to implement legislation and policies that address global challenges and societal issues. By doing so, it can offer coherent and comprehensive solutions to matters requiring collective action and transnational governance. The EU's institutional strength, coupled with its ability to craft responses to cross-border challenges, provides it with a unique advantage in responding to the evolving societal demands for human rights protection.[15] Consider, for instance, the protection of fundamental rights in the digital sphere, the safeguarding of social rights within the Internal Market, or the defence of rights related to health and environmental protection. In such domains, the EU clearly emerges as the primary actor able to confront these challenges. This will be examined further

[13] N Daminova, 'The European Court of Human Rights on the "Stockholm's Roadmap Directives": the quest for a coherent application of "due process" rights in Europe?' (2023) Weekend Edition n°156, *EU Law Live*, 15.

[14] A Bradford, *The Brussels Effect: How the European Union Rules the World* (Oxford University Press, 2020).

[15] I thank George Letsas for suggesting that I should make this stance more explicit and bold.

in the final section of this chapter, where I argue that the EU must engage more robustly with issues relating to fundamental rights, harnessing its power and capacity to protect these rights more effectively.

That said, this does not extend to all fields indiscriminately; rather, it applies to specific domains where the EU possesses the necessary capacity to act effectively, notably in a global context. The protection of human rights does not necessarily always have to be carried out at the EU level. In international human rights law, it is in fact considered that states are the natural protectors of human rights. The international level steps in only in cases of failure at the national level.

The principle of subsidiarity is, in this regard, key to allocating responsibilities for the protection of fundamental rights among the different players, in particular when EU institutions consider legislating in the field.[16] This principle, which constitutes a legal obligation to be respected by EU institutions, was addressed in chapter one of this book. It asserts that EU action should only be pursued when the objectives of the proposed action cannot be adequately achieved by the Member States alone, and when action at EU level provides added value, thereby ensuring that decisions are made at the most effective level of governance.[17]

Section II – A Field of Tensions and Contradictions

In certain cases and to a certain extent, EU law has the potential to bring genuine added value to the protection of fundamental rights within its Member States. Yet, as this book has demonstrated, the EU's contribution to fundamental rights also reveals a deeper and more complex tension – one that has underpinned the analysis throughout. While the EU can indeed act as a powerful driver for the advancement of human rights, and enforcement of them, in one way, it may also, paradoxically, make it seriously difficult for them to be effectively safeguarded in another way. This ambivalence is rooted in the very nature of the European project. The EU is not, nor was it ever intended to be, an international organisation dedicated to the protection of human rights. Its role in this domain is inherently limited by design. This is, first, due to the absence of a general competence in matters of fundamental rights (section II.1). And second, even where the EU is entitled to act, it does so within a framework that is often marked by contradictions: the protection of

[16] See ch 1, s IV of this book, 'Limitation: A Paradoxically Restricted Mandate'.

[17] It should be noted that this limitation, which is addressed to the EU and to all its institutions in the Treaties, is in practice only implemented by the political institutions, and in particular by the European legislature. Indeed, it is generally considered that the CJEU is not bound by this principle insofar as its interpretative function is concerned. The CJEU does not really apply this reasoning, which it regards as political. I am grateful to Orlando Scarcello for having suggested this very useful clarification. For further discussion, see G de Búrca, 'Reappraising Subsidiarity's Significance after Amsterdam' (Jean Monnet Working Paper 7/99, Harvard, 2000).

fundamental rights is not its sole, nor indeed its primary, objective (section II.2). One of the most inherent, enduring, and complex challenges of the European integration process – particularly acute in the field of human rights – is the pursuit of an equilibrium between the need for unity and the imperative to respect and preserve diversity, in particular regarding national particularities (section II.3). Finally, the question of the effectiveness of this new layer of protection – although it arises in a different way than in international human rights law – remains central (section II.4).

II.1. A Fragmented Layer of Protection with Blurred Boundaries

As discussed in chapter one of this book, while the EU possesses a certain capacity to protect fundamental rights, this capacity remains constrained.[18] The EU does not have a general mandate in the field of fundamental rights protection. This is, arguably, a significant limitation of its action in this area, and a key distinction from other systems such as that of the ECHR, the main objective of which is the protection of those rights. As a consequence, the EU Charter has a limited scope of application. It applies to Member States only when they implement EU law (Article 51).[19]

This limitation, naturally, restricts the scope of the EU's potential contribution to fundamental rights protection. Furthermore, even within the scope of EU law, the EU's actions in the field of fundamental rights protection are not uniform in the degree to which they apply. As examined in chapter one, EU Fundamental Rights legislation, in particular, exhibits differing levels of density. As previously underlined,[20] European legislation can go remarkably far in what it regulates. For instance, some provisions include rules on the burden of proof, deadlines to provide legal remedies, and even the obligation to establish independent authorities to ensure the enforcement of these fundamental rights. This approach is undeniably innovative when compared with traditional international human rights law, which generally refrains from specifying obligations with such precision, especially because of the margin of discretion left to national authorities.

The dividing line between the scope of EU Fundamental Rights Law and national law can, however, be difficult to delineate at times, particularly in light of the varying intensity of regulation across EU legislative acts.

This fragmented situation gives rise to a host of ambiguities that undermine the overall coherence and intelligibility of the EU's Fundamental Rights regime.

[18] See ch 1, ss IV–VI of this book.

[19] With the interpretative difficulties arising from the definition of this scope, which involves many borderline cases.

[20] See ch 1, s VI of this book, 'Emancipation: A new Norm-maker'.

This issue has long been acknowledged by numerous scholars and commentators. Indeed, it results in uncertainties regarding the scope of application of EU Fundamental Rights Law. In turn, these uncertainties generate significant challenges regarding consistency and clarity for those seeking to rely upon these rights. Users and beneficiaries of the system, whether Member States, national or European courts, or individuals, often face difficulties in determining the precise scope of the EU's powers in this field, leading to both legal and administrative confusion. In addition to creating difficulties in terms of clarity for the beneficiaries of rights, this situation also significantly affects the balance of powers between the EU and the Member States.

In addition, the emergence of new forms of governance in the field of fundamental rights – particularly in the budgetary sphere – further complicates the legal landscape. A notable example is the cross-sectoral applicability of the so-called enabling conditions linked to compliance with the EU Charter of Fundamental Rights, introduced in the framework of EU funding programmes governed by the Common Provisions Regulation.[21] These mechanisms, which condition access to EU structural and investment funds on compliance with fundamental rights obligations, are strikingly broad in scope. While their stated aim is to strengthen the enforcement of fundamental rights, they also contribute to blurring the lines between the competences of the EU and those of the Member States.

This ambiguity is not merely a matter of legal interpretation; it has profound constitutional implications. As the EU expands its influence into domains traditionally falling within national responsibility, it risks disturbing the delicate balance of competences enshrined in the EU's constitutional architecture.[22]

I will illustrate this with one example, the creation of residential facilities for persons with disabilities. On its face, the establishment of such facilities falls neither within the scope of EU law nor within the EU's competence. However, the situation becomes far more complex when Member States decide to finance these facilities using EU structural funds, such as the European Social Fund Plus (ESF+). In such cases, EU law may suddenly become relevant. The European Ombudsman has considered that, where EU funds are used for such purposes, the European Commission must ensure that Member States comply with their obligations under the EU Charter and the UN Convention on the Rights of Persons with Disabilities (UNCRPD), to which the EU is itself a party. Specifically, Article 19 of the UNCRPD requires progress towards independent

[21] Regulation (EU) 2021/1060 of the European Parliament and of the Council of 24 June 2021 laying down common provisions on the European Regional Development Fund, the European Social Fund Plus, the Cohesion Fund, the Just Transition Fund and the European Maritime, Fisheries and Aquaculture Fund and financial rules for those and for the Asylum, Migration and Integration Fund, the Internal Security Fund and the Instrument for Financial Support for Border Management and Visa Policy [2021] OJ L231/159 (CPR Regulation); see ch 3 of this book, 'A Sophisticated Oversight over Fundamental Rights'.

[22] M Fisicaro, 'Conditionality and the making of the EU spending power: the question of competence' (2026) *Common Market Law Review*, forthcoming.

living and deinstitutionalisation. In its 2022 inquiry,[23] the Ombudsman called on the European Commission to strengthen its oversight and to equip its staff with clear, up-to-date, and operational guidance.

But this example raises further questions. Suppose a residential facility is built with EU funding and is fully compliant with the requirements of Article 19 of the UNCRPD. Does everything that happens within that facility fall within the scope of application of the EU Charter, simply because of the initial EU financial contribution? Does the EU Charter apply to daily practices, internal rules, or the conduct of staff operating within such an institution by virtue of EU funding having been involved at the outset?[24]

Such an interpretation would, in my view, constitute an unduly expansive understanding of the scope of EU law. Nonetheless, these hypothetical scenarios serve to underscore the significant legal and constitutional uncertainty that continues to surround the precise boundaries of the EU Charter's applicability, particularly under its Article 51(1). They raise difficult and unresolved questions about the temporal and material scope of EU Fundamental Rights obligations when national actions are supported – wholly or partially – by EU instruments. Such ambiguities not only challenge the coherence of the EU's Fundamental Rights architecture but also place both Member States and individuals in a state of uncertainty regarding the standards to which they are held accountable.

II.2. A Site of Conflict

It has been repeatedly emphasised throughout this book that the protection of fundamental rights has never been the sole or even primary objective of the EU. At the time of its creation, the protection of these rights was not even included in its declared aims. Today, however, the situation has evolved. Fundamental rights now constitute one of the EU's foundational values and their protection lies among its objectives, albeit alongside a range of diverse political goals.

Article 3 TEU, which enumerates the EU's objectives, explicitly affirms that the EU should promote its founding values – which include fundamental rights – and the wellbeing of its peoples,[25] and establish an area of freedom (and security, and justice).[26] Furthermore, Article 3(3) states that the EU 'shall combat social

[23] Ombudsman Decision on the own-initiative inquiry into how the European Commission monitors EU Structural and Investment funds to ensure they are used to promote the right of persons with disabilities to independent living and inclusion in the community (OI/2/2021/MHZ).

[24] On this issue, the CJEU seems to indicate that the mere use of EU funding does not automatically bring a situation within the scope of application of the EU Charter. See, for instance, Case C-117/14 *Poclava* EU:C:2015:60 [2015] and Case C-562/12 *Liivimaa* EU:C:2014:2229 [2014], as well as I Gambardella, 'EU Governance through Funding: What Consequences for the Scope of Application of EU Fundamental Rights?' (2024) 31(2) *Maastricht Journal of European and Comparative Law* 215–231.

[25] TEU, art 3(1).

[26] ibid, art 3(2). In my view, however, it would be reductive to oppose these various objectives, as security and justice directly contribute to the effectiveness of fundamental rights. See, for instance, the judgment of the ECtHR, *Romeo Castaño v Spain & Belgium* App no. 8351/17 (ECHR, 9 July 2019).

exclusion and discrimination, and shall promote social justice and protection, equality between women and men, solidarity between generations and the protection of the rights of the child'. The EU should also promote human rights in the context of the EU's 'relations with the wider world'.[27]

Thus, the protection of fundamental rights has, for about three decades, been leading up to now officially being a recognised objective of the EU. It is also increasingly reflected in the EU's policy actions, which are more frequently and explicitly aimed at furthering fundamental rights.

However, the EU's ambitions are by no means confined to the protection of fundamental rights; they extend to other broad and complex objectives that are, in many respects, comparable to those pursued by a state. The EU is not, and should not be conceived of as, a human rights organisation which has the primary function to establish inviolable red lines such as those delineated by the ECtHR. Rather, akin to a state, it must navigate and reconcile competing interests within the parameters set by those red lines. These balancing exercises are conducted, first and foremost, by the EU's political institutions, but they are also subject to judicial scrutiny. The CJEU, as a particular guardian of the EU Charter of Fundamental Rights – the EU's own 'Bill of Rights' – plays a central role in this regard. That said, the role of the CJEU is to ensure that the law of the EU as a whole is upheld,[28] not only the EU Charter of Fundamental Rights. As such, it is frequently required to arbitrate the balancing of fundamental rights against other objectives pursued by the EU. This is precisely why accession to the ECHR, and the external scrutiny offered by the ECtHR, would bring genuine added value. The EU has indeed committed itself to acceding to the ECHR, as stated in Article 6(2) TEU. This prospective accession is of great significance, as it would provide an external framework within which such balancing of rights and interests may take place.

The theoretical framework of balancing competing interests is well established in legal discourse.[29] Yet this balancing act is not merely theoretical; it is consistently observable in practice. Whenever the legislature adopts provisions intended to give concrete expression to fundamental rights, it inevitably also limits their ambit – depending on how it implements other, often competing, policy objectives.

A recent and salient example of this dynamic is found in the New Pact on Migration and Asylum.[30] This legislative package introduces a comprehensive reform of EU secondary legislation and directly addresses the fundamental rights of asylum seekers within the EU as ancillary to other goals.[31] However, the Pact

[27] TEU, art 3(5).

[28] ibid, art 19(1).

[29] See, for instance, R Alexy, *Theory of Constitutional Rights* (Oxford University Press, 2009).

[30] Communication from the European Commission to the European Parliament, the Council of the EU, the European Economic and Social Committee and the Committee of the Regions on a New Pact on Migration and Asylum COM/2020/609 final.

[31] For a detailed discussion on how the EU relies on its legal bases to act subsidiarily in the protection of fundamental rights, see ch 1 of this book, 'A Simultaneously Strong and Limited Human Rights Protector'.

also pursues other objectives that come into immediate tension with human rights protection, notably those of ensuring 'more secure European borders' and enabling 'faster and more efficient procedures for asylum and return'. It is well documented that measures adopted under the Common European Asylum System have, at times, imposed serious limitations on migrants' fundamental rights, even resulting in egregious violations.

Such tensions between fundamental rights objectives and competing objectives are equally present in the EU's mechanisms for legal, political, and financial oversight of its Member States' compliance with fundamental rights obligations. In this context, as well, it is apparent that the EU's monitoring framework – though robust in principle – suffers from the influence of political pragmatism.[32] This has been particularly visible in the role of the European Commission, which, as the Guardian of the Treaties, is responsible for oversight and for initiating infringement proceedings. The limitations of this role were powerfully highlighted by Daniel Kelemen and Tommaso Pavone in their seminal article, 'Where Have the Guardians Gone?'.[33] The authors point to what they term a supranational politics of forbearance – the deliberate underenforcement of EU law due to the politicisation of international institutions and the trade-offs confronting executives who act simultaneously as prosecutors and policymakers.

Another clear illustration of this tension is the use of financial conditionality – and, more specifically, the manner in which such tools have, at times, been employed as leverage in negotiations. A notable political episode is the partial, but nonetheless significant, lifting of financial measures imposed in response to national human rights violations in Hungary.[34] This concession was reportedly granted in order to secure Hungary's withdrawal of its veto against the adoption of sanctions on Russia under the Common and Foreign Security Policy, which requires unanimity among the Member States to proceed. This practice has been aptly theorised and labelled as 'soft hostage-taking' by Patrick Müller and Peter Slominski.[35] The authors precisely identify the systemic issues that may arise from the interplay between different strands of EU policymaking – particularly those governed by an intergovernmental logic and subject to unanimity requirements. In such contexts, a Member State may strategically resort to the implicit threat of

[32] See ch 2, s II.2 of this book, 'Institutional Enforcement to Protect EU Fundamental Rights Protection'.

[33] D Kelemen and T Pavone, *Where Have the Guardians Gone? Law Enforcement and the Politics of Supranational Forbearance in the European Union* (Johns Hopkins University Press, 2023) 779–825.

[34] 'Hungary agrees deal and lifts veto on €18bn EU aid package for Ukraine' (*Euronews*, 13 December 2022), https://www.euronews.com/my-europe/2022/12/13/hungary-lifts-vetoes-on-ukraine-aid-and-corporate-tax-to-lower-frozen-eu-funds.

[35] P Müller and P Slominski, 'The soft hostage-taking of EU foreign policy: Hungary's rule of law conflict with the EU and Russia's war against Ukraine' (2025) *Journal of European Public Policy* 1–27. See also K Lane Scheppele and J Morijn, 'Money for nothing? EU institutions' uneven record of freezing EU funds to enforce EU values' (2024) *Journal of European Public Policy* 474–97. The European Parliament has, moreover, challenged the European Commission's margin of discretion that allowed Hungary to exert pressure, and the action for annulment is still pending before the CJEU.

a veto, often as a bargaining tool to advance its interests in areas connected to the protection of fundamental rights and EU values. Notably, this is typically done without explicitly linking these concerns in formal discourse, allowing the Member State to exert pressure while maintaining plausible deniability. Such dynamics reveal how human rights conditionality can become entangled in broader political negotiations, undermining the coherence and credibility of the EU's fundamental rights commitments.

In this light, EU Fundamental Rights Law is, by its very nature, a site of tensions, negotiations, and conflicts. It is not merely a catalogue of guarantees, but a dynamic legal space in which the founding values of the EU, including fundamental rights, are interpreted, challenged, and balanced against its other objectives. Understanding this complexity is essential to grasping the true nature of fundamental rights within the EU legal order. In this regard, one is naturally reminded of the situation in states, which do not require an explicit conferral of powers to regulate rights: such trade-offs are routine. Any state would encounter analogous difficulties in regulating, for example, migration flows.

II.3. The Challenge of Unity and Diversity

Beyond the questions of fragmentation and conflict, one of the greatest challenges of EU Fundamental Rights Law lies in how it is articulated in national systems of human rights protection. As already underlined, the state and the national judiciary have traditionally been regarded as the *principal* guardians of human rights. International human rights law is designed to operate *subsidiarily*; it comes into play only when national protection mechanisms fail. The ECHR's margin of appreciation doctrine is a representation of this conception.[36] It reflects, on the one hand, the ethical imperative of respecting pluralism and cultural diversity, which gives concrete expression to the principle of subsidiarity; and, on the other hand, the functional consequence of dividing responsibility for implementing the ECHR between national and ECHR authorities. In pragmatic terms, national authorities are deemed better positioned to evaluate the legitimacy of interferences in the rights the ECHR protects. Recourse to the ECtHR should serve as a safety net where there are deficiencies in following the national legal route.

The EU framework, however, disrupts this traditional binary architecture. The EU Fundamental Rights Law system does not merely set minimum 'red lines'. It increasingly makes autonomous political choices about the level and scope of fundamental rights protection; choices which may, in certain cases, take precedence over national standards. This complex dynamic reflects a broader tension

[36] G Letsas, 'Two Concepts of the Margin of Appreciation' (2006) 26(4) *Oxford Journal of Legal Studies* 705–32.

that runs through many areas of EU law: the ambition to achieve unity *and* diversity. This tension partly explains the considerable complexity inherent in EU Fundamental Rights Law.

As analysed in chapter one of this book, the relationship between unity and diversity is more intricate within the EU framework, due to the existence of competing objectives pursued by the EU. Indeed, there are cases where EU Fundamental Rights Law does not only act as a floor for human rights protection, but also as a ceiling. In such instances, Member States are no longer permitted to exceed that ceiling, in order not to jeopardise other provisions or objectives of EU law.

The balance between promoting unity and respecting diversity depends notably on the presence or absence of legislative measures harmonising the requirements imposed by fundamental rights, as well as on the extent of such legislation. Where such legislation exists, it generally determines the degree of tolerance for diversity. In the absence of such legislation, it falls to the CJEU to establish the threshold of acceptable diversity within the common area of fundamental rights protection, taking into account other imperatives such as the protection of the EU's financial interests and the freedoms of movement.[37]

When engaging with EU Fundamental Rights Law, it is, therefore, essential to keep in mind that its underlying logic differs significantly from that of traditional international human rights law. The 'human rights' principle of subsidiarity does not, in this context, allow Member States to exceed the minimum standards established by EU law in all circumstances. In certain cases, this minimum standard also becomes a maximum standard – a feature that is quite specific to the EU system of fundamental rights protection.

II.4. The Fragile Effectiveness of (EU) Fundamental Rights Law

Throughout this book, I have examined the singularities of the EU Fundamental Rights system, which stem, in particular, from its innovative institutional architecture and its distinctive legal characteristics. These features clearly set EU Fundamental Rights Law apart from international human rights law. They are designed to strengthen the effectiveness and enforcement of these rights within national legal orders. In this respect, it is beyond doubt that EU law possesses genuine normative force.

However, the question of effectiveness remains highly relevant. Far from being immune to the challenges typically encountered in the implementation of international law, the application of EU law also faces significant difficulties. These difficulties are of two main kinds: first, the general problem of implementation that

[37] For a detailed analysis, see ch 1, ss III and IV of this book.

affects many legal norms; and second, the growing resistance of national authorities to the implementation of international and EU law itself.

The first challenge is, in a sense, inherent to all legal systems. The mere adoption of a legal norm does not, *ipso facto*, guarantee its enforcement. This is true of EU law as well, and perhaps even more so, given its complexity and the persistent lack of familiarity with EU legal principles among many national legal actors. The EU's institutional architecture seeks to mitigate these difficulties, but it cannot entirely overcome them. Such challenges arise even in relation to some of the most sophisticated areas of EU law. The General Data Protection Regulation (GDPR) is a striking example: as scholars have noted, serious concerns remain regarding its enforcement.[38] Thus, although the EU's data protection framework represents one of the most innovative systems for the implementation of human rights standards, it is by no means immune to practical flaws.

The second type of difficulty stems from a growing resistance towards both international law and European human rights law more broadly. A recent example is the open letter signed by nine heads of government addressed to the ECtHR, urging that Court to reconsider its interpretation of the ECHR.[39] These leaders criticised the ECtHR for allegedly extending the ECHR beyond the intentions of its drafters, to the detriment of national concerns such as security and the control of irregular migration. This letter, which constitutes a direct affront to the independence of the ECtHR, is far from an isolated act.[40] It forms part of a broader movement of delegitimation of international human rights law and liberal values, both in Europe and beyond. EU Fundamental Rights Law is, of course, not immune to this trend.

I shall return, in the epilogue of this book, to the broader and troubling context in which the EU Fundamental Rights system is currently evolving. It must, nevertheless, be emphasised from the outset that recognising the distinctive features of the EU's legal structure should not obscure the broader current environment that endangers it.

Section III Fundamental Rights as a Political Project for the EU

A thorough understanding of the strengths and complexities inherent in EU Fundamental Rights Law is essential to fully appreciate the nature and

[38] G Gentile and O Lynskey, 'Deficient by design? The transnational enforcement of the GDPR' (2022) 71(4) *International and Comparative Law Quarterly* 799–830.

[39] 'Open Letter to the European Court of Human Rights' (22 May 2025), available at https://www.governo.it/sites/governo.it/files/Lettera_aperta_22052025.pdf.

[40] On this broader trend and the reactions it has provoked, see S Van Drooghenbroeck and F Tulkens, 'Les dégoûtants et les dégoûtés Doit-on continuer à critiquer la Cour européenne des droits de l'homme?' (2025) *Revue trimestrielle des droits de l'Homme* 939–63.

functioning of the EU's role in the protection of human rights in Europe. EU Fundamental Rights Law both provides a substantial opportunity and presents a complex challenge, as it may, at times, give rise to tension. This is an undeniable reality. It is, therefore, imperative to engage with this framework in a constructive and principled manner, with the ultimate aim of ensuring that individuals entitled to these rights can enjoy the fullest possible protection under EU law.

Yet this is only part of the picture. Beneath these questions lies another fundamental inquiry – one that has quietly underpinned the reflections throughout this book: what is the future of EU Fundamental Rights Law in an era marked by turbulence, when both the EU itself and the liberal values that are the foundation of human rights are increasingly being challenged? In addressing this question, I would like to use the final part of this book to advance a strong stance: fundamental rights must be embraced as a genuine political project by 'European society'.[41]

In my view, redefining the EU's action in the field of fundamental rights protection has, in fact, become vital: not only for the long-term coherence and credibility of EU Fundamental Rights Law itself, but, just as crucially, for the future of the EU as a political project. It is no secret that both the EU and human rights are increasingly the target of public scepticism, even disillusionment, among European citizens. In light of this growing disconnect, might this be the moment to reconceive the protection of fundamental rights as a central political project of the EU?

The strategic necessity of addressing certain rights at the supranational level is already established, as previously underlined. Think, for instance, of the protection of children and consumers in the digital sphere, the right to a healthy environment, media freedom, and essential social rights in the context of a deeply globalised market. The type of protection afforded in this context should no longer be perceived merely as remote legal obligations; rather, it requires political choices that shape the kind of society the EU aspires to build. Could this not serve as a foundation for a renewed European public sphere – one in which citizens collectively deliberate on the normative commitments of their EU? Reframing fundamental rights as a shared political endeavour may well be essential to restoring democratic legitimacy and reinforcing the EU's cohesion in the face of fragmentation.

Against this backdrop, I argue that the politicisation of EU Fundamental Rights Law – undertaken within the boundaries established by international human rights law – may well constitute its only viable path to sustainability (section III.1). Achieving this, however, will require a reassessment of the EU's capacity in this domain (section III.2).

[41] I borrow this term from L Azoulaï, 'The Law of the European Society' (2022) 59(4) *Common Market Law Review* 203–14.

III.1. Towards a Political Turn in EU Fundamental Rights Law

In the previous chapters of this book, I critically examined the singularity of EU Fundamental Rights Law – its distinctive features, its particular mode of functioning, the strengths it may offer, but also its inherent limitations. This analytical groundwork is, in my view, essential: after all, does it not contribute to reinforcing the international protection of human rights by rendering the structure and logic of one of its key components more intelligible?

Yet this technical and structural analysis cannot be meaningfully separated from a broader reflection on the evolving condition of human rights in Europe. Today, human rights are not only increasingly questioned and criticised, but in some cases systematically challenged as foundational principles of our democratic systems. This is also confirmed in the European context. One need only consider the explicit agendas of certain political leaders who openly advocate for the establishment of so-called 'illiberal democracies': political regimes in which electoral processes may formally remain in place, yet where the protection of individual liberties and the system of checks and balances are systematically weakened or altogether disregarded.[42]

This trend reveals, among other things, a deeper crisis within constitutional liberalism – particularly its rationalist and individualist underpinnings. Human rights have long been situated within a rationalist framework, rooted in the belief in the possibility of a universal consensus based on reason.[43] From this perspective, the sphere of fundamental rights is conceived as one that should remain insulated from being a political topic.

In my view, *politics* – understood as the arena through which 'people make, preserve and amend the general rules under which they live'[44] – should operate within normative boundaries. I also believe that fundamental rights should now be approached from a different perspective, particularly at the level of the EU. Alongside other scholars, I wish to emphasise that the practical implementation of human rights obligations cannot – and should not – be entirely insulated from the political forum. Put differently, liberal constitutionalism should not exclude from

[42] On this concept, see F Zakaria, 'The Rise of Illiberal Democracy' (1997) 76(6) *Foreign Affairs* 22–43. The concept was initially used to describe political regimes in Latin America, and has since been applied to developments in Europe; see A Buzogány and M Varga, 'The Ideational Foundations of the Illiberal Backlash in Central and Eastern Europe: The Case of Hungary' (2018) 25(6) *Review of International Political Economy* 811–28. More generally, on the degradation of liberal values in the EU, see M Wind, *The Tribalization of Europe: A Defence of Our Liberal Values* (Polity Press, 2020); and R Drinóczi and A Bień-Kacała, *Illiberal Constitutionalism in Poland and Hungary: The Deterioration of Democracy, Misuse of Human Rights and Abuse of the Rule of Law* (Routledge, 2021).

[43] J Habermas, *Between Facts and Norms: Contributions to a Discourse Theory of Law and Democracy* (MIT Press, 1996); J Rawls, *Political Liberalism* (Columbia University Press, 1993).

[44] A Heywood, *Politics* (Macmillan Education Limited, 1997), quoted by R Coman, *The Politics of the Rule of Law in the EU Polity* (Palgrave Macmillan, 2022) 14.

the political sphere the normative and institutional choices that are inherently implicated in the enactment and enforcement of human rights, including at the level of the EU. More precisely, the way these rights are enforced and achieved ought to be subject to open and transparent political debate, particularly when it comes to conferring substantive meaning upon these rights and reconciling them with competing societal interests. Within this context, disagreements must be recognised, as Rawls underscores, as 'the normal result of the exercise of human reason within the framework of the free institutions of a constitutional democratic regime'.[45]

These conflicting perspectives – advocating for the politicisation of human rights while simultaneously upholding the principle that they should remain beyond the political realm – are particularly pronounced at the EU level. The EU is not an international human rights organisation whose sole mandate is the protection of human rights. Rather, the EU should be understood as a political organisation, in which fundamental rights must be situated within a broader constellation of objectives, priorities, and institutional constraints. This essential distinction calls for a shift in perspective, but it may also encounter the challenges posed by the politicisation of issues within the EU's complex architecture and delicate balance. The 'severity of the transformations'[46] in our societies nevertheless calls, in my view, for a political awakening in the system of protection of fundamental rights within the EU.

The implementation of EU Fundamental Rights Law should, therefore, be conceived as encompassing 'constitutional negotiations'[47] (section III.1(a)). Within this framework, the protection of fundamental rights within the EU should be regarded as a political project in its own right (section III.1(b)). At the same time, this perspective must be situated within the normative framework of the EU Charter of Fundamental Rights and international human rights law, which defines the boundaries within which such politicisation may legitimately occur (section III.1(c)).

III.1.a. The Politicisation of EU Fundamental Rights Law

Given the broad relevance of human rights and the complexity of their implementation, I believe we must move beyond a purely consensual understanding and acknowledge the need for negotiation over their concrete implications. Rather, it ought to be approached as a subject for legitimate political challenge, where divergent interpretations and competing normative priorities can be openly debated. In other words, I call for a politicisation of EU Fundamental Rights Law. As put by de Wilde and Zürn, 'politicisation' in general terms means 'the demand for or the

[45] Rawls, *Political Liberalism* (n 43).
[46] Wind, *The Tribalization of Europe* (n 42) 10.
[47] GCN Webber, *The Negotiable Constitution: On the Limitation of Rights* (Cambridge University Press, 2009) 29.

act of transporting an issue into the field of *politics* – making previously apolitical matters political'.[48] Within this framework, the decision-making subject is shifted into the 'sphere of public choice', implying that collectively binding decisions on the matter can be made by and for the *polity*.[49]

The question of the politicisation of human rights is far from straightforward. Comparative law reveals significant variation in how institutional arrangements are conceived. As Tim Koopmans notes, although the judiciary is typically seen as the foremost guardian of human rights in most states, in some, such as the United Kingdom, this role is largely attributed to the parliament.[50] At the national level, the issue of politicisation, though not always explicitly framed in these terms, forms part of the routine operation of political institutions. Within human rights law, it is well established that the definition of limitations – and, consequently, the implementation of rights – is, in principle, reserved to the legislature. Such restrictions must, after all, be 'prescribed by law'. However, this does not necessarily entail that the discourse surrounding these processes is explicitly characterised as one of politicisation. By entrusting the practical realisation of fundamental rights to the legislative process, legal systems implicitly acknowledge the political nature of rights enforcement. From this perspective, it may be accurate to conceptualise the discourse surrounding EU Fundamental Rights Law through a similar analytical framework. Determining the proper scope of fundamental rights involves complex political decisions, as these rights are not absolute. They must often be weighed both against competing public interests – such as, for instance, public security, public health, etc. – and against other rights.[51] Yet, there are no straightforward or uniquely correct answers to these normative trade-offs.

More precisely, a balanced approach appears to be the most appropriate: legislative action to implement human rights, coupled with judicial oversight to ensure that such measures are enacted within a framework that allows political processes to function effectively. This dynamic can likewise be observed at the national level.

In this framework, one way to conceive of the vitality of a democratic order is to see it as premised upon the institutionalisation of structured debate among actors who, while bound by a shared commitment to democratic principles, fundamentally disagree as to the content of the decisions.[52] Conflicting views do not undermine democracy; they constitute the very condition of its resilience.

[48] P de Wilde and M Zürn, 'Can the Politicization of European Integration be Reversed?' (2012) 50(1) *Journal of Common Market Studies* 137, 139.

[49] M Zürn, 'Opening up Europe: next steps in politicisation research' (2016) 39(1) *West European Politics* 164, 167.

[50] T Koopmans, *Courts and Political Institutions* (Cambridge University Press, 2003) 223. For a more in-depth analysis of the system, see S Gardbaum, *The New Commonwealth Model of Constitutionalism: Theory and Practice* (Cambridge University Press, 2013).

[51] M van den Brink, *Legislative Authority and Interpretation in the European Union* (Oxford University Press 2024) 104.

[52] J Waldron, 'The Dignity of Legislation' (1995) 54(2) *Maryland Law Review* 153–54; and C Mouffe, *Agonistique. Penser politiquement le monde* (Beaux-Arts de Paris éditions, 2014) 29.

As Kalypso Nicolaïdis, building on Rawlsian thought, has observed, 'any regime which guarantees the respect of basic rights will also be marked by an unavoidable share of disagreement, antagonism and conflict on the ultimate questions of what is "good" – good for the group and good for individuals'.[53] In the same vein, Waldron's view of politics is grounded in the pervasive nature of disagreement – whether about the common good, the meaning of justice, or even the fundamental moral rights that a just society ought to protect.[54]

From this perspective, the content and operationalisation of EU Fundamental Rights Law should not be depoliticised in the pursuit of consensus. On the contrary, the way they are implemented should remain open to political consideration at the EU level. It is precisely for this reason that I advocate a political aspect in the approach to EU Fundamental Rights Law. Persistent disagreement among participants should not be seen as a sign that deliberations have failed. On the contrary, the articulation of irreconcilable differences can be highly valuable, as it helps to clarify the conceptual and practical boundaries of the debate and enables citizens to make more informed judgements on the issues at hand. The deliberations should not be regarded solely as a process for achieving consensus. Rather, they serve a dual purpose: to define the contours of disagreement and to contribute to the development of a collectively informed, though not necessarily unanimous, common understanding.[55] The dynamism of democratic life indeed hinges on the recognition and articulation of clearly differentiated political positions. Democracy thrives not in the absence of conflict, but through the structured and constructive engagement of competing viewpoints. To deny this 'agonistic' dimension, which conceives of conflict as constitutive of democracy, is to risk allowing political disagreement to degenerate into destructive antagonisms, grounded not in negotiable policy differences but in non-negotiable moral convictions or rigid, essentialist identities. In other words, the healthy functioning of a democratic system requires that conflict be channelled through mechanisms of deliberations and challenge rather than being repressed, which would render society vulnerable to polarisation and social fragmentation.[56] Democracy requires conflictual engagement and must offer forms of identification grounded in distinct, yet democratic, political projects – including within the institutional framework of the EU.[57]

The call for the politicisation of EU Fundamental Rights Law also seems particularly relevant in the context of the current 'crisis of values' that the EU is facing. In particular, I believe, following the proposal of Édouard Dubout, that we must adopt a 'pragmatist approach' to values – one that does not regard them as abstract and universal ideals, but rather as practical guides to action, the

[53] K Nicolaidis and J Pelabay, 'One Union, One Story? In Praise of Europe's Narrative Diversity' in A Warleigh-Lack (ed), *Reflections on European Integration* (Palgrave, 2008) 3.

[54] J Waldron, *Law and Disagreement* (Oxford University Press, 1999).

[55] J Clarenne, *Delibérer au Parlement* (Larcier, 2022) 152.

[56] Mouffe, *Agonistique* (n 52) 29.

[57] ibid.

evolving content of which must be the result of collective choice.[58] European law can, in this sense, serve as a tool through which European society defines and reshapes the meaning of its liberal values – especially human rights – according to changing contexts and historical moments. Thus, as Dubout suggests, European Fundamental Rights Law may serve as an 'existential' field of experimentation, within which the transformations of European ways of life and collective imaginaries are projected.[59]

III.1.b. A Political Project for the European Demoï-cracy

Actually achieving a political shift at the level of the EU is by no means straightforward. Its well-known institutional weaknesses make the organisation of democratic life within it particularly challenging.

In this regard, the well-established and influential work of Kalypso Nicolaïdis on the notion of 'demoï-cracy' proves particularly illuminating. This concept envisions the EU as a political entity that acknowledges and embraces the plurality of *demoï* – that is, the diverse peoples and democratic communities that compose it. Democratic engagement at such a supranational scale is inherently complex; however, Nicolaïdis offers conceptual tools to render it conceivable. Among these is the crucial shift from a community grounded in shared identity to one oriented around a shared project – a 'community of project'.[60] The EU, as has been widely discussed, fundamentally differs from political communities rooted in the framework of nation-states. Rather than being bound by a singular, shared identity, the EU is held together by common projects and collectively defined objectives.[61] In this respect, Article 1 TEU explicitly states that the EU is established as 'a union on which the Member States confer competences to attain objectives they have in common'. This formulation underscores the functional and purposive nature of the EU's political architecture. Foremost among these objectives, as enumerated in Article 3 TEU, is that the 'Union's aim is to promote peace, its values and the well-being of its peoples'. The promotion of fundamental rights and values is, thus, not incidental but central to the EU's raison d'être. Accordingly, the EU is mandated to 'pursue its objectives by appropriate means commensurate with the competences which are conferred upon it in the Treaties'.[62] This legal framework reflects a model of integration grounded not in uniformity of identity, but in the pursuit of shared normative

[58] É Dubout, 'Peut-on défendre les valeurs de l'Union européenne par le droit' (2025) *Revue des droits et libertés fondamentaux* 1, 9.

[59] ibid, 9.

[60] Own translation. O Jouanjan, 'Ce que "donner une constitution à l'Europe" veut dire' (2003) *Cités* 21, 23.

[61] K Nicolaïdis, 'Notre Demoï-cratie européenne: La Constellation Transnationale à l'horizon du Patriotisme Constitutionnel' (*Politique européenne*, 2016) 45, 61.

[62] TEU, art 5(1).

commitments and collective aspirations.[63] As Nicolaïdis aptly puts it: 'In a community of project, the sense of belonging to – and commitment towards – the EU must be grounded in *doing* rather than *being*.'[64]

Moreover, the EU, unlike a traditional international organisation, establishes itself not as a co-operation of Member States, but rather as an organisation that directly addresses its citizens. Olivier Jouanjan rightly points out that the EU 'is not simply an "international organisation" *but a polity*, a political body, a kind of *res publica*'.[65]

Within this conceptual framework, the domain of fundamental rights should be more compellingly framed as a genuine political project for the EU *polity* – one that the EU is not only empowered to pursue, but also uniquely positioned to bring to life.[66] Rather than a static expression of shared identity, fundamental rights protection should become a dynamic field of collective action, emblematic of the EU's capacity to translate common values into tangible commitments. Assuming this shift and embracing such a mission would provide the EU with a critical opportunity to mitigate the risks it currently faces – risks that stem, in part, from an essentialist interpretation of its founding values. By moving beyond a static conception of identity, the EU could instead articulate a praxis rooted in a democratically endorsed political project.

In this light, values – and, in particular, fundamental rights – should no longer be considered only as markers of belonging, but be mobilised as catalysts for collective and inclusive political engagement. There is a pressing need for deeper political discussion and structured deliberation on how fundamental rights are to be implemented within the EU. Too often, these questions are treated as purely technical or legal matters, left to experts or institutions far removed from citizens' everyday concerns. Yet, issues such as the protection of children on social media, the safeguarding of free elections against foreign interference, or the guarantee of a free and independent press are inherently political questions: the way in which they are implemented must ultimately be the subject of collective choice by the citizens themselves.

For instance, when we ask which rules should govern social media platforms to protect younger generations, we are not merely engaging in a debate about regulation or digital innovation. We are deciding how to balance different fundamental rights and freedoms, including the freedom of expression, the protection of personal data and privacy, the freedom to conduct a business, the right to security, and so on. Similarly, discussions on how to shield elections

[63] Nevertheless, a discernible evolutionary trend has emerged in this area, with the CJEU affirming the existence of 'the very identity of the European Union as a common legal order'. See, inter alia, Case C-156/21 *Hungary v European Parliament and Council of the European Union* EU:C:2022:197 [2022], para 127.

[64] Own translation. Nicolaïdis, 'Notre Demoï-cratie européenne' (n 61) 61. Emphasis in original.

[65] Own translation and emphasis added. Jouanjan, 'Ce que "donner une constitution à l'Europe" veut dire' (n 60) 23.

[66] See, above, the strategic positioning of the EU.

from cyberattacks or disinformation campaigns are not technical details but essential to preserving European democracies. The same applies to the protection of media freedom and pluralism, which is crucial so that citizens can make informed choices, as well as to the respect for fundamental rights in trade and the circulation of goods, where questions of ethics, human dignity, and global justice are at stake.

All these issues require collective deliberation and, inevitably, political arbitration. Politicisation should not be seen only as a threat to fundamental rights, but also as the necessary condition for these debates to take place openly, where different perspectives can confront one another and compromises can be reached. By bringing such discussions into the political sphere, citizens are not only given a voice but also the opportunity to recognise the tangible ways in which the EU contributes to shaping their daily lives. In this sense, politicisation is not merely a theoretical ideal; it is the path towards bringing the EU closer to the people it serves.

Nevertheless, a close examination of the EU's Fundamental Rights framework reveals a persistent gap: the absence of a fully explicit and politically embraced vision of human rights as a collective undertaking. While a series of legislative instruments have indeed been adopted by EU political institutions to implement fundamental rights law – such as the GDPR, the Digital Services Act, and the Artificial Intelligence Act – the explicit articulation of their connection to human rights as a political project remains underdeveloped. The acknowledgement of the necessary politicisation of human rights is, in fact, essential – particularly in the case of open-ended human rights standards that require further normative and institutional specification. As Webber and Yowell put it, 'they leave open answers to the questions: what do my rights entitle me to do (or be free from)? Who is to do (or forbear from) what in satisfaction of my rights?'.[67] Answering such questions requires legislative measures that arbitrate between reasonable and morally underdetermined alternatives, 'within a zone demarcated on one side, by what reason requires and, on the other, by what reason prohibits'.[68] Moreover, articulating the politicisation of EU Fundamental Rights Law could contribute to strengthening the very cement of European society – whose destiny is to endure not through a unified cultural or social system,[69] but thanks to a common programme for the 'social life of European individuals'.[70]

The engagement of political debate at the European level with questions of fundamental rights is not without precedent. As previously discussed, there has

[67] GCN Webber and P Yowell, 'Introduction: Securing Human Rights through Legislation' in GCN Webber et al, *Legislated Rights: Securing Human Rights through Legislation* (Cambridge University Press, 2018) 11.

[68] ibid.

[69] Azoulaï, 'The Law of the European Society' (n 41) 205.

[70] ibid, 206.

been political deliberation on matters such as equality, non-discrimination, and data protection. These developments attest to the EU's capacity to act meaningfully within the field of fundamental rights. It nonetheless appears desirable to underscore more explicitly that the institutional mandate in this area is firmly established, thereby offering a legitimate foundation for a more overtly political articulation of the EU's Fundamental Rights project. Indeed, what appears to be lacking is a deeper politicisation of fundamental rights in the strongest sense of the term. One may legitimately ask whether European citizens are aware that the EU is a global pioneer in these fields. Do these policies give rise to public debate among those they are intended to serve? In the absence of such democratic engagement, the transformative potential of the EU's fundamental rights framework risks remaining both underutilised and insufficiently visible within the public sphere. As previously noted, one of the EU's enduring challenges lies in reconciling unity with diversity – in other words, in 'creating a form of community that makes room for heterogeneity'.[71] In this context, the political project of fundamental rights within the EU could serve as a crucial means of reinforcing the connection between the EU and its citizens, who ought to be more effectively informed and engaged on these issues. By articulating rights not merely as individual entitlements but as expressions of shared values and mutual responsibilities, such a project possesses the potential to foster social and political cohesion without suppressing diversity or difference.

III.1.c. The EU Charter and the European Convention on Human Rights as a Framework

If there is to be democratic debate, there must nonetheless remain an anchor in the form of minimum consensus on the constitutive institutions of liberal democracy and the ethico-political values that sustain democratic co-existence. This minimum consensus corresponds to the legal principle of the rule of law, and to human rights as normative constraints on the exercise of political power.[72]

At the level of the EU, from an internal perspective, these boundaries are established by the EU Charter of Fundamental Rights. Beyond that, I would argue for the establishment of an external framework, which entails the EU's formal commitment to the ECHR. Such a dual framework should ensure that the politicisation of EU Fundamental Rights Law remains fully consistent with international human rights standards.

In this respect, the EU Charter provides a relatively open normative framework within which the EU's competences may be exercised. As Justine Lacroix

[71] Mouffe, *Agonistique* (n 52) 68.

[72] For a discussion on the potential existence of a 'dissensus' in the EU, involving an irreconcilable clash over these liberal values, see R Coman, *The Politics of the Rule of Law in the EU Polity* (Palgrave Macmillan, 2022) 14.

has argued, the EU Charter remains ideologically open and normatively flexible.[73] This openness implies that a range of political choices remains available and could be meaningfully pursued, should the legislature choose to do so.[74] The EU Charter thus offers not only a legal foundation but also a space for democratic deliberation and political imagination.

The interpretive openness surrounding the EU's Bill of Rights could illustrate, as underlined by Lacroix, one of its most distinctive features:

> Rather than constituting a homogeneous community unified around ostensibly consensual and uniquely 'European' values, the EU ought to be understood as a space of civilised contestation among diverse normative traditions – libertarian, liberal, socialist, and radical – each offering competing visions of human rights.[75]

In this light, the European project should not be considered as the expression of a fixed identity, but rather a democratic arena in which the meaning of liberty and equality is continuously negotiated.[76] The EU Charter is amenable to such an undertaking, insofar as it does not merely articulate the rights it enshrines as individual entitlements,[77] but rather conceives them as constitutive elements of a broader social fabric.[78] This thesis resonates with Claude Lefort's thesis that human rights should not be interpreted as mechanisms of individual isolation, but rather as supports for the network of relations through which individuals contribute to the construction of a shared world.[79] The relational dimension of fundamental rights is explicitly affirmed in the EU Charter, the preamble of which underscores that the 'Enjoyment of these rights entails responsibilities and duties with regard to other persons, to the human community and to future generations'. While the EU Charter does not impose a single essentialist or universalist vision of human rights for Europe, nor does it confine itself to enshrining purely individual rights for 'atomised monads'.[80] To borrow the words of Édouard Dubout, one might consider it as expressing – albeit still in a nascent form – 'a certain conception of relating to and uniting with others'.[81] It is, in this sense, a Charter for the 'Union'.[82]

[73] J Lacroix, 'Ouvrir les portes de l'interprétation: la Charte et l'inscription sociale des droits' (2021) *Cahiers de droit européen* 114

[74] A Bailleux, 'Préambule' in F Picod, C Rizcallah, and S Van Drooghenbroeck, *La Charte des droits fondamentaux de l'Union européenne. Commentaire article par article*, 3rd edn (Bruylant, 2023) 28.

[75] Lacroix, 'Ouvrir les portes de l'interprétation' (n 73) 115. Own translation.

[76] ibid.

[77] It should be noted, however, that the individual dimension of rights is also strongly present in the EU Charter, which enshrines numerous aspects of individual liberty, particularly in the economic sphere. This is exemplified, for instance, by art 16 of the EU Charter, which guarantees the freedom to conduct a business. On this point, see É Dubout, 'Le sujet des droits de la Charte. De l'être universel à l'être relationnel' in A Iliopoulou-Penot and L Xerou, *La Charte des droits fondamentaux de l'Union européenne, source de renouveau constitutionnel?* (Bruylant, 2020) 279–96.

[78] Lacroix, 'Ouvrir les portes de l'interprétation' (n 73) 117.

[79] C Lefort, 'Démocratie et globalisation' in *Le Temps Présent* (Berlin, 2007), quoted by Lacroix, 'Ouvrir les portes de l'interprétation' (n 73).

[80] In a Leibnizian sense.

[81] Dubout, 'Le sujet des droits de la Charte' (n 77) 296.

[82] ibid.

Such an understanding of rights – one that integrates the demands of community and intergenerational responsibility – necessarily presupposes a form of political mediation.

Political decisions, while necessarily made within the framework established by the EU Charter as an internal legal guideline, should also be clearly subject to external oversight. Analogous to states in contemporary democracies that develop their own systems for the protection of fundamental rights while accepting external scrutiny, the EU ought similarly to adhere to an external normative framework, notably the ECHR system.

As Laurence Burgorgue-Larsen observes, 'human rights justice is singular'.[83] By ratifying international human rights treaties, states consent to subordinate themselves to shared values that transcend their domestic legal orders, thereby legitimising external review of their actions. In this respect, international human rights law diverges from 'traditional' international law: it is less concerned with regulating relations between treaty-contributing states than with governing the interactions between individuals, and between individuals and the state.[84] Nonetheless, states continue to exercise their sovereignty, not by negating international law, but by actively implementing it in practice. In this regard, the role of the national legislature is crucial: through democratic procedures, it clarifies the content, scope, and limits of human rights, thereby transforming them from 'indeterminate' rights into 'determinate' rights.[85] The European Court of Human Rights fully endorses this view, recently affirming in a judgment handed down in the Grand Chamber formation that, 'Judicial intervention, including by this Court, cannot replace or provide any substitute for the action which must be taken by the legislative and executive branches of government.'[86]

In the same vein, as I explained earlier, the role of the EU in this context may be compared to that of a state: namely, an arena for the politicisation of human rights. The implementation of human rights must, at least in part, be accompanied by democratic legitimation, and it is through democratic procedures within given legal communities that such rights must be realised. In this regard, the legislature is the central politically legitimate authority for undertaking the constitutional negotiations 'necessary to complete the specifications of rights'.[87]

Whereas the regime of international human rights law cannot provide such a forum – precisely because of its global and depoliticised character – the legal order of the EU, by contrast, encompasses spaces dedicated to the exercise of political action. It is worth recalling that the functioning of the EU is grounded

[83] L Burgorgue Larsen, *The 3 Regional Human Rights Courts in Context. Justice That Cannot Be Taken for Granted* (Oxford University Press, 2024), 1.

[84] H Dumont and I Hachez, 'Repenser la souveraineté à la lumière du droit international des droits de l'homme' (2017) *Revue belge de droit constitutionnel* 315–63.

[85] Webber, *The Negotiable Constitution* (n 47) 8.

[86] Case *Verein Klimaseniorinnen Schweiz and others v Switzerland* App no. 53600/20 (ECHR, 9 April 2024), ECLI:CE:ECHR:2024:0409JUD005360020, para 412.

[87] Webber, *The Negotiable Constitution* (n 47) 8.

in the principle of representative democracy.[88] European citizens are represented in the directly elected European Parliament (and have been since 1979),[89] as well as in the Council of the EU, composed of ministerial representatives of Member States who are democratically accountable before their respective parliaments, and who jointly exercise legislative power within the EU. Although the institutional system of the EU is, of course, subject to criticism with respect to its functioning – debates we shall not revisit here – it can, nevertheless, be reasonably maintained that its decision-making processes now offer sufficient guarantees to be regarded as democratic.[90]

There is, therefore, a fundamental divergence in nature between, on the one hand, the legal order of the EU and, on the other, international human rights law. While the latter serves to delineate the 'red lines' within which states may exercise political authority, the law of the EU is intended to emanate from – and contribute to the development of – a European political space. As Gret Haller observed in 2012, 'at the international level, no Parliament is elected to deliberate and decide on human rights', and that 'such premises exist in Europe, though without final competence in the field of fundamental rights'.[91] Nonetheless, as the chapter one of this book has demonstrated, the EU has undergone a significant evolution in this respect. Today, it both possesses and exercises competences across a broad range of policy areas, thereby enabling it to engage with questions that are directly pertinent to the protection of fundamental rights through political processes.

It is, however, crucial that political deliberations within the EU occur within the framework of international human rights law. Since the Treaty of Lisbon, Article 6 TEU has enshrined the imperative for the EU to accede to the ECHR, making such accession an obligation. This process, envisioned for several decades, has already given rise to considerable debate.[92] Following years of negotiation, marked by numerous legal and political obstacles, a new draft agreement on the EU's accession to the ECHR was eventually submitted for an Opinion from the CJEU. The story is well known: the previous draft agreement was halted by *Opinion 2/13*, delivered by the CJEU in 2014.[93] Despite the multiple deadlocks identified by the CJEU, EU institutions and the Council of Europe decided in 2019 to relaunch

[88] TEU, art 10.

[89] TEU, art 14(3).

[90] On the legitimacy of the EU legislator, see, among others, M van den Brink, 'Justice, Legitimacy and the Authority of Legislation' (2019) 82(2) *Modern Law Review* 293–318; and, more specifically within the field of fundamental rights protection, Y Lorans, *Le juge et le législateur de l'Union européenne: étude d'une protection collaborative des droits fondamentaux* (Bruylant, 2026).

[91] G Haller, *Droits de l'homme, révolution et démocratie* (Economica, 2015) 132. See also A Buchanan, *Justice, Legitimacy, and Self-Determination: Moral Foundations for International Law* (Oxford University Press, 2007) 330.

[92] See, among others, D Halberstam, '"It's the Autonomy, Stupid!" A Modest Defense of *Opinion 2/13* on EU Accession to the ECHR, and the Way Forward' (2015) 16 *German Law Journal* 105–46, and F Ronkes Agerbeek, 'EU Accession to the European Convention on Human Rights: A New Hope' (2024) *European Papers* 695–713.

[93] Opinion 2/13 ECLI:EU:C:2014:2454 [2014].

the negotiations, resulting in the elaboration of a revised text intended to address the objections previously raised. Among the most significant obstacles identified was the issue arising from the CJEU's limited jurisdiction over matters falling within the Common Foreign and Security Policy (CFSP). In this regard, and drawing in particular on the principle of the rule of law, the CJEU has, in its more recent case law – such as in *KS and KD*[94] – interpreted the Treaties as conferring upon it a broader competence in CFSP-related matters. It is, therefore, reasonable to expect that this development will facilitate the recognition that the CFSP jurisdictional issue no longer constitutes an insurmountable obstacle to accession.

Time will tell whether the new draft agreement will ultimately be found compatible with primary law by the CJEU. Nevertheless, it seems to me indispensable – both for legal and legitimacy reasons – that the EU should eventually accede to the ECHR. Such accession would ensure that its political and legal action, including in the field of fundamental rights protection, remains coherent with international human rights law and thereby enhances the EU's credibility as a global human rights player.

The EU Charter of Fundamental Rights and the European Convention on Human Rights thus constitute the normative framework within which the politicisation of EU Fundamental Rights ought to be envisaged. In this respect, it appears that the CJEU has increasingly embraced this understanding, recognising a wide margin of discretion for the legislature in the implementation of human rights – one that, however, cannot be exceeded, particularly where such action would contravene the EU Charter itself.

III.2. Rethinking the EU's Capacity in the Field of Fundamental Rights Protection

Enabling such a political turn in the field of fundamental rights protection, in turn, requires a reassessment of the EU's institutional architecture. In this framework, the absence of a general competence in the field of fundamental rights protection represents a significant structural gap for the EU. While the promotion and protection of fundamental rights constitutes one of the EU's declared objectives, it can act only within the limits of the competences conferred upon it by the Treaties. Like any international organisation, the EU is, therefore, bound by the principle of conferral. The adoption of the EU Charter, and its elevation to the status of primary law, has not altered this foundational limitation. The drafting and incorporation of the EU Charter were presented as neutral with regard to the division of competences between the EU and the Member States.[95] Nevertheless, it is difficult

[94] Joined Cases C-29/22 P and C-44/22 P, *KS and KD v Council and Others* ECLI:EU:C:2024:725 [2024].

[95] The Member States feared that the EU Charter might be invoked by the EU legislature as a direct source of legal authority. In response, art 51(2) was meticulously crafted and repeatedly revised to guarantee that it remained entirely neutral in this regard.

to ignore that a certain centralising effect has resulted from the development of an EU Fundamental Rights Law framework.[96] Moreover, as previously emphasised, the boundary between the national and EU spheres of application remains remarkably blurred. This lack of clarity raises serious concerns regarding both legal certainty and the intelligibility of EU action in this area.

While I do not consider it necessary to confer a general competence on the EU in the field of human rights protection, I regard it as essential to delineate more clearly the EU's capacities in relation to fundamental rights, for two principal reasons: first, to reduce legal uncertainty; and second, to facilitate what I regard as a necessary and desirable 'political pivot' in the domain of EU Fundamental Rights Law.

For this stance, one may recall the argument advanced almost three decades ago by Philip Alston and Joseph Weiler, who advocated the establishment of a coherent and comprehensive 'Human Rights Policy' at the EU level.[97] Even at that time, this proposition posed complex institutional and conceptual challenges. How, for instance, could a general policy on fundamental rights be effectively operationalised? In response, Armin von Bogdandy noted that persistent doubts surround the justification for treating human rights as a single unified policy domain, given that fundamental rights cut across an exceptionally wide array of EU competences. He further emphasised the difficulty of envisaging a coherent administrative structure capable of implementing such a policy in a consistent and effective manner.[98]

I concur, to a large extent, with the view that the EU should not be conceived as developing a general overarching 'policy' in the field of human rights. Such an undertaking does not correspond to its primary purpose. Moreover, it would imply granting the EU a cross-cutting competence in this domain – one that would, in fact, profoundly alter its very nature. Indeed, the attribution of a general competence in the field of fundamental rights could be tantamount to reversing the principle of conferral that defines the EU's legal order, thereby moving it closer to the nature of a state rather than an international organisation. A general and positive competence in the field of fundamental rights would, in practice, enable the EU to intervene in almost any area of policy, for virtually all matters can be framed in terms of human rights. The defining feature of an international organisation, however, is the possession of competences that are both attributed and specific. It is true, as has been acknowledged,[99] that nothing precludes an international organisation from being vested with a broad range of powers; yet

[96] On this, see O Scarcello, 'Fundamental rights and the federal equilibrium: Comparing the doctrines of incorporation in the USA and the EU' (2023) 30(6) *Maastricht Journal of European and Comparative Law* 729–59; and, earlier, J-P Jacqué, 'Back to Philadelphia' (2002) *Revue du Marché Commun* 661–69.

[97] P Alston and JHH Weiler, 'An "Ever Closer Union" in Need of a Human Rights Policy' (1998) 9(4) *European Journal of International Law* 658–723.

[98] A von Bogdandy, 'The European Union as a Human Rights Organization? Human Rights and the Core of the European Union' (2000) 37(6) *Common Market Law Review* 1307, 1311.

[99] See s II of the Introduction to this book.

such competences must remain materially limited – they cannot, in my view, be unlimited. Furthermore, any such attribution of competence would necessitate a unanimously agreed amendment of the Treaties – an outcome which, for political reasons, appears highly improbable.

The so-called 'political shift' in the field of fundamental rights should, thus, not be understood as requiring the creation of a centralised overarching human rights policy at the EU level. Rather, it should be seen as a deeper politicisation of fundamental rights issues – integrating them more explicitly and transparently into the exercise of the EU's existing competences. This approach does not require a reallocation of powers but instead calls for greater clarity and political responsibility in the way rights-based considerations are handled within the EU's policy frameworks.

This proposal could materialise in several ways.

First, it may be envisaged that the institutions of the EU – particularly those vested with legislative power – could adopt policy-oriented legal instruments designed to more clearly articulate the fundamental rights dimension of certain measures they intend to pursue within the framework of the EU's competences. Put differently, such instruments could render explicit, and more firmly embed, the fundamental rights considerations inherent in specific policy areas.

A considerable proportion of current legislative proposals and acts integrate human rights considerations, even when their principal legal basis is found in areas unrelated to human rights, such as the Internal Market.[100] Nevertheless, there would be considerable merit in establishing a more cross-cutting political instrument through which the institutions could expressly delineate their approach in relation to fundamental rights. Such an initiative might even take the form of an interpretative regulation clarifying the relevant legal bases, thereby enhancing both legal certainty and transparency with respect to the fundamental rights implications in these fields. This proposition draws inspiration from a call already advanced by Gareth Davies in 2015, when he observed, in the context of the Internal Market, that 'the most urgent need, if we are not to entirely rewrite the Treaties, is for more precision about what an Internal Market needs'.[101] In this vein, he proposed the adoption of an interpretative EU Regulation, pursuant to Article 114 TFEU, to provide greater clarity as to the meaning of the Internal Market, free movement, and undistorted competition. By analogy, could one not envisage the adoption of one or more legislative instruments, based on those legal provisions commonly invoked for measures relating to human rights, that would explicitly articulate the fundamental rights dimension within these frameworks? The objective is not to constrain

[100] See ch 1. On this, see, among others, V Delhomme and C Rizcallah, 'Internal Market Legislation and Dissensus over Liberal Democracy' in R Coman et al, *The Palgrave Handbook of Dissensus over Liberal Democracy* (Palgrave, forthcoming).

[101] G Davies, 'Democracy and Legitimacy in the Shadow of Purposive Competence' (2015) 21(1) *European Law Journal* 2, 21.

the use of Article 114 for this purpose, but to render explicit that fundamental rights are integral to legislation designed to ensure the proper functioning of the Internal Market. In adopting such an interpretative EU Regulation, the institutions would have the opportunity to deliberate on their priorities in this domain, thereby promoting greater transparency and informing citizens more comprehensively, including regarding the positions adopted by various stakeholders. In a perhaps less ambitious vein, one might, at the very least, envisage the adoption of a Communication by the Commission, which would serve to elucidate its approach to the protection of human rights when developing legislative proposals pertaining to the Internal Market or to the Area of Freedom, Security, and Justice.

Second, such a reorientation towards a policy framework that more overtly incorporates fundamental rights considerations might equally call for a more systematic and substantive deliberation of these matters at all stages of the legislative process. This line of thought has been advanced by a group of scholars within the framework of the Proposals for Ex Ante Review of EU Legislation (PEARL) project.[102] Their central contention is that the EU ought to ensure the compatibility of legislative measures with fundamental rights prior to their adoption. This proposal aims to complement the existing *ex post* judicial review mechanisms by establishing *ex ante* mechanisms of a political, rather than strictly judicial, nature. Within this perspective, they advocate for the systematic mainstreaming of fundamental rights protection from the very earliest stages of legislative drafting, going beyond the formalistic checklist approach currently employed by the Council of the EU and the European Commission within the framework of the Better Regulation strategy.[103] In particular, they call for fundamental rights to be integrated in a more coherent and transversal manner within the impact assessments of legislative initiatives. To operationalise this vision, they propose the conclusion of a new Interinstitutional Agreement on 'Better Fundamental Rights Compliant Regulation', designed to facilitate the centralisation and dissemination of best practices pertaining to fundamental rights protection, shared among the European Commission, the European Parliament, and the Council of the EU. In this context, it appears both necessary and appropriate to cultivate a measured degree of politicisation with regard to questions pertaining to fundamental rights, as previously emphasised, insofar as political determinations will, by their very nature, be unavoidable. Within the framework of such interinstitutional arrangements, it is therefore imperative to establish structured fora for deliberation, wherein the fundamental rights

[102] I Gambardella et al, 'Enhancing Fundamental Rights Protection: Proposals for Ex Ante Review of EU Legislation (PEARL)' (*Verfassungsblog*, 4 November 2024), https://verfassungsblog.de/enhancing-fundamental-rights-protection/.

[103] European Commission, 'Better Regulation Toolbox', July 2023, available at https://commission.europa.eu/document/download/9c8d2189-8abd-4f29-84e9-abc843cc68e0_en?filename=BR%20toolbox%20-%20Jul%202023%20-%20FINAL.pdf.

implications of the measures under consideration are accorded a prominent and clearly delineated position within the decision-making process.

Third, it appears essential, in the context of a more explicit emphasis on the fundamental rights dimension of certain European policies, that the allocation of responsibilities between the EU, on the one hand, and the Member States, on the other, be more clearly defined. As noted above, there remains considerable ambiguity concerning which matters fall within the remit of EU law and, conversely, the extent to which Member States retain discretion under this common framework. To ensure the coherence and integrity of these multiple layers, it would be necessary to delineate more precisely the margin of discretion left to national authorities under each harmonisation instrument. This could, for instance, be achieved by specifying within legislative acts both: (i) the degree of harmonisation envisaged, and, conversely (ii) the margin of manoeuvre available to Member States when implementing this measure. Too often, indeed, uncertainties persist as to the nature and extent of the harmonisation pursued by a given piece of EU legislation. By clearly and unambiguously indicating, for instance, whether a measure seeks to achieve minimum (or maximum) harmonisation, such doubts could be alleviated.

Finally, this political activation, and the clarification of the EU's capacity in the field of fundamental rights protection, cannot be seriously contemplated without the EU's accession to the ECHR. As previously emphasised, such accession is indispensable from two perspectives: (i) legal coherence, as it is essential to avoid the risk of conflicting obligations arising from two international organisations (all Member States are parties to the ECHR); and (ii) from the standpoint of legitimacy. The EU can only aspire to be recognised as a legitimate international actor in the protection of human rights if it commits to operating within the framework established by the ECHR, as interpreted by the ECtHR – the pre-eminent instrument for human rights protection on the European continent.

Conclusion

This final chapter has sought to move beyond the descriptive analysis of the framework and particularities of EU Fundamental Rights Law towards a more reflective and forward-looking inquiry. Having examined both the added value and the limitations of EU law for the protection of human rights – for individuals seeking to better access their rights, as well as for international human rights practitioners aiming to appreciate its potential – it was necessary to take stock of the state of EU Fundamental Rights Law, and to consider what this field reveals about the EU itself and its contribution to the broader process of European integration.

In this regard, EU Fundamental Rights Law emerges as both a resonance chamber for human rights and a dynamic arena for normative development. It provides a site where competing legal orders and political visions intersect, allowing for the advancement of – yet also the challenge to – rights. This duality reflects the very nature of the European project: the EU's pursuit of multiple, sometimes competing, objectives within a composite constitutional order.

At a more prescriptive level, EU Fundamental Rights Law should now be regarded as an opportunity for renewal in the integration process. It ought henceforth to be conceived as a genuinely political project – one directed towards the construction of a European society founded upon shared principles and values. As the growing prominence of fundamental rights questions within EU governance and the establishment of a Commission priority for 2019–24 on the promotion of a 'European way of life' demonstrate, these issues are no longer peripheral, but lie at the very core of the European project.[104] Yet this prompts a crucial question: what place should fundamental rights occupy within this vision of a European way of life, and how can they be meaningfully implemented within it?

These issues, in my view, make political arbitration that is grounded in sound deliberation necessary. Within this context, EU Fundamental Rights Law should constitute a true political project for European 'demoï-cracy', providing the normative foundations of a European society. In an era marked by political attacks on democracy and liberal values, it is crucial to articulate the principles that unite this society. As Azoulaï observes, we are witnessing a 'Europeanisation of everyday life', where 'the sharing of material realities, modes of living, and socio-economic and political ideals is undeniable, and Europe has, in many respects, become a sociological reality'.[105] It is precisely for this reason that the EU has a central role to play – one that must be rendered more explicit and comprehensible. European citizens should be made aware that, at the level of the EU, far-reaching political choices are being made which directly affect the protection of their most fundamental and everyday rights. Enhancing public understanding of this dimension is essential if the EU is to strengthen its democratic legitimacy and foster a sense of shared ownership over the values it seeks to uphold.

Accordingly, the institutional architecture of the EU should more clearly reflect the role it is called upon to play in the everyday realities of European life, while providing a coherent and legitimate foundation for collective governance, democratic participation, and social cohesion. As Armin von Bogdandy has emphasised, human rights function, across many legal orders, as 'instruments for continuous adaptation to changing social needs, fears and convictions'.[106]

Might it not, therefore, be time to fully embrace this dynamic within the EU's legal order, which has now attained a considerable degree of institutional and

[104] Margaritis Schinas was the European Commission Vice-President for Promoting our European Way of Life until 2024. The role has now been split between different commissioners.

[105] Azoulaï, 'The Law of the European Society' (n 41) 210, quoting E Recchi, A Favell, F Apaydin et al (eds), *Everyday Europe: Social Transnationalism in an Unsettled Continent* (Policy Press, 2019).

[106] von Bogdandy, 'The European Union as a Human Rights Organization?' (n 98) 1338.

normative maturity? Might this not represent, among other possible avenues, a means of bringing the Union closer to its citizens, by allowing them genuinely to apprehend and take ownership of the human rights issues that the European level is particularly well placed to address? It is my contention that this is indeed the case, and it is for this reason that I argue in favour of an explicit political shift in the EU's approach to human rights.

Concluding Remarks

EU Fundamental Rights Law, a Cluster of Raw Diamonds

As we conclude this study, it is worth pausing to reflect on the path we have travelled across the landscape of the EU Fundamental Rights system.

If, as I hope, the journey has been engaging, it must also be acknowledged that it has often been a winding one. The reason is simple: the EU's fundamental rights architecture is difficult to navigate and has evolved in a particularly complex and uncertain context.

The ambiguities underpinning this framework stem, in part, from its fragmented and technically dense nature. The intricacy of EU Fundamental Rights Law is one of its principal weaknesses, and it is a legitimate target of criticism. Complexity in law is never desirable, even if it is sometimes unavoidable, as legal rules must grapple with the increasingly elaborate structure of our societies. Yet its presence feels particularly regrettable in the domain of human rights: rights so essential, and so closely tied to the human person, ought to be accessible and intelligible. In this book, I have therefore sought to contribute – modestly – to a clearer understanding of the EU Fundamental Rights framework.

A further difficulty lies in the fact that the EU's action in the field of human rights, although pervasive, remains insufficiently known. It manifests itself across policies and sectors, yet is rarely acknowledged as the action of a fully-fledged human rights player. One of the aims of this study has, therefore, also been to unravel the true scope of EU Fundamental Rights Law and to make visible what too often remains overlooked. This study also calls for a firmer political commitment in this domain. It is now time for the EU to explicitly assume the role that it plays – or ought to play – in the field of human rights protection in Europe.

EU Fundamental Rights Law, I argue, possesses distinctive and considerable value within the human rights landscape; a value comparable to that of raw diamonds. It may offer resources that are rare and precious, and that cannot always be found in traditional human rights instruments. These resources are, however, not uniform; they are faceted and fragmented. Their value, moreover, depends on the density of the applicable EU rules in the domain concerned. The richness of EU law can only be fully appreciated once it is polished and used appropriately. These rules can also be sharp, capable of cutting, and may thus become a sword rather than a safeguard for human rights. Like a cluster of diamonds, EU Fundamental Rights Law can thus, at times, enhance protection – depending on the density of the resource in a given area – but it can also be intrusive and abrasive. Moreover, the EU's current approach to human rights is far from exemplary, and the full potential of these diamonds has certainly not (yet?) been revealed.

I believe that this cluster of diamonds would benefit from being studied more closely, polished with greater care, and more fully grasped by the EU institutions and the Member States themselves, so that its richness and potential may be fully realised.

To support a deeper understanding of this particular system, I shall offer below a brief reminder of the key stages of our journey, before a short epilogue situating this study within the current political context.

Chapter one set the scene for the architecture of EU Fundamental Rights: a system that is simultaneously strong and limited. The EU has become an essential player in the field of human rights protection in Europe. Its contribution can be significant – indeed, at times more robust than international human rights law. Yet this source of protection is often insufficiently mobilised. This is regrettable, although understandable: while its effects can be strong, the scope of EU Fundamental Rights Law is limited. This system cannot be invoked in all circumstances, unlike, for example, the European Convention on Human Rights, which applies whenever the acts or omissions at issue fall within the jurisdiction of a contracting party. Nevertheless, it seems important to emphasise the transformative potential of EU law in this field, particularly in areas where EU harmonisation exists. In several domains, a highly developed body of law has emerged, allowing the EU to act as a genuine standard-setter in the field of human rights. This is particularly evident in the fields of anti-discrimination and data protection, but it also extends to less explored areas, such as the protection of fundamental rights within criminal procedure. This is the message I sought to convey in the first chapter: EU Fundamental Rights Law – although limited in scope and multifaceted – can, in certain contexts, offer significant resources.

Chapter two explored in greater depth the special features of EU Fundamental Rights Law. This layer of protection can be particularly strong, thanks to the characteristics of EU law and the comprehensive system of judicial remedies that supports it. Effectiveness is often the point at which international law reveals its limitations, including in the field of human rights. By contrast, the EU framework can demonstrate a degree of authority that surpasses that of other international human rights instruments. The chapter, therefore, examined how these features and the EU system of judicial remedies may generate genuine added value to the EU Fundamental Rights system. Yet this very structure also renders the system strikingly incisive. Like an uncut diamond, EU law must be handled with caution: in certain circumstances, it may restrict or even undermine human rights protections stemming from other legal sources, whether national or international.

Chapter three was devoted to the oversight of EU Fundamental Rights Law. As a highly complex international organisation, the EU has developed a multifaceted system to ensure respect for this body of law within the Member States. This system may be described as comprising three levels. The first is the strictly political level, which includes the accession process, ongoing but limited scrutiny by the EU institutions (in particular the European Parliament, the European Commission, and the Council of the EU), and the well-known procedure under Article 7 TEU. A second, more innovative, layer consists of financial instruments designed both to support human rights protection in the Member States and to sanction violations in the context of the use of EU funds. Finally, an independent monitoring and supervisory system – most notably the Fundamental Rights Agency and, at national level, equality bodies and data protection authorities – completes the architecture. This system is sophisticated and complex, but this does not mean that it is fully effective. Significant progress remains to be made, and certain reforms may well be required.

Finally, chapter four issued a call to engage more fully with the EU's Fundamental Rights system. The development of EU Fundamental Rights Law should become a genuine political project for the EU's demoï-cracy, as it is capable of providing the normative foundations of a European society. In a period marked by political pressure on democracy and liberal values, articulating the principles that bind us together is more crucial than ever.

In this spirit, I advocate a renewed political engagement with human rights at EU level – one in which EU institutions, the Member States, and citizens themselves consciously take part in the choices inherent in shaping a EU Fundamental Rights policy. Such a policy will inevitably remain limited, and I do not argue in favour of granting the EU a general competence in this field. EU action in the field of human rights protection, already exists, but it remains insufficiently visible, and the political choices it entails are not sufficiently spelled out. Are citizens aware that essential decisions concerning their human rights are taken, at least in part, within the EU framework? – not enough. It is, therefore, necessary, in my view, to give clearer expression to the fact that fundamental choices about the substance of these rights are made at EU level.

This is a wager – a risky one, particularly in the current context. Yet it is vital for the future of the EU as we know it today, founded on the values of liberal democracy. These values, including human rights, must be given substance, so that they can no longer be so easily appropriated – or hollowed out – by their adversaries.

Epilogue

A Risky but Vital Wager

I opened the concluding remarks by acknowledging the sinuous nature of this writing journey. It was not merely winding: at times, it became a corridor of mist. Doubt accompanied me like a quiet travelling companion. The EU Fundamental Rights Law system is not simply a complex edifice – it is a fragile architecture, buffeted by crosswinds and now cast into a political climate that has turned openly hostile.

It would be illusory to ignore that human rights are no longer considered as being a shared foundation and ideal. I had already sensed as much in the Introduction. Much the same can be said of the EU, which is increasingly subject to sharp criticism that questions the very legitimacy of the integration project. It was a distant rumble, at times, yet now close enough to make the walls of the European edifice tremble.

These voices challenging the EU and its liberal values no longer only murmur beyond its borders, but they now also resonate very loudly within its own chambers.

A few days before completing the writing of this monograph, on 13 November 2025, an unprecedented event occurred: for the first time in the history of the European Parliament, a text implying a significant rollback of regulations enshrined under the Green Deal was adopted, thanks to an alliance between the European People's Party (EPP) and the far-right groups of the European Conservatives and Reformists Group (ECR). This is a coalition once unimaginable – the confluence of two rivers that had long carved parallel and incompatible courses. One of these currents, previously shunned, now feeds the same legislative basin.

Without venturing into the political details of this regrettable moment, I could not bring this book to a close without acknowledging the shadow it casts. This political development challenges, of course, the call for a political shift in EU Fundamental Rights Law that I advance in this book. It also echoes the doubt that accompanied me throughout the writing: is this truly the right moment to focus on the special characteristics, the technical artefacts, the sometimes arid subtleties of the EU Fundamental Rights system, when the very foundations of our liberal democracies are under threat?

This book does not claim to offer a magical remedy for the crisis gripping our liberal societies, in Europe or beyond. Nevertheless, it ultimately seemed to me that it is perhaps precisely in these moments of near-existential crisis, which call into question the resilience of our liberal democracies, that the need to continue to work and reflect on the values that sustain them becomes most compelling. It is precisely when the foundations begin to quake that we must continue to illuminate the cogs, uncover the mechanisms, and offer some clarity amidst the turmoil.

I am convinced that by sincerely re-engaging with the values of liberal democracy, those who wish to defend them may yet succeed. Perhaps we have taken these values for granted for too long, abandoning the debate over the real demands they entail. In the silence we left behind, others found the space to seize the words, twist them, stain them, and turn them against what they once signified.

Today, I believe that the level of the European Union is perhaps the last remaining space where one can still aspire to a political project that places human rights firmly at its core. At the international level, the United States has, in recent times, gravely jeopardized that very project. As for the broader "Greater Europe" of forty-six states within the Council of Europe, it appears deeply weakened and less able than before to embody a clear and authoritative point of reference in this field. One need only recall that Russia was still a member at the time of its invasion of Ukraine; or consider the "Letter of the Nine" and the joint declaration of twenty-seven states openly questioning the legitimacy of the European Court of Human Rights. At this juncture, the only bulwark that continues to withstand the tide – and one that must be strengthened with determination – is the European Union itself.

Some will call this naïveté. Perhaps it is. Yet it is precisely this demanding and persistent naïveté that kept me at my desk, and which grounds my final, unequivocal claim: the need to embrace a genuine political shift in the EU's approach to fundamental rights. This wager is undoubtedly a risky one, but it is, in my view, nothing less than vital for the future of the European project.

SELECTED BIBLIOGRAPHY IN EU FUNDAMENTAL RIGHTS LAW

This bibliography does not seek to provide an exhaustive account of the existing scholarship. Its purpose is instead to highlight a curated selection of additional works that engage with the protection of fundamental rights within the European Union and related issues.

Monographs

Beijer, Malu, *The Limits of Fundamental Rights Protection by the EU: The Scope for the Development of Positive Obligations* (Intersentia, 2017).

Burgorgue-Larsen, Laurence, *The 3 Regional Human Rights Courts in Context: Justice That Cannot Be Taken for Granted* (Oxford University Press, 2024).

Coman, Ramona, *The Politics of the Rule of Law in the EU Polity* (Palgrave Macmillan, 2022).

Costello, Cathryn, *The Human Rights of Migrants and Refugees in European Law* (Oxford University Press, 2015).

Dawson, Mark, *The Governance of EU Fundamental Rights* (Cambridge University Press, 2017).

Davio, Victor, *EU Fundamental Rights: A Source of Special Significance for the European Court of Human Rights* (Larcier, 2026).

De Coninck, Joyce, *The EU's Human Rights Responsibility Gap: Deconstructing Human Rights Impunity of International Organisations* (Hart Publishing, 2024).

Dubout, Édouard, *Droit constitutionnel de l'Union européenne*, 1st edn (Bruylant, 2021).

Fink, Melanie, *Frontex and Human Rights: Responsibility in 'Multi-Actor Situations' under the ECHR and EU Public Liability Law* (Oxford University Press, 2018).

Frantziou, Eleni, *The Horizontal Effect of Fundamental Rights in the European Union: A Constitutional Analysis* (Oxford University Press, 2019).

Imamovic, Sejla, *The Architecture of Fundamental Rights in the European Union* (Hart, 2022).

Kosta, Vasiliki, *Fundamental Rights in EU Internal Market Legislation* (Hart Publishing, 2015).

Lynskey, Orla, *The Foundations of EU Data Protection Law* (Oxford University Press, 2015).

Muir, Elise, *EU Equality Law: The First Fundamental Rights Policy of the EU*, 1st edn (Oxford University Press, 2018).

Raimondo, Giulia, *The European Integrated Border Management: Frontex, Human Rights and International Responsibility* (Hart Publishing, 2024).

Rizcallah, Cecilia, *The Principle of Mutual Trust in European Union Law. An essential principle facing a crisis of values* (Bruylant, 2022).

Tinière, Romain and Vial, Claire, *Droit de l'Union européenne des droits fondamentaux* (Bruylant, 2023).

Williams, Andrew, *EU Human Rights Policies: A Study in Irony* (Oxford University Press, 2004).

——, *The Ethos of Europe: Values, Law and Justice in the EU*, 1st edn (Cambridge University Press, 2010).

Wind, Marlene, *The Tribalization of Europe: A Defence of Liberal Values* (Polity Press, 2020).

Wouters, Jan and Ovádek, Michal, *The European Union and Human Rights: Analysis, Cases, and Materials* (Oxford University Press, 2021).

Edited volumes and special issues

Bast, Jürgen and von Bogdandy, Armin (eds), *Principles of European Constitutional Law*, 2nd edn (Hart, 2011).

Bonelli, Matteo, Eliantonio, Mariolina, and Gentile, Giulia (eds), *Article 47 of the EU Charter and Effective Judicial Protection, Volume 1: The Court of Justice's Perspective* (Hart Publishing, 2022).

Bribosia, Emmanuelle, Rizcallah, Cecilia, and Van Drooghenbroeck, Sébastien, 'Special Issue: "La Charte a vingt ans. Regards croisés pour un anniversaire"' (2021) *Cahiers de droit européen* 1–218.

Closa, Carlos and Kochenov, Dimitry (eds), *Reinforcing Rule of Law Oversight in the European Union* (Cambridge University Press, 2016).

Iliopoulou-Penot, Anastasia and Xenou, Lamprini (eds), *La Charte des droits fondamentaux, source de renouveau constitutionnel européen?* (Bruylant, 2020).

Muir, Elise, Garben, Sacha and Govaere, Inge (eds), *Activating Human and Fundamental Rights Before the European Courts* (Hart Publishing, 2026).

Pascual, Maribel González and Sánchez, Sara Iglesias (eds), *Fundamental Rights in the EU Area of Freedom, Security and Justice* (Cambridge University Press, 2021).

Peers, Steve et al (eds), *The EU Charter of Fundamental Rights: A Commentary*, 2nd edn (Hart Publishing, 2021).

Picod, Fabrice, Rizcallah, Cecilia, and Van Drooghenbroeck, Sébastien (eds), *La Charte des droits fondamentaux de l'Union européenne. Commentaire article par article*, 3rd edn (Bruylant, 2023).

Tinière, Romain and Vial, Claire (eds), *Les dix ans de la Charte des droits fondamentaux de l'Union européenne: bilan et perspectives* (Bruylant, 2020).

Journal articles and Chapters in edited volumes

Alston, Philip and de Schutter, Olivier (eds), *Monitoring Fundamental Rights in the EU: The Contribution of the Fundamental Rights Agency* (Hart, 2005).

Alston, Philip and Weiler, Joseph HH, 'An "Ever Closer Union" in Need of a Human Rights Policy' (1998) *European Journal of International Law* 658–723.

Azoulai, Loïc, 'The Law of the European Society' (2022) *Common Market Law Review* 203–14.

Baraggia, Antonia and Bonelli, Matteo, 'Linking Money to Values: The New Rule of Law Conditionality Regulation and Its Constitutional Challenges' (2022) 23 *German Law Journal* 131–56.

Bogdandy, Armin von, 'The European Union as a Human Rights Organization? Human Rights and the Core of the European Union' (2000) *Common Market Law Review* 1307, 1311.

Bonelli, Matteo, 'Effective Judicial Protection in EU Law: An Evolving Principle of a Constitutional Nature' (2019) 12 *Review of European Administrative Law* 35–62.

——, 'Infringement Actions 2.0: How to Protect EU Values before the Court of Justice' (2022) 18 *European Constitutional Law Review* 30–58.

——, 'Growing pains: Direct effect, primacy and fundamental rights after *Lin*' (2024) *Common Market Law Review* 1045–76.

Bribosia, Emmanuelle, 'La protection des droits fondamentaux' in Magnette, Paul (ed), *La constitution de l'Europe* (Éditions de l'Université de Bruxelles, 2000) 107–27.

Callewaert, Johan, 'Do we still need Article 6(2) TEU? Considerations on the Absence of EU Accession to the ECHR and its Consequences' (2018) *Common Market Law Review* 1685–1716.

Coppel, Jason and O'Neill, Aidan, 'The European Court of Justice: Taking Rights Seriously?' (1992) *Common Market Law Review* 669–92.

Davio, Victor, 'Detention in the Hungarian Transit Zones: A Case of Higher Fundamental Rights Protection by EU Law vis-a-vis the ECHR' (2022) *European Law Review* 393–409.

Dawson, Mark and Muir, Elise, 'Individual, Institutional and Collective Vigilance in Protecting Fundamental Rights in the EU: Lessons from the Roma' (2011) 48 *Common Market Law Review* 751–75.

de Búrca Gráinne, 'After the EU Charter of Fundamental Rights: The Court of Justice as a Human Rights Adjudicator' (2013) *Maastricht Journal of European and Comparative Law* 168–84.

——, 'The Evolution of EU Human Rights Law' in Craig, Paul and de Búrca, Gráinne (eds), *The Evolution of EU Law*, 3rd edn (Oxford University Press, 2021) 480–505.

de Witte, Bruno, 'The Relative Autonomy of the European Union's Fundamental Rights' (2019) *Nordic Journal of International Law* 65–85.

——, 'EU Law: Is It International Law?' in Barnard, Catherine and Peers, Steve (eds), *European Union Law*, 3rd edn (Oxford University Press, 2020) 191–210.

Delhomme, Vincent and Rizcallah, Cecilia, 'Internal Market Legislation and Dissensus over Liberal Democracy' in Coman, Ramona et al, *The Palgrave Handbook of Dissensus over Liberal Democracy*, Palgrave, forthcoming.

Douglas-Scott, Sionaidh and Hatziz, Nicholas, *Research Handbook on EU Law and Human Rights* (Routledge, 2017).

——, 'Peut-on défendre les valeurs de l'Union européenne par le droit' (2025) *Revue des droits et libertés fondamentaux*

Eeckout, Piet, 'Opinion 2/13 on EU Accession to the ECHR and Judicial Dialogue: Autonomy or Autarky' (2015) *Fordham International Law Journal* 955–92.

Feenstra, Sjoerd, 'How Can the Viking/Laval Conundrum Be Resolved? Balancing the Economic and the Social: One Bed for Two Dreams?' in Vandenbroucke, Frank, Barnard, Catherine and De Baere, Geert (eds), *A European Social Union after the Crisis*, 1st edn (Cambridge University Press, 2017) 308–43.

Fisicaro, Marco, 'Beyond the Rule of Law Conditionality: Exploiting the EU Spending Power to Foster the Union's Values' (2022) 7 *European Papers – A Journal on Law and Integration* 697–719.

Frantziou, Eleni, 'Human Rights as an Example of Cooperative Federalism? A Chronology of the Use of the Preliminary Reference Procedure in Human Rights Cases between 1957 and 2023' (2023) *European Journal of Legal Studies* 189–220.

Fromont, Louise and Van Waeyenberge, Arnaud, 'Trading Rule of Law for Recovery? The New EU Strategy in the post-Covid Era' (2021) *European Law Journal* 132–47.

Gambardella, Ilaria, 'EU Governance Through Funding: What consequences for the scope of application of EU fundamental rights?' (2024) 31 *Maastricht Journal of European and Comparative Law* 215–33.

Halberstam, Daniel, '"It's the Autonomy, Stupid!" A Modest Defense of *Opinion 2/13* on EU Accession to the ECHR, and the Way Forward' (2015) 16 *German Law Journal* 105–46.

Hillion, Christopher, 'Enlarging the European Union and Deepening Its Fundamental Rights Protection' (2013) 11 *Swedish Institute for Policy Studies* 1–16.

Jacqué, Jean-Paul, 'Pride and/or prejudice? Les lectures possibles de l'avis 2/13 de la Cour de justice' (2015) 1 *Cahiers de droit européen* 19–45.

Jakab, András and Kochenov, Dimitry (eds), *The Enforcement of EU Law and Values* (Oxford University Press, 2017).

Khabirpour, Nabil, 'The Principles of Effectiveness, Effective Judicial Protection and the Rule of Law' (2023) 5 *European Human Rights Law Review* 477–81.

Kochenov, Dimitry, *EU Enlargement and the Failure of Conditionality: Pre-Accession Conditionality in the Fields of Democracy and the Rule of Law* (Kluwer Law International, 2008).

Kosta, Vasiliki, 'Investigating Lessons for the EU's Fundamental Rights Policies' (2023) 19 *European Constitutional Law Review* 371–89.

Krommendijk, Jasper, 'The Use of ECtHR Case Law by the Court of Justice after Lisbon: The View of Luxembourg Insiders' (2015) *Maastricht Journal of European and Comparative Law* 812–35.

Lenaerts, Koen, 'Limits on Limitations: The Essence of Fundamental Rights in the EU' (2019) 20 *German Law Journal* 779–93.

Lenaerts, Koen and Gutiérrez-Fons, José Antonio, 'The Place of the Charter in the European Legal Space' in Peers, Steve et al (eds), *The EU Charter of Fundamental Rights: A Commentary*, 2nd edn (Bloomsbury, 2021) 1711–34.

Muir, Elise, 'Fundamental Rights: An Unsettling EU Competence' (2014) 15 *Human Rights Review* 25–37.

——, 'The Fundamental Rights Implications of EU Legislation: Some Constitutional Challenges' (2014) 51 *Common Market Law Review* 219–46.

——, 'Reshuffling Our Understanding of Fundamental Rights Law in Europe: An EU Lawyer's Research Agenda' (2021) *European Human Rights Law Review* 142–48.

O'Leary, Siofra, 'A Tale of Two Cities – Fundamental Rights Protection in Strasbourg and in Luxembourg' (2018) *Cambridge Yearbook of European Legal Studies* 3.

Ovadek, Michal, 'The Curious Case of the Fundamental Rights Agency's Mandate: Legal Shrouding and Democratic Politics' (2019) 25(4) *European Public Law* 517–34.

Passalacqua, Virginia, 'Legal Mobilization via Preliminary Reference: Insights from the Case of Migrant Rights' (2021) 58 *Common Market Law Review* 751–76.

Pech, Laurent and Scheppele, Kim Lane, 'Illiberalism Within: Rule of Law Backsliding in the EU' (2017) 19 *Cambridge Yearbook of European Legal Studies* 3–47.

Plat, Théodore, 'The Effectiveness of Social Directives in the Light of the Charter of Fundamental Rights of the European Union – A Mirage on the Social Horizon?' (2023) *Revue des Affaires Européennes* 771–82.

Rizcallah, Cecilia, 'La protection des droits fondamentaux dans l'Union européenne: l'immuable poids des origines?' (2015) *Cahiers de droit européen* 399–427.

——, 'The Principle of Mutual Trust and the Protection of Fundamental Rights in the Area of Freedom, Security and Justice: A critical look at the Court of Justice's stone-by-stone approach' (2023) *Maastricht Journal of European and Comparative Law* 255–72.

Robin-Olivier, Sophie, 'The Power of the Right to an Effective Remedy to Horizontalize Directives. Comment on Case C-715/20, X (Absence de motif de résiliation), 20 February 2024' (2025) 32(1) *Maastricht Journal of European and Comparative Law* 65–77.

Scarcello, Orlando, 'Fundamental rights and the federal equilibrium: Comparing the doctrines of incorporation in the USA and the EU' (2024) 30(6) *Maastricht Journal of European and Comparative Law* 729–59.

Scheppele, Kim Lane, Kochenov, Dimitry and Grabowska-Moroz, Barbara, 'EU Values Are Law, After All: Enforcing EU Values through Systemic Infringement Actions by the European Commission and the Member States of the European Union' (2021) 39 *Yearbook of European Law* 3–121.

Scheppele, Kim Lane and Morijn, John, 'What Price Rule of Law?' in Södersten, Anna and Hercock, Edwin (eds), *The Rule of Law in the EU: Crisis and Solutions*, Swedish Institute for European Policy Studies, Report no 1, April 2023) 29–36.

Smismans, Stijn, 'The European Union's Fundamental Rights Myth' (2010) 48 *Journal of Common Market Studies* 46–69.

Spaventa, Eleanor, 'Fundamental Rights in the European Union' in Barnard, Catherine and Peers, Steve (eds), *European Union Law*, 4th edn (Oxford University Press, 2023) 242–83.

Tinière, Romain, 'Le Parlement européen et la protection des droits fondamentaux ou le chevalier blanc des droits de l'homme à l'épreuve de la réalité' in Marguery, Tony, Platon, Sébastien and van Eijken, Hanneke, *Les élections européennes, 40 ans après: bilan, enjeux et perspectives* (Bruylant, 2020) 69–84.

Van Drooghenbroeck, Sébastien, 'Vérité à Luxembourg, erreur à Strasbourg. A propos de certaines plus-values discrètes de la Charte des droits fondamentaux de l'Union européenne' in Picod, Fabrice and Blumann, Claude, *Annuaire de droit de l'Union européenne 2021* (Editions Panthéon Assas, 2021) 173–92.

Van Drooghenbroeck, Sébastien and Rizcallah, Cecilia, 'The ECHR and the Essence of Fundamental Rights: Searching for Sugar in Hot Milk?' (2019) 20 *German Law Journal* 904–23.

Weiler, Joseph HH and Lockhart, Nicholas JS, '"Taking Rights Seriously?" Seriously: The European Court and Its Fundamental Rights Jurisprudence', published in two parts in the *Common Market Law Review* (1995) 51–94 and 579–627.

Williams, Andrew, 'Human Rights in the EU' in Chalmers, Damian and Arnull, Anthony (eds), *The Oxford Handbook of European Union Law* (Oxford University Press, 2015) 249–70.

Xenou, Lamprini, 'Right to paid annual leave: The Cour de cassation recognized the direct horizontal effect of Article 31(2) of the EU Charter and strengthened the protection of employees' rights' (2025) 32(1) *Maastricht Journal of European and Comparative Law* 78–88.

INDEX

accelerated procedure, 143–44
accession of the EU to ECHR, 3, 27, 71–72, 233, 254
  Opinion 2/13, 6, 22–23, 41, 76, 249–50
accession to EU:
  imposition of EU fundamental rights, 25–26, 160–64
***Achbita* case,** 86–87
African Commission on Human and Peoples' Rights, 7–8
age discrimination, 49, 118
***Akerberg Fransson* judgment,** 28–29, 77–78
***Alemo-Herron* case,** 86
***Almonacid Arellano* case,** 102–3
American Convention on Human Rights (ACHR), 102–3
anti-discrimination, 48, 60, 84–85, 123, 126–28, 183–84, 212, 213–15, 258
anti-SLAPP Directive, 57
Area of Freedom, Security, and Justice (AFSJ), 2–3, 10, 23–24, 39–41, 46, 89, 170
  harmonisation, 55–56, 128
  mutual recognition system, 130
  preliminary rulings
    accelerated procedure, 143–44
    expedited procedure, 144
Asylum, Migration and Integration Fund (AMIF), 177–78, 185, 187
asylum law, *see* **immigration and asylum**
attributed competences principle, 26
  see **conferral principle**
austerity, 37, 199–200
autonomous logic, 34–35, 43, 56
autonomy of EU law, 38, 41–42, 50, 70–72, 103, 123, 125–26
  European Monitoring Centre on Racism and Xenophobia, 208–9

balancing competing interests, 41, 45, 46–47, 56, 80–84, 121, 123–24, 152–53, 231, 233
  promoting unity versus respecting diversity, 236, 241–42, 244–45
  violations of ECHR, 74–75
***Białowieża case*,** 153–54
Border Management and Visa Instruments Fund (BMVI), 177–78, 185, 187
***BPC Lux 2 and Others* case,** 80
Brussels IIb Regulation, 57
'Brussels Effect', 228
***Bauer* case,** 119–20, 122–23
  Cooperation and Verification Mechanism, 163–64
  substantive criminal law, 78
burden of proof, 48–49, 124, 125–26, 230

Charter of Fundamental Rights of the EU (CFREU), 2–3, 5, 11, 21–22, 26, 27–28
  ECHR, relationship with, 70–71
  limits to scope, 28–30
  level of protection, 79–82
    absence of EU harmonisation, 79–82
    with EU harmonisation, 83–88
  scope of application, 76–77
    absence of EU harmonisation, 77–82
    with EU harmonisation, 82–88
Citizens, Equality Rights and Values (CERV) programme, 194–95
civil matters:
  judicial co-operation, 56–57, 168–69
  mutual recognition, 57
Cohesion Fund (CF), 176–78, 178–81, 183–85, 188, 191, 198, 231
cohesion policy:
  Common Provision Regulation, 176–78, 182–83
  European Regional Development Fund, 179–80
***Commission v Hungary (Higher Education)*,** 72
Committee on Legal Affairs (JURI), 166–67
Common Agricultural Policy (CAP), 176–77
'Common Area for the Protection of Fundamental Rights', 4, 9–12, 13, 140, 236

Common European Asylum System (CEAS), 60, 61, 65–66, 129, 227, 233–34
Common Foreign and Security Policy (CFSP), 210–11, 250
Common Provision Regulation (CPR), 176–78, **207**
funds supporting fundamental rights protection, 178–81
sanctions to ensure respect of fundamental rights, 182–94
see also CPR funds
competing objectives within EU, 12, 38–42, 71–72, 94–95, 157–58, 234–35, 236, 254–55
Conditionality Regulation, 174–75, 202–3, 203–5, **207**
conferral principle, 26, 27, 30, 93, 131, 150–51, 235, 250–51
consolidation of fundamental rights protection, 4–6, 11, 20–23, 24–26
consumer protection, 52
CFREU Art 38, 115, 127
***contra legem* interpretation,** 98
Convention on the Rights of Persons with Disabilities (CRPD), 53, 183–84, 187–88, 231–32
conventionality control doctrine, 102–4
***Costa v Enel*,** 19, 94, 104–5
Council of Europe, 1, 4, 5–6, 7–9, 19, 23, 26, 65, 161, 220–21, 249–50
see also European Convention on Human Rights
Council of the European Union, 21, 23, 48, 53, 65, 68–69, 164–65, 170–71
country-specific recommendations (CSRs), 188, 198, 199–200
Court of Justice of the European Union (CJEU), 2, 5, 8–9, 20, 91–92, 202–3
infringement proceedings, 152–53, 164–65
interpretation of EU law, 70–76
Opinion 2/13, 6, 22–23, 41, 76, 249–50
preliminary reference procedure, 95, 97, 105, 108, 141–45, 225–26
CPR funds, 177–78
funds supporting rights protection, 178–81
sanctions to ensure respect of rights, 182–94
criminal matters, 24
Area of Freedom, Security, and Justice, 130
effectiveness principle, 81–82
inter-state co-operation, 87–88
judicial co-operation, 56, 57–60, 168–69, 210–11
legality principle, 81
limitation periods, 81
mutual trust, 59
primacy of EU law, 81–82
procedural rights, 58–60
unity principle, 81–82

data protection, 129, 214–15, 222, 227, 245–46, 258–59
data protection authorities, 216, 217–18
data protection officers, 217–18
European Data Protection Board, 217–18
European Data Protection Supervisor, 50, 212, 216
General Data Protection Regulation, 50–51, 110, 126–27, 215–18, 237, 245
see also personal data
data protection authorities (DPAs), 216, 217–18
data protection officers (DPO), 217–18
***Defrenne* judgment,** 47–48, 114
***Deldits* case,** 51
democracy principle, 7–8, 20–21, 22, 24–25, 150–52, 161, 163–64, 241–43, 246, 248–49, 255, 259, 261
Democracy, Rule of Law and Fundamental Rights monitoring group, 165–66
demoi-cracy concept, 243–44
derogations, 28–29, 186
direct effect of EU law, 93–95, 97–98, 105–6, 107
ECHR, relationship with, 100–1
horizontal effect, 112–23
vertical direct effect, 108–12
disability discrimination, 49, 53, 86–87, 124, 183–84, 186, 214–15
distortion of competition, 1, 47, 66, 252
Dublin Regulation, 40, 133

economic crisis, 37, 68–69, 168–69
economic integration, 5, 23–24, 38–39, 66
effective judicial protection principle, 42, 78–79, 106–7, 115, 120, 131–39, 144–45, 149–50, 168–69, 197, 199–200, 201–2, 204, **207**
effective remedy, 58, 62, 63–64, 109, 128–30, 132–33, 138–39

effectiveness principle, 41–42, 94–95, 98–99, 138–39
effectiveness through CJEU case law, 130–39
effectiveness through legislation, 123–30
effet utile, 92–93, 94–95, 100–1, 123, 130–31, 135
employee rights, *see* **labour law; worker rights**
Employment Equality Directive 2000/78, 48
enforcement of an EU Fundamental Rights Law framework, 140
institutional enforcement, 145–56
judicial enforcement, 141–45
equal opportunities, 47–48, 68, 180, 182, 198, 213–14
equal pay, 47–48, 112–13, 114, 125–26
equal treatment, 47–48, 69, 85–87, 105, 117–19, 121–22, 124, 147, 212, 213–14
equality between men and women, 67, 182–83, 186
CFREU Art. 23, 69
equality principle:
harmonisation, 47–49
equivalence principle, 99, 123, 131–32, 145
EU as 'norm-maker', 45, 89, 226, 227
harmonisation, 45–47
area freedom, security, and justice, 55–66
equality and non-discrimination, 47–49
internal market, development of, 51–55
protection of personal data, 50–51
social policy and emergence social rights, 66–70
EU enlargement, 162–64
EU Justice, Rights and Values Fund, 176, 194–96
Eurojust, 212, 218
European Accessibility Act, 52, 53–54
European Arrest Warrant system, 58–59, 130
criminal judicial co-operation, 135
Framework Decision, 24
Melloni judgement, 41–42
mutual trust principle, 40
European Central Bank (ECB):
tensions between economic integration and social rights, 38–39
European Coal and Steel Community (ECSC), 1
European Commission, 145–46
Annual Report on application of CFREU, 167–68
Annual Rule of Law Report, 169–70
EU Justice Scoreboard, 168–69
political oversight over fundamental rights, 167–70
tensions between economic integration and social rights, 38–39
European Convention on Human Rights (ECHR), 2–3, 19–20, 27, 225
accession of the EU to ECHR, 3, 27, 71–72, 161, 233, 254
Opinion 2/13, 6, 22–23, 41, 76, 249–50
European Court of Human Rights (ECtHR), 9, 13–14, 19–20, 248
European Court of Justice (ECJ), 2, 19–20, 36, 47–48, 71, 91, 202–3
CJEU interpretation, 70–76
European Data Protection Board (EDPB), 217–18
European Data Protection Supervisor (EDPS), 50, 212, 216
European Economic Community, 1
European identity, 20–21, 44
European Maritime, Fisheries and Aquaculture Fund (EMFAF), 177–78, 185, 188
European Media Freedom Act, 52, 54–55
European Ombudsman, 231–32
European Parliament, 21–22, 156, 161–62, 248–49, 258–59
Democracy, Rule of Law and Fundamental Rights monitoring group, 165–67
European Pillar of Social Rights, 68–69
political oversight over fundamental rights, 165–67
European Pillar of Social Rights, 68–69, 175, 180, 188, 200, **207**
European Political Community:
failure of, 18–19
European Regional Development Fund (ERDF), 177–80, 181, 185, 188
European Semester, 168–69, 188, 198, 199–200
European Social Fund Plus (ESF+), 177–78, 180–81, 185, 188, 231–32
Europeanisation, 255
Europol, 212, 218
Euroscepticism:
growth of, 14, 237
expedited procedure, 144, 153
external border management, 37, 61, 73, 155–56, 218–20
external relations, 10–11, 173–74

***F.M.S. and others* case,** 73–74
***Factortame I* judgment,** 99
fair and just working conditions (CFREU Art. 31), 67–68, 105–6, 115, 119–20, 225–26
family and professional life (CFREU Art. 33), 68–69
financial conditionality, 234–35
financial sanctions for violations, 166–67
flexibility clause, 210–11
Framework Employment Directive, 213
***Francovich* judgment,** 107
free movement of capital, 148
freedom of expression and information (CFREU Art. 11), 55
freedom of movement, 73–74, 148
freedom of the arts and sciences (CFREU Art. 13):
  academic freedom, 149
freedom of thought, conscience and religion (CFREU Art. 10), 84
freedom of thought, conscience and religion (ECHR Art. 9), 84
freedom to choose an occupation and right to engage in work (CFREU Art. 15), 181
freedom to conduct a business (CFREU Art. 16), 86, 149
Frontex, 212, 218–20, 222
Fundamental Rights Agency (FRA), 166, 206, 208–9
  advisory function, 209–10
  scope of action, 210
  strategic framework, 211
Fundamental Rights Officer (FRO), 212, 218–19

gender discrimination, 49, 125, 213
gender equality, 67–70, 125, 182–84, 187, 192, 195, 198
gender reassignment, 51
General Data Protection Regulation (GDPR), 50–51, 110, 126–27, 215–18, 237, 245
general principles of EU law, 2, 19–20, 21–22, 28–30, 70–71, 225
***Google Spain* case,** 121

Habitats Directive, 153–54
Hague Programme (2004), 2–3, 57–58
harmonisation, 45–47
  absence of EU harmonisation
    level of protection, 79–82
    scope of application of CFREU, 77–82
  area freedom, security, and justice, 55–66
  equality and non-discrimination, 47–49
  internal market, development of, 51–55
  protection of personal data, 50–51
  social policy and emergence social rights, 66–70
health care (CFREU Art. 35), 179, 198
horizontal effects of fundamental rights, 112
  CJEU case law, through, 114–23
    age-based discrimination, 117–18
    disputes between individuals, 121
    essential/non-essential content, 116–17
    paid annual leave, 119
    rights of disabled persons, 115
    workers' rights, 114–20
  legislation, through, 112–13
human dignity, 113, 150, 245
  CFREU Art. 1, 180–81
Hungary:
  conditionality mechanism, 166–67, 173, 192–94
  judicial independence, 147, 198–99, 201–2
  Recovery and Resilience Plan, 193
  rule of law reforms, 147, 203, 204–5, 221, 234–35
  violations of EU values, 166, 221, 234–35
    academic freedom, 72
    higher education, 72, 148–49
    judicial reforms, 147
    transit zones for asylum seekers, 73–74
    transparency of civil society organisations, 148
    usufruct rights on agricultural land, 147–48
    violations of LGBTIQ+ rights, 150–51, 193

***Ilias and Ahmed v Hungary*,** 73–74
immigration and asylum:
  Asylum, Migration and Integration Fund, 177–78, 185, 187
  Common European Asylum System (CEAS), 60, 61, 65–66, 129, 227, 233–34
  New Pact on Asylum and Migration, 61, 233–34
  right to asylum (CFREU Art. 18), 63–64

right to liberty, 72–73
transit zones for asylum seekers, 73–74
imputability, 30
infringement proceedings, 140, 145–46, 147–52, 154–56, 157–58, 164–65, 166–67, 221, 234
instrumental logic, 43, 55–57, 130
integration of persons with disabilities (CFREU Art. 26), 115, 179–81
Inter-American Commission on Human Rights (IAComHR), 7–8
Inter-American Court of Human Rights (IACtHR), 102–4
internal market, 5, 46, 51–55, 149, 228–29, 252–53
anti-discrimination measures, 47–48
competing objectives, 38–39
harmonisation, 51–55
integration, 9–10, 38–39, 66
protection of personal data, 50, 127–28
Internal Security Fund (ISF), 177–78, 185
International Covenant on Civil and Political Rights (ICCPR), 7
International Covenant on Economic, Social and Cultural Rights (ICESCR), 7
International Monetary Fund (IMF):
tensions between economic integration and social rights, 38–39

judicial activism, 141–45
judicial co-operation, 55–56
civil matters, 55–57, 227
criminal matters, 55–56, 57–60, 135, 143–44, 210
family matters, 143, 227
judicial independence, 78–79, 106–7, 138, 147, 149–50, 154, 164, 192–94, 196, 198–99, 201–2, 205
judicial remedies, 91–92, 95, 140, 159
accelerated procedure, 143–44
European Commission, 145–48, 149–56
expedited procedure, 144
institutional enforcement, 145–56
preliminary ruling proceeding, 143, 145
vigilance of individuals, 141–45
jurisdiction, 29–30
Brussels IIb Regulation, 57
CJEU jurisdiction, 71–72, 140
European Convention on Human Rights, 100–1
Just Transition Fund (JTF), 177–78, 185
Justice Programme, 194, 196–97

labour law, 49, 66–70, 115, 119–20
Employment Equality Directive 2000/78, 48
Framework Employment Directive, 213
***Laval* case,** 39
legitimate interest, 85–86, 121, 125
level of protection (CFREU Art. 53), 79–80
LGBTIQ+ rights, 85, 150, 193, 204
liberal democracy, 246, 259
limitations of fundamental rights protection, 26–28, 250–54
***Lin* case,** 42, 81–82
loyal co-operation, 142, 144–45

Maastricht Treaty (1992), 21
margin of appreciation, 33, 64, 80, 84, 235
margin of discretion of Member States, 79, 82, 83–85, 86, 108, 230, 234, 250, 254
***Melloni* case,** 41, 80
migrant crisis, 37
minimum safeguards, 55, 69–70, 111
minimum standards, 46, 55–66, 79, *88*, 214–15, 227, 236
Multiannual Financial Framework (MFF), 175, 194–95, 197
mutual recognition of decisions, 24, 39–40, 55–56
civil matters, 57
criminal law, 43, 130, 227
mutual trust principle, 24, 39–41, 58–59, 150–51

national autonomy, 80, 83
national human rights institutions (NHRIs), 167–68, 187–89, *190*
National Recovery and Resilience Plans (NRRPs), 197, 198, 199–201, **207**
national security, 110
national standards of protection, 77, 82, 87
***nature spécifique*,** 92–93
***ne bis in idem* principle,** 9–10, 72, 106, 109
NextGenerationEU (NGEU) programme, 175
New Pact on Asylum and Migration, 61, 233–34
non-discrimination principle, 89, 183, 186, 212, 227, 245–46
CFREU Art. 21, 115, 179–80, 183–84
Citizens, Equality Rights and Values programme, 195

employers' duties, 113
equality bodies, 213–15
general principle of EU law, 118–19
harmonisation, 47–49, 51
rights of persons of disabilities, 179–80, 183
non-*refoulement* principle, 111–12
***nullum crimen, nulla poena sine lege*,** 81

obligation to respect human rights (ECHR Art. 1), 29–30, 138

partnership agreements and programmes, 186, 188–89, *190*, 192–93, **207**
Patient's Rights Directive, 52–53
personal data, *see* **protection of personal data**
Poland:
Broniowski v Poland, 101
Common Provision Regulation, 192–93
democracy principle, 151
judicial independence, 149–50, 198–99, 202
partnership agreements, 192–93
preventive procedure against Poland, 173
safeguarding the rule of law, 153–54, 202–3
violations of Habitats Directive and Birds Directive, 153–54
political oversight, 160, 164–65
accession to EU and imposition of EU fundamental rights, 160–64
Council of the European Union, 170–71
European Commission, 167–70
European Parliament, 165–67
serious and persistent breach of fundamental rights
Art. 7 TEU, 171–72
preventive procedure, 172
remedial procedure, 172
political turn in fundamental rights protection, 237–40, 250–54
CFREU and ECHR, role of, 246–50
demoï-cracy concept, 243–46
politicisation of EU Fundamental Rights Law, 240–43
preliminary reference procedure, 95, 97, 105, 108, 141–45, 225–26
presumption of innocence and right of defence (CFREU Art. 48), 58, 129–30, 136
primacy of EU law, 19, 34–35, 94, 95–96
principles of legality and proportionality of criminal offences and penalties (CFREU Art. 49), 81, 129
prohibition of discrimination on grounds of age, 118
prohibition of discrimination on grounds of nationality, 1–2
prohibition of discrimination on grounds of racial or ethnic origin, 49, 213
prohibition of discrimination on the grounds of religion or belief, 49
proportionality principle, 27, 33–34, 39, 74, 129–30, 184–85
protection of personal data:
harmonisation, 50–51
internal market, 50, 127–28
non-discrimination principle, 47–49, 51, 113, 215–18
public law, 74–75, 146

Qualification Directive, 62–63, 65–66

Racial Equality Directive, 48
Reception Conditions Directive, 61–62, 71–72, 73–74
refugee crisis, 37
religious discrimination, 49
Recovery and Resilience Facility (RRF), 193, **207**
carrot-and-stick approach, 175, 197, 205
RRF-funded initiatives supporting rights protection, 198–99
RRF sanctions ensuring respect of rights, 199–203
National Recovery and Resilience Plans, 197
resistance to fundamental and human rights protection, 11, 14–15, 17–18, 34–38, 237
Return Directive, 111
***Rewe* effectiveness,** 99, 123, 131–32
right not to be tried or punished twice in criminal proceedings for the same criminal offence (CFREU Art. 50), 106, 109
right to a fair trial (ECHR Art. 6), 79, 139
right to a legal remedy, 75
right to asylum (CFREU Art. 18), 63
right to education (CFREU Art. 14), 149, 179–80, 198
right to effective remedy:
CFREU Art. 47, 40, 58, 63–64, 78–79, 106–7, 109–10, 115, 120, 129, 131–39, 202
ECHR Art. 13, 100–1, 139

right to family reunification, 64
right to health (CFREU Art. 35), 179, 198
right to property (CFREU Art. 17), 147–48
right to respect for private and family life (ECHR Art. 8), 65
rights of people with disabilities, 54, 181, 183–84, 199
rights of the child, 227, 232–33
  CFREU Art. 24, 181
rights of the elderly (CFREU Art. 25), 54, 179–80, 199
right-wing populism, 15
  rule of law reforms, 15, 147, 203, 204–5, 221, 234–35
ritual slaughter, 83–84
Romania:
  Cooperation and Verification Mechanism, 163–64
  judicial independence, 198
  limitation periods, 81
  rule of law, 203
rule of law, 42, 153–54, 202–3
  European Commission Annual Rule of Law Report, 169–70
  Democracy, Rule of Law and Fundamental Rights monitoring group, 165–66
  right-wing popularism rule of law reforms, 15, 147, 203, 204–5, 221, 234–35
Rule of Law Report, 169–70

sanctions (financial), 152–56, 165–67, 174–75
  ensuring respect of fundamental rights, 182–83
    fundamental rights conditionalities, 182–86, 189–92
    partnership agreements and programmes, 188–89, 192–93
    respect of *all* fundamental rights, 186
    respect of the EU Charter, 186
    UN Convention on the Rights of Persons with Disabilities, 187–88
  non-compliance, 151–53
scope of application (CFREU Art. 51), 27–28, 28, 29–30, 77–79, 210–11, 230, 232
  scope with EU Harmonisation, 82–88
  scope with no EU Harmonisation, 77–82
    level of protection, 83–89
    scope of application, 82–83
scope of guaranteed rights (CFREU Art. 52), 22, 70–72, 79, 227
sexual orientation discrimination, 49, 64, 124, 151, 182–83, 186, 214–15
shared values, 150–51, 195, 245–46, 248
shared identity, 44–45
***Simmenthal* case,** 105–6
Single European Act (1986), 21
Single Market, 38, 43–44
social exclusion, 37, 66–67, 180–81
social justice, 21, 66–67, 232–33
social policy and social rights, 66–70
social security and social assistance (CFREU Art. 34), 179
***source autonome*,** 92–93
Spain, 25
  Google Spain case, 121
standard-setting, 7–8, 18, 89
  EU as 'norm-maker', 45, 89, 226, 227
    area freedom, security, and justice, 55–66
    CJEU interpretation, 70–76
    equality and non-discrimination, 47–49
    EU harmonisation, 45–70
    internal market, development of, 51–55
    protection of personal data, 50–51
    scope with EU Harmonisation, 82–88
    scope with no EU Harmonisation, 77–82
    social policy and emergence social rights, 66–70
subsidiarity principle, 27, 28, 30–34, 139, 229, 235–36
supranational nature, 6–9, 137, 140, 156, 169, 221, 228, 234, 238, 243
supremacy of EU law, *see* **primacy of EU law**
supremacy principle (federal countries), 104
sustainability, 238

***Tarrico* case,** 42
territorial scope of EU law, 29–30, 157
***Test-Achats* case,** 121–22
transparency, 156
  civil society organisations, 148–49
  EU budget and implementation of funds, 191–92
  general principles of EU law, 22
  legal certainty and transparency, 252–53
  media service providers, 55

pay transparency and enforcement mechanisms, 47–48, 112–13, 125
accession to the ECHR, 249–50, 258–59
see also accession of the EU to ECHR

UN Convention on the Rights of Persons with Disabilities (UNCRPD), 183–84, 187–88, **207**, 231–32
UN High Commissioner for Refugees (UNHCR), 128
unanimity requirement, 53, 172, 234–35
uniformity of protection, 29, 43–44, 50, 80, 83, 88, 124, 141–42, 227, 230, 257–58
uniqueness of EU Law, 91, 100–5, 146
unity of responsibility in international law principle, 74
Universal Declaration on Human Rights (UDHR), 7

values crisis within EU, 164–65, 205, 221–22, 242–43
***Van Gend en Loos* case,** 91, 93–94, 104–5, 109, 141
***Viking* judgment,** 39

worker rights, 66–68, 69–70, 106, 136–37
equal pay, 47–48, 112–13, 114, 125–26
free movement of workers, 182–83
informing and consulting workers, 120
older employees, 117–18
religious employers, 84–85
see also labour law
workers' right to information and consultation within the undertaking (CFREU Art. 27), 115, 120
Working Time Directive, 67–68, 69–70, 105–6, 119

www.ingramcontent.com/pod-product-compliance
Ingram Content Group UK Ltd.
Pitfield, Milton Keynes, MK11 3LW, UK
UKHW020242290926
15470UKWH00002B/690

9 781509 989102